Econometrics

Econometrics
Theory and Applications with EViews

Ben Vogelvang

Harlow, England · London · New York · Boston · San Francisco · Toronto
Sydney · Tokyo · Singapore · Hong Kong · Seoul · Taipei · New Delhi
Cape Town · Madrid · Mexico City · Amsterdam · Munich · Paris · Milan

Pearson Education Limited
Edinburgh Gate
Harlow
Essex CM20 2JE
England

and Associated Companies throughout the world

Visit us on the World Wide Web at:
www.pearsoned.co.uk

First published 2005

ISBN 0 273 68374 8

British Library Cataloguing-in-Publication Data

A catalogue record for this book is available from the British Library

Library of Congress Cataloging-in-Publication Data

A catalogue record for this book is available from the Library of Congress

10 9 8 7 6 5 4 3 2 1
09 08 07 06 05

Typeset in 10/12 pt. Times by 59
Printed and bound by   Henry Ling Ltd., at the Dorset Press, Dorchester, Dorset

The publisher's policy is to use paper manufactured from sustainable forests.

Dedicated to my fine small family:
Yvonne,
Astrid and Valentijn,
Michiel

Contents

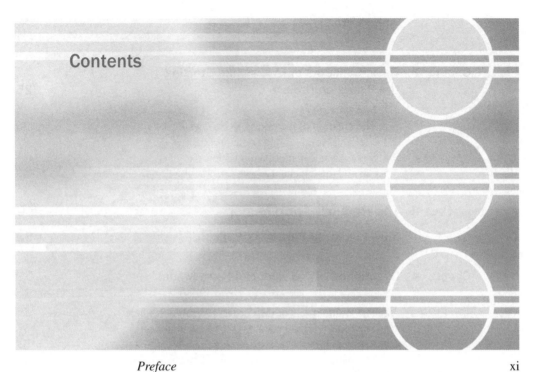

Companion Website and Instructor resources

Visit the Companion Website at **www.pearsoned.co.uk/vogelvang**

For students

■   Empirical data sets for practical learning, as described in Chapter 2 of the book

For lecturers

■   Downloadable Case Notes to assist in using the data sets to carry out the case
exercises described in the book

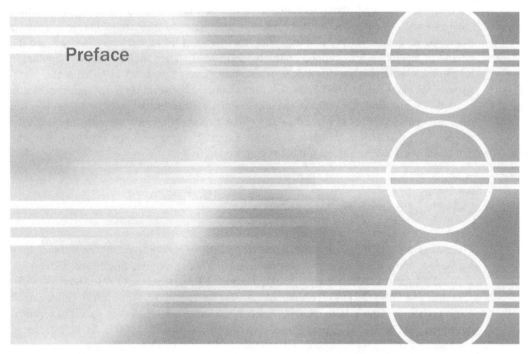

Preface

About this first course in econometrics

Economists will regularly be confronted with results of quantitative economic research. Therefore they should have knowledge about quantitative economic methods: they should know how models arise, what the underlying assumptions are, and in what way estimates of parameters or other economic quantities are computed. In this book, 'a first course in econometrics' is presented that meets all these requirements. In this course, econometric theory is combined with econometric practice by showing and exercising its use with software package EViews.

Basic knowledge of econometric theory is necessary to understand what may (or may not) be done in applied quantitative economic research. It is not imperative that students can prove all the underlying statistical theorems that are necessary to derive estimators and statistics. In other words, the aim of this econometrics course is to make students aware of the underlying statistical assumptions of the methods they want to use or that others have used. It is very important to recognise which assumptions have been made by an author, whether these assumptions have been tested in a correct way, etc. In this book, many exact derivations are given, but in some cases it is sufficient just to explain what is going on in that particular situation. References to the econometrics literature, for more detailed information on any subject, are given in throughout the text and are listed at the end of this book.

Econometrics is not mathematics or statistics only, but econometrics clearly belongs to the economic discipline; this starting-point is obviously recognisable in the text. With this approach to teaching econometrics, students will get a clear understanding of econometric practice and the underlying econometric theory. The integration of econometric theory, its application and the use of econometric software distinguishes this book from existing econometric texts.

The best way to learn about doing quantitative economic research is to study econometrics where theory and empirical work alternate in an integrated way: immediately applying a discussed procedure on economic data by using econometric software. Students see the benefit of theoretically explained methods more clearly when they are directly applied in an empirical example. For this reason, a number of cases have been included in this book. Most of the cases can be considered as a 'simulation' of performing quantitative economic research. A case does not concern the solving of a mathematical or statistical problem; it uses real economic data to solve an economic question. The cases will help to realise the target of this first course, which is to learn what can be done with econometrics, and why econometrics is a compulsory subject for an economist.

Features and objectives of this book

The main feature of the book is the strong integration of econometric theory and matching software to apply the theory. This distinguishes this book from existing econometric texts, such as Dougherty (2002), Greene (2000), Gujarati (2003), Hamilton (1994), Hendry (1995), Johnston and DiNardo (1997), Maddala (2001), Stock and Watson (2003), Studenmund (2001), Thomas (1997), Verbeek (2000) and Wooldridge (1999). A very short but practical introduction to get a first impression of econometrics is Franses (2002). In the mentioned textbooks, the theory is discussed and illustrated with empirical examples and exercises that are often mathematical or statistical calculations.

The objective of this book is learning 'to correctly perform quantitative economic research' by means of showing elaborated examples from econometric practice and by working through cases. For this purpose, the use of EViews is discussed in detail in connection with the econometric theory. With empirical data sets students act as if they were doing a quantitative economic project. Such a project is evaluated throughout the book because the same data will be used in successive chapters. Earlier obtained results will be reconsidered in following chapters. It is the auther's experience that this approach to teaching econometrics is very effective in understanding the use of econometric methods.

After this 'first course in econometrics' students will have the following skills. They will be able to specify simple linear economic models, to estimate their parameters in a correct way by using economic data and econometric software (EViews), to test the underlying assumptions, and to evaluate the computer results. They will have learned to compute elasticities empirically, to test simple hypotheses about economic behaviour, to forecast economic variables and to simulate an economic policy. Finally, they will be acquainted with a variety of econometric models and methods.

This book offers a complete text for a 'first course', as a broad number of econometric topics is introduced and discussed with their applications. The total number of subjects can be too much for one course, so the text has been written in a way that various selections of chapters can be made for a desired level of the course in question. However, Parts I and II have to be discussed and studied completely, after which the course can be extended with chapters from Parts III and IV.

This book is suitable for self-study because of the extensive and integrated discussion of econometric methods and their use with EViews, together with the included examples, data and exercises. Therefore, the use of this book is not limited to university courses in econometrics. It can very well be studied by economists in trade and industry, or government institutions, who have an interest in quantitative economic research.

EViews (Econometric Views)

Various econometric software packages are available. Some examples of well-known packages that can be used under Windows are EViews, Microfit, OxMetrics (which has a number of known modules like PcGive, PcGets, STAMP and TSP/GiveWin), RATS and Stata. EViews has been chosen for this course as it is the author's experience that it is the most suitable software for realising the objectives stated above.

The use and output from EViews is extensively described in this text. Each time an estimator or a statistic is discussed, its application with EViews will be demonstrated by showing the specific EViews windows. The way to use the software for estimating parameters of economic models and for testing hypotheses, by simply 'clicking' on the procedure names, will be described. However, the application of methods in EViews is not an automatic affair: each time a student has to take decisions him or herself about the next step that has to be done.

EViews is published by Quantitative Micro Software (QMS). Students can buy the EViews 3.1 Student Version at a very low price, provided they can submit a proof of academic affiliation. For detailed information see the 'QMS Home Page' at http://www.eviews.com/. In this book, the use of EViews 4.1 has been discussed. Finishing this manuscript coincided with the release of EViews 5 by QMS. The discussion of EViews in this book concerns the basic procedures for analysing economic data, estimating simple models and testing the underlying statistical and economic assumptions. For that purpose, it makes hardly any difference which level of EViews is used. The appearance of a window can differ slightly in various versions of EViews, but this is not confusing. Interesting aspects of updates of procedures, which are discussed in this book, will be described on the website related to this book.

Prerequisites for this econometrics course

Basic knowledge of matrix algebra and statistics (distributions, estimation and test principles) is required. If you do not have this knowledge and cannot take a course in statistics or mathematics, then you are advised to read the statistical and/or mathematical chapters that are often found in various available econometrics textbooks. Such compact chapters provide adequate knowledge to study this introductory course in econometrics.

Organisation and contents

This book has four parts. Part I consists of three preparatory chapters. In the first chapter some basic concepts of economic and econometric models are briefly summarised.

Chapter 2 introduces the cases and describes the data that will be used throughout the book. In Chapter 3, EViews is introduced and extensively discussed.

Part II concerns the 'reduced-form model'. This model is discussed in detail in Chapters 4 to 7. All the necessary assumptions that have to be made for estimating the parameters of the model, and many statistical tests concerning the validity of the assumptions, come up for discussion. Applications with EViews are presented whenever possible and useful. Parts I and II form already a minimal but complete basic econometrics course. To give an idea of timing, it is possible to do such a course in about 14 or 15 two-hour lessons.

With a selection of the subjects in Part III the basic course can be extended. In Part III, a number of specific models are discussed. It concerns issues like what to do when some of the assumptions concerning the reduced-form model, from Part II, have been rejected or when they are not valid. For these reasons, different estimators are introduced in Chapters 8 and 9. In Chapters 8, 10 and 11, different models with their own specific properties will be introduced. These chapters concern the model with a qualitative dependent variable, and two multiple equation models: the seemingly unrelated regression model (SUR) and the simultaneous equation model (SEM). It will take about seven, two-hour lessons to discuss all the subjects of Part III in an extended course.

Part IV pays attention to the dynamic behaviour of economic models for time-series data. Various types of dynamic models will be discussed. Chapter 12 discusses the estimation of coherent short-run and long-run models. This discussion is important for knowing in which way correct dynamic model specifications for time-series data can be obtained. Subjects that come up are 'unit-root tests', 'cointegration' and 'error-correction' models. All these topics belong in a contemporary basic course in econometrics. Chapter 13 discusses some 'distributed lag models', which are the last dynamic causal models discussed in this book. Finally, Chapter 14 presents the univariate time-series models (ARIMA models). If the course should be extended with all the subjects of this time-series block, eight, two-hour lessons would be needed.

Website

All the data that are used in the examples and cases in the book can be found on the related website:

www.booksites.net/vogelvang

By using a website for additional information, data is easily updated when new and interesting information becomes available. Other information that is relevant after the book has been printed and live updates of EViews will also be placed on the site.

Acknowledgments

The text of this book has benefited very much from the comments and suggestions that I have received from colleagues and ex-quantitative-economics students at the Vrije Universiteit Amsterdam. In alphabetical order, I am very grateful to Jonneke Bolhaar, Hidde Smit, Koos Sneek and Job Zinkstok who have all read the complete manuscript. This resulted in many comments and suggestions, which have clearly contributed to the many text improvements. Koos Sneek has very carefully read the text, and guarded me against formulating a number of statistical statements in a 'too casual' and therefore sometimes non-exact way. His detailed comments and suggestions have been of inestimable value. I am grateful to Hidde Smit for his ideas about a clear order in discussing a number of subjects, and for his sharp eye in judging the empirical oriented topics in the book which yielded many improvements. I thank two of my ex-students, Jonneke Bolhaar and Job Zinkstok, who have 'voluntarily' spent a lot of their time in judging the book from the point of view of potential users – the students – which also resulted in many improvements. The final text has benefited greatly from all the mentioned contributions.

I thank Kees van Montfort for providing me with the interesting cross-section data set about the Dutch firms that is used in the cases in Chapters 8 and 11. I thank Bernd Heidergott, with whom I share an office at our Department of Econometrics, for always having time to answer all my varied questions.

I want to thank various Pearson Education personnel for their guidance during the entire project. I appreciate the informal but constructive way in which everything was discussed. Especially, I am very indebted to the guidance of Justinia Seaman and Janey Webb. Janey was very helpful during the first part of the project in particular. They always quickly and adequately answered my e-mail questions.

Finally, I am thankful to Quantitative Micro Software for their support and for giving me permission to include all the EViews screen shots in this book.

Only I am responsible for the remaining errors in the text.

Ben Vogelvang

Preparatory Work

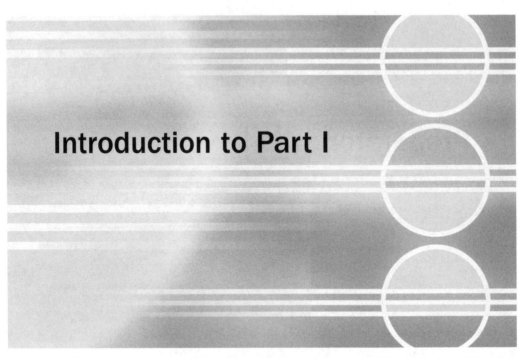

Introduction to Part I

In this part some necessary basic concepts concerning econometric research are discussed. Before a serious start can be made with learning econometrics you need to know about basic aspects of economic and econometric models, about the sorts of economic data that exist and about the use of a software package like EViews that is discussed in this book. In Chapter 1, the basic concepts of econometric models are introduced. The chapter contains a discussion of important aspects of the linear economic and econometric model. The different types of data that can be collected and the different kinds of economic variables and equations that are distinguished will also be discussed. The relationship between the parameters of the model and elasticities is emphasised. Different phases in an econometric research can be distinguished. These phases are schematically presented at the end of Chapter 1. Each phase consists of a number of topics or procedures that have to be done or can be done; this has been summarised. In fact, this scheme indicates the way empirical research is done, from the beginning to the end. These aspects determine the contents of Part II.

The cases and the available data are introduced in Chapter 2. The data that have been used in the examples in the text are also available and this makes it possible for the reader to reproduce the examples.

In Chapter 3, the last chapter of Part I, a number of basic concepts of EViews are introduced. These basic EViews operations are extensively discussed with many examples of the windows that are opened by EViews. Information is given about what can be done in those windows. The procedures in EViews have more interesting and useful aspects than just their easy use for computational work. The graphical output from EViews can be directly inserted into a text editor like Word or Scientific WorkPlace (LaTex). In the last section of Chapter 3, the first exercise is formulated as the start of an empirical econometric research project. This exercise corresponds with the first phase in an empirical study, namely a data analysis.

The knowledge obtained from this part will be sufficient to start you on the discussion of the first econometric model, the 'reduced-form model', that is introduced in Part II, and the empirical applications using EViews.

Chapter 1

Basic Concepts of Econometric Models

1.1 Scientific quantitative economic research

In economic research, as in other disciplines of science, the distinction can be made between theoretical and empirical research. Theoretical economic research in general concerns the development of economic theories. In quantitative economics or in econometrics, it also concerns the development of statistical methods to test the validity of economic theories. These methods fill the tool-box for econometricians. The tool-box mainly consists of statistical and econometric methods, estimators to estimate unknown parameters of economic models, and test statistics to test hypotheses about economic behaviour. Many methods have been made operational in software packages.

Empirical quantitative economic research consists of confronting a hypothesis, formulated from the economic theory, with the reality of the economic world. The hypothesis is tested by using real economic data. In this text, the emphasis is on correctly performing applied econometric research and on the notion that some tools can be used whereas others yield incorrect results.

When doing research it is important to adhere to a number of methodological rules. Research must be objective and reliable. The results have to be capable of being reproduced by other researchers. For example, when a research paper is submitted to a journal for publication, you may be asked to put the used economic data at the editor's disposal, so that other people can check the reliability of the results. Another methodological aspect is to keep the finally obtained result, like an estimated model, as parsimonious as possible to present a transparent analysis of the investigated economy. The research has to be done in an ethically wise manner. 'Data mining' as a method of obtaining results predetermined by the researcher is potentially an unethical method of empirical research. Data mining has to do with estimating many regression equations in a non-structural manner – just every possible combination of explanatory variables can be used – and then choosing subjectively the result that confirms the idea that the researcher wants to prove. If that happens, the result deserves the title 'How to lie with statistics'! Correctly found scientific evidence to support the original hypothesis stemming from the economic theory has *not* been found; in fact the final result will be worthless in many cases.

If you want to prove an economic theory then you have to find a parsimonious econometric model in a structural way, which does not reject the economic and statistical assumptions that have been made to obtain this model. That model can be used to test the hypothesis. If such a model cannot be found then the conclusion should be drawn that the hypothesis is probably not valid and has to be rejected.

In obtaining an econometric model for time-series data, the approach of David Hendry will be used: structural modelling from general to specific. With this approach the data is analysed and modelled in a structural and objective way. (See, for example, Hendry (1995), and also Charemza and Deadman (1992) for a discussion on this topic.)

Naturally, it is also important to write a research paper in a clear, transparent and systematic way. A number of rules exist to help you write in a systematic way. Attention to this stage of a research project will be given in Section 6.6, before the first case that simulates a research project, Case 2, is introduced.

1.2 Economic and econometric models

A quantitative economic research project starts with an economic theory. Hypotheses can be formulated from the economic theory about the economic behaviour of economic agents in the real world. Hypotheses can also be formulated on the basis of people's own observations. The model of the economic behaviour that has been derived from a theory is the *economic model*. The model consists of mathematical equations with economic variables and unknown parameters. Statistical assumptions about the model will be made and tested afterwards. After the unknown parameters have been estimated by using economic data for the variables and by using an appropriate econometric estimation method, one has obtained an *econometric model*. Often it is possible to derive properties of the model a priori, by looking at the theory only. These properties are relevant for the evaluation of the estimation result later on. In Stewart and Wallis (1981, pp.3–4) a simple clarifying example is given with a macroeconomic consumption function that is shown below. In its most simple form, consumption is determined by income only. In the literature it is customary to use the notation C for consumption and Y for income. Then the consumption function is written as a function of income:

$$C = f(Y).   \tag{1.1}$$

Equation (1.1) is specified as a *linear economic model* by writing:

$$C = \beta_1 + \beta_2 Y.   \tag{1.2}$$

It is common to use Greek characters to denote the parameters. The parameters β_1 and β_2 are unknown and have to be estimated. Notice that this equation has not been correctly specified: an exact relationship between consumption and income does not exist. The correct way of specifying a causal model for economic variables will be introduced in Section 4.2. It is possible to look already at some properties of this function that are known from the economic (Keynesian) theory. For example: consumption increases as income increases, but consumption increases less than income does. This implies for equation (1.1) that the first derivative of consumption with respect to income is positive and smaller than 1. If both variables are expressed in identical units then these restrictions imply:

$$0 < \frac{dC}{dY} < 1. \tag{1.3}$$

Inequality (1.3) results in a restriction on the parameters β_2 of the consumption equation (1.2):

$$0 < \beta_2 < 1.$$

Further, you may expect a positive value for the intercept: $\beta_1 > 0$. These inequalities will be used in the 'economic evaluation' of the econometric model after the parameters of the model have been estimated. It is also known that the part of the income that will be consumed will decrease when income rises, or formulated in mathematical terms:

$$\frac{d\,(C/Y)}{dY} < 0.$$

Differentiation of the quotient C/Y gives:

$$\frac{d\,(C/Y)}{dY} = \frac{1}{Y}\frac{dC}{dY} - \frac{C}{Y^2} < 0.$$

Elaboration of the inequality, with the assumption that $Y > 0$ and $C > 0$, yields:

$$\frac{1}{Y}\frac{dC}{dY} < \frac{C}{Y^2},$$
$$\frac{dC}{dY} < \frac{C}{Y},$$
$$\frac{Y}{C}\frac{dC}{dY} < 1. \tag{1.4}$$

The left-hand side of inequality (1.4) is the mathematical expression of the income elasticity. The last inequality states that the income elasticity is less than 1.

Suppose that the parameters have been estimated with the resulting values $\widehat{\beta}_1 = 15.4$ and $\widehat{\beta}_2 = 0.81$, then the model is written as

$$\widehat{C} = 15.4 + 0.81Y,$$

which is the *econometric model*. The usual notation for publishing an econometric model is discussed in Section 6.6 (and the 'hat' above the C in Section 4.3).

1.3   Economic data

The unknown parameters of a proper economic model can be estimated if sufficient data on the variables are available. The collected data form the *sample*. The data are considered as drawn from populations. Each observation is:

- ■   a realisation of a variable at a certain moment, for example, personal income, company's production, country's GDP, etc. or
- ■   a realisation for a certain object or subject such as the sales of firms in the same business or the ownership of a PC by a student.

Three main types of economic data can be distinguished: *time-series data*, *cross-section data* and *panel data*. In this book, attention is only paid to the analysis of time-series data and cross-section data.

Time-series data are historical data. Historical data can be observed at different frequencies, like annual data, quarterly data, etc. Often, published time-series data concern average values of the variables during a year or a quarter, but alternatively it is also possible to analyse end-of-the-period data. This can sometimes be observed for high-frequency data such as weekly or daily data: for example, stock market data, or futures prices on commodity exchanges.

Cross-section data are data collected during one period, for example, for people, companies or countries. Cross-section data are then collected typically in one month or one quarter. Panel data are cross-section data that are collected at various points of time, but the data concern the same panel of subjects or objects in every period. In most studies, large cross-sections are found collected for only a few points of time. (See, for example, Baltagi (2001) for an extensive discussion about modelling panel data.)

An important difference between time-series data and cross-section data is that time-series data have a fixed ordering in time. Cross-section data do not have a fixed ordering, the researcher determines a logical ordering, for example, from low to high income. The difference between time-series data and cross-section data is also seen in the notation. For time-series data the subscript t is added to the variable (e.g. C_t and Y_t), whereas for cross-section data the subscript i is used (C_i and Y_i).

Economic data can be collected in different ways. Data are published in national and international statistical periodicals. If data have to be collected in this way, then they have to be manually input to a computer file, which is not a convenient way of importing data. Now it is often possible to get the data in electronic form, for example, from international organisations by using the internet. (See Chapter 2 for some examples.) Sometimes data is free to download but sometimes you have to pay for data. The data that are necessary to do the exercises included in this book can be downloaded from the internet (see Chapter 2).

1.4   Variables of an economic model

In an economic model there is one variable on the left-hand side of the equation, called the *dependent variable*. Variables on the right-hand side of the equation are the *explanatory variables*. The nature of economic variables can be *endogenous*, *exogenous* or *lagged dependent.* A variable is an endogenous variable if the variable is determined in the model in question. Therefore the dependent variable is always an endogenous variable. The exogenous variables are determined outside the model. Lagged dependent (or lagged endogenous) variables are 'predetermined' in the model. In fact they are endogenous, but their values have already been realised. Knowledge about the nature of the variables, especially of the explanatory variables, is of importance for the choice of an estimator for the unknown parameters and for knowing the properties of the estimator.

The model is not necessarily a model of only one equation. One equation can often be considered as part of a larger model where other variables are determined too. If more equations have been specified to determine other endogenous variables of the system then the system is called a *simultaneous equation model* (SEM); this model is the subject of Chapter 10. In such a model it is possible to simulate any policy for a more or less completely specified economy. For example, one can change the percentage of any tax variable and compute the effect on consumption, etc. If the number of equations is identical to the number of endogenous variables, then that system of equations is called *complete.* A complete model can be solved for the endogenous variables. This is necessary if one wishes to perform simulations with the model as mentioned above. (See the next section for more discussion on this topic.)

Although it is not necessary to specify a complete model for all the endogenous variables, if you are only interested in the study of one of the equations of that model, it is always important to judge the nature of all the explanatory variables of that equation. It is an open door, but it is clear that lagged variables only can occur in time-series models. Below two examples are given to highlight these points.

Example 1.1   A simple Keynesian macro model

In the macro-consumption equation, model (1.2), both the variables C_t and Y_t are endogenous variables, because they are determined in the same macroeconomic model, but an equation for income was not considered yet as so far the 'research interest' concerned consumption only. For example, an equation for Y_t can be added in the form of an identity, which gives the following most simple Keynesian model as an example of a complete SEM:

$$C_t = \beta_1 + \beta_2 Y_t,$$
$$Y_t = C_t + I_t,$$

where I_t is the variable for the investments, which is considered as an exogenous variable in this model specification. The subscript t indicates that the variables are observed as time-series with, for example, annual, quarterly or monthly observations. In general notation, t runs from 1 to n: $t = 1, \ldots, n$.

Example 1.2   A model for coffee consumption in a country

In Vogelvang (1988) an econometric model for the world coffee market has been developed. That is the reason why many examples in this book relate to the coffee market. This example concerns a quarterly model for the consumption of coffee in a coffee-importing country. It is assumed that coffee consumption $\left(C_t^{cof}\right)$ depends on the coffee price $\left(P_t^{cof}\right)$, the price of tea (P_t^{tea}), as tea can be a substitute for coffee, and income (Y_t). Of course more economic variables can be relevant in explaining coffee consumption, but this is just an example to illustrate the discussed topics of an economic model. (See also Remark 1.2 below.) The coffee consumption equation can be written as:

$$C_t^{cof} = \beta_1 + \beta_2 P_t^{cof} + \beta_3 P_t^{tea} + \beta_4 Y_t.$$

In this model, C_t^{cof} and P_t^{cof} are two endogenous variables because both variables will be determined in a complete model for the world coffee market. An equation explaining P_t^{cof} is not specified as only the consumption of coffee is 'studied' here. P_t^{tea} and Y_t are two exogenous variables because they are not determined in a model for the coffee market. Notice that the expected signs of the parameters are: $\beta_2 < 0$, $\beta_3 > 0$, $\beta_4 > 0$. No a priori restrictions exist on the constant term β_1.

The models are *static models* in the examples so far. The implication of a static model is that a change of an explanatory variable in period t is fully reflected in the dependent variable in the same period t. That can sometimes be considered as a strong restriction on the model. When the price increases with one unit in period t the consumption of coffee decreases with β_2 in period t. Such a change can be unrealistic for economic reasons. Although that depends on the frequency of the data, for annual data it is not a problem, but for monthly data this can be different. For example, consumption can be based on the current price but also on the price from the (recent) past. In that case, the prices from previous periods, called *lagged variables*, are also specified in the equation. For example:

$$C_t^{cof} = \beta_1 + \beta_2 P_t^{cof} + \beta_3 P_t^{tea} + \beta_4 Y_t + \beta_5 P_{t-1}^{cof} + \beta_6 P_{t-2}^{cof}.$$

When the price increases with one unit in period t the consumption of coffee has decreased with β_2 in period t, with $\beta_2 + \beta_5$ in period $t + 1$, and with $\beta_2 + \beta_5 + \beta_6$ in period $t + 2$. In other words, the short-run price response is β_2 and the long-run price response is $\beta_2 + \beta_5 + \beta_6$. (A detailed discussion about short-run and long-run models is given in Part IV.)

The parameter β_2 is negative, the signs of β_5 and β_6 are not known a priori. If β_5 and β_6 are negative, then a new price needs three periods before the adjustment in consumption is complete and the long-run price response is larger than the short-run price response. Opposite signs of a lagged variable indicate a correction on the adjustment in the previous period(s). For that reason, it is possible that the long-run price response is less than the short-run price response. Other explanatory variables can be specified with lags too. The equation is called a *dynamic model* when lagged variables have been specified.

It is also possible that lags of the dependent variable are specified as explanatory variables, as in the following specification:

$$C_t^{cof} = \beta_1 + \beta_2 P_t^{cof} + \beta_3 P_t^{tea} + \beta_4 Y_t + \beta_5 C_{t-1}^{cof}.$$

In this model, the quantity of consumed coffee from the previous period $(t - 1)$ influences the coffee consumption in the present period (t). This variable C_{t-1} represents the habit formation or the (stochastic) trend in consumption, which is clearly not unrealistic from an economic point of view. The variable C_{t-1}^{cof} is a lagged endogenous variable, just as the variables

P_{t-i}^{cof}, but in this equation C_{t-1}^{cof} is called a *lagged dependent variable*. The specification of lagged endogenous variables does have its own statistical problems, as will be explained in Chapter 4. A model with a lagged dependent variable is, mathematically seen, a difference equation. The parameter β_5 has the restriction $0 \leq \beta_5 < 1$, otherwise the difference equation will explode, or will show an unrealistic alternating influence of C_{t-1}^{cof}. A short-term price change will have less effect on consumption when the trend is strong (β_5 close to 1).

Note that the specification of lags decreases the sample length that is used to estimate the parameters. The frequency of the data is important for the specification of the dynamics in a model. Many lags can be expected in a model for high-frequency data, or just a few or no lags are expected in a model for low-frequency data. A model for variables measured in monthly averages will have more dynamics than a model for variables with an annual frequency.

Remark 1.1 Warning

Be aware of specifying strange restrictions in the model, like 'holes' in lag patterns. For example, an equation like:

$$C_t = \beta_1 + \beta_2 Y_t + \beta_3 Y_{t-2}$$

has a remarkable restriction: consumption in period t is determined by income from the periods t and $t - 2$, but not by income from period $t - 1$! That is clearly not a realistic model. For example, this can happen when it is observed that the influence of Y_{t-1} is not significantly different from zero after the parameters have been estimated, and the variable is mindlessly deleted. This point will discussed in more detail later on.

Remark 1.2 Is the specification of the coffee consumption equation realistic?

Income (Y_t) has been linearly specified in the coffee consumption equation. The utmost consequence of this specification is that enormous quantities of coffee are consumed at very high income levels! That is actually not very realistic. A model is just valid in a certain sample and within a certain range of the variables. One has to be cautious with computing predictions for an endogenous variable for extreme values of the explanatory variables by using an estimated econometric model. The same is true for long-term model simulations.

Other variables can be relevant in explaining coffee consumption, like the price of soft drinks as one more possible substitute for coffee.

Trends in a country's population might also influence the total coffee consumption. Then it is better to specify consumption and income per capita.

1.5 Structural and reduced-form equations

The equations of the economic model as specified in the economic theory, are called the *structural equations*. A complete model of a number of structural equations is the *structural form* of the model. Different types of structural equations can be distinguished. An equation like the consumption equation is called a *behavioural equation*. Other relationships are, for example, *technical relationships* (like production functions) and *identities* (as in Example 1.1). Unknown parameters do not occur in an identity.

A complete SEM can be solved for the endogenous variables. The solution is called the *reduced-form model*. The reduced-form model consists of *reduced-form equations*. The SEM in Example 1.1 is a complete structural form with two equations for the two endogenous variables C_t and Y_t, The investment variable I_t is supposed to be exogenous. Solving that model for C_t and Y_t gives the two reduced-form equations:

$$C_t = \frac{\beta_1}{1 - \beta_2} + \frac{\beta_2}{1 - \beta_2} I_t,$$

$$Y_t = \frac{\beta_1}{1 - \beta_2} + \frac{1}{1 - \beta_2} I_t.$$

Or in general notation:

$$C_t = \pi_{11} + \pi_{12} I_t,$$

$$Y_t = \pi_{21} + \pi_{22} I_t.$$

The reduced form will be used to simulate a policy or to compute forecasts for the endogenous variables, of course after the estimated reduced form parameters have been inserted.

The equations for time-series data that have been considered so far are models that describe the behaviour of the economic variables in the short run. Lagged endogenous and lagged exogenous variables in a structural model are predetermined, so they will be found as explanatory variables in reduced-form equations. When lagged endogenous variables are specified in a structural form, some of the reduced-form equations will be difference equations that can be solved to compute long-run effects. Without lagged dependent variables the reduced-form equations show the long-run effect too, as seen in Example 1.2. If a static specification is a correct model for the short run, then it is also a specification for the long-run model.

1.6   Parameters and elasticities

It is useful to look at the parameters, the coefficients of the variables, in more detail. In a first econometrics course it is usual to assume that parameters are constant in the model, implying that the economic structure of the model is assumed to be constant in the sample. Other assumptions about the parameters can be made, but not in this book.

The following terminology is used. The parameters are estimated by an *estimator* and the result is called an *estimate*. The magnitude of the parameters depends on the units of the variables. The values of the estimated parameters can hardly be interpreted when the units of the various variables are different. Therefore, it is often better to check the validity of the estimates by computing and evaluating the magnitude of elasticities, which are free of units. It is important to be aware of the following point. Below it is shown that restrictions on elasticities are imposed by the log transformation of the variables. The log transformation is a popular transformation in econometric research: because it removes non-linearities to some extent, it has a dimming influence on changes of the variance of the variables, and because the coefficients can easily be interpreted as elasticities.

The following specifications can be distinguished and are illustrated with a simple linear bivariate model.

■ The model has been linearly specified in the observed two variables:

$$Y_t = \beta_1 + \beta_2 X_t.$$

The definition of the elasticity e_{yx} of Y with respect to X is:

$$e_{yx} = \frac{\partial Y_t}{\partial X_t} \frac{X_t}{Y_t}.$$

So, when using the bivariate model, the elasticity e_{yx} is computed as:

$$e_{yx} = \beta_2 \frac{X_t}{Y_t}.$$

The elasticity varies in the sample with both the variables Y_t and X_t. The elasticity can be computed for all the points of time of the sample period. Then it is interesting to look at a graph of the elasticity. The quantities that can be reported in a paper are, for example, the maximum, minimum and mean value of the elasticity in the sample period. This can be done in EViews in a simple way. Regularly, you find that only the sample means are substituted for X_t and Y_t, but presenting only an average elasticity can be less informative. What you want to compute depends on what has happened in the sample period. If the economy was rather quiet in that period it can be sufficient to compute the mean elasticity only. But in a period with heavy price changes on a commodity market, for example, you may expect that the price elasticity with respect to demand has not been very constant. Then it is more informative to publish more statistics than just a mean. An example of the computation of an income elasticity in EViews is given in Section 3.4.

■ The variables X_t and Y_t have been transformed in their (natural) logarithms. The model is:

$$ln\,(Y_t) = \beta_1 + \beta_2 ln\,(X_t) \tag{1.5}$$

Differentiating (1.5) with respect to X_t gives the elasticity e_{yx} of Y with respect to X:

$$e_{yx} = \frac{\partial Y_t}{\partial X_t} \frac{X_t}{Y_t} = \beta_2 \frac{Y_t}{X_t} \frac{X_t}{Y_t} = \beta_2.$$

This means that the coefficient β_2 of model (1.5) has become an elasticity and this elasticity no longer varies with any variable. The elasticity is *constant* in the sample as the parameter β_2 is assumed to be constant. This is a restriction! Be aware before the application of the log transformation whether or not this restriction is an economically realistic restriction in the sample period that is analysed.

Two other possible specifications can be distinguished, which are the following semi-logarithmic models.

■   The model is:

$$Y_t = \beta_1 + \beta_2 ln\,(X_t)\,.$$

In this situation the elasticity e_{yx} is:

$$e_{yx} = \frac{\partial Y_t}{\partial X_t}\frac{X_t}{Y_t} = \beta_2 \frac{1}{X_t}\frac{X_t}{Y_t} = \beta_2 \frac{1}{Y_t}.$$

This elasticity only varies with Y_t.

■   The model is:

$$ln\,(Y_t) = \beta_1 + \beta_2 X_t.$$

The elasticity e_{yx} is now computed as:

$$e_{yx} = \frac{\partial Y_t}{\partial X_t}\frac{X_t}{Y_t} = \beta_2 Y_t \frac{X_t}{Y_t} = \beta_2 X_t,$$

and this elasticity varies with X_t only.

Conclusion

The conclusion is that one has to be aware of the consequences when transforming variables to their logarithms. Is it realistic, for economic reasons, to restrict the elasticity to be constant, or to vary with only one of the variables, in that particular sample period? If the answer is yes, then it is not a problem but if this is not the case then the log transformation should not be applied.

1.7   Stochastic models

Until now, the models were discussed as exactly determined mathematical equations. That is possible in the 'natural sciences' where exact relationships are derived between physical variables. However, it is not the case in economics. Economic relationships are not exact relationships so they need to be written in a different way. A *disturbance term* will be included at the right-hand side of the equation to complete the equation. A disturbance term is a stochastic variable that is not observed. At the right-hand side of the equation, two parts of the specification will be distinguished: the *systematic part,* which concerns the specification of variables, based on the economic theory; and the *non-systematic* part, which is the remaining random non-systematic variation, to make it a valid equation. All variables that are known to be relevant for the explanation of the endogenous variable have to be specified in the model, but then the equation between the variables is still not an exact relationship. In a well-specified model, the difference between the systematic part and the endogenous dependent variable will be random without any systematic behaviour. When that is not the case, the systematic part has not been correctly specified and has to be respecified.

For example, a linear bivariate model is specified in *general notation* as follows.

$$Y_t = \beta_1 + \beta_2 X_t + u_t. \tag{1.6}$$

The variable Y_t is the dependent (endogenous) variable, X_t is an exogenous explanatory variable, the variable u_t is the disturbance term representing the non-systematic part of the equation. As mentioned above, the disturbance term u_t cannot be observed. The disturbance term is a stochastic variable and assumptions will be made with respect to its probability distribution. These assumptions are introduced in Section 4.2 and will be considered in more detail in Chapter 6. The stochastic behaviour of the disturbance term implies that the endogenous variable is a stochastic variable too. All endogenous variables, whether they are dependent or explanatory variables, are stochastic variables. It will be clear that model (1.6) with only one explanatory variable is rather limited in explaining the behaviour of an economic variable. When introducing the general linear model in Section 4.2, the specification will be more generally discussed.

1.8   Applied quantitative economic research

In this section, the process of an econometric research project is schematically summarised. As introduced earlier, the aim of empirical econometric research is the analysis of an economic phenomenon by specifying an economic model (the economic theory), estimating its parameters and testing the assumptions that have been made by using common sense, economic knowledge and statistical methods. The resulting model will be an econometric model. This model can be used to compute elasticities, to test economic hypotheses, to simulate policies, to compute forecasts, etc. First a number of assumptions of the model have to be formulated after which the unknown parameters will be estimated. This concerns deterministic assumptions as well as stochastic assumptions. By using the estimates, the validity of the assumptions will be tested. If some of them are rejected then the model has to be reformulated. This process can be characterised by the following scheme of stages in an empirical research project. All the points mentioned will be discussed in following chapters.

The deterministic assumptions

The deterministic assumptions concern the specification of the economic model, which is the formulation of the null hypothesis about the relationship between the economic variables of interest. The basic specification of the model originates from the economic theory. An important decision is made about the size of the model, whether one or more equations have to be specified. In other words, does the analysis concern a single equation model or a multiple equation model? A different question is: at what economic level has the model to be formulated, at micro or macro level, etc.

The choice of which variables have to be included in the model stems also from the economic theory. For a time-series model, an adequate choice of the time frequency must be made, which is in accordance with the research objective. For example, a model that has to explain short-run stock market prices should be estimated by using daily or weekly data (average or closing prices), whereas long-term economic cycles can be analysed with a macroeconomic model that has been estimated by using annual data. A coffee consumption equation, like the one in Example 1.2, will probably adequately be estimated for monthly or quarterly data. The availability of data can influence the assumptions that have to be made about the specification of the equation. If no sufficient data are available at the desired time frequency, then it is possible that the research objective has to be reformulated.

The mathematical form of the model has to be determined. Is it possible to assume that the model is linear or is it necessary to specify a non-linear model? A linear model is more convenient to analyse, but it has to be based on a realistic assumption. Distinction can be made between linearity in the parameters and linearity in the variables. This can be shown with an example of the following non-linear model (e.g. a Cob–Douglas production function). The non-linear model:

$$Y_t = \beta_1 X_t^{\beta_2} Z_t^{\beta_3} e^{u_t}$$

can be linearised by the log transformation:

$$\ln(Y_t) = \ln(\beta_1) + \beta_2 \ln(X_t) + \beta_3 \ln(Z_t) + u_t \text{ or}$$
$$\ln(Y_t) = \beta_1^* + \beta_2 \ln(X_t) + \beta_3 \ln(Z_t) + u_t.$$

This model is non-linear in the variables but it is linear in the parameters. When we are talking about a linear model this concerns a model that is *linear in the parameters*. The parameters of this model can be estimated with a linear estimator like the ordinary-least squares estimator. The following non-linear model cannot be linearised by a simple log transformation:

$$Y_t = \beta_1 X_t^{\beta_2} Z_t^{\beta_3} + u_t.$$

Specific reasons must exist to specify an additional disturbance term here. The parameters have to be estimated by a non-linear estimation method.

The stochastic assumptions and estimation of the parameters

Statistical assumptions need to be formulated about the stochastic variables in the model with respect to the distributions and/or their moments. What is important regarding the choice of an estimator for the parameters is that you have knowledge about the nature of the explanatory variables: are these variables endogenous or exogenous, as was explained in Section 1.4?

A data analysis is important at the beginning of the research project. It provides information about the behaviour of the economic variables in the sample period. Do the variables correlate as expected? Are trends or other systematic patterns, like seasonal patterns, economic fluctuations or cycles, present in the time-series data? Is the variance of the disturbance term in a model with cross-section data constant or is the variance proportional to the variance of one or more of the explanatory variables? Conclusions from such an analysis give rise to action: for example, the elimination of systematic behaviour from the variables or the choice of a specific estimator for the parameters. An estimation method will be chosen on the basis of these assumptions. Then the unknown parameters are estimated and test statistics are calculated to evaluate the results, as described in the next stage below.

Evaluation of the estimation results

The evaluation concerns the verification of the validity and reliability of all the assumptions that have been made. This concerns the unsystematic part as well as the systematic part of the model. The evaluation of the results takes place in various ways. A first evaluation is obtained by using common sense and economic knowledge, for example when looking at the sign and magnitude of the parameters or elasticities. This is followed by testing the stochastic assumptions that have been made by using a normality test, autocorrelation tests, heteroskedasticity tests, etc. Looking at a plot of the residuals can be very informative about cycles or outliers that have not been observed before. Attention must be paid to the hypothesis that the structure is linear and constant in the sample period.

If the stochastic assumptions have not been rejected, the deterministic assumptions can be tested by using statistical tests to test for restrictions on parameters: for example, the t-test and F-test can be performed, the coefficient of determination R^2 can be interpreted, etc.

In some projects, it is relevant to evaluate the forecasting power or simulation properties of the model by simulating the estimated model for either the entire sample period or for only a part of the sample period.

The continuation of the project

The rejection of some of the preceding assumptions may give rise to returning to the specification or estimation stage. Often the systematic part of the model has to be respecified during the process of achieving a final parsimonious model. But when the evaluation is satisfactory, then it is time to write the final version of the research report.

Conclusion

The scheme given above will be elaborated in Chapter 4. In Chapter 4, the 'reduced-form model' will be introduced and discussed. This model encompasses 'the classical regression model' which is a linear static model with exogenous explanatory variables only.

The 'reduced-form model' can be a more general and dynamic model with lags of the dependent variable as explanatory variables too. Later on, 'structural models', which are models that have also endogenous explanatory variables, are discussed (see Chapter 9). These three types of models have different properties. Their parameters have to be estimated in a different way and the used estimators have different properties. It will be shown that the choice of an estimator that has to be used is dependent on the stochastic properties of the model specification.

Chapter 2

Description of the Data Sets and Introduction to the Cases

2.1 Introduction

In this chapter, a description is given of the available data that will be used in the cases. These cases are an introduction to performing empirical econometric research. The cases do not concern mathematical or statistical exercises with one solution, but they give rise to economic questions that can be answered with econometric modelling and statistical testing, by using the provided real economic data. The result of econometric research is not one unique answer, which is in contrast to the mentioned exercises. The cases have been formulated in a way that lets the student perform empirical econometric research, not yet in an autonomous way but according to the questions or assignments formulated in the case. In fact it is simulated empirical work that is guided by the points that are mentioned in the cases. In an applied econometric research project, time-series or cross-section data are analysed and modelled. Both types of data come up in the relevant chapters. The data files are Microsoft Excel files that can be downloaded from the accompanying website.

The aims of this book are not achieved by including a huge number of data sets. A number of files are offered that will be sufficient to use on many aspects of the discussed econometric themes. Sometimes a choice between a couple of sets can be made. Of course, it is not necessary to use the provided data. It could be more interesting or exciting to use data that has been collected from your own research instead of the provided data sets. Then you can kill two birds with one stone: studying applied econometrics and starting your own research at the same time!

In the next section, the data set that contains the time-series data that has been used in the examples throughout the text will be introduced. The reader can reproduce these examples by using the data which will contribute to a better understanding of the text. Subsequently, the accompanying data sets are introduced in consecutive sections. In sections with time-series data an introductory guidance is given concerning possible models that can be estimated. In Section 3.5, one of the data sets will be selected for a data analysis as formulated in Case 1. The complete first exercise starts in Case 2 at the end of Chapter 6. That is quite a way ahead, therefore the reader is advised to use the examples given in the text when studying the first six chapters. What to do with the cross-section data set is formulated in the relevant Cases 4 and 9, after the specific models for these cases have been discussed.

In Chapter 3, the procedure for importing data in an EViews 'workfile' is described. Each research project has its own workfile. If you want to include any variable from a different workfile in the workfile that is currently being used, then that is no problem. It is possible to exchange variables between various workfiles of EViews. In an easy and convenient way variables can be copied from one EViews workfile into another. This is explained in Remark 3.6 in Section 3.2. So you are not limited to using only variables from one of the offered data files that are discussed in this chapter.

2.2   Data set 1: commodity prices

The time-series data that will be used in the examples originate from former research on international agricultural commodity markets as done by the author in the past, see, for example, Vogelvang (1994). The data set has been updated with recent data and data are available in the file *pcoccoftea.xls*.

This data set concerns the following monthly data on the price of cocoa, coffee and tea:

- the coffee price is the Composite Indicator Price (according to the definition in the International Coffee Agreement 1976) in US$ cents per pound, for the sample period January 1960 to September 2002;
- the cocoa price is the Cocoa NY/London 3-month futures price also in US$ cents per pound and for the sample period 1960(01)–2002(09);
- the tea price is the London price in US$/tonne for the sample period 1960(01)–1998(06).

The data are from the UNCTAD, *Monthly Commodity Price Bulletin*. The following considerations have played a role in analysing a relationship between these prices. Coffee, cocoa (beside other uses) and tea are beverages that may be considered, to a certain extent, as substitutes for each other. An important property of these commodities is that they are all commodities that can be stored. Another important feature is that coffee and cocoa have been involved in an international commodity agreement (with varying success). Tea is traded unrestrictedly. Further, it is well-known that some of the commodities are often traded on the same futures exchange, like the New York Board of Trade, which is also a reason for price interrelationships.

The idea behind these data is as follows. When studying the price formation of these commodities, price movements on the cocoa market were observed that were not caused by circumstances in the world cocoa market, but probably by economic developments in the world coffee market. The data on the commodity prices show more or less similar developments in some sub-periods, of course beside specific price movements of the particular commodities themselves in other periods. For instance, the high prices of all the commodities in 1976 and 1977 were caused by occurrences on the coffee market (see Figure 3.20). More facts about the prices are given in the examples.

For these reasons, a simple relationship can be used to illustrate many of the items discussed in several chapters.

2.3 Data set 2: macroeconomic data

Macroeconomic data sets are offered for the USA, the UK, France, Australia and Japan. These data have been collected from the website of the Organization of Economic Co-operation and Development (OECD), http://www.oecd.org/, and the Bureau of Economic Analysis (BEA), http://www.bea.doc.gov/. They concern quarterly data for sample periods between 1980 and 2003. The data files are Excel files; you always have to create your own EViews workfiles. The files with OECD data are defined as:

- *Macro_USA.xls*, sample period: 1980(01)–2003(01);
- *Macro_UK.xls*, sample period: 1980(01)–2003(01);
- *Macro_France.xls*, sample period: 1979(04)–2003(01);
- *Macro_Australia.xls*, sample period: 1979(04)–2003(01);
- *Macro_Japan.xls*, sample period: 1980(01)–2003(01).

The selected variables, with their names in parentheses as they are shown in the files, are:

- gross domestic product (*gdp*);
- private final consumption expenditures (*cons*);
- government final consumption expenditure (*gov*);
- investments (private and government) (*inv*).

These variables contain the nominal values in domestic currencies, but for Japan are in billions of yen. Where real data are also provided, the names are preceded with an r as in r_gdp, r_cons, etc. The real data of the USA are expressed in the currency value of 1996 and for the other countries in the 1995 value (Australia 2000(01)). The units of the OECD data are millions of the national currencies; for the USA and Japan the units are in billions. The data are seasonally adjusted.

These data sets can be used individually to estimate simple models for the economy of one country, but they can also be used together to estimate one model (a SUR model) for a number of countries simultaneously, as will be introduced in Section 8.3. For example, as a basis model a simple SEM can look like:

$$C_t = \gamma_{11} + \beta_{11}Y_t + u_{t1}$$
$$I_t = \gamma_{21} + \beta_{21}Y_t + \gamma_{22}Y_{t-1} + u_{t2}$$
$$Y_t = C_t + I_t + G_t,$$

with $C_t = cons_t$, $Y_t = gdp_t$, $I_t = inv_t$, and $G_t = gov_t$.

Parameters of endogenous variables are denoted by β_{ij}s, and parameters of exogenous or predetermined variables by γ_{ij}s. Dynamic consumption and investment equations can be estimated with the provided data. A 'discrepancy variable' has to be added to make the identity balanced as the involved variables are not all the variables in the 'national accounts' that determine Y_t. This discrepancy variable is needed in Case 8. An exercise to model one of the equations is formulated in Case 2. Case 5 is an exercise with a SUR model. The data is used again in Case 8 where system estimation methods are applied to estimate the parameters of the SEM simultaneously. The data will also be used in other more specific exercises.

One more data file concerning the USA has been included for a long sample period: *Macro_USA_long.xls*. It concerns quarterly data (at annual levels) for the same and for some more variables observed in the period 1946(01)–2003(01). These data are obtained from the National Income and Product Accounts tables (NIPA-tables) of the BEA. Two separate variables are included for the investments representing private (*gross_private_inv*) and government (*gross_gov_inv*) investment. The net exports of goods and services are also included. One more GDP variable is found in this file: *gdp_nsa_q* representing the GDP that is not seasonally adjusted and measured at quarterly levels. The variables are measured in billions of US dollars. More information about the data, such as the computation of index figures and the seasonal adjustment, and of course more data, can be found at the mentioned websites. With this more extensive data set it is possible to refine the macro model and to investigate this long sample for the presence of structural breaks.

2.4   Data set 3: oil market-related data

Two data files related to the oil market in the USA are provided: *Vehicles_USA.xls,* and *Oil_gas_USA.xls*. The file *Vehicles_USA.xls* contains quarterly observations that are seasonally adjusted at annual rates, for the following variables:

- '*exp_vehicles*': expenditures on vehicles and parts, 1946(01)–2003(02);
- '*price_vehicles*': price index (1996 = 100) of vehicles and parts, 1947(01)–2003(02);
- '*quant_vehicles*': quantity index (1996 = 100) of vehicles and parts, 1947(01)–2003(02);
- '*price_gas_oil*': price index (1996 = 100) of gasoline and oil, 1947(01)–2003(02);
- '*quant_gas_oil*': quantity index (1996 = 100) of gasoline and oil, 1947(01)–2003(02);
- '*price_defl_pc*': price deflator for personal consumption expenditures, 1947(01)–2003(02);
- '*price_defl_dg*': price deflator for durable goods, 1947(01)–2003(02).

Also included are the GDP and the real GDP from the file *Macro_USA_long.xls*.

All the data have been obtained from the NIPA-tables. They are seasonally adjusted, at annual rates, and measured in billions of US dollars. With this data set the expenditures on vehicles in the USA can be analysed.

The file *oil_gas_usa.xls* contains monthly data on crude oil prices and retail gas prices. These data have been obtained from the website of the Energy Information Administration

(EIA), http://www.eia.doe.gov/. The following variables are included in the Excel file:

- 'crude oil domestic first purchase price' in cents per barrel: 1974:(01)–2003(04); ($p\_crudeoil\_us$);
- 'F.O.B. cost of crude oil imports', in cents per barrel: 1973(10)–2003(04); (fob_imp);
- 'landed cost of crude oil imports', in cents per barrel: 1973(10)–2003(04); ($landed\_imp$);
- 'leaded regular gasoline, US city average retail price', in tenth cent per gallon: 1973(10)–1991(04); (p_lead_reg);
- 'unleaded regular gasoline, US city average retail price', in tenth cent per gallon: 1976(01)–2003(05); (p_unlead_reg);
- 'unleaded premium gasoline, US city average retail price', in tenth cent per gallon: 1981(09)–2003(05); ($p\_unlead\_premium$);
- 'all types of gasoline, US city average retail price', in tenth cent per gallon: 1978(01)–2003(05); (p_all).

With the data from this file a similar analysis can be done as given in the examples, but now concerning a relationship between world market prices of crude oil and retail prices of gasoline.

In Case 1, an economic model has to be formulated and these data can be analysed, after which an econometric model will be estimated in Case 2. For comparing these prices be aware of the different units of the variables: 1 barrel = 42 US gallons.

2.5   Data set 4: money market

A file with monetary data from the USA has been included to analyse the demand for money. The data have been obtained from the economic database FREDII of the Federal Reserve Bank of St. Louis that can be found at http://research.stlouisfed.org/. A lot of economic data with long time-series can be found in that database. The selected monetary data for performing a case concerning the American money demand is available in the file: *money_usa.xls*.

The original monetary data from FREDII have a monthly frequency, but as the GDP was only encountered as quarterly data, all the data has been rendered into quarterly data. The following variables are available for the period 1959(01)–2003(02).

- the money stock M1, M2 and M3, not seasonally adjusted ($m1$, $m2$, $m3$);
- GDP, the same variable as before, which has been seasonally adjusted at annual levels (gdp);
- price index of the GDP, seasonal adjusted ($price\_defl\_gdp$);
- consumer price index, not seasonal adjusted (cpi);
- an interest variable, the 3-Month Treasury Bill market rates (tbr).

The money stock will be used as an approximation for the demand for money that can be explained by the GDP and the interest rate. If these data will be used, then the formulation of an economic model for the money demand is done in Case 1 together with a data analysis, whereas in Case 2 an econometric model is determined.

2.6 Data set 5: cross-section data

Two data files with cross-section data are used. One file concerns simulated data that is used in an example in Chapter 11. The other data file consists of business-economic data that will be used for cases in Section 8.6 (heteroskedasticity) and in Section 11.5 for a model with a qualitative dependent variable. The files are: *pcdata.xls* and *business.xls*.

The simulated data in the file *pcdata.xls* are described in Section 11.4. The business economic data originates from the study by Van Montfort, Ridder and Kleinknecht (2002). Two cases are formulated in Part III, where some of the variables from the original file will be used. The cases are not corresponding to the original study, they only use the data in more simple formulated cases. The file consists of cross-section data from 2886 firms in the Netherlands that were collected in 1992. The following variables will be used.

■ percentage of sales of products that are new to the firm (new_s_firm);
■ percentage of sales of products that are new to the industry ($new\_s\_industry$);
■ number of employees in full-time employment ($empl$);
■ R&D costs in proportion to sales (rd_s);
■ sales growth in percentages between 1990 and 1992 (gr_s).

A number of dummy variables are included in the data set:

■ The dummy variable '$modern$' is equal to one if the firm is a modern company and equal to zero if that is not the case.
■ The dummy variable '$incentr$' is equal to one if the firm is located in a central region and otherwise equal to zero.
■ The dummy variable '$rdcoop$' is equal to one if the firm is engaged in R&D co-operation and otherwise equal to zero.
■ The dummy variable '$extech$' is equal to one if the firm acquires external techno-logical knowledge and otherwise equal to zero.

The concept of dummy variables is explained in Section 7.5.

In Case 9 (Chapter 11) we will analyse whether the need for external technological knowledge (the variable $extech$) can be explained by variables from this data set. Modelling of the dummy variable $extech$ concerns the problem of estimating a model for a qualitative dependent variable, a topic which is discussed in Chapter 11. With such a model, the probability can be estimated that a firm needs external technological knowledge given a number of characteristics of that firm. In Case 4, the variable 'percentage of sales of products new to the industry' ($new\_s\_industry$) will be explained by a causal model. That case is an application of the subjects that are discussed in Chapter 8.

Chapter 3

Basic Concepts of EViews and Starting the Research Project

3.1 Introduction

In this chapter the use of a number of general basic procedures from EViews is introduced as a start to learning the principles of this software package. Version 4.1 of EViews is used to describe the procedures in this book.

For this purpose the data on world-market commodity prices, as introduced in the preceding chapter, will be used. Many examples of EViews procedures will be given by using these data. A relationship between these variables yields a simple but useful 'model' to illustrate applications from econometric theory. Besides the use of EViews, we will look at the output, especially pictures, that can easily be imported in a text editor. In fact, a preliminary data analysis will be done in this chapter. We will see how graphs can be made, correlations can be computed, data can be seasonally adjusted, elasticities can be calculated, etc.

However, this book is not an EViews manual. A complete description of all the procedures in EViews is found in its help file. The help function in EViews is very instructive and is identical to the EViews 4 User's Guide that is also available as a pdf file under the help button. As this book offers a first course in econometrics with the accent on showing the use of econometric methods in the economic practice of doing research, only the most important or relevant procedures are discussed in detail. After becoming acquainted with EViews in this and following chapters, you will be able to use EViews autonomously.

3.2   The creation of a workfile in EViews

The basis in EViews is the *workfile*. For every research topic or project a workfile is created. An EViews workfile contains *objects*, like *series, equations, groups of variables, graphs, tables*, etc. All these objects are part of the workfile. So the first thing to do in EViews is to create the workfile and to import the data that creates the first objects: the variables as a number of series. An existing workfile will be opened in following EViews sessions to continue the research project. The data will be imported in the workfile in the first EViews session, but additional data can be imported at any time. To import the data, you have to know how the data has been organised in the original data file that has to be read. The data files can be organised by variable or by date. The names of the variables can precede the series in the data file or can be given when importing data in EViews. In the example below, the data are organised by observation, the names are in the file, and the data are in an Excel file. EViews can read various types of data files.

The following points have to be done to start working with EViews. First, start EViews in Windows. Next click on 'File' and 'New', and select 'Workfile'; this is shown in Figure 3.1.

Notice at the bottom of Figure 3.1 that a *history list* exists with the names of recently used workfiles. Various data sets will be used in this book, so a workfile has to be made for each data set. In a next EViews session, start again by clicking on 'File'. The names of recently used workfiles are visible in the history list and one can select directly a workfile from this list. It is also possible to double-click on the name of the workfile in a file-management program like Windows Explorer or Total Commander (Ghisler (2003), see: http://www.ghisler.com/) if the extension (.wf1) has been associated with the EViews program. Then EViews starts with that workfile.

A window appears (see Figure 3.2) with questions about the data: the frequency and the sample period. Most of the options concern time-series data. 'Undated or irregular' concerns the import of cross-section data.

If cross-section data has been selected the range changes in 'Start observation', which will be equal to one and 'End observation', which is equal to the number of the last observation.

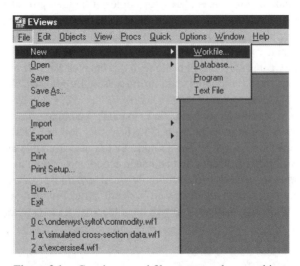

Figure 3.1:   Creating a workfile, step one: the new object

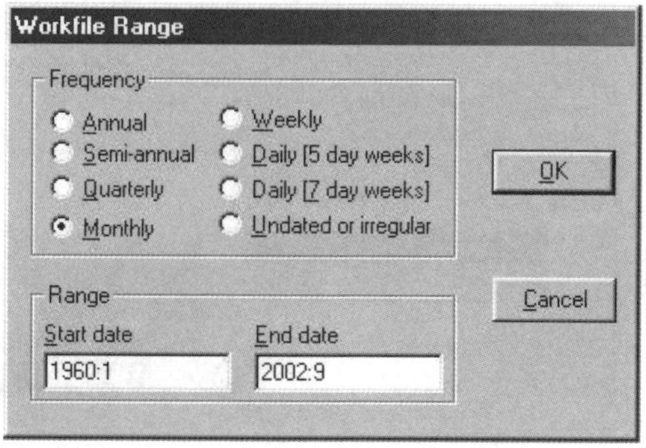

Figure 3.2: Creating a workfile, step two: defining the frequency

For time-series data, mark the correct frequency and fill in the 'Start date' and 'End date'. Three series of monthly data as mentioned in the introduction will be imported. So select 'Monthly' and type the 'Start date' and the 'End date', and click OK.

The window in Figure 3.3 shows the new workfile. In this window, two variable names appear: a vector (c) that will contain estimation results, and a series with the name resid that

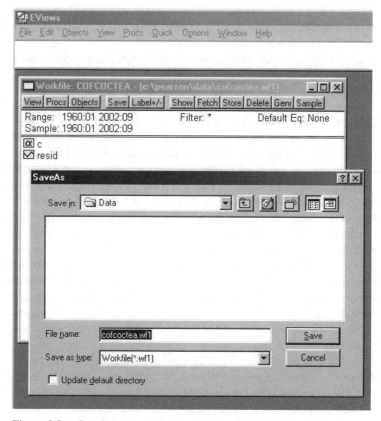

Figure 3.3: Creating a workfile, step three: saving the file in a directory

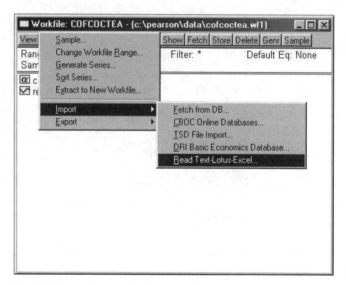

Figure 3.4:   Importing data in the workfile

will contain the residuals after the parameters of a model have been estimated. The vector c will be used for testing restrictions on parameters or for specifying equations. The residuals in resid will be used to test statistical assumptions, among other things. Click 'Save as' from the file menu, and change the name 'Untitled' to a suitable name. In Figure 3.3 the name cofcoctea has been chosen.

The workfile gets the extension .wf1. It is convenient to check the box 'Update default directory' at the bottom of the 'Save as' window: then EViews starts in the same directory in a follow-up session when the program is started in general without linking to a file. That is usually easier than browsing through the directory structure to find the workfile every time you continue working with EViews.

At this stage, the data can be imported in the workfile. Click on 'Procs' and select 'Import' and then select the type of data file: a database file, an ASCII file or an Excel file (which is a convenient way to import the data) as shown in Figure 3.4. Two screen shots are given; one for reading an Excel file in Figure 3.5 and one for reading a text file in Figure 3.6. So select 'Read Text-Lotus-Excel', and browse for the data file that has to be imported. The data on the commodity prices are read from an Excel data file as shown in Figure 3.5.

EViews 'asks' whether the data file has been organised by observation or by series (in 'Columns' or in 'Rows'). In this example, the data that will be imported are three series with the monthly world-market prices of cocoa, coffee and tea, organised in columns. In Figure 3.5 we see that the data are in sheet2 of the Excel file. If the data file contains the names of the variables, only the number of variables in the file has to be entered. The names are in the first row, so the first data cell is cell B2 (the first column contains the dates).

When the data are in a text file a different window is opened; this window is shown in Figure 3.6.

In this window one has to fill in similar information as mentioned before concerning Figure 3.5. There is a *preview window*, so that it is possible to check whether the correct data will be imported and to see that the data are organised by observation. If the data are not neatly organised in a matrix, do not mark 'File laid out as rectangle'. Next click OK.

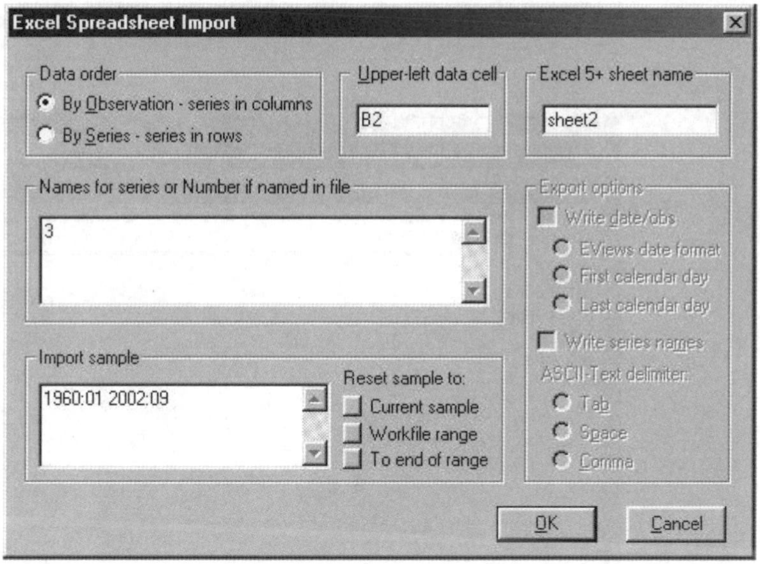

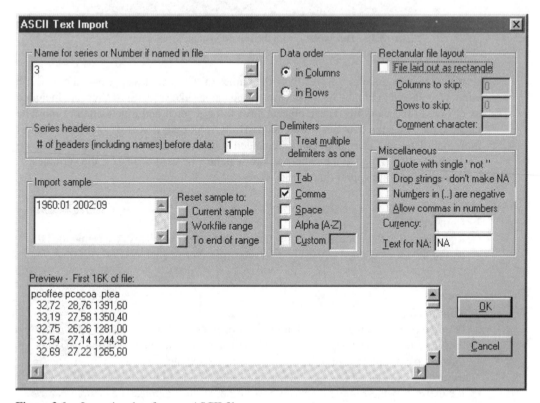

Figure 3.5: Importing data from sheet2 from an Excel file

Figure 3.6: Importing data from an ASCII file

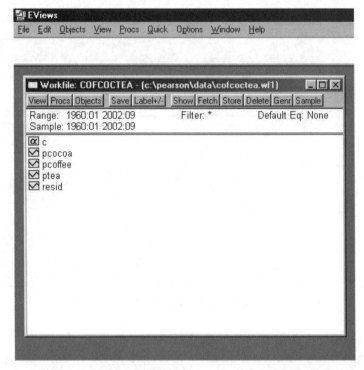

Figure 3.7:   The workfile with the imported data

If all has been done in a correct way the names of the variables appear in the workfile window as shown in Figure 3.7, otherwise wrong names like *ser01, ser02,* etc. are included as objects in the workfile. These objects have to be deleted and a new attempt must be undertaken. After the data have been successfully imported, it is still possible to import more data later on. The range can be changed (under 'Procs') or new variables can be imported. Statistical and graphical procedures can now be used to analyse the variables.

Some remarks are appropriate at this stage.

Remark 3.1
Remember that the price of tea is given until June 1998 only. This means that the last part of the series is filled with a code for missing ('Not Available') observations: *NA*.

Remark 3.2
Observe that a 'Range' and a 'Sample' has been defined. In the displayed window they are equal, but that depends on what has to be done. The range is the entire sample that has been imported into the workfile. But, for example, if you are interested in estimating a model for only part of the sample and forecasting the dependent variable for the rest of the sample then you have to adjust the sample. The sample can be redefined by clicking the button 'Sample'.

Remark 3.3

The blank space on top of the EViews window is the *command window*, where commands can be typed in. Examples are given later on. The space for this window can be adjusted by dragging the bottom line of the command window up or down.

Remark 3.4

It is useful to click on the button 'Options' to install or redefine default options. For example, the option 'Graphics Defaults' is used to make a default installation for the appearance of figures.

Remark 3.5

At the end of the session the workfile *has to be saved*, so that everything that has been done (transformations of variables, specification of equations, maybe formations of groups, etc.) is available in the workfile in the next session. Each result (object) can be sent to the printer for a printout by clicking on 'Print' in the toolbar of that particular window. One word of advice: do not wait to save the workfile until the end of the session, but click regularly on the *save-button* of the workfile, as it would be a pity if your work gets lost when your PC unexpectedly hangs up!

Remark 3.6

In Section 2.1 it was noted that variables can easily be exchanged between different workfiles. That is done by opening more than one workfile inside the same EViews window. Click with the right-hand mouse button on the variable that has to be copied, and select 'Copy'. Next activate the other workfile by clicking with the right-hand mouse button in an empty space of that window, and select 'Paste'. This might be a useful action in Case 5, for example, where data from a number of workfiles have to be combined.

Remark 3.7

It is possible that you have data with different frequencies, for example, monthly and quarterly data, in which case EViews can convert the data to a common frequency. For example, this has been done with Data set 4 concerning the money market. The money stock has been observed monthly, whereas the other variables have quarterly data. This can be solved in the following way. Make a workfile defined for quarterly data and another for monthly data. Import the money stock data into the monthly workfile. Select 'Store to DB' under 'Object' in the 'Series window'. Select 'Individual.DB? files' in the 'Store window' that has appeared. Browse for the correct directory and click 'Yes'. The variable is saved with the extension .db. This variable can be imported in the quarterly workfile by selecting 'Import' and 'Fetch from DB'. EViews automatically computes quarterly averages of the monthly data. More conversion options are available; see 'Conversion Options' under 'View' in the 'Series window'. You always recognise the conversion in the series sheet as shown in Figure 3.8. The way to display a series is discussed in Section 3.3.

When EViews is used in a more advanced manner, it is useful to create a real database for many economic variables instead of individual variables stored in any

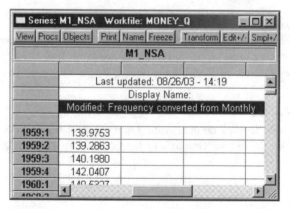

Figure 3.8:   Example of frequency conversion when importing data

directory. More detailed information about the use of a database can be found in the EViews User's Guide.

3.3   Viewing variables and some procedures

In the upper-left corner of the window of any EViews object two important buttons are found, the buttons 'View' and 'Procs'. With the options under 'View' you can look at various representations of the object. Using 'View' in the 'Series window' options is useful for data analysis involving graphs, descriptive statistics, etc. The options under 'Procs' provide a number of procedures that can be applied on that particular object. In the 'Series window' procedures like seasonal adjustment are found that can be used when quarterly or monthly data have been collected showing a seasonal pattern.

In this section, you will see what these options result in. Their use will be illustrated by applying some of the options on the imported commodity prices. Of course it is not the intention to discuss all the options that are available, but only those which are most frequently used in a research project. More specific options that are not discussed in this section can be encountered in following chapters, whereas an explanation of the remaining options can be found in the EViews User's Guide. A variable (series) is selected by one click, and its window is opened by double clicking on the series name. After double clicking on the series name the series is seen in a new window (the 'Series window'), like a spreadsheet. See the window in Figure 3.9, where part of the spreadsheet is visible. We will look at the results of some possible options that can be chosen in this window. Before using the 'View' button see the 'Edit +/−' button in the series window. After clicking on that button the series window will look like an Excel sheet where the series can be edited, which is useful when errors in the data occur, for example, or when new data become available.

First, the available options are considered that are found under 'View' and these are shown in Figure 3.9. In that figure, the option to make a 'Graph' of the cocoa price series has been selected.

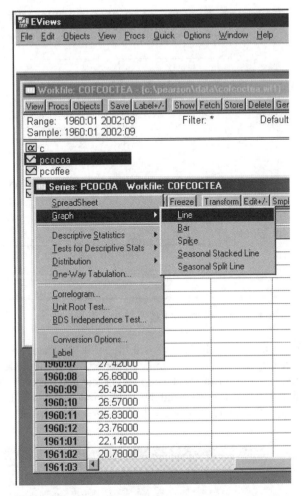

Figure 3.9: Preparing a graph

Also look at the other possibilities under the 'View' button. Some of them are obvious, others will be discussed later on, for example, the 'Unit Root Test...' will be introduced in Chapter 12. The graph is shown in Figure 3.10.

However, Figure 3.10 does not have the appearance of a figure an author would like to have in his article. The appearance of this graph can be changed by double clicking on any part of the graph you would like to change, like the labels, or the axis, or the graph itself. After such a double-click the 'Graph options window' opens, as shown in Figure 3.11. In that window a number of tabs appear corresponding to the various parts of the graph. In Figure 3.11 the tab 'Legend' has been selected, where among others the name of the variable has been replaced by a suitable name that is understandable in a publication, namely 'Cocoa price' instead of PCOCOA.

The meaning of every tab speaks for itself. When you are satisfied with the result, the graph can be imported into a text editor like MS Word, LaTex or Scientific WorkPlace. The figure can also be included as a *graph object* in the workfile by clicking on 'Freeze'

Figure 3.10:   A graph of P_t^{coc}

and giving it a name with 'Name'; see Figure 3.12 where a graph object can be found. The picture can be saved on disk to be imported into the text file that contains your paper afterwards. In Word it can also be copied via 'cut and paste'. To save the file on disk you can use both the series window and the graph window. Click 'Edit' in the upper toolbar and select 'Copy'. This yields a window like the one in Figure 3.12.

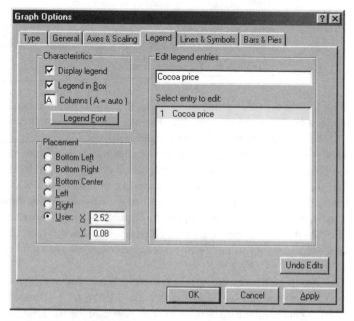

Figure 3.11:   Adjusting the graph

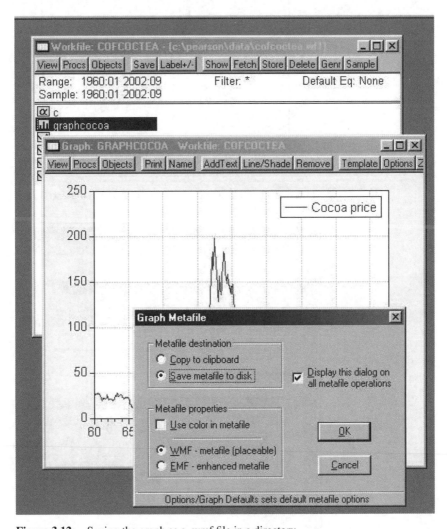

Figure 3.12: Saving the graph as a .wmf file in a directory

Click OK and browse the directories to select the directory where the file has to be saved. An example of an adjusted and imported figure of the cocoa price, which is a .wmf file, is given in Figure 3.13.

Observe in Figure 3.13 all the changes that have been made; and compare Figure 3.13 with Figure 3.10. The Y-axis has been manually scaled. The label name has been changed into a clear name for the text, the label has been dragged into the figure and has got a box. Gridlines have been plotted and text has been added at the bottom of the picture.

In a similar way, the procedures that are found under 'Procs' can be used. The procedures that can be applied on a variable are shown in the window of Figure 3.14.

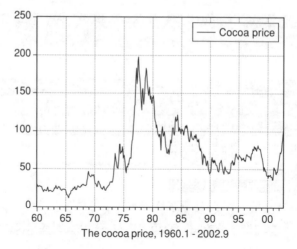

The cocoa price, 1960.1 - 2002.9

Figure 3.13:   The graph of P_t^{coc} as imported in this text

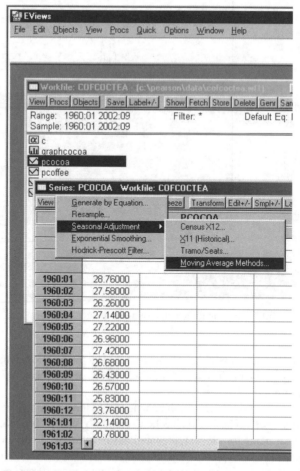

Figure 3.14:   Procedures in the 'Series' window

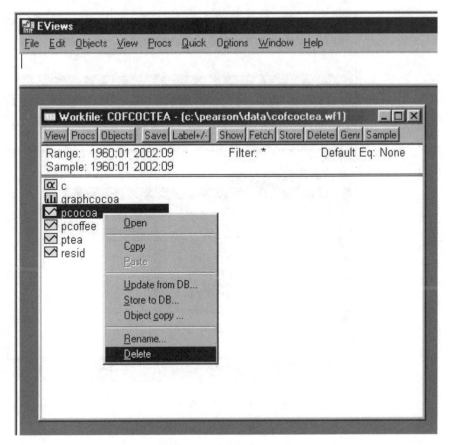

Figure 3.15: Options for an object 'Series', here P_t^{coc}

The procedure that has been selected is seasonal adjustment. Seasonal adjustment is one of the topics that will be discussed in Chapter 7. It is a rather useless option for this variable, as P_t^{coc} has no seasonal pattern, as we have seen in the graph. Under 'Quick' in the upper toolbar of the workfile, procedures can also be found to analyse the data.

Different options appear by clicking with the *right-hand mouse button* on the names of one or more marked variables. In Figure 3.15 an example is given of a right-click on the cocoa price. Displayed in that example is the way to delete an object from the workfile.

The contents under buttons like 'View' and 'Procs' is not identical in the windows of each object: it depends on which procedures make sense for the data in that particular window. In an 'Equation' window other views and procedures are available than those in a 'Series' or a 'Group' window. We have seen the available options that can be selected under 'View' and 'Procs' in the 'Series' window. As an example, compare the options of 'View' in the 'Series' window with those under 'View' of the 'Group' window in Figure 3.17 later.

Also other objects are created in a workfile. For example, we have created the object 'graphcocoa' in the example shown in Figure 3.15. The 'Group object' is a very useful object. Various objects can be opened as a *group of objects*, for example, a group of variables, but also a group of graphs can be created, which becomes a new graph, etc. The use of a group

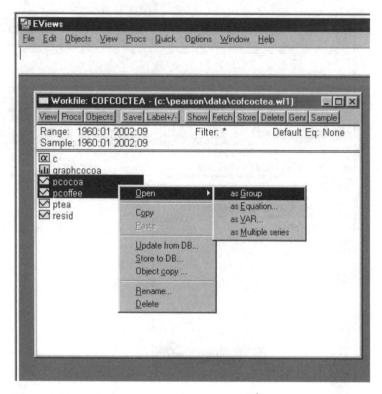

Figure 3.16: Creating a group with P_t^{coc} and P_t^{cof}

of variables is very convenient during an EViews session. For example, it is possible to make all kind of multiple graphs, to compute group statistics, etc. In many cases, it is not necessary to save a group with a name because a group is very easily created again and the workfile will become too disorderly and large by including every object that has been created.

How is a group created? Only one object (e.g. a series) is selected with the left-hand mouse button. To create a group of objects keep the 'Ctrl' button pushed down and click with the left-hand mouse button on the relevant object names. It will become a 'Group' by selecting 'Open' (under 'View'), and selecting 'as Group'. See also the other possibilities in Figure 3.16. Another convenient and fast way to create a group is clicking with the right-hand mouse button on the selection of variables, after which the same options appear.

Notice in Figure 3.16 the 'Open' option 'as Equation ...'. Selection of this option yields a static regression equation in the 'Equation Specification' window. If an equation is specified in this manner the order of the selection is important. The first variable that is selected is the dependent variable in the regression equation. However, this is a subject that will be discussed in Chapter 4. A display of the options that are available under 'View' in the groups window is given in Figure 3.17. The different views of the group are various types of graphs, descriptive (group and series) statistics, sample correlations, etc. The first option 'Group Members' is useful in order to alter the members of the group; existing members

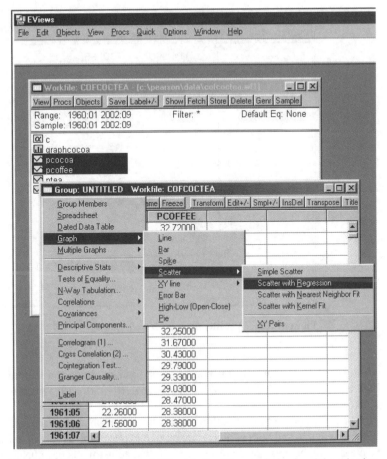

Figure 3.17: The contents of 'View' in the 'Group window' and the selection of a 'Scatter with Regression'

can be deleted from the group and new members can be added to the group. In Figure 3.17 a scatter diagram with a regression line has been selected. The resulting scatter diagram is given in Figure 3.18. Just like the corrections made for the graph of P_t^{coc}, it is better to make changes to this picture too, before including it in a paper.

Figure 3.18 clearly shows that a linear relationship between the two prices exists. Furthermore you can observe a clustering of points at low prices and an increasing variance around the regression line when prices are high. These observations are, from an economic perspective, not unexpected. The high prices (and heavy price changes) correspond to the disturbed and uncertain market during the 1970s, caused by the devastation of coffee trees in Brazil as a result of very cold weather. The variances of the two prices are much higher at high prices than at low prices. The interpretation and the consequences of this last observation will be considered in Part II.

The next option that is selected in 'View' is 'Multiple Graphs'. The choice 'Line' in 'Multiple Graphs' yields a picture with two separate graphs in one figure. After manual

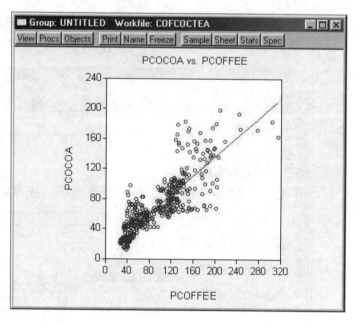

Figure 3.18: A scatter diagram of P_t^{coc} and P_t^{cof}

scaling and some other adjustments the graph has been imported into this text as shown in Figure 3.19. Both variables have the same range (0–350 \$ct/lb) by manual scaling of the Y-axis.

It is also possible to plot both variables in one graph. Select the option 'Graph' in the 'Group' window and both variables are plotted in one graph as shown in Figure 3.20. It will be clear from the appearance of Figure 3.20 that adjustments have been made to the initial picture.

Figure 3.20 clarifies the idea behind the relationship between P_t^{coc} and P_t^{cof} that is used in the examples in this book. It is obvious to see that the two prices have a similar pattern,

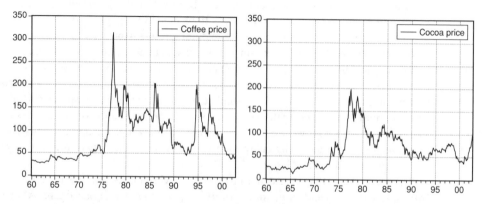

Figure 3.19: Multiple graphs of P_t^{coc} and P_t^{cof} made from a group, identically scaled

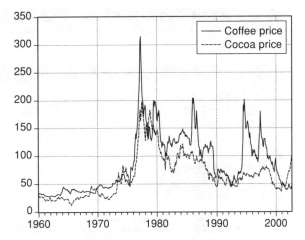

Figure 3.20: A combined graph of P_t^{coc} and P_t^{cof} made from a group

whereas the 'basics' for the price formation of both commodities are not identical. Review Section 2.2 again for some arguments as to why these prices move together.

After these examples from the 'View' options, we look at the procedures under 'Procs' in the 'Group' window. Clicking on 'Procs' has made these group procedures available. See these possible procedures in 'Procs' on your own PC. The best way to learn the various possibilities of a procedure, or to see the possible view options, is to select one of the various buttons and to try out the options. The structure of successive windows is logical and, if necessary, the help function is adequate, as mentioned earlier.

Finally two more examples of EViews output are given. In Figure 3.21, the workfile shows that the three price variables have been selected as a group after which the *correlation matrix* and the *group statistics* (select 'Descriptive Stats') have been computed. Because the 'common sample' has been used it was not a problem to include the price of tea in the group too. The total sample has 513 observations and, as seen in Figure 3.22, from the *group statistics* the common sample has 462 observations.

The prices of cocoa and coffee are rather strongly correlated, the price of tea correlates less with the other prices. When this correlation matrix is computed for a number of sub-samples of the range, remarkable changes in the values of the correlation between the price of tea and those of coffee and cocoa can be observed, whereas the correlation between the coffee and cocoa price remains stable. This is useful knowledge regarding the analysis of the relationship between these prices.

3.4 Some basic calculations in EViews

When performing empirical econometric research, it frequently happens that variables have to be transformed, or that some number (a scalar) like an elasticity has to be calculated. Variables can be transformed or generated with the command 'genr' or by using a

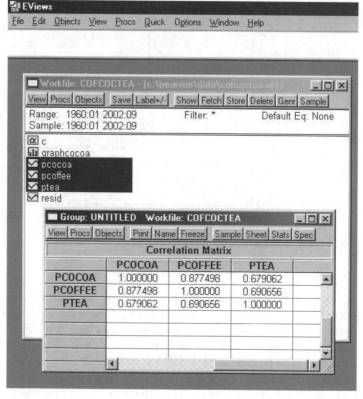

Figure 3.21:   The correlation matrix selected in the 'Group' window

'Genr-button'. A scalar can be computed with the command 'scalar'. Examples are given in this section.

A well-known transformation is the log transformation. Later on in the course, models with variables specified in first differences will also be encountered. These transformations are easily performed in EViews. Transformations of variables can be specified in various ways. The *command* for a transformation can be typed into the *command window* at the top of the EViews window. For example, two new variables *lpcocoa* or *dlpcocoa* are generated by typing:

$$genr\ lpcocoa = log\,(pcocoa)\,,$$

or

$$genr\ dlpcocoa = lpcocoa - lpcocoa\,(-1)\,.$$

The command window keeps a record of the commands by maintaining a *history list* during an EViews session, which can be an advantage if one has to do a number of similar transformations for more than one variable, because the command can be adjusted to transform another variable. A second possibility to compute transformations is by clicking on the

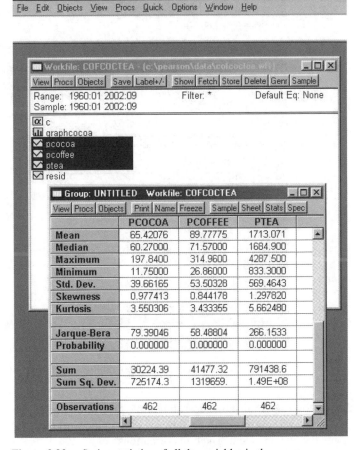

Figure 3.22: Series statistics of all the variables in the group

button 'Genr' in the workfile. Next the window 'Generate Series by Equation' opens. In that window only

$$lpcocoa = log(pcocoa)$$

has to be specified, using the same example as above. But in this way no history list is created. Both possibilities of creating the log of the cocoa price are shown in Figure 3.23.

It is not always necessary to transform variables in advance by creating new objects. All these transformations enlarge the contents of the workfile. Often it is possible to use an *operator* within a window. For example in an 'Equation Specification' window operators can be used. In an equation specification window the model is specified and an estimator is chosen to estimate the parameters (discussed in Part II). The *log* and *difference operators* are used in the following way. The specification of

$$log(pcocoa) \text{ or } d(pcocoa)$$

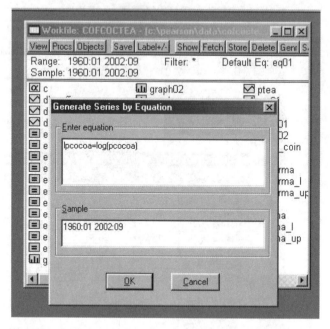

Figure 3.23: Illustration of two possibilities to generate $\ln(P_t^{coc})$

in the window implies that the logarithm or the first differences of the cocoa prices are used in the model, without generating a new variable in the workfile. And it is even possible to combine the two operators. The transformations

$$d(log(pcocoa)) \text{ or } dlog(pcocoa)$$

yield the first differences of the logarithms of the cocoa price in the model.

Other manipulations with objects can be found under 'Objects' in the upper toolbar: for example, the option 'Delete'. As mentioned earlier, 'Delete' is also found in the toolbar of the workfile, and the right-hand mouse button can also be used.

Not only transformed variables but also scalars can be computed. The computation of an income elasticity will serve as example. Suppose that the parameters of the following dynamic consumption equation has been estimated.

$$\widehat{CONS}_t = \widehat{\beta}_1 + \widehat{\beta}_2 Y_t + \widehat{\beta}_3 CONS_{t-1}.$$

The name $CONS$ is used instead of C, because in EViews the name C is used for a vector with estimation results, as immediately seen below in equation (3.1). In the notation of EViews, the estimation result is explicitly written in the following way.

$$\widehat{CONS}_t = c\,(1) + c\,(2) * Y_t + c\,(3) * CONS_{t-1}. \tag{3.1}$$

This means that the vector elements $c(1)$, $c(2)$ and $c(3)$ contain the numerical values of the estimated parameters. It is simple to compute an income elasticity with this result. The formula to compute an income elasticity (el_y) with respect to the sample means of consumption and income (see Section 1.6) is:

$$el\_y = \widehat{\beta}_2 \cdot \frac{\overline{Y}}{\overline{CONS}},\qquad(3.2)$$

where $\overline{Y}$ and $\overline{CONS}$ are the sample means. This elasticity can be computed in EViews by using the facility that many computational results are available with the prefix @. So the sample mean of the series Y is known as $@mean(Y)$ and the sample mean of the series $CONS$ is known as $@mean(CONS)$. (See the EViews User's Guide for other available statistics.)

Compute the income elasticity by typing the following expression in the command window:

$$\text{scalar } el\_y = c(2) * @mean(y)/@mean(cons).\qquad(3.3)$$

The object el_y is included in the workfile, with the symbol # as prefix. Double-clicking on the scalar name results in showing its value at the bottom of the EViews window. In Figure 3.24 a part of the estimation result of the consumption equation (3.1) is shown in an 'Equation' window (using a small data set from Thomas (1997): Appendix III, Table AIII.4). The two variables $cons_t$ and y_t have been seasonally adjusted, which yields the variables $conssa$ and ysa in the workfile. The estimation procedure will be discussed in Section 4.9.

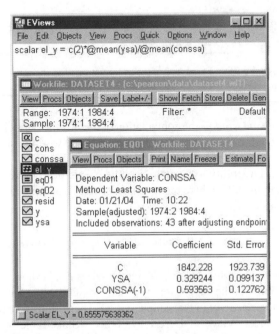

Figure 3.24: Example 1 of the computation of an income elasticity

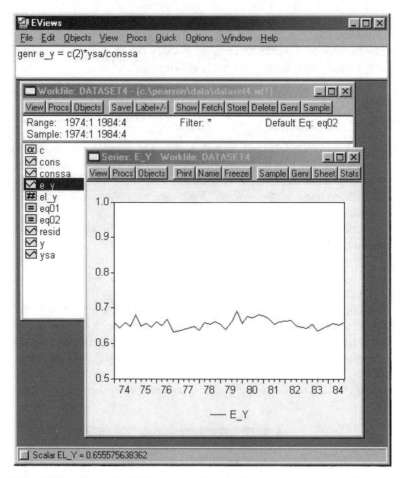

Figure 3.25: Example 2 of the computation of an income elasticity (e_y) for every observation

In the *command window* the computation of the income elasticity (3.3) is demonstrated. For example, double-clicking on the object el_y in the workfile shows the result at the bottom of the window in Figure 3.24: $el\_y = 0.6556$.

Another possibility to compute income elasticities is given by the following example, given in Figure 3.25, where the income elasticity has been computed for all the quarters in a new series (e_y),

$$genr\ e\_y = c\,(2) * ysa/conssa,$$

see the command window, after which the series e_y is shown as a graph.

In Section 1.6, the suggestion was made to publish the mean, maximum and minimum values of the elasticity in the sample period. These statistics are immediately found in the summary under 'View' – 'Descriptive Stats', 'Stats Table' – see Figure 3.26 where the values are shown. The mean of the elasticity is 0.6555 and the elasticity varies between 0.6323 and 0.6924.

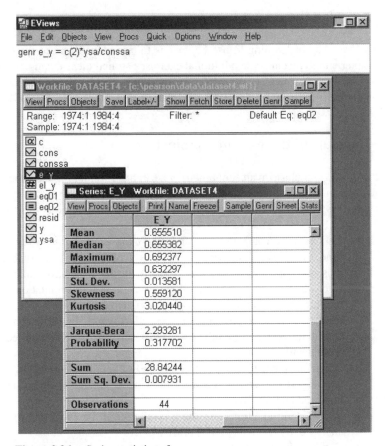

Figure 3.26: Series statistics of e_y

Notice that the mean elasticity in Figure 3.26 is different than the value of el_y in Figure 3.24, because the formulae are different: the quotient of means versus the mean of quotients!

In this section enough of an introduction to the use of EViews has been provided to make a viable start with the econometrics course in Part II. More general and additional information can be found in the EViews User's Guide. The EViews introduction, as discussed in this chapter, will be applied in Case 1. This concerns a data analysis that precedes the estimation stage.

3.5 Case 1: the data analysis

In this exercise the accent is

- on learning the use of EViews, and
- making a start with an econometric research project.

These points are combined in this first case.

Learning the use of EViews

The best way of learning to use EViews is to reproduce some of the examples from this chapter and to invent some additional exercises around these examples. Download the file 'pcoccoftea.xls', make a workfile and import the variables. Perform a number of exercises on the basis of the examples in this chapter.

The start of the research project

Part of the first phase in an econometric research is formulating the economic problem and writing an introduction for the research paper. The economic data is collected and a data analysis is done. The following assignments can be used as directions for the exercise.

- Choose a 'research project' and select the accompanying data set. The relevant time-series data, Data set 2, 3 or 4, have been described in Chapter 2. Of course it is also possible to use time-series data that you have collected for your own research. Some concrete directions concerning the formulation of a model for the accompanying data have been given in Chapter 2 together with the introduction of the data. Formulate your research objective(s) with the chosen data set. You can also look at the formulation of Case 2, where the first 'research project' is elaborated in more detail.

- Download the data into your computer. Start EViews on your PC, create a workfile, and import the data in the workfile. Check whether the data have been correctly imported and save the workfile.

- Write an introduction with the formulation of the economic problem that will be analysed, by using any word processor.

- Generate transformed variables when you expect that they will probably be used in the project too, such as deflating variables when you would like to model the economic variables in real terms. Often it is useful to model the logs of the variables as discussed in Chapter 1.

- Examine the variables by making graphs. In case the data are monthly or quarterly, data check whether seasonal patterns exist in the series and decide what to do if they are present. Do this for all the relevant variables. Adjust the appearance of the graphs, which are candidates for your draft paper, in a way that they are suitable to import into your paper.

- Make a group of relevant variables. Decide which graphs you like to see of these variables: multiple or combined graphs, scatter diagrams, etc. Look at 'Descriptive Statistics' and 'Correlations' and decide which information is useful for the next section in your paper concerning data analysis.

- Make a start with writing the second section of your paper that will focus on the data analysis.

The Reduced-Form Model

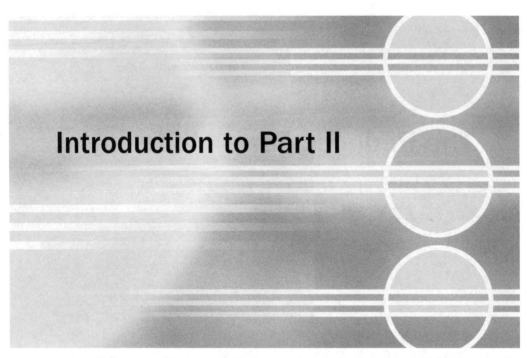

Introduction to Part II

In Part II, the general linear model is discussed in detail. It concerns the linear model for one endogenous variable that is explained by exogenous and/or lagged variables (when the sample concerns time-series data). Remember Section 1.8 where the scheme with the stages of an econometric research project was given. The first two stages concern the deterministic and stochastic assumptions that have to be made for the model. These stages are discussed in Chapter 4 where the model is defined and the ordinary least squares (OLS) estimator with some of its properties is introduced. Chapters 5 and 6 concern the evaluation phase where statistical tests are introduced to test the stochastic and deterministic assumptions that have been made with respect to the specification of the model.

In Chapter 7, the last chapter of Part II, a number of different specific topics around the linear model are discussed and the consequences of specification errors are considered. We will also look at forecasting problems. Which additional assumptions have to be made so that the estimated model can be used for out-of-sample forecasting? Multicollinearity is the issue of high sample correlation between the explanatory variables that can bring about inaccurate or wrong estimates; this will be demonstrated. One of the deterministic assumptions is that the structure of the model is constant in the sample period. This assumption is tested in Sections 6.5 and 7.5. The modelling of structural breaks is a subject that will come up at the end of Chapter 7. General to specific modelling as a procedure to estimate a model in a structural way and all the other discussed items are applied in the cases.

In the Preface, it has already been indicated that Parts I and II can be seen as a complete basic course concerning the linear regression model. After these two parts have been studied you will know whether or not OLS may be applied as an estimator of the parameters, because the properties of this estimator will be known. You will also be able to estimate and test simple linear equations, with exogenous and lagged explanatory variables (for time-series data), in a correct way. Part II provides a lot of insight into many aspects of this linear model.

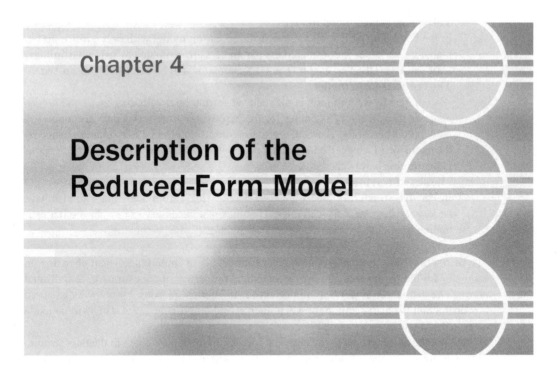

Chapter 4

Description of the Reduced-Form Model

4.1 Introduction

An economic model is the result of economic theoretical considerations or stems from ideas based on empirical research. Such a model is called a *structural model*, as it describes the structure of the economic phenomenon that is studied. In this chapter, all models are *linear* models. In Chapter 1, the structural economic model was introduced; this showed relationships between endogenous and exogenous variables. In Section 1.5, we considered a structural model that consists of more than one equation. That model can be solved for the endogenous variables when the number of endogenous variables is equal to the number of equations. The solution for the endogenous variables is the *reduced-form model*. In the reduced-form equations the endogenous variables are expressed in terms of the exogenous and lagged variables. A special reduced-form model is the model with only exogenous explanatory variables. Such a model is called *the classical regression model*. This model is regularly discussed as one of the first topics in econometric textbooks, as is done in this chapter also. It is a clear model to start with for didactical reasons; it is a restrictive model as all the explanatory variables have to be exogenous. *Reduced-form models* are more general because lagged dependent (and lagged exogenous) explanatory variables are involved allowing for dynamic economic behaviour in the model. It is true that it is good to start with discussing the classical regression model for didactical reasons, but it is also useful to discuss deviations from that model immediately where relevant, for example, to observe changes in the properties of an estimator. The following three specifications of the linear model are distinguished and discussed in detail in Parts II and III of this text.

■ **The classical regression model**
In the beginning of Part II, the classical regression model with only *exogenous* explanatory variables is considered. Its parameters are estimated by using the ordinary least squares (OLS) estimator. The OLS estimator will be extensively discussed.

■ **The reduced-form model**
Also in Part II, we will look at the reduced-form model with *exogenous* and *lagged dependent* explanatory variables for the case where time-series data are modelled. How properties of the classical regression model and the OLS estimator change by the inclusion of a lagged endogenous explanatory variable will be clarified at various places in this part of the book.

■ **The structural model**
In Part III, structural models are considered, which are models that can also have *endogenous* explanatory variables. That makes it necessary to introduce other estimation methods like the two-stage least squares (2SLS) estimator.

The distinction between these three types of models is of importance when choosing an estimator for the parameters and for the statistical properties of the estimator, as indicated above. The distinction is not only important for theoretical reasons, but knowledge about this distinction is clearly important when interpreting empirical results. This will be made clear in this chapter.

First, all the assumptions of the classical regression model are given in the next section. This is followed by the introduction of the OLS estimator in Section 4.3. After that some statistical properties of estimators in general and of the OLS estimator in particular are discussed in Sections 4.4–4.7. In Section 4.8 the principle of maximum likelihood estimation is introduced. Finally, in Section 4.9 the applications with EViews are discussed.

4.2   The assumptions of the classical regression model

In this section, all the assumptions of the classical regression model, with additional comments are given. The specification of the linear model is:

$$Y_t = \beta_1 + \beta_2 X_{t2} + \ldots + \beta_K X_{tK} + u_t, \tag{4.1}$$

$$u_t \sim NID\left(0, \sigma_u^2\right), \text{ for every } t. \tag{4.2}$$

NID in (4.2) means normally, independently distributed. All the assumptions concerning this model will be explained below.

First, the assumptions concerning the specification of the equation, the *deterministic assumptions*, are introduced.

■ Y_t is the endogenous, dependent variable.
■ Y_t is explained by K linearly independent exogenous explanatory variables X_{tk}, with $k = 1, \ldots, K$.
■ The first explanatory variable is: $X_{t1} = 1$ for all t. This is the constant term. In general it will be assumed that a constant term is included in the model.

■ The number of observations in the sample period is equal to $n : t = 1, \ldots, n$; for an accurate estimation result it is desirable that n is clearly larger than K.

■ The difference between the number of observations and the number of explanatory variables $n - K$, is the number of degrees of freedom of the model. The estimation results generally improve as $n - K$ increases.

■ The structure is constant in the sample period, or in other words all the parameters β_k are constant in the sample period. In general, this has consequences for the choice of n. The length of the sample period must be chosen such that the economic structure has not changed in that period.

■ The K explanatory variables X_{tK} are linearly independent and form the *systematic part* of the model.

Next consider the *stochastic assumptions*.

■ The variable u_t is the disturbance term, which is the *non-systematic part* of the model. The disturbance term is not observed. Assumptions about u_t are made and will be tested after the parameters have been estimated. Often these tests will be interpreted as model-specification tests, as will be explained in Chapter 6.

■ The variable u_t is assumed to be normally, independently distributed. This assumption means that all the n disturbances have been drawn from independent, identical normal distributions. The normality assumption is not necessary to estimate the parameters with the ordinary least squares estimator (see Section 4.3) but it is required when assumptions or hypotheses are to be tested. The moments of the disturbance term in model (4.1) have to be constant, as u_t may have no systematic influence. The mean, variance and autocovariance of u_t are (with E as the expectations operator):

$$E(u_t) = 0; \; t = 1, \ldots, n$$

$$E(u_t u_s) = \begin{cases} \sigma_u^2, & \text{if } t = s, \quad \text{for all } t \text{ and } s, \\ 0, & \text{if } t \neq s, \quad t, s = 1, \ldots, n. \end{cases}$$

The variance σ_u^2 is constant, or in other words the disturbance term is *homoskedastic* or *not heteroskedastic*. The autocovariances are zero, which means that no *autocorrelation* is present; of course, this is relevant for time-series models only. Then we also know the expectation of the endogenous variable Y_t, conditional on the explanatory variables.

$$Y_t = \beta_1 + \beta_2 X_{t2} + \ldots + \beta_K X_{tK} + u_t,$$
$$E(Y_t) = \beta_1 + \beta_2 X_{t2} + \ldots + \beta_K X_{tK} + E(u_t),$$
$$E(Y_t) = \beta_1 + \beta_2 X_{t2} + \ldots + \beta_K X_{tK}.$$

An exact linear relationship exists between the expectation of Y_t and the explanatory variables.

In Chapter 8, the linear model with different disturbance-term assumptions will be discussed. There the general least squares (GLS) estimator instead of the OLS estimator can be used to estimate the parameters.

■ After the parameters β_K have been estimated, the *residuals* e_t can be computed. The residuals are defined as:

$$e_t = Y_t - \widehat{\beta}_1 - \widehat{\beta}_2 X_{t2} - \ldots - \widehat{\beta}_K X_{tK}.$$

When the economic model is correctly specified there is no significant autocorrelation or heteroskedasticity found in the residuals by the statistical tests that will be used to test the assumption that u_t is random.

This linear model and its assumptions can be written in matrix notation, which is a clear and simple notation and more convenient for analytical purposes. In general, the following notation will be used:

■ bold face and capital letters for matrices,
■ bold face and lower case letters for vectors,
■ the vector $\mathbf{y}$ is a column vector and $\mathbf{y}'$ is a row vector.

The linear model (4.1) and the stochastic assumptions (4.2) are written in matrix notation as follows.

$$\mathbf{y} = \mathbf{X}\boldsymbol{\beta} + \mathbf{u} \tag{4.3}$$

$$\mathbf{u} \sim N\left(\mathbf{0}, \sigma_u^2 \mathbf{I}_n\right). \tag{4.4}$$

The vector $\mathbf{y}$ is an $(n \times 1)$ vector with observations on the dependent variable, and $\mathbf{X}$ is an $(n \times K)$ matrix with observations on all the explanatory variables. The parameter vector $\boldsymbol{\beta}$ is a $(K \times 1)$ vector with K unknown parameters. The vector $\mathbf{u}$ is an $(n \times 1)$ vector with n non-observed disturbances. The matrix $\mathbf{I}_n$ is the $(n \times n)$ identity matrix. The explanatory variables are linearly independent, which means that the rank $r(\mathbf{X}) = K$. Notice that all the assumptions have been specified in the matrix notation as introduced above. To illustrate the notation in more detail, the vectors and matrices are shown below.

$$\mathbf{y} = \begin{pmatrix} Y_1 \\ Y_2 \\ Y_3 \\ \cdot \\ \cdot \\ \vdots \\ \vdots \\ Y_n \end{pmatrix}, \mathbf{X} = \begin{pmatrix} 1 & X_{12} & X_{13} & \cdot & \cdot & X_{1K} \\ 1 & X_{22} & X_{23} & \cdot & \cdot & X_{2K} \\ 1 & X_{32} & X_{33} & \cdot & \cdot & X_{3K} \\ \cdot & \cdot & \cdot & \cdot & \cdot & \cdot \\ \cdot & \cdot & \cdot & \cdot & \cdot & \cdot \\ \vdots & \vdots & \vdots & \vdots & \vdots & \vdots \\ \vdots & \vdots & \vdots & \vdots & \vdots & \vdots \\ 1 & X_{n2} & X_{n3} & \cdot & \cdot & X_{nK} \end{pmatrix}, \boldsymbol{\beta} = \begin{pmatrix} \beta_1 \\ \beta_2 \\ \cdot \\ \vdots \\ \beta_K \end{pmatrix}, \mathbf{u} = \begin{pmatrix} u_1 \\ u_2 \\ u_3 \\ \cdot \\ \vdots \\ \vdots \\ u_n \end{pmatrix}.$$

The collected data on the economic variables $Y_t, X_{t1}, X_{t2}, \ldots, X_{tK}$ are in the columns of the vector $\mathbf{y}$ and the matrix $\mathbf{X}$.

The disturbances are assumed to be *uncorrelated* (covariances are zero) and *homoskedastic*, they all have the same variance σ_u^2. Therefore the $(n \times n)$ variance-covariance matrix of the disturbances $Var(\mathbf{u})$ has been written as $\sigma_u^2 \mathbf{I}_n$ in (4.4). The notation is clarified below.

$$Var(\mathbf{u}) = E[(\mathbf{u} - E(\mathbf{u}))][(\mathbf{u} - E(\mathbf{u}))]' = E\mathbf{u}\mathbf{u}'$$

$$= E \begin{pmatrix} u_1 \\ u_2 \\ u_3 \\ \cdot \\ \cdot \\ u_n \end{pmatrix} \begin{pmatrix} u_1 & u_2 & u_3 & \cdot & \cdot & u_n \end{pmatrix}$$

$$= \begin{pmatrix} Eu_1^2 & Eu_1u_2 & Eu_1u_3 & \cdot & \cdot & Eu_1u_n \\ Eu_2u_1 & Eu_2^2 & Eu_2u_3 & \cdot & \cdot & \cdot \\ Eu_3u_1 & Eu_3u_2 & Eu_3^2 & \cdot & \cdot & \cdot \\ \cdot & \cdot & \cdot & \cdot & \cdot & \cdot \\ \cdot & \cdot & \cdot & \cdot & \cdot & \cdot \\ Eu_nu_1 & \cdot & & \cdot & \cdot & Eu_n^2 \end{pmatrix}$$

$$= \begin{pmatrix} \sigma_u^2 & 0 & 0 & \cdot & \cdot & 0 \\ 0 & \sigma_u^2 & 0 & \cdot & \cdot & 0 \\ 0 & 0 & \sigma_u^2 & \cdot & \cdot & 0 \\ \cdot & \cdot & \cdot & \cdot & \cdot & \cdot \\ \cdot & \cdot & \cdot & \cdot & \cdot & 0 \\ 0 & 0 & 0 & \cdot & 0 & \sigma_u^2 \end{pmatrix} = \sigma_u^2 \mathbf{I}_n.$$

The $K+1$ parameters $\beta_1, \ldots, \beta_K$ and σ_u^2 are unknown and have to be estimated from the data. All the assumptions will be tested when estimates of the unknown parameters have been obtained and the residuals have been calculated. If (some of) the assumptions are rejected then this rejection will be interpreted as an indication that the model has been mis-specified. The implication is that the systematic part of the model has to be respecified in most cases. Notice that the examples discussed in Chapter 1, the macroeconomic consumption equation and the coffee-consumption equation, do not satisfy the assumptions of the classical regression model, as endogenous explanatory variables occur.

4.3   The ordinary least squares (OLS) estimator

The least squares principle yields an estimator that minimises the squared differences between the observed Y_t and the predicted $\widehat{Y}_t$ from the estimated model. These differences are called the *residuals*. If estimates $\widehat{\beta}_1, \widehat{\beta}_2, \ldots, \widehat{\beta}_K$ have been computed then *predicted values* $\widehat{Y}_t$ are computed as:

$$\widehat{Y}_t = \widehat{\beta}_1 + \widehat{\beta}_2 X_{t2} + \ldots + \widehat{\beta}_K X_{tK}, \ t = 1, \ldots, n$$

and the *residuals* e_t are computed as:

$$e_t = Y_t - \widehat{Y}_t, \ t = 1, \ldots, n.$$

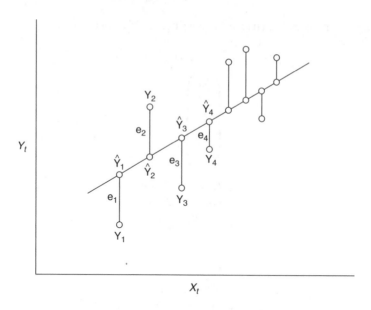

Figure 4.1:   Illustration of the bivariate regression $\widehat{Y}_t = \widehat{\beta}_1 + \widehat{\beta}_2 X_t$

For illustration, a picture with the observations Y_t, the regression line, the predicted values $\widehat{Y}_t$, and the residuals e_t is given in Figure 4.1.

We want to have a model with the best fit to the observed data. That best fit is obtained by using an estimator for the unknown parameters that ensures that we get a model with residuals e_t that are as small as possible. The residuals are a function of the parameter estimates. The problem is solved by minimising the sum of the squares of the residuals as a function of the parameter estimates. The sum of the squared residuals is used to avoid cancelling of positive and negative residuals.

Define the function of the squared residuals as:

$$f\left(\widehat{\beta}_1, \widehat{\beta}_2, \ldots, \widehat{\beta}_K\right) = \sum_{t=1}^{n} e_t^2,$$

and determine the minimum of f with respect to $\widehat{\beta}_1, \widehat{\beta}_2, \ldots, \widehat{\beta}_K$.

For didactical reasons the OLS estimator will first be derived for the bivariate regression model in a rather extensive way, after which we look at the OLS estimator for the general multivariate model in matrix notation.

The bivariate regression model

The following bivariate regression model is used to derive the OLS estimator:

$$Y_t = \beta_1 + \beta_2 X_t + u_t.$$

The function that has to be minimised is:

$$f\left(\widehat{\beta}_1, \widehat{\beta}_2\right) = \sum_{t=1}^{n} e_t^2$$

$$= \sum_{t=1}^{n} \left(Y_t - \widehat{Y}_t\right)^2$$

$$= \sum_{t=1}^{n} \left(Y_t - \widehat{\beta}_1 - \widehat{\beta}_2 X_t\right)^2.$$

Differentiating $f\left(\widehat{\beta}_1, \widehat{\beta}_2\right)$ with respect to $\widehat{\beta}_1$ and $\widehat{\beta}_2$ yields the following first order conditions.

$$\frac{\partial f\left(\widehat{\beta}_1, \widehat{\beta}_2\right)}{\partial \widehat{\beta}_1} = \sum_{t=1}^{n} 2\left(Y_t - \widehat{\beta}_1 - \widehat{\beta}_2 X_t\right)(-1) = 0 \qquad (4.5)$$

$$\frac{\partial f\left(\widehat{\beta}_1, \widehat{\beta}_2\right)}{\partial \widehat{\beta}_2} = \sum_{t=1}^{n} 2\left(Y_t - \widehat{\beta}_1 - \widehat{\beta}_2 X_t\right)(-X_t) = 0. \qquad (4.6)$$

These two equations are rewritten and called the normal equations:

$$\sum_{t=1}^{n} Y_t = n\widehat{\beta}_1 + \widehat{\beta}_2 \sum_{t=1}^{n} X_t \qquad (4.7)$$

$$\sum_{t=1}^{n} Y_t X_t = \widehat{\beta}_1 \sum_{t=1}^{n} X_t + \widehat{\beta}_2 \sum_{t=1}^{n} X_t^2. \qquad (4.8)$$

Solving the normal equations for the unknown parameter estimates $\widehat{\beta}_1$ and $\widehat{\beta}_2$ results in expressions for $\widehat{\beta}_1$ and $\widehat{\beta}_2$ that can be computed from the data.

Two well-known expressions for $\widehat{\beta}_1$ and $\widehat{\beta}_2$ can be calculated from (4.7) and (4.8):

$$\widehat{\beta}_2 = \frac{\sum_{t=1}^{n} \left(Y_t - \overline{Y}\right)\left(X_t - \overline{X}\right)}{\sum_{t=1}^{n} \left(X_t - \overline{X}\right)^2},$$

$$\widehat{\beta}_1 = \overline{Y} - \widehat{\beta}_2 \overline{X}.$$

with $\overline{X}$ and $\overline{Y}$ as the sample means of X and Y (notation: $\overline{X} = \frac{1}{n} \sum_{t=1}^{n} X_t$, etc.).

Proof The following two relationships between variables in *deviation form* (in deviation from their sample means) and their *levels* will be used in the derivation that is given below.

$$\sum_{t=1}^{n} \left(X_t - \overline{X}\right)^2 = \sum_{t=1}^{n} X_t^2 - n\overline{X}^2, \tag{4.9}$$

$$\sum_{t=1}^{n} \left(X_t - \overline{X}\right)\left(Y_t - \overline{Y}\right) = \sum_{t=1}^{n} X_t Y_t - n\overline{X}\,\overline{Y}. \tag{4.10}$$

The two relationships (4.9) and (4.10) are obtained by rewriting the summations at the left-hand side of the equations, and by using substitutions of the mean in the following way:

$$\sum_{t=1}^{n} X_t = n\overline{X}, \text{ etc.}$$

Rewrite equation (4.7):

$$\widehat{\beta}_1 = \frac{1}{n} \sum_{t=1}^{n} Y - \widehat{\beta}_2 \frac{1}{n} \sum_{t=1}^{n} X_t$$
$$= \overline{Y} - \widehat{\beta}_2 \overline{X}. \tag{4.11}$$

Substitute $\widehat{\beta}_1$ in (4.8) and solve the equation for $\widehat{\beta}_2$:

$$\sum_{t=1}^{n} Y_t X_t = \left(\overline{Y} - \widehat{\beta}_2 \overline{X}\right) \sum_{t=1}^{n} X_t + \widehat{\beta}_2 \sum_{t=1}^{n} X_t^2,$$

$$\sum_{t=1}^{n} Y_t X_t = \overline{Y} \sum_{t=1}^{n} X_t - \widehat{\beta}_2 \overline{X} \sum_{t=1}^{n} X_t + \widehat{\beta}_2 \sum_{t=1}^{n} X_t^2,$$

$$\sum_{t=1}^{n} Y_t X_t = n\overline{Y}\,\overline{X} - n\widehat{\beta}_2 \overline{X}^2 + \widehat{\beta}_2 \sum_{t=1}^{n} X_t^2,$$

$$\sum_{t=1}^{n} Y_t X_t - n\overline{Y}\overline{X} = \widehat{\beta}_2 \left(\sum_{t=1}^{n} X_t^2 - n\overline{X}^2\right).$$

Next substitute the equations (4.9) and (4.10), which gives:

$$\sum_{t=1}^{n} \left(X_t - \overline{X}\right)\left(Y_t - \overline{Y}\right) = \widehat{\beta}_2 \sum_{t=1}^{n} \left(X_t - \overline{X}\right)^2.$$

Thus the solution for $\widehat{\beta}_2$ has been obtained:

$$\widehat{\beta}_2 = \frac{\sum\limits_{t=1}^{n} \left(X_t - \overline{X} \right) \left(Y_t - \overline{Y} \right)}{\sum\limits_{t=1}^{n} \left(X_t - \overline{X} \right)^2}. \tag{4.12}$$

The estimate $\widehat{\beta}_1$ can be computed by substitution of the estimate $\widehat{\beta}_2$ in equation (4.11):

$$\widehat{\beta}_1 = \overline{Y} - \widehat{\beta}_2 \overline{X}. \tag{4.13}$$

Of course, other expressions can be written for $\widehat{\beta}_1$ and $\widehat{\beta}_2$. Values for (4.13) and (4.12) can be calculated when economic data for Y_t and X_t have been collected. Expression (4.13) implies that the regression line passes through $\left(\overline{X}, \overline{Y} \right)$, the point determined by the sample means of X and Y; see also Section 5.2.

The multivariate regression model

For the multivariate case it is more convenient to proceed with the model in matrix notation (4.3):

$$\mathbf{y} = \mathbf{X}\boldsymbol{\beta} + \mathbf{u}.$$

Then it is not necessary to write all the sums of squares and products of variables for solving the minimisation problem to get the OLS estimator. Write the predicted values and residuals as $(n \times 1)$ vectors $\widehat{\mathbf{y}}$ and $\mathbf{e}$:

$$\widehat{\mathbf{y}} = \mathbf{X}\widehat{\boldsymbol{\beta}},$$

and

$$\mathbf{e} = \mathbf{y} - \widehat{\mathbf{y}}.$$

As before, the sum of the squared residuals has to be minimised as a function of the K parameter estimates defined as:

$$f\left(\widehat{\beta}_1, \widehat{\beta}_2, \ldots, \widehat{\beta}_K \right) = \sum_{t=1}^{n} e_t^2,$$

or in matrix notation:

$$f\left(\widehat{\boldsymbol{\beta}} \right) = \mathbf{e}'\mathbf{e}. \tag{4.14}$$

First, rewrite the function (4.14) as an explicit function of the estimates:

$$f\left(\widehat{\beta}\right) = \mathbf{e}'\mathbf{e}$$
$$= (\mathbf{y} - \widehat{\mathbf{y}})' (\mathbf{y} - \widehat{\mathbf{y}})$$
$$= \left(\mathbf{y} - \mathbf{X}\widehat{\beta}\right)' \left(\mathbf{y} - \mathbf{X}\widehat{\beta}\right)$$
$$= \mathbf{y}'\mathbf{y} - 2\widehat{\beta}'\mathbf{X}'\mathbf{y} + \widehat{\beta}'\mathbf{X}'\mathbf{X}\widehat{\beta}.$$

This is a quadratic function in $\widehat{\beta}$. Obtain the first-order conditions by differentiating $f\left(\widehat{\beta}\right)$ with respect to $\widehat{\beta}$. (See, for example, Johnston and DiNardo (1997) p. 464 for some rules concerning matrix differentiation.)

$$\frac{\partial f\left(\widehat{\beta}\right)}{\partial \widehat{\beta}} = -2\mathbf{X}'\mathbf{y} + 2\mathbf{X}'\mathbf{X}\widehat{\beta} = \mathbf{0}.$$

Solving for $\widehat{\beta}$ immediately gives the *normal equations*:

$$\mathbf{X}'\mathbf{y} = \mathbf{X}'\mathbf{X}\widehat{\beta}. \tag{4.15}$$

Notice the similarity with the normal equations (4.7) and (4.8) for the bivariate model, which can be written in matrix notation as:

$$\begin{pmatrix} \sum\limits_{t=1}^{n} Y_t \\ \sum\limits_{t=1}^{n} Y_t X_t \end{pmatrix} = \begin{pmatrix} n & \sum\limits_{t=1}^{n} X_t \\ \sum\limits_{t=1}^{n} X_t & \sum\limits_{t=1}^{n} X_t^2 \end{pmatrix} \begin{pmatrix} \widehat{\beta}_1 \\ \widehat{\beta}_2 \end{pmatrix}.$$

The equations (4.15) consist of K linear equations in K unknown parameters $\widehat{\beta}_k$. Because the explanatory variables X_{tk} are linearly independent we know for the rank of $\mathbf{X}$ that $r(\mathbf{X}) = K$, and $r(\mathbf{X}'\mathbf{X}) = K$. Therefore the inverse matrix $(\mathbf{X}'\mathbf{X})^{-1}$ exists. Multiply equation (4.15) by $(\mathbf{X}'\mathbf{X})^{-1}$ on both sides, and the OLS estimator can be written as:

$$\widehat{\beta} = (\mathbf{X}'\mathbf{X})^{-1} \mathbf{X}'\mathbf{y}. \tag{4.16}$$

Notice the similarity of this expression in matrix notation for the entire parameter vector $\widehat{\beta}$ and expression (4.12) for the parameter $\widehat{\beta}_1$ in the bivariate model. Before going on, it is necessary to check whether this solution is a minimum indeed, by deriving the second-order conditions:

$$\frac{\partial f\left(\widehat{\beta}\right)}{\partial \widehat{\beta}\partial \widehat{\beta}'} = 2\mathbf{X}'\mathbf{X}.$$

The matrix $\mathbf{X}'\mathbf{X}$ is a positive definite matrix, so the least squares solution determines the minimum of the function (4.14).

Notice that $\widehat{\beta}$ is linear in the endogenous (stochastic) variable $\mathbf{y}$, which is important in analysing the stochastic properties of $\widehat{\beta}$. The vector $\widehat{\beta}$ contains *the point estimates* of the parameters β. *Interval estimates* will be determined in Chapter 5. The vector $\widehat{\beta}$ is printed as the first column in the EViews regression output; see Figure 4.4 later.

In Section 5.2, a number of relationships among variables of the model and the OLS estimator will be considered. These concern relationships that we use at various stages later in the course or which are useful to know for empirical work. In the following sections, some properties of the OLS estimator are discussed, after which the computation of the OLS estimator in EViews will be considered in Section 4.9.

4.4 Relationship between disturbances and residuals

In this section, the relationship between the unobserved variable $\mathbf{u}$ and the calculated residuals $\mathbf{e}$ will be derived. But first a matrix will be introduced for notational convenience that is often used in analytical considerations of relationships among economic variables. The matrix expression $\mathbf{I}_n - \mathbf{X}\left(\mathbf{X}'\mathbf{X}\right)^{-1}\mathbf{X}'$ is frequently encountered in all kinds of analytical derivations. Examples that make use of this matrix are also found in this section. For this reason the notation $\mathbf{M}_X$ for this expression – which is standard notation for this matrix in the econometrics literature – is introduced and the properties of $\mathbf{M}_X$ are determined. The subscript X is used to show clearly that $\mathbf{M}_X$ is an expression in the matrix $\mathbf{X}$. The matrix $\mathbf{M}_X$ has no economic relevance. So, the definition of the $(n \times n)$ matrix $\mathbf{M}_X$ is:

$$\mathbf{M}_X = \mathbf{I}_n - \mathbf{X}\left(\mathbf{X}'\mathbf{X}\right)^{-1}\mathbf{X}',$$

and its properties are:

- $\mathbf{M}_X$ is symmetric and idempotent: $\mathbf{M}_X = \mathbf{M}'_X, \mathbf{M}_X\mathbf{M}_X = \mathbf{M}_X$, which can easily be checked;
- $\mathbf{M}_X$ is singular, it has rank equal to $n - K$ (see the next section);
- $\mathbf{M}_X$ and the explanatory variables are orthogonal: $\mathbf{M}_X\mathbf{X} = \mathbf{0}$, which is verified by computing the product.

The second term in the definition of $\mathbf{M}$ is frequently denoted as the matrix $\mathbf{P}_X$ in the econometrics literature.

$$\mathbf{P}_X = \mathbf{X}\left(\mathbf{X}'\mathbf{X}\right)^{-1}\mathbf{X}',$$
$$\mathbf{M}_X = \mathbf{I}_n - \mathbf{P}_X.$$

Sometimes it is convenient to use $\mathbf{P}_X$ in analytical derivations. Just like $\mathbf{M}_X$, the matrix $\mathbf{P}_X$ is a symmetric idempotent matrix.

The following two interesting relationships can simply be derived:

$$\mathbf{e} = \mathbf{M}_X\mathbf{y}, \tag{4.17}$$
$$\mathbf{e} = \mathbf{M}_X\mathbf{u}. \tag{4.18}$$

Equation (4.18) means that the residuals are a linear combination of the unknown disturbances. The disturbances are not observed themselves, but a linear combination of the disturbances is observed. The relationships (4.17) and (4.18) are obtained as follows.

$$
\begin{aligned}
\mathbf{e} &= \mathbf{y} - \hat{\mathbf{y}} \\
&= \mathbf{y} - \mathbf{X}\hat{\beta} \\
&= \mathbf{y} - \mathbf{X}\left(\mathbf{X}'\mathbf{X}\right)^{-1}\mathbf{X}'\mathbf{y} \\
&= \left(\mathbf{I}_n - \mathbf{X}\left(\mathbf{X}'\mathbf{X}\right)^{-1}\mathbf{X}'\right)\mathbf{y} \\
&= \mathbf{M}_X\mathbf{y} \\
&= \mathbf{M}_X\left(\mathbf{X}\beta + \mathbf{u}\right) \\
&= \mathbf{M}_X\mathbf{u}.
\end{aligned}
$$

The residuals will be used to test the disturbance-term assumptions. Therefore, we need to know the distribution of the residual vector e. Under the assumption that u is normally distributed, e is normally distributed too, because of the linear relation (4.18). In the steps to obtain expressions for the vector $E\left(\mathbf{e}\right)$ and the matrix $Var\left(\mathbf{e}\right)$ the assumption that all the explanatory variables are exogenous is used explicitly.

$$
\underset{(n\times 1)}{E\left(\mathbf{e}\right)} = E\left(\mathbf{M}_X\mathbf{u}\right)
$$

$$
= \mathbf{M}_X E\left(\mathbf{u}\right)
$$

$$
= \mathbf{0};
$$

$$
\underset{(n\times n)}{Var\left(\mathbf{e}\right)} = E\mathbf{e}\mathbf{e}'
$$

$$
= E\mathbf{M}_X\mathbf{u}\mathbf{u}'\mathbf{M}_X'
$$

$$
= \mathbf{M}_X\left(E\mathbf{u}\mathbf{u}'\right)\mathbf{M}_X'
$$

$$
= \mathbf{M}_X\left(\sigma_u^2\mathbf{I}_n\right)\mathbf{M}_X'
$$

$$
= \sigma_u^2\mathbf{M}_X.
$$

This implies the following sampling distribution for the residual vector e:

$$
\mathbf{e} \sim N(\mathbf{0}, \sigma_u^2\mathbf{M}_X).
$$

It is a degenerated distribution as the variance-covariance matrix is singular. Notice that this result has been obtained by using all the assumptions of the classical regression model. Notice also, that under the assumption that u is homoskedastic and not-autocorrelated, the residuals e are heteroskedastic and autocorrelated. So, if the covariances of the disturbances are zero and the variances are identical then this is not valid for the residuals!

4.5 Estimation of the variance of the disturbance term

One parameter of the linear model has still to be estimated – the variance of the disturbance term σ_u^2. In this section, an unbiased estimator of σ_u^2 is derived by using the OLS residuals. The following result will be proved:

$$\widehat{\sigma}_u^2 = \frac{1}{n-K} \sum_{t=1}^{n} e_t^2,$$

is an unbiased estimator of σ_u^2 :

$$E\left(\widehat{\sigma}_u^2\right) = \sigma_u^2.$$

Proof From (4.18) it follows that:

$$\sum_{t=1}^{n} e_t^2 = \mathbf{e}'\mathbf{e}$$

$$= \mathbf{u}'\mathbf{M}_X\mathbf{u}.$$

Next the expectation $E\left(\mathbf{e}'\mathbf{e}\right)$ is determined by using straightforward matrix algebra. The notation $tr\left(\mathbf{M}\right)$ means the trace of the matrix $\mathbf{M}$, which is equal to the sum of the elements of the main diagonal of $\mathbf{M}$.

$$E\left(\mathbf{e}'\mathbf{e}\right) = E\left(\mathbf{u}'\mathbf{M}_X\mathbf{u}\right)$$

$$= E\left(tr\left(\mathbf{u}'\mathbf{M}_X\mathbf{u}\right)\right), \text{ as } \mathbf{u}'\mathbf{M}_X\mathbf{u} \text{ is a scalar}$$

$$= E\left(tr\left(\mathbf{M}_X\mathbf{u}\mathbf{u}'\right)\right), \text{ cyclical change in the multiplication}$$

$$= tr\left(\mathbf{M}_X\left(E\mathbf{u}\mathbf{u}'\right)\right), \text{ as } \mathbf{X} \text{ is exogenous}$$

$$= tr\left(\mathbf{M}_X\left(\sigma_u^2\mathbf{I}_n\right)\right), \text{ the disturbance-term assumptions are substituted}$$

$$= \sigma_u^2 \cdot tr\left(\mathbf{M}_X\right),$$

$$= \sigma_u^2\left(tr\left(\mathbf{I}_n\right) - tr\left(\mathbf{X}\left(\mathbf{X}'\mathbf{X}\right)^{-1}\mathbf{X}'\right)\right), \text{ using its definition}$$

$$= \sigma_u^2\left(tr\left(\mathbf{I}_n\right) - tr\left(\left(\mathbf{X}'\mathbf{X}\right)^{-1}\mathbf{X}'\mathbf{X}\right)\right), \text{ cyclical change in the multiplication}$$

$$= \sigma_u^2\left(tr\left(\mathbf{I}_n\right) - tr\left(\mathbf{I}_K\right)\right)$$

$$= \sigma_u^2\left(n-K\right).$$

This also proves that $r\left(\mathbf{M}_X\right) = n - K$, because $r\left(\mathbf{M}_X\right) = tr\left(\mathbf{M}_X\right)$, as $\mathbf{M}_X$ is an idempotent matrix (see e.g.: Johnston and DiNardo (1997), p.483). Rewriting the result gives:

$$E\left(\frac{1}{n-K}e'e\right) = \sigma_u^2.$$

Define:

$$\widehat{\sigma}_u^2 = \frac{1}{n-K}e'e$$

$$= \frac{1}{n-K}\sum_{t=1}^{n} e_t^2,$$

then it follows that:

$$E\left(\widehat{\sigma}_u^2\right) = \sigma_u^2.$$

The estimator $\widehat{\sigma}_u^2$ is an unbiased estimator of the disturbance variance σ_u^2.

See Section 5.5 for a simpler proof of the unbiasedness of $\widehat{\sigma}_u^2$, after the distribution of $\widehat{\sigma}_u^2$ has been determined. In the regression output of EViews, the value of $\widehat{\sigma}_u$ is printed and it is called the *standard error of regression* (S.E. of regression); see Figure 4.4 later.

4.6 Desirable statistical properties of estimators

In this section, we look at some properties of estimators in general, which are considered as desirable. Then, in the following section, we check whether the OLS estimator has these properties. Also, the usual notation will be introduced. Knowledge of these properties is desirable when doing empirical research, because one has to know about the interpretation and quality of the estimation results. In fact, familiarity with basic statistics for econometrics is essential. This book does not discuss statistics, but some statistical concepts will be outlined for a better understanding of the econometric methods and their properties. These concepts are important for reviewing estimation results and writing a research paper correctly.

The introduction will be done for the parameter β_2 in the simple bivariate linear model (1.6):

$$Y_t = \beta_1 + \beta_2 X_t + u_t.$$

An *estimator* is a stochastic variable. The estimator of β_2 is written as $\widehat{\beta}_2$. The estimator $\widehat{\beta}_2$ has a probability distribution which is written as $f_{\widehat{\beta}_2}$. The computation of a point *estimate* $\widehat{\beta}_2$ for β_2, based on a random sample, is identical to drawing a number from this distribution. The notation for an estimator and an estimate is identical, but it will be clear from the text what is meant.

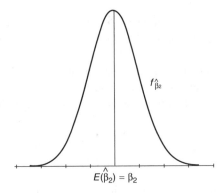

Figure 4.2: The sampling distribution of $\widehat{\beta}_2 : f_{\widehat{\beta}_2}$, with $E(\widehat{\beta}_2) = \beta_2$

Unbiasedness

If an estimator $\widehat{\beta}_2$ has the property that the mean $E(\widehat{\beta}_2)$ of its distribution function $f_{\widehat{\beta}_2}$ is equal to the unknown parameter β_2, then the estimator is called an *unbiased estimator*. This is written as:

$$E(\widehat{\beta}_2) = \beta_2.$$

The sampling distribution $f_{\widehat{\beta}_2}$ of $\widehat{\beta}_2$ may look as shown in Figure 4.2.

The difference between the estimate $\widehat{\beta}_2$ (the draw from the sampling distribution) and the mean β_2 is called the *sampling bias* or *sampling error*. If it is possible to take many draws from this distribution, then the mean value of these draws should be in the neighbourhood of β_2, or the mean of the sampling errors should be close to zero. However, observations on economic variables, the data, are only realised once, so only one estimate of β_2 is obtained.

Efficiency

An estimator is an *efficient* estimator if, in some well-defined class of estimators (e.g. the class of linear unbiased estimators), it is the estimator with the smallest variance.

Consistency

The estimator $\widehat{\beta}_2$ is a consistent estimator of β_2 if the distribution $f_{\widehat{\beta}_2}$ collapses at the point β_2 into a straight line when the sample size n goes to infinity. This means that, for increasing n, the variance of $\widehat{\beta}_2$ goes to zero, and in cases where the estimator is biased, the bias also goes to zero. The distribution of the estimator, like the one in Figure 4.2, becomes narrower and narrower when n increases, and becomes degenerate at the point β_2. The usual notation to show that an estimator is consistent is:

$$\underset{n \to \infty}{P \lim} \left(\widehat{\beta}_{2,n} \right) = \beta_2.$$

The notation $\widehat{\beta}_{2,n}$ stands for the OLS estimator of β_2 applied for a sample with n observations. $P\lim$ stands for *probability limit*. The series $\widehat{\beta}_{2,n}$ converges in probability to β_2 if n goes to infinity.[*]

Some properties of the $P\lim$ operator are summarised and then used to consider the (in)consistency of the OLS estimator in Section 4.7. The following rules are valid. Not all rules hold for the expectations operator E, except when the variables are independent.

$$P\lim_{n\to\infty} (x_n + y_n) = P\lim_{n\to\infty} (x_n) + P\lim_{n\to\infty} (y_n)$$

$$P\lim_{n\to\infty} (x_n - y_n) = P\lim_{n\to\infty} (x_n) - P\lim_{n\to\infty} (y_n)$$

$$P\lim_{n\to\infty} (x_n \cdot y_n) = P\lim_{n\to\infty} (x_n) \cdot P\lim_{n\to\infty} (y_n)$$

$$P\lim_{n\to\infty} (x_n/y_n) = P\lim_{n\to\infty} (x_n) / P\lim_{n\to\infty} (y_n), \text{ if } P\lim_{n\to\infty} (y_n) \neq 0.$$

Similar rules can be given for random matrices or vectors, if the multiplication is possible, and the matrix $\mathbf{X}$ is not singular:

$$P\lim_{n\to\infty} (\mathbf{X}\mathbf{y}) = P\lim_{n\to\infty} (\mathbf{X}) \cdot P\lim_{n\to\infty} (\mathbf{y})$$

$$P\lim_{n\to\infty} (\mathbf{X}^{-1}) = \left(P\lim_{n\to\infty} (\mathbf{X}) \right)^{-1}, \text{ etc.}$$

Only minor attention to asymptotic behaviour of estimators is given in this book, as asymptotic theory is a topic that is beyond its scope.

The consistency property implies that the estimator $\widehat{\beta}_2$ itself does not have an *asymptotic distribution*. If asymptotic behaviour of the estimator is to be studied, the estimator must be rescaled and the asymptotic distribution of $\sqrt{n}\left(\widehat{\beta}_{2,n} - \beta_2\right)$ is to be determined. This will not be discussed further; only passive knowledge is needed to understand the practical implications for the estimation result of some model specifications. (See other econometric or statistical textbooks for a more theoretical discussion on this topic.) Example 4.1 is given to illustrate the above introduced concept.

---

[*] See the difference between the definition of the concept 'limit' and 'probability limit'. For a deterministic variable the limit x of the series x_n is defined as: $\lim_{n\to\infty} x_n = x$ if for every $\varepsilon > 0$, there is a number N such that

$$\text{for every } n > N : |x_n - x| < \varepsilon.$$

In case the variable x_i is a stochastic variable, it can be true that for any $\varepsilon > 0$ with positive probability $|x_n - x| > \varepsilon$ for all n. Therefore the concept 'converging in probability' is introduced. If x_n is a sequence of stochastic variables, then the x_n converge in probability to a constant x for $n \to \infty$ if for every ε and $\delta > 0$, there is a number N such that

$$\text{for every } n > N : Prob\left(|x_n - x| < \varepsilon\right) > 1 - \delta.$$

The number x is called the 'probability limit' (the $P\lim$) of x_n; in notation:

$$P\lim_{n\to\infty} x_n = x.$$

Example 4.1 The sample mean as estimator of the population mean

In general, if $\widehat{\theta}_n$ is a consistent estimator of the parameter θ, with sampling distribution: $N(\theta, q/n)$, then it is easy to show that $\sqrt{n}\left(\widehat{\theta}_n - \theta\right) \sim N(0, q)$. The estimator $\widehat{\theta}$ is said to have an asymptotic normal distribution:

$$\widehat{\theta} \overset{A}{\sim} N\left(\theta, \frac{q}{n}\right).$$

A simple example is the sample mean as estimator of the population mean. If $x_1, x_2, \ldots, x_n$ is a sample from a normally distributed population with mean μ and variance σ^2, then it is well-known that the sample mean: $\overline{x} = \frac{1}{n}\sum x_i$ is distributed as $\overline{x} \sim N(\mu, \sigma^2/n)$ with mean μ and variance σ^2/n. Then, according to the above:

$$\sqrt{n}(\overline{x} - \mu) \sim N(0, \sigma^2),$$

implying:

$$(\overline{x} - \mu) \overset{A}{\sim} N\left(0, \frac{\sigma^2}{n}\right) \text{ or: } \overline{x} \overset{A}{\sim} N\left(\mu, \frac{\sigma^2}{n}\right).$$

4.7 The distribution and some properties of the OLS estimator

In this section, the distribution of $\widehat{\beta}$ is derived. But first we consider distributions of linearly transformed stochastic variables (vectors), the results of which will be applied in determining the distribution of $\widehat{\beta}$. In upcoming analytical derivations the following three transformed distributions will be used directly when the occasion should arise.

A linear transformation of a stochastic vector

Let $\mathbf{y}$ be an $(n \times 1)$ random vector, $\mathbf{c}$ an $(m \times 1)$ vector with constants, and $\mathbf{C}$ an $(m \times n)$ matrix with constants. Define the $(m \times 1)$ vector $\mathbf{z}$ as a linear transformation of $\mathbf{y}$:

$$\mathbf{z} = \mathbf{c} + \mathbf{C}\mathbf{y},$$

then the first two moments of the linear transformed vector $\mathbf{z}$ look like:

$$E(\mathbf{z}) = \mathbf{c} + \mathbf{C} \cdot E(\mathbf{y}),$$
$$Var(\mathbf{z}) = \mathbf{C} \cdot Var(\mathbf{y}) \cdot \mathbf{C}'.$$

If $\mathbf{y}$ is normally distributed, then $\mathbf{z}$ is also normally distributed, or more explicitly:

if

$$\mathbf{y} \sim N\left(\boldsymbol{\mu}_y, \boldsymbol{\Omega}_y\right),$$

and

$$\mathbf{z} = \mathbf{c} + \mathbf{C}\mathbf{y},$$

then **z** is distributed as follows:

$$\mathbf{z} \sim N\left(\mathbf{c} + \mathbf{C}\boldsymbol{\mu}_y, \mathbf{C}\boldsymbol{\Omega}_y\mathbf{C}'\right). \tag{4.19}$$

For clarification, we consider the following bivariate example. Let two dependently distributed stochastic variables x and y be given by:

$$x \sim N\left(\mu_x, \sigma_x^2\right), \; y \sim N\left(\mu_y, \sigma_y^2\right), \text{ and } cov\left(x, y\right) = \sigma_{xy}.$$

Next look at the distribution of the following linear transformation of these variables:

$$z = c_1 x + c_2 y.$$

From basic statistics it is known that:

$$z \sim N\left(\mu_z, \sigma_z^2\right), \text{ with} \tag{4.20}$$

$$\mu_z = c_1 \mu_x + c_2 \mu_y \tag{4.21}$$

$$\sigma_z^2 = c_1^2 \sigma_x^2 + c_2^2 \sigma_y^2 + 2c_1 c_2 \sigma_{xy}. \tag{4.22}$$

These expressions can be written in matrix notation. Define the vectors $\mathbf{c}'$ and $\boldsymbol{\mu}'$:

$$\mathbf{c}' = \begin{pmatrix} c_1 & c_2 \end{pmatrix} \text{ and } \boldsymbol{\mu}' = \begin{pmatrix} \mu_x & \mu_y \end{pmatrix},$$

and the covariance matrix $\boldsymbol{\Omega}$:

$$\boldsymbol{\Omega} = \begin{pmatrix} \sigma_1^2 & \sigma_{12} \\ \sigma_{12} & \sigma_2^2 \end{pmatrix}.$$

Then the equations (4.21) and (4.22) for μ_z and σ_z^2 can be written as follows:

$$\mu_z = \begin{pmatrix} c_1 & c_2 \end{pmatrix} \begin{pmatrix} \mu_x \\ \mu_y \end{pmatrix},$$

$$\mu_z = \mathbf{c}'\boldsymbol{\mu},$$

$$\sigma_z^2 = \begin{pmatrix} c_1 & c_2 \end{pmatrix} \begin{pmatrix} \sigma_1^2 & \sigma_{12} \\ \sigma_{12} & \sigma_2^2 \end{pmatrix} \begin{pmatrix} c_1 \\ c_2 \end{pmatrix},$$

$$\sigma_z^2 = \mathbf{c}'\boldsymbol{\Omega}\mathbf{c}.$$

So the distribution (4.20) of z is written in matrix notation:

$$z \sim N\left(\mathbf{c}'\boldsymbol{\mu}, \mathbf{c}'\boldsymbol{\Omega}\mathbf{c}\right). \tag{4.23}$$

When this result (4.23) is generalised for a multivariate distribution with more than two variables, we write the distribution of z as shown in (4.19).

Two linear transformations of the same stochastic vector

In the second situation, we have the two $(m \times 1)$ vectors z_1 and z_2 that are linear functions of the *same* stochastic $(n \times 1)$ vector y with covariance matrix $Var(y) = \Omega_y$:

$$z_1 = c_1 + C_1 y$$
$$z_2 = c_2 + C_2 y,$$

with $(m \times n)$ matrices C_1 and C_2 with constants. The transformation are written as follows:

$$\begin{pmatrix} z_1 \\ z_2 \end{pmatrix} = \begin{pmatrix} c_1 \\ c_2 \end{pmatrix} + \begin{pmatrix} C_1 \\ C_2 \end{pmatrix} y.$$

Then the distribution of $\begin{pmatrix} z_1 & z_2 \end{pmatrix}'$ is:

$$\begin{pmatrix} z_1 \\ z_2 \end{pmatrix} \sim N \left(\begin{pmatrix} c_1 + C_1 \mu_y \\ c_2 + C_2 \mu_y \end{pmatrix}, \begin{pmatrix} C_1 \Omega_y C_1' & C_1 \Omega_y C_2' \\ C_1 \Omega_y C_2' & C_2 \Omega_y C_2' \end{pmatrix} \right).$$

A linear transformation of two dependently distributed stochastic vectors

Finally, consider two stochastic $(n \times 1)$ vectors y_1 and y_2 that are dependently distributed as follows:

$$\begin{pmatrix} y_1 \\ y_2 \end{pmatrix} \sim N \left(\begin{pmatrix} \mu_{y_1} \\ \mu_{y_2} \end{pmatrix}, \begin{pmatrix} \Omega_{y_1} & \Omega_{y_1,y_2} \\ \Omega_{y_1,y_2} & \Omega_{y_2} \end{pmatrix} \right),$$

where the $(n \times n)$ covariance matrices have been defined as follows.

$$\Omega_{y_1} = Var(y_1),$$
$$\Omega_{y_2} = Var(y_2),$$
$$\Omega_{y_1,y_2} = Cov(y_1, y_2).$$

We consider two vectors z_1 and z_2 that are linear functions of the stochastic vectors y_1 and y_2, defined as:

$$z_1 = c_1 + C_1 y_1$$
$$z_2 = c_2 + C_2 y_2,$$

or put together as:

$$\begin{pmatrix} z_1 \\ z_2 \end{pmatrix} = \begin{pmatrix} c_1 \\ c_2 \end{pmatrix} + \begin{pmatrix} C_1 & 0 \\ 0 & C_2 \end{pmatrix} \begin{pmatrix} y_1 \\ y_2 \end{pmatrix}.$$

Then the distribution of $\begin{pmatrix} \mathbf{z}_1 & \mathbf{z}_2 \end{pmatrix}'$ is:

$$\begin{pmatrix} \mathbf{z}_1 \\ \mathbf{z}_2 \end{pmatrix} \sim N \left(\begin{pmatrix} \mathbf{c}_1 + \mathbf{C}_1 \boldsymbol{\mu}_{y_1} \\ \mathbf{c}_2 + \mathbf{C}_2 \boldsymbol{\mu}_{y_2} \end{pmatrix}, \begin{pmatrix} \mathbf{C}_1 \boldsymbol{\Omega}_{y_1} \mathbf{C}_1' & \mathbf{C}_1 \boldsymbol{\Omega}_{y_1,y_2} \mathbf{C}_2' \\ \mathbf{C}_1 \boldsymbol{\Omega}_{y_1,y_2} \mathbf{C}_2' & \mathbf{C}_2 \boldsymbol{\Omega}_{y_2} \mathbf{C}_2' \end{pmatrix} \right).$$

In the next subsection, we encounter a linear transformation of the vector $\mathbf{u}$ with disturbances when deriving the distribution of the OLS estimator $\widehat{\beta}$.

Unbiasedness and variance of the OLS estimator

By using the notation introduced above, the distribution of $\widehat{\beta}$ will be determined. This distribution is necessary for computing the standard errors for the individual parameter estimates. The expectation and the covariance matrix of $\widehat{\beta}$ will be computed. The distribution is also used for testing hypotheses concerning possible values of the parameters β_k. As will be seen below, the OLS estimator $\widehat{\beta}$ is an unbiased estimator of β with exogenous explanatory variables. The well-known form used to analyse the properties of $\widehat{\beta}$ is the expression of $\widehat{\beta}$ in β and its *sampling error* as obtained in equation (4.24).

$$\begin{aligned} \widehat{\beta} &= (\mathbf{X}'\mathbf{X})^{-1} \mathbf{X}'\mathbf{y}, \\ &= (\mathbf{X}'\mathbf{X})^{-1} \mathbf{X}' (\mathbf{X}\beta + \mathbf{u}) \\ &= (\mathbf{X}'\mathbf{X})^{-1} \mathbf{X}'\mathbf{X}\beta + (\mathbf{X}'\mathbf{X})^{-1} \mathbf{X}'\mathbf{u} \\ &= \beta + (\mathbf{X}'\mathbf{X})^{-1} \mathbf{X}'\mathbf{u}. \end{aligned} \tag{4.24}$$

The second term in expression (4.24) $(\mathbf{X}'\mathbf{X})^{-1} \mathbf{X}'\mathbf{u}$ is the *sampling error* of the estimator $\widehat{\beta}$. With expression (4.24) the moments of the OLS estimator $\widehat{\beta}$ are derived. The vector $\widehat{\beta}$ has been written as a linear transformation of the vector $\mathbf{u}$. By using the distribution (4.19), the expressions for the mean vector and covariance matrix of $\widehat{\beta}$ are easily obtained.

$$\begin{aligned} E\left(\widehat{\beta}\right) &= \beta + (\mathbf{X}'\mathbf{X})^{-1} \mathbf{X}' \cdot E\mathbf{u} \\ &= \beta + (\mathbf{X}'\mathbf{X})^{-1} \mathbf{X}' \cdot \mathbf{0} \\ &= \beta. \end{aligned}$$

This proves that the OLS estimator $\widehat{\beta}$ is an unbiased estimator of the parameter vector β in the classical regression model. The covariance matrix is:

$$\begin{aligned} Var\left(\widehat{\beta}\right) &= Var\left((\mathbf{X}'\mathbf{X})^{-1} \mathbf{X}'\mathbf{u}\right) \\ &= (\mathbf{X}'\mathbf{X})^{-1} \mathbf{X}' \cdot Var(\mathbf{u}) \cdot \mathbf{X} (\mathbf{X}'\mathbf{X})^{-1} \\ &= (\mathbf{X}'\mathbf{X})^{-1} \mathbf{X}' \cdot \sigma_u^2 \mathbf{I}_n \cdot \mathbf{X} (\mathbf{X}'\mathbf{X})^{-1} \qquad (\leftarrow \text{Notice!}) \\ &= \sigma_u^2 (\mathbf{X}'\mathbf{X})^{-1}. \end{aligned}$$

Notice that the disturbance-term assumptions have been substituted above to obtain the covariance matrix of the distribution (4.25)! The covariance matrix of $\widehat{\beta}$ shows that the estimates of the parameters are usually not independently distributed. So, in the classical regression model, $\widehat{\beta}$ is an unbiased estimator of β, and the sampling distribution of $\widehat{\beta}$ is:

$$\widehat{\beta} \sim N\left(\beta, \sigma_u^2 \left(\mathbf{X}'\mathbf{X}\right)^{-1}\right). \tag{4.25}$$

Once more, notice that this is the sampling distribution of $\widehat{\beta}$ derived for exogenous $\mathbf{X}$, and it is conditional that *all* the disturbance-term assumptions are valid. Later on, when we look at the more general reduced-form model, we will see that these sampling results for the parameters of the reduced-form model only hold for very large samples or, in other words, we then have asymptotic results for the OLS estimator.

However, the distribution of $\widehat{\beta}$ cannot be used directly to compute interval estimates because it contains the unknown variance σ_u^2. By using the estimate $\widehat{\sigma}_u^2$ for σ_u^2, feasible standard errors of the parameter estimates are computed in practice, but *interval estimates* cannot be computed by using the distribution (4.25) because σ_u^2 is the parameter of the distribution and not $\widehat{\sigma}_u^2$. In Section 5.6, interval estimates are derived by using the Student's t-distribution. The *estimated covariance matrix* of the parameter estimates is:

$$\widehat{Var\left(\widehat{\beta}\right)} = \widehat{\sigma}_u^2 \left(\mathbf{X}'\mathbf{X}\right)^{-1}. \tag{4.26}$$

In EViews this matrix is shown in the 'Equation' window under 'View' with the option 'Covariance Matrix'. The diagonal elements of $\widehat{\sigma}_u^2 \left(\mathbf{X}'\mathbf{X}\right)^{-1}$ contain the estimated variances of the estimates and the elements outside the diagonal are the estimated covariances between the estimates. Sometimes it is necessary to use the covariances of the parameter estimates for a statistical test.

The distribution (4.25) can be written for an individual parameter estimate $\widehat{\beta}_k$ as:

$$\widehat{\beta}_k \sim N\left(\beta_k, \sigma_u^2 x^{kk}\right),$$

where x^{kk} is the k-th diagonal element of $\left(\mathbf{X}'\mathbf{X}\right)^{-1}$; superscripts have been used to denote that they are elements of the inverse matrix. Then the *standard errors* of $\widehat{\beta}_k$ $(k = 1, \ldots, K)$ are written as:

$$se\left(\widehat{\beta}_k\right) = \widehat{\sigma}_u \sqrt{x^{kk}},$$

where *se* stands for 'standard error'. The standard errors $se\left(\widehat{\beta}_k\right)$ are the square roots of the elements on the main diagonal of the estimated covariance matrix (4.26). The second column of the EViews regression output, in Figure 4.4, contains the standard errors $se\left(\widehat{\beta}_k\right)$ of the estimates $\widehat{\beta}_k$.

Remark 4.1 Inaccurately calculated standard errors
We have seen that the results in the regression output are only valid if the disturbance-term assumptions are not violated. The absence of autocorrelation and heteroskedasticity has been used to get expression (4.26) for the variance-covariance matrix of the OLS estimator. Your computer does not know whether the hypotheses about the disturbance term **u** have or have not been rejected, so EViews always computes the matrix (4.26). If the disturbance-term assumptions have been rejected, then EViews (and every other software package) does not calculate the correct covariance matrix! In fact, the standard errors are underestimated in that case and the estimation result looks better than it is. That is the reason that we first need an estimated model where the disturbance-term assumptions are not rejected, before we can look at the 'quality' of the estimated parameters in a correct way.

The efficiency property of the OLS estimator

The OLS estimator is efficient in the class of linear unbiased estimators. With this property the OLS estimator is called BLUE (best linear unbiased estimator). In the econometrics literature, the efficiency theorem in the linear model is called the Gauss–Markov theorem, which is a historical name. The theorem is proved by showing that the OLS estimator $\hat{\beta}$ has a smaller variance than any other linear unbiased estimator $\tilde{\beta}$ of β. Or, in matrix terms: the difference between the covariance matrix of $\tilde{\beta}$ and $\hat{\beta}$ is a positive definite matrix written as $\left(Var\left(\tilde{\beta}\right) - Var\left(\hat{\beta}\right) \right)$.

Proof   Define $\tilde{\beta}$ as a different linear unbiased estimator of β:

$$\tilde{\beta} = \mathbf{C}\mathbf{y}.$$

$\mathbf{C}$ is a $(K \times n)$ matrix with constants, just as the $(K \times n)$ matrix $(\mathbf{X}'\mathbf{X})^{-1}\mathbf{X}'$ of the OLS estimator. The estimator $\tilde{\beta}$ is unbiased:

$$E\tilde{\beta} = \beta.$$

This property implies restrictions on the coefficient matrix $\mathbf{C}$:

$$
\begin{aligned}
E\tilde{\beta} &= E\left(\mathbf{C}\mathbf{y}\right) \\
&= E\left(\mathbf{C}(\mathbf{X}\beta + \mathbf{u})\right) \\
&= E\left(\mathbf{C}\mathbf{X}\beta + \mathbf{C}\mathbf{u}\right) \\
&= \mathbf{C}\mathbf{X}\beta + \mathbf{C}E\mathbf{u} \\
&= \mathbf{C}\mathbf{X}\beta.
\end{aligned}
$$

$\tilde{\beta}$ is an unbiased estimator if

$$\mathbf{C}\mathbf{X} = \mathbf{I}_K.$$

For the covariance matrix of $\widetilde{\beta}$ one finds:

$$\begin{aligned}
Var\left(\widetilde{\beta}\right) &= Var\left(\mathbf{CX}\beta + \mathbf{Cu}\right) \\
&= Var(\mathbf{Cu}) \\
&= \mathbf{C}{\cdot}Var\left(\mathbf{u}\right){\cdot}\mathbf{C'} \\
&= \mathbf{C}{\cdot}\sigma_u^2\mathbf{I}_n{\cdot}\mathbf{C'} \\
&= \sigma_u^2\mathbf{CC'}.
\end{aligned}$$

Remember the expression of the covariance matrix of the OLS estimator

$$Var\left(\widehat{\beta}\right) = \sigma_u^2\left(\mathbf{X'X}\right)^{-1}.$$

Look at the difference of $\left(\mathbf{X'X}\right)^{-1}\mathbf{X'}$ and $\mathbf{C}$ to link the two covariance matrices. Define this difference as the $(K \times n)$ matrix $\mathbf{D}$:

$$\mathbf{D} = \mathbf{C} - \left(\mathbf{X'X}\right)^{-1}\mathbf{X'}$$

or

$$\mathbf{C} = \left(\mathbf{X'X}\right)^{-1}\mathbf{X'} + \mathbf{D}.$$

By using $\mathbf{CX} = \mathbf{I}_K$ the following property of the matrix $\mathbf{D}$ is derived:

$$\begin{aligned}
\left(\mathbf{X'X}\right)^{-1}\mathbf{X'X} + \mathbf{DX} &= \mathbf{I}_K \\
\mathbf{I}_K + \mathbf{DX} &= \mathbf{I}_K \\
\mathbf{DX} &= \mathbf{0}.
\end{aligned}$$

Using this property yields:

$$\begin{aligned}
\mathbf{CC'} &= \left(\left(\mathbf{X'X}\right)^{-1}\mathbf{X'} + \mathbf{D}\right)\left(\left(\mathbf{X'X}\right)^{-1}\mathbf{X'} + \mathbf{D}\right)' \\
&= \left(\mathbf{X'X}\right)^{-1}\mathbf{X'X}\left(\mathbf{X'X}\right)^{-1} + \mathbf{DD'} \\
&= \left(\mathbf{X'X}\right)^{-1} + \mathbf{DD'}.
\end{aligned}$$

So the difference between the $(K \times K)$ matrices $\mathbf{CC'}$ and $\left(\mathbf{X'X}\right)^{-1}$ is the positive definite matrix $\mathbf{DD'}$. Hence:

$$\begin{aligned}
Var\left(\widetilde{\beta}\right) &= \sigma_u^2\mathbf{CC'} \\
&= \sigma_u^2\left(\left(\mathbf{X'X}\right)^{-1} + \mathbf{DD'}\right) \\
&= Var\left(\widehat{\beta}\right) + \sigma_u^2\mathbf{DD'}.
\end{aligned}$$

The difference $Var\left(\widetilde{\beta}\right) - Var\left(\widehat{\beta}\right)$ is equal to the positive definite matrix $\sigma_u^2\mathbf{DD'}$, which means that the OLS estimator has the smallest variance in the class of linear unbiased estimators. The OLS estimator is an efficient estimator in that class. Then the OLS estimator is called BLUE: best linear unbiased estimator.

The consistency property of the OLS estimator

Asymptotic theory is not a topic in this book, but with the concept of consistency and the $P\lim$ operator as introduced in Section 4.6 we are able to look at the large sample properties of estimators. (See the statistical literature or any of the references to more theoretical econometric textbooks, for a more detailed discussion on this subject.)

To prove the consistency of the OLS estimator, the following additional assumptions are made about the covariances of the explanatory variables. The $(K \times K)$ matrix with sample moments of the explanatory variables (with respect to zero) is $(\mathbf{X}'\mathbf{X})/n$. To be clear, the matrix is written in more detail (all summations run from 1 till n):

$$\frac{1}{n}\mathbf{X}'\mathbf{X} = \frac{1}{n}\begin{pmatrix} n & \sum X_{t2} & \sum X_{t3} & \cdots & \sum X_{tK} \\ \sum X_{t2} & \sum X_{t2}^2 & \sum X_{t3}X_{t2} & \cdots & \sum X_{tK}X_{t2} \\ \sum X_{t3} & \sum X_{t2}X_{t3} & \sum X_{t3}^2 & \cdots & \vdots \\ \vdots & \vdots & \vdots & \ddots & \vdots \\ \sum X_{tK} & \sum X_{t2}X_{tK} & \cdots & \cdots & \sum X_{tK}^2 \end{pmatrix}.$$

A necessary requirement is that all the elements of the matrix converge to finite constants for increasing n. The matrix $(\mathbf{X}'\mathbf{X})/n$ converges to a matrix $\mathbf{\Omega}_{XX}$ that has elements equal to population moments, in the case of random variables, or equal to finite constants in the case of deterministic variables. This distinction is elaborated in Examples 4.2–4.4. The usual notation for this property is:

$$P\lim_{n\to\infty}\left(\frac{1}{n}\mathbf{X}'\mathbf{X}\right) = \mathbf{\Omega}_{XX}.$$

And because of the properties of the probability limit mentioned in Section 4.6, the $P\lim$ of the inverse matrix is the inverse of the $P\lim$:

$$P\lim_{n\to\infty}\left(\frac{1}{n}\mathbf{X}'\mathbf{X}\right)^{-1} = \mathbf{\Omega}_{XX}^{-1}.$$

Further, consider the $(K \times 1)$ vector $(\mathbf{X}'\mathbf{u})/n$ with sample covariances (with respect to zero) of the explanatory variables and the disturbance term.

$$\frac{1}{n}\mathbf{X}'\mathbf{u} = \frac{1}{n}\begin{pmatrix} \sum u_t \\ \sum u_t X_{t2} \\ \sum u_t X_{t3} \\ \vdots \\ \sum u_t X_{tK} \end{pmatrix}.$$

The K elements of this vector are the sample covariances between the explanatory variables (X_{tk}) and the disturbance term (u_t). If the disturbance term and the explanatory variables are independently distributed, then these covariances converge to zero for increasing n:

$$P \lim_{n \to \infty} \left(\frac{1}{n} \mathbf{X}'\mathbf{u} \right) = \mathbf{0}. \tag{4.27}$$

Otherwise some of the elements are finite constants unequal to zero:

$$P \lim_{n \to \infty} \left(\frac{1}{n} \mathbf{X}'\mathbf{u} \right) = \mathbf{q}. \tag{4.28}$$

Three examples (Examples 4.2–4.4) concerning the large sample properties of the OLS estimator will be given, that are in accordance with the three types of models that were introduced in Section 4.1:

■ the classical regression model,
■ the reduced-form model, and
■ the structural form model.

Example 4.2   Exogenous explanatory variables (classical regression model)

In this example, we consider the classical regression model, where all the explanatory variables are exogenous, so expression (4.27) is valid. The following result for the OLS estimator is obtained. The starting-point is again the expression

$$\widehat{\beta} = \beta + (\mathbf{X}'\mathbf{X})^{-1} \mathbf{X}'\mathbf{u}.$$

Next compute the probability limit $P \lim_{n \to \infty} \widehat{\beta}_n$.

$$
\begin{aligned}
P \lim_{n \to \infty} \widehat{\beta}_n &= \beta + P \lim_{n \to \infty} \left((\mathbf{X}'\mathbf{X})^{-1} \mathbf{X}'\mathbf{u} \right) \\
&= \beta + P \lim_{n \to \infty} \left(\left(\frac{1}{n} \mathbf{X}'\mathbf{X} \right)^{-1} \cdot \left(\frac{1}{n} \mathbf{X}'\mathbf{u} \right) \right) \\
&= \beta + P \lim_{n \to \infty} \left(\frac{1}{n} \mathbf{X}'\mathbf{X} \right)^{-1} \cdot P \lim_{n \to \infty} \left(\frac{1}{n} \mathbf{X}'\mathbf{u} \right) \\
&= \beta + \Omega_{XX}^{-1} \cdot \mathbf{0} \\
&= \beta.
\end{aligned}
$$

The OLS estimator is consistent.

We clearly see that the crucial prerequisite for $\widehat{\beta}$ to be consistent is that the explanatory variables and the disturbance term are independently distributed.

Example 4.3   A lagged dependent explanatory variable (reduced-form model)

If lagged dependent variables are included as explanatory variables, the OLS estimator is biased but it is still a consistent estimator. In this case, only asymptotic properties of the estimation result can be obtained. To demonstrate these properties of the OLS estimator we look at the following dynamic model

$$Y_t = \beta_1 + \beta_2 X_t + \beta_3 Y_{t-1} + u_t, \ u_t \sim NID\left(0, \sigma_u^2\right) \text{ for all } t.$$

The expression $\widehat{\beta} = \beta + (X'X)^{-1} X'u$ of the OLS estimator for this specific equation is written below:

$$\begin{pmatrix} \widehat{\beta}_1 \\ \widehat{\beta}_2 \\ \widehat{\beta}_3 \end{pmatrix} = \begin{pmatrix} \beta_1 \\ \beta_2 \\ \beta_3 \end{pmatrix} + \begin{pmatrix} n & \sum X_t & \sum Y_{t-1} \\ \sum X_t & \sum X_t^2 & \sum X_t Y_{t-1} \\ \sum Y_{t-1} & \sum X_t Y_{t-1} & \sum Y_{t-1}^2 \end{pmatrix}^{-1} \begin{pmatrix} \sum u_t \\ \sum X_t u_t \\ \sum Y_{t-1} u_t \end{pmatrix}.$$

Look at the expectation of $\widehat{\beta}$ to see whether the OLS estimator is unbiased or not.

$$E \begin{pmatrix} \widehat{\beta}_1 \\ \widehat{\beta}_2 \\ \widehat{\beta}_3 \end{pmatrix} = \begin{pmatrix} \beta_1 \\ \beta_2 \\ \beta_3 \end{pmatrix} + E \begin{pmatrix} n & \sum X_t & \sum Y_{t-1} \\ \sum X_t & \sum X_t^2 & \sum X_t Y_{t-1} \\ \sum Y_{t-1} & \sum X_t Y_{t-1} & \sum Y_{t-1}^2 \end{pmatrix}^{-1} \begin{pmatrix} \sum u_t \\ \sum X_t u_t \\ \sum Y_{t-1} u_t \end{pmatrix}.$$

Because of *contemporaneous* non-zero correlations between elements of the matrix $(X'X)^{-1}$ with elements of the vector $X'u$ (the matrix/vector elements contain all the observations because of the summations) the expectations operator cannot be moved into the last column. This implies biased results in small samples.

However, property (4.27) is still valid because Y_{t-1} and u_t are independently distributed. The OLS estimator is still consistent. For a first course it is sufficient to establish the conclusion that all the results are asymptotic now. This has to be mentioned in a research paper too, when the estimated model is not a classical regression model. To show the consistency property, the probability limit of $\widehat{\beta}$ is determined:

$$\underset{n\to\infty}{P \lim} \begin{pmatrix} \widehat{\beta}_1 \\ \widehat{\beta}_2 \\ \widehat{\beta}_3 \end{pmatrix}_n = \begin{pmatrix} \beta_1 \\ \beta_2 \\ \beta_3 \end{pmatrix} + \underset{n\to\infty}{P \lim} \left(\frac{1}{n} \begin{pmatrix} n & \sum X_t & \sum Y_{t-1} \\ \sum X_t & \sum X_t^2 & \sum X_t Y_{t-1} \\ \sum Y_{t-1} & \sum X_t Y_{t-1} & \sum Y_{t-1}^2 \end{pmatrix} \right)^{-1}$$
$$\times \underset{n\to\infty}{P \lim} \begin{pmatrix} \frac{1}{n} \sum u_t \\ \frac{1}{n} \sum X_t u_t \\ \frac{1}{n} \sum Y_{t-1} u_t \end{pmatrix},$$

then it follows that:

$$P \lim_{n \to \infty} \begin{pmatrix} \widehat{\beta}_1 \\ \widehat{\beta}_2 \\ \widehat{\beta}_3 \end{pmatrix}_n = \begin{pmatrix} \beta_1 \\ \beta_2 \\ \beta_3 \end{pmatrix} + \Omega_{XX}^{-1} \cdot \begin{pmatrix} 0 \\ 0 \\ 0 \end{pmatrix} = \begin{pmatrix} \beta_1 \\ \beta_2 \\ \beta_3 \end{pmatrix}.$$

The variables Y_t and u_t are dependently distributed but Y_{t-1} and u_t are independently distributed, so the OLS estimator is still a consistent estimator.

Example 4.4   An endogenous explanatory variable (structural-form model)

Finally, we consider the model with endogenous explanatory variables, then the OLS estimator is inconsistent as property (4.28) is valid instead of property (4.27).

$$P \lim_{n \to \infty} \widehat{\beta}_n = \beta + P \lim_{n \to \infty} \left(\frac{1}{n} \mathbf{X'X} \right)^{-1} \cdot P \lim_{n \to \infty} \left(\frac{1}{n} \mathbf{X'u} \right)$$
$$= \beta + \Omega_{XX}^{-1} \cdot \mathbf{q}$$
$$\neq \beta.$$

At least one element of the vector $\mathbf{q}$ is not equal to zero. In this situation, the use of another and consistent estimator is necessary, as will be introduced in Chapter 9. In this example, the most simple Keynesian model is used again. The structural equations are:

$$C_t = \beta_1 + \beta_2 Y_t + u_t$$
$$Y_t = C_t + I_t.$$

Consumption (C_t) and income (Y_t) are assumed to be endogenous variables and investment (I_t) an exogenous variable. In the consumption equation the income variable (Y_t) is an endogenous explanatory variable. The inconsistency of the OLS estimator $\widehat{\beta}_2$ will be demonstrated in this example.

The relationship between Y_t and u_t is easily observed in the reduced-form equation for income. Reduced-form equations are the model solutions for the endogenous variables (they are expressed in the exogenous and lagged dependent variables) as introduced in Section 1.5. The reduced-form equation for income is:

$$Y_t = \frac{\beta_1}{1 - \beta_2} + \frac{1}{1 - \beta_2} I_t + \frac{u_t}{1 - \beta_2},$$

which shows that u_t is related to Y_t.

It is not difficult to compute the covariance between Y_t and u_t:

$$E\left((Y_t - EY_t)(u_t - Eu_t) \right).$$

First find an expression for the first term:

$$EY_t = \frac{\beta_1}{1 - \beta_2} + \frac{1}{1 - \beta_2} I_t,$$

so:

$$Y_t - EY_t = \frac{u_t}{1 - \beta_2}.$$

Substitute this term and evaluate the covariance between Y_t and u_t:

$$E\left((Y_t - EY_t)(u_t - Eu_t)\right) = E\left(\left(\frac{u_t}{1 - \beta_2}\right)u_t\right)$$

$$= \frac{\sigma_u^2}{1 - \beta_2}.$$

Next we observe that the OLS estimator is inconsistent.

$$P\lim_{n \to \infty}\begin{pmatrix}\widehat{\beta}_1 \\ \widehat{\beta}_2\end{pmatrix} = \begin{pmatrix}\beta_1 \\ \beta_2\end{pmatrix} + \Omega_{XX}^{-1} \cdot P\lim_{n \to \infty}\begin{pmatrix}\frac{1}{n}\sum u_t \\ \frac{1}{n}\sum Y_t u_t\end{pmatrix}$$

$$= \begin{pmatrix}\beta_1 \\ \beta_2\end{pmatrix} + \Omega_{XX}^{-1} \cdot \begin{pmatrix}0 \\ \sigma_u^2(1 - \beta_2)^{-1}\end{pmatrix}$$

$$= \begin{pmatrix}\beta_1 \\ \beta_2\end{pmatrix} + \begin{pmatrix}c_1 \\ c_2\end{pmatrix}.$$

The inconsistencies c_1 and c_2 are the result from the matrix multiplication

$$\Omega_{XX}^{-1} \cdot \begin{pmatrix}0 \\ \sigma_u^2(1 - \beta_2)^{-1}\end{pmatrix}.$$

In the Examples 4.2–4.4, properties of the OLS estimator have been established for the three different types of models. The relevance of this knowledge for empirical work is evident. A summary of the results is given below.

- **The classical regression model**
  The linear model has exogenous explanatory variables, which are considered as deterministic variables in the equation: the OLS estimator is unbiased, consistent and efficient in the class of linear unbiased estimators.
- **The reduced-form model**
  The linear model has exogenous and lagged dependent explanatory variables: the OLS estimator is biased, consistent and asymptotically efficient (in the class of linear consistent estimators). The properties of the OLS estimator are interpreted for large samples. The bias goes to zero for increasing sample size.

■ **The structural model**
The linear model has exogenous, lagged dependent and endogenous explanatory variables: the OLS estimator is biased and inconsistent. Another estimator has to be used to obtain at least consistent estimation results.

4.8   Maximum likelihood estimation

In following chapters, the maximum likelihood (ML) estimator will occasionally be referred to. ML is a general statistical principle to estimate the parameters of (non-)linear models. See any statistical/econometrics textbook, for example, Cramer (1989), to become familiar with ML estimation procedures. In this section, a short description concerning the ML principle is given for the general linear model. For estimating the parameters with ML, some specific probability distribution needs to be assumed for the disturbance term. As usual, the assumption will be made that the disturbances are normally distributed.

$$\mathbf{y} = \mathbf{X}\boldsymbol{\beta} + \mathbf{u}, \text{ with } \mathbf{u} \sim N\left(\mathbf{0}, \sigma_u^2 \mathbf{I}_n\right).$$

The multivariate density function for the observations of the endogenous variable is:

$$f\left(\mathbf{y}'; \boldsymbol{\beta}', \sigma_u^2\right) = \frac{1}{(2\pi\sigma_u^2)^{n/2}} e^{-\left((\mathbf{y}-\mathbf{X}\boldsymbol{\beta})'(\mathbf{y}-\mathbf{X}\boldsymbol{\beta})/2\sigma_u^2\right)},$$

This is a function of $\mathbf{y}$ for given values of the parameters $\boldsymbol{\beta}'$ and σ_u^2. The multivariate normal density in terms of $\mathbf{u}$ is:

$$f\left(\mathbf{u}'; \boldsymbol{\beta}', \sigma_u^2\right) = \frac{1}{(2\pi\sigma_u^2)^{n/2}} e^{-\mathbf{u}'\mathbf{u}/2\sigma_u^2}.$$

The likelihood function has the same form, but is interpreted as a function of the parameters for given observations:

$$L = L\left(\boldsymbol{\beta}', \sigma_u^2; \mathbf{u}'\right) = \frac{1}{(2\pi\sigma_u^2)^{n/2}} e^{-\mathbf{u}'\mathbf{u}/2\sigma_u^2}.$$

It is more convenient to work with the log-likelihood function.

$$ln\left(L\right) = ln\left((2\pi\sigma_u^2)^{-n/2} e^{-\mathbf{u}'\mathbf{u}/2\sigma_u^2}\right)$$

$$= -\frac{n}{2}ln\left(2\pi\right) - \frac{n}{2}ln\left(\sigma_u^2\right) - \frac{\mathbf{u}'\mathbf{u}}{2\sigma_u^2}.$$

The likelihood function has to be maximised. Differentiation with respect to $\boldsymbol{\beta}$ first gives the following first-order condition:

$$\frac{\partial ln\left(L\right)}{\partial \boldsymbol{\beta}} = -\frac{\partial \mathbf{u}'\mathbf{u}}{\partial \boldsymbol{\beta}} \cdot \frac{1}{2\sigma_u^2} = 0.$$

In this condition, we see that maximising the likelihood function with respect to the parameters β is identical to minimising the sum of squared residuals. This implies that the maximum likelihood estimator $\widetilde{\beta}$ of the parameter vector β is identical to the OLS estimator $\widehat{\beta}$ of β, if $u_t \sim NID\left(0, \sigma_u^2\right)$.

To obtain the ML estimator of σ_u^2, $ln\left(L\right)$ is differentiated with respect to σ_u^2, which yields the second first-order condition:

$$\frac{\partial ln\left(L\right)}{\partial \sigma_u^2} = -\frac{n}{2\sigma_u^2} + \frac{\mathbf{u'u}}{2\sigma_u^4} = 0.$$

Solving this equation for σ_u^2 gives the solution:

$$\sigma_u^2 = \frac{1}{n}\mathbf{u'u}.$$

The ML estimator of σ_u^2, defined as $\widetilde{\sigma}_u^2$, is different from the OLS estimator $\widehat{\sigma}_u^2$ of σ_u^2:

$$\widetilde{\sigma}_u^2 = \frac{1}{n}\sum_{t=1}^{n} e_t^2$$

$$\widehat{\sigma}_u^2 = \frac{1}{n-K}\sum_{t=1}^{n} e_t^2.$$

The ML estimator $\widetilde{\sigma}_u^2$ is a biased estimator of σ_u^2. From statistical theory it is well-known that the ML estimator is always consistent and efficient within the class of consistent and asymptotically normally distributed estimators, but it can be biased in finite samples. We have established that minimising the sum of squared residuals yields ML estimates. For linear models it makes no difference whether the parameters are estimated with OLS or ML. The ML principle will be used in this way for non-linear models that are found later in the text.

EViews regression output always gives the value of the maximum of the log-likelihood function; see Figure 4.4 later. The value of the log-likelihood function will be used for hypotheses testing with the likelihood ratio test, which is one of the topics of the next chapter.

4.9   Regression analysis with EViews

To perform a regression analysis in EViews one has to specify the equation in an 'Equation Specification' window. The estimation procedure will be explained by using the workfile from Figure 3.7. The hypothesis that will be investigated is a simple relationship where coffee prices influence the price of cocoa on the world market. The model that will be estimated is a *reduced-form model* because lagged dependent variables are included in the equation. We use Hendry's approach of modelling from general to specific. This is a recommended procedure to determine structural or reduced-form models for time-series data. (In Chapter 7, this procedure will be considered in more detail.)

The relationship is analysed for the variables transformed into their logarithms. A general specification for this relationship is:

$$\ln(P_t^{coc}) = \beta_1 + \sum_{i=0}^{L} \beta_{1i} \ln\left(P_{t-i}^{cof}\right) + \sum_{j=1}^{L} \beta_{2j} \ln\left(P_{t-j}^{coc}\right) + \sum_{h=0}^{L} \beta_{3h} \ln\left(P_{t-h}^{tea}\right) + u_t$$

(4.29)

with, for example, three lags ($L = 3$) for each explanatory variable. The sample concerns monthly data and because prices react quickly to each other, just a few lags for the variables should be sufficient. The estimation result (not reproduced here) shows that this number of lags is sufficient to have non-autocorrelated residuals. The price of tea has no influence on the cocoa price and the inclusion of P_t^{cof} and P_{t-1}^{cof} is sufficient to show the influence of the coffee price on the cocoa price. Estimation of this last regression model will be demonstrated here.

The following steps are examples of what can be done:

- Start EViews.
- Open your workfile; in this example the workfile 'cofcoctea' is opened (Figure 3.7).
- The commodity prices are transformed into their logs and the new variables get the names *lpcocoa*, *lpcoffee* and *lptea*.

Next, the regression equation is specified. The specification of the equation that will be estimated in this example is:

$$\ln(P_t^{coc}) = \beta_1 + \beta_2 \ln\left(P_t^{cof}\right) + \beta_3 \ln\left(P_{t-1}^{cof}\right)$$
$$+ \beta_4 \ln\left(P_{t-1}^{coc}\right) + \beta_5 \ln\left(P_{t-2}^{coc}\right) + \beta_6 \ln\left(P_{t-3}^{coc}\right) + u_t.$$

It is a specific model, its specification has been obtained in a couple of steps by reducing the general model (4.29). Notice that this equation is not a classical regression model but a reduced-form model because of the lags of the cocoa price. The equation can be specified in the 'Equation Specification window' as follows:

lpcocoa c lpcoffee lpcoffee(−1) lpcocoa(−1) lpcocoa(−2) lpcocoa(−3).

This specification can also be written in a more convenient way:

lpcocoa c lpcoffee(0 to −1) lpcocoa(−1 to −3).

This has been done in the window from Figure 4.3. It has been obtained in the following way.

- Click the 'Quick button' in the EViews window and select 'Estimate Equation'. Next the 'Equation Specification' window opens. Another way to open an equation window is to select the variables involved. Next click with the right-hand mouse

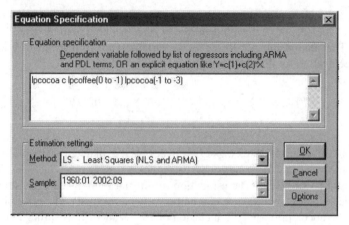

Figure 4.3:   Specification of a regression equation

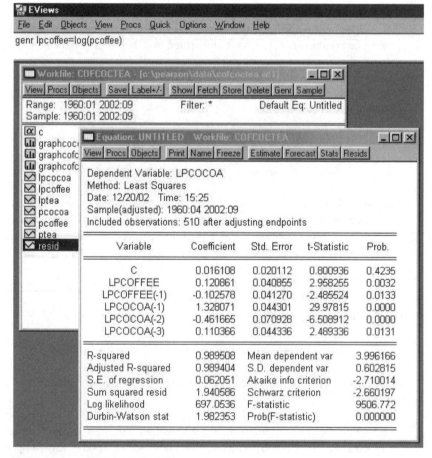

Figure 4.4:   Regression output

button on the selection and click 'Open as Equation'; see the other options in Figure 3.16. With this option, only a static equation is specified, the lags have to be filled in subsequently.

■ Specify the regression equation in that window. An example has been given in Figure 4.3.

■ Choose an estimation method and click OK. The indicated default method is OLS; other estimators will be encountered in Part III. It is also possible to change the estimation period in this window. This change does not influence the sample in the workfile. The estimation result is presented in the 'Equation' window. The output belonging to the specified relationship in Figure 4.3 is shown in Figure 4.4.

Let us take a look at Figure 4.4. Many results in the output have still to be explained. The (6×1) vector $\widehat{\beta}$ with the point estimates is found under *Coefficient*. The standard errors of the estimates $se\left(\widehat{\beta}_k\right)$, as determined in Section 4.7, are given in the second column: *Std. Error*. The other columns will be explained later on. When the tests for the disturbance-term assumptions and restrictions on parameters have been introduced in the following chapters, this example will be elaborated further to explain the other computed statistics in Figure 4.4. When hypotheses are tested, EViews computes the value of the test statistic and generally its 'probability' or 'p-value' too. A number of those probabilities can be found in the output in Figure 4.4. This implies that the use of statistical tables will be hardly necessary. In the heading of the 'Equation' window you can observe that the sample has been adjusted and starts in 1960:04. EViews automatically adjusts the sample when time-lags are specified in the equation. We have lost three observations by making the model dynamic with the specification of lags. The maximum lag is 3 in this regression. Looking at the statistics given at the bottom of the window you may not recognise them all at this stage of the course, but they will be explained in following chapters.

If it is relevant to print the results, click on 'Print' in the window in question. The results can be copied into the text file via the clipboard as well.

Chapter 5

Testing the Deterministic Assumptions

5.1 Introduction

In the previous chapter, the general linear model, its stochastic assumptions, and the OLS estimator for its parameters have been discussed. Based on these assumptions the distribution of the OLS estimator has been derived. This means that standard errors can be computed for the OLS estimates. In Chapter 1, the arguments were given that it is necessary to get a model where the disturbance-term assumptions are not rejected. From the previous chapter, we know that only in that case are the standard errors of the OLS estimator correctly calculated. It is clear that when the stochastic assumptions have not been rejected, we can correctly perform statistical tests for hypotheses about the parameters. Therefore, the logical follow up to Chapter 4 is a chapter where a number of tests are introduced for testing the disturbance-term assumptions. After these 'tools' are known, a chapter where tests can be discussed, which are needed for testing the specification of the systematic part of the model, could follow. However, knowing these facts, the tests will be discussed the other way around! The reason is that some of the tests for testing the disturbance-term assumptions are, for example, Student's t-tests or Fisher F-tests. These tests are more conveniently introduced in a chapter with statistical tests for the deterministic assumptions and can sometimes be used in a similar way when testing disturbance-term assumptions. This is why we will first discuss the tests for deterministic assumptions, in this chapter. The t-, F- and LM-tests are discussed, but only under the strict assumption that the disturbance-term assumptions are true. With the knowledge about the tests obtained in this chapter, it is possible to discuss the tests for the stochastic assumptions in a clearer way in Chapter 6.

Besides a discussion about various types of tests concerning possible values of the parameters, we will consider a well-known statistic regarding the quality of the linear fit to the data: the coefficient of determination R^2. This statistic can only be interpreted correctly if the disturbance-term assumptions are met. Because R^2 is also used as a quality measure for the systematic part of the model it will be introduced in this chapter, in Section 5.3. Some arithmetical problems, which will be explained in that section, exist around this measure. First, in Section 5.2 relationships among the variables of the linear model are discussed that are relevant to the topics that come afterwards. The remaining sections of this chapter concern the above-mentioned tests.

Let there be no misunderstanding that in practice one has to test the disturbance-term assumptions first. This will be done in Case 2 when the first research paper will be written. This is why the formulation of Case 2 is found at the end of Chapter 6. Therefore, it is mentioned once again that in this chapter it is assumed that the assumption

$$u_t \sim NID\left(0, \sigma_u^2\right)$$

holds!

5.2   Relationships among variables of the linear model

Some relationships among the variables of the linear model are relevant for the derivation of test statistics or have interesting computational consequences. In this section we look at these relationships. First, we show that the residuals e are orthogonal to the explanatory variables that are in the columns of $\mathbf{X}$. Rewrite the normal equations (4.15) from Section 4.4 in the following way.

$$\mathbf{X'y} = \mathbf{X'X}\widehat{\beta}$$
$$\mathbf{X'y} - \mathbf{X'X}\widehat{\beta} = \mathbf{0}$$
$$\mathbf{X'}\left(\mathbf{y} - \mathbf{X}\widehat{\beta}\right) = \mathbf{0}$$
$$\mathbf{X'e} = \mathbf{0}. \tag{5.1}$$

In the matrix $\mathbf{X'}$ the variables are in the rows, so all the explanatory variables are multiplied with e in equation (5.1) and all these products are zero. All the explanatory variables are *orthogonal* to the OLS residuals. For example, this *orthogonality property* will be used in the derivation of the F-statistic in Section 5.7. The orthogonality property is also true for the predicted values of the dependent variable, as this variable is a linear combination of the explanatory variables:

$$\widehat{\mathbf{y}}'\mathbf{e} = \widehat{\beta}'\mathbf{X'e}$$
$$= \widehat{\beta}' \cdot \mathbf{0}$$
$$= 0.$$

The presence or absence of a constant term in the model has arithmetical consequences for some relationships or statistics. In this section, some important consequences are shown.

If the model contains a constant term then the elements in the first row of $\mathbf{X}'$ are all equal to 1. The orthogonality property can be schematically shown in the following way:

$$
\begin{pmatrix}
1 & 1 & \cdots & 1 \\
X_{12} & X_{22} & \cdots & X_{n2} \\
\vdots & \vdots & \vdots & \vdots \\
X_{1K} & X_{2K} & \cdots & X_{nK}
\end{pmatrix}
\cdot
\begin{pmatrix}
e_1 \\ e_2 \\ \vdots \\ e_n
\end{pmatrix}
=
\begin{pmatrix}
\sum_{t=1}^{n} e_t \\
\sum_{t=1}^{n} e_t X_{t2} \\
\vdots \\
\sum_{t=1}^{n} e_t X_{tK}
\end{pmatrix}
=
\begin{pmatrix}
0 \\ 0 \\ \vdots \\ 0
\end{pmatrix}.
$$

Define a vector ι with all elements equal to 1:

$$
\iota' = \begin{pmatrix} 1 & 1 & . & . & 1 \end{pmatrix}'.
$$

Then, the multiplication of the first row with the residual vector shows:

$$
\iota' \mathbf{e} = 0 \Longrightarrow \sum_{t=1}^{n} e_t = 0 \Longrightarrow \bar{e} = 0.
$$

The sum and the mean of the residuals are equal to zero if a constant term has been included in the model. In general, this is not the case without a constant term in the model. Some of the effects around the specification or non-specification of a constant term will be discussed here. They concern arithmetic problems with practical implications when estimating a homogeneous relationship.

First, use this property to show that $\overline{Y} = \overline{\widehat{Y}}$ when an intercept is included in the equation:

$$
Y_t = \widehat{Y}_t + e_t,
$$

$$
\frac{1}{n} \sum_{t=1}^{n} Y_t = \frac{1}{n} \sum_{t=1}^{n} \widehat{Y}_t + \frac{1}{n} \sum_{t=1}^{n} e_t
$$

$$
\overline{Y} = \overline{\widehat{Y}} + 0
$$

$$
\overline{Y} = \overline{\widehat{Y}}.
$$

The means of the observed and predicted values of the dependent variable are identical.

With an intercept in the equation it is simple to demonstrate that the sample means of the variables are on the regression plane, because $\bar{e} = 0$:

$$
Y_t = \widehat{\beta}_1 + \widehat{\beta}_2 X_{t2} + \widehat{\beta}_3 X_{t3} + \ldots + \widehat{\beta}_K X_{tK} + e_t,
$$

$$
\frac{1}{n} \sum_{t=1}^{n} Y_t = \widehat{\beta}_1 + \widehat{\beta}_2 \frac{1}{n} \sum_{t=1}^{n} X_{t2} + \widehat{\beta}_3 \frac{1}{n} \sum_{t=1}^{n} X_{t3} + \ldots + \widehat{\beta}_K \frac{1}{n} \sum_{t=1}^{n} X_{tK} + \frac{1}{n} \sum_{t=1}^{n} e_t,
$$

$$
\overline{Y} = \widehat{\beta}_1 + \widehat{\beta}_2 \overline{X}_2 + \widehat{\beta}_3 \overline{X}_3 + \ldots + \widehat{\beta}_K \overline{X}_K.
$$

This property can be used in a model in 'deviation form'. Such a specification has an *implicit constant term*. A model in deviation form is a model for the variables in deviation from their sample means. See, for example, the bivariate model:

$$Y_t = \beta_1 + \beta_2 X_t + u_t.$$

In deviation form, the model is:

$$\left(Y_t - \overline{Y}\right) = \beta_2 \left(X_t - \overline{X}\right) + \left(u_t - \overline{u}\right).$$

The estimate $\widehat{\beta}_1$ of the constant term can always be computed from:

$$\widehat{\beta}_1 = \overline{Y} - \widehat{\beta}_2 \overline{X}.$$

In fact, to compute a regression in deviation form has historical interest only, because a model in deviation form has one normal equation less to solve, an advantage in the past.

The following expression is *always* true because of the orthogonality property $\left(\sum\limits_{t=1}^{n} \widehat{Y}_t e_t = 0\right)$.

$$Y_t = \widehat{Y}_t + e_t$$

$$\sum_{t=1}^{n} Y_t^2 = \sum_{t=1}^{n} \widehat{Y}_t^2 + \sum_{t=1}^{n} e_t^2 + 2 \sum_{t=1}^{n} \widehat{Y}_t e_t$$

$$\sum_{t=1}^{n} Y_t^2 = \sum_{t=1}^{n} \widehat{Y}_t^2 + \sum_{t=1}^{n} e_t^2. \tag{5.2}$$

It can happen during the derivation of a statistic that we can use an expression like (5.2) in 'deviation form'. The following relationship (5.3), in deviation form, is true with a constant term in the model:

$$\sum_{t=1}^{n} \left(Y_t - \overline{Y}\right)^2 = \sum_{t=1}^{n} \left(\widehat{Y}_t - \overline{Y}\right)^2 + \sum_{t=1}^{n} e_t^2. \tag{5.3}$$

This can be established in a similar way.

$$Y_t = \widehat{Y}_t + e_t$$

$$\left(Y_t - \overline{Y}\right) = \left(\widehat{Y}_t - \overline{Y}\right) + e_t$$

$$\sum_{t=1}^{n} \left(Y_t - \overline{Y}\right)^2 = \sum_{t=1}^{n} \left(\widehat{Y}_t - \overline{Y}\right)^2 + \sum_{t=1}^{n} e_t^2 + 2 \sum_{t=1}^{n} \left(\widehat{Y}_t - \overline{Y}\right) e_t$$

$$\sum_{t=1}^{n} \left(Y_t - \overline{Y}\right)^2 = \sum_{t=1}^{n} \left(\widehat{Y}_t - \overline{Y}\right)^2 + \sum_{t=1}^{n} e_t^2.$$

The last relationship has been obtained by substituting the following quantities

$$\sum_{t=1}^{n} \widehat{Y}_t e_t = 0$$

and

$$\sum_{t=1}^{n} \overline{Y} e_t = \overline{Y} \sum_{t=1}^{n} e_t = 0.$$

Relationship (5.3), which is only valid with a constant term in the model, is frequently denoted as:

$$TSS = ESS + RSS.$$

The total sum of squares (TSS) equals the explained sum of squares (ESS) plus the residual sum of squares (RSS). Multiplied by $1/n$ it is an expression of the variances of the variables; the (total) variance of Y_t is split into the 'explained variance' and the 'unexplained variance'.

5.3 The coefficient of determination

The considerations of the previous section influence the computation of the following statistic, the *coefficient of determination,* often just called *R-squared.* The coefficient of determination R^2 is a measure of the goodness-of-fit of the estimated model to the data. This coefficient can be considered as an indicator concerning the quality of the estimated linear model. When R^2 is close to 1 it can be an indication that the estimated *linear* model gives a good description of the economy, and when R^2 is close to zero it can be an indication that this is not the case. R^2 can be used as such if the disturbance-term assumptions have not been rejected.

R^2 can be expressed in three ways, therefore a subscript is added:

$$R_1^2 = 1 - \frac{RSS}{TSS} = 1 - \frac{\sum_{t=1}^{n} e_t^2}{\sum_{t=1}^{n} (Y_t - \overline{Y})^2},$$

$$R_2^2 = \frac{ESS}{TSS} = \frac{\sum_{t=1}^{n} (\widehat{Y}_t - \overline{Y})^2}{\sum_{t=1}^{n} (Y_t - \overline{Y})^2},$$

$$R_3^2 = r_{Y\widehat{Y}}^2 = \frac{\left(\sum_{t=1}^{n} (\widehat{Y}_t - \overline{Y}) (Y_t - \overline{Y}) \right)^2}{\sum_{t=1}^{n} (\widehat{Y}_t - \overline{Y})^2 \sum_{t=1}^{n} (Y_t - \overline{Y})^2}.$$

The following word expressions for R^2 clarify the definitions:

$$R_1^2 = 1 - \frac{\text{Unexplained variance of } Y_t}{\text{Total variance of } Y_t},$$

$$R_2^2 = \frac{\text{Explained variance of } Y_t}{\text{Total variance of } Y_t},$$

R_3^2 = The squared linear correlation coefficient between Y_t and $\widehat{Y}_t$.

If a constant term is in the equation, then the three expressions are identical to each other: demonstrated by using the expression $TSS = ESS + RSS$. Then R^2 has also the property:

$$0 \le R^2 \le 1.$$

The definition of R_1^2 is frequently used to compute R^2, as is the case in EViews. It is easy to see that the statistic R^2 is not useful in the bivariate model, because R^2 is always equal to the value r_{YX}^2, the correlation coefficient between Y_t and X_t. So, in the bivariate model R^2 is independent of the parameter estimates and cannot give information about the 'quality' of the model. This is conveniently demonstrated by evaluating the third expression R_3^2:

$$R^2 = r_{Y\widehat{Y}}^2 = r_{Y,\beta_1 + \beta_2 X_t}^2 = r_{YX}^2,$$

because $\widehat{Y}_t = \widehat{\beta}_1 + \widehat{\beta}_2 X_t$ is a linear transformation of X_t.

The statistic is not useful in a model without a constant term. Then it can be shown that:

■   the three definitions of R^2 are not equal to each other;
■ R_1^2 can become *negative*; and
■ R_2^2 can become *larger than* 1.

However, R_3^2 is always between 0 and 1 because it is the squared correlation coefficient of Y_t and $\widehat{Y}_t$, which gives information about the fit of the model to the data. So, in a model without a constant term or with one explanatory variable, R^2 has no meaning and should *not* be included in a paper reporting the econometric results. In EViews R_1^2 is computed, so does not report this statistic in the above described situations. In a model estimated without an intercept it is always possible to compute R_3^2 yourself $(K \ge 2)$ and to report its value if you wish to publish an R^2. (Then mention in your paper the definition of R^2 you have used.)

The behaviour of the R_i^2 can be demonstrated with the following simulated example. Two series Y_{t1} and X_t have been generated, with only 14 observations, which is sufficient for this purpose. Next three other 'dependent' variables have been computed by linear transformations of Y_t to make it all much worse:

$$Y_{t2} = Y_{t1} - 20$$

$$Y_{t3} = Y_{t1} - \frac{1}{2}\left(Y_{t1} - min\left(Y_{t1}\right)\right)$$

$$Y_{t4} = Y_{t1} - \frac{3}{5}\left(Y_{t1} - min\left(Y_{t1}\right)\right).$$

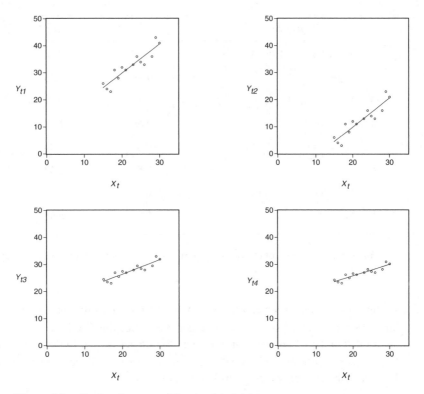

Figure 5.1: Scatter diagrams of the simulated data

Scatter diagrams (see Figure 5.1) will show that it is very odd to estimate relationships between these dependent variables Y_{ti} and X_t without using a constant term.

In Table 5.1, the regression results are given for the four relationships estimated with and without a constant term, with standard errors in parentheses. The results speak for themselves. Everything that has been discussed in the text can be found in Table 5.1.

One more annoying aspect of the determination coefficient is its property to increase when arbitrary variables are added to the model. This is caused by the fact that $\sum\limits_{t=1}^{n} e_t^2$ decreases when variables are added; see Remark 5.7 later. This is a bad property for an indicator about the quality of the estimation result of a model and is the reason that the *adjusted determination coefficient* $\left(\overline{R}^2\right)$ is introduced. The nominator and denominator of R_1^2 are corrected for degrees of freedom:

$$\overline{R}^2 = 1 - \frac{\sum\limits_{t=1}^{n} e_t^2 / (n-K)}{\sum\limits_{t=1}^{n} (Y_t - \overline{Y})^2 / (n-1)},$$

or

$$\overline{R}^2 = 1 - \left[(1 - R^2)(n-1)/(n-K)\right].$$

Regression	R_1^2	R_2^2	R_3^2
1 $\widehat{Y}_{t1} = 8.26 + 1.08\ X_t$ (3.03) (0.13)	0.84	0.84	0.84
2 $\widehat{Y}_{t1} = 1.43\ X_t$ (0.03)	**0.75**	**1.23**	**0.84**
3 $\widehat{Y}_{t2} = -11.74 + 1.08\ X_t$ (3.03) (0.13)	0.84	0.84	0.84
4 $\widehat{Y}_{t2} = 0.57\ X_t$ (0.04)	**0.65**	**1.32**	**0.84**
5 $\widehat{Y}_{t3} = 15.63 + 0.54\ X_t$ (1.52) (0.07)	0.84	0.84	0.84
6 $\widehat{Y}_{t3} = 1.21\ X_t$ (0.04)	**-0.53**	**2.42**	**0.84**
7 $\widehat{Y}_{t4} = 17.10 + 0.43\ X_t$ (1.21) (0.05)	0.84	0.84	0.84
8 $\widehat{Y}_{t4} = 1.17\ X_t$ (0.05)	**-1.73**	**3.53**	**0.84**

Table 5.1: Examples of the varying determination coefficient for models with and without an intercept

$\overline{R}^2$ increases when variables are added whose parameter estimates have a t-value that is larger than one. The t-statistic will be derived in Section 5.6. Both statistics R^2 and $\overline{R}^2$ are printed in the EViews output; see again Figure 4.4 earlier. In the regression showed in Figure 4.4 the difference between R^2 and $\overline{R}^2$ is rather small, because of the large sample. In small samples, larger deviations will be observed.

5.4 Survey of some useful distributions and test principles

We will consider some necessary statistical topics as preparatory work before interval estimates can be computed and restrictions can be tested. A more detailed discussion and proofs regarding the issues in this section can be found in the statistical literature or in a statistical chapter in a more theoretical econometrics book. Such proofs concern a number of χ^2-distributions that are needed to obtain the Student t- and Fisher F-distributions for testing restrictions on parameters.

First, the definitions of the Student t- and Fisher F-distribution must be memorised, because these definitions will be applied to derive the test statistics.

■ The definition of the Student t-distribution with r degrees of freedom is as follows. If $x \sim N(0,1)$, $v^2 \sim \chi^2(r)$, and x and v are independently distributed, then the following quotient has a Student's t-distribution with r degrees of freedom:

$$\frac{x}{\sqrt{v^2/r}} \sim t(r), \tag{5.4}$$

or

$$(x/v)\sqrt{r} \sim t(r).$$

■ The definition of the Fisher F-distribution with p and q degrees of freedom is as follows. If $x^2 \sim \chi^2(p)$, $y^2 \sim \chi^2(q)$, and x^2 and y^2 are independently distributed, then the following quotient has a Fisher F-distribution with p and q degrees of freedom:

$$[(x^2/p) / (y^2/q)] \sim F(p, q). \tag{5.5}$$

From these definitions, it is clear that we will need χ^2-distributions, in addition to the normally distributed OLS estimator, for deriving t- and F-distributions. Therefore, a helpful summary of four useful χ^2 distributions, which will be used to derive the test statistics, is given below. (See, for example, Johnston and DiNardo (1997: pp.493–495).)

■ First, consider a variable x_i with n independent observations from a standard normal distribution. Use the notation (4.4) from Section 4.2:

$$\underset{(n\times 1)}{\mathbf{x}} \sim N\left(\mathbf{0}, \mathbf{I}_n\right).$$

Then, by definition, the sum of squares $\sum_{i=1}^{n} x_i^2$ has a $\chi^2(n)$ distribution:

$$\mathbf{x}'\mathbf{x} = \sum_{i=1}^{n} x_i^2 \sim \chi^2(n). \tag{5.6}$$

■ Secondly, consider a variable x_i with n observations that is normally independently distributed with mean 0 and variance σ^2. Then the $(n \times 1)$ vector $\mathbf{x}$ is distributed as:

$$\underset{(n\times 1)}{\mathbf{x}} \sim N\left(\mathbf{0}, \sigma^2\mathbf{I}_n\right)$$

Standardise the x_i, and the sum of squares $\sum_{i=1}^{n} (x_i/\sigma)^2$ has again a $\chi^2(n)$ distribution:

$$\frac{1}{\sigma^2}\mathbf{x}'\mathbf{x} = \sum_{i=1}^{n} (x_i/\sigma)^2 \sim \chi^2(n). \tag{5.7}$$

Now write $(\mathbf{x}'\mathbf{x})/\sigma^2$ in a different way, in matrix notation:

$$\frac{1}{\sigma^2}\mathbf{x}'\mathbf{x} = \mathbf{x}'\left(\sigma^2\mathbf{I}_n\right)^{-1}\mathbf{x}, \tag{5.8}$$

and see the benefit of this notation in the following situation.

■ Thirdly, consider an $(n \times 1)$ vector $\mathbf{x}$, containing n observations on the variable x_i, which is normally distributed with zero mean and an $(n \times n)$ covariance matrix $\mathbf{\Omega}$:

$$\underset{(n\times 1)}{\mathbf{x}} \sim N\left(\mathbf{0}, \mathbf{\Omega}\right).$$

It can be shown that:

$$\mathbf{x}'\mathbf{\Omega}^{-1}\mathbf{x} \sim \chi^2(n). \tag{5.9}$$

See the analogy with the notation in (5.8).

■ Finally, we consider the following situation. We have a variable x_i with n observations that is normally independently distributed with mean 0 and variance σ^2:

$$\underset{(n\times 1)}{\mathbf{x}} \sim N\left(\mathbf{0}, \sigma^2 \mathbf{I}_n\right).$$

Further we have an $(n \times n)$ idempotent matrix $\mathbf{A}$ with rank $r \leq n$. Then the following χ^2-distribution can be derived:

$$\frac{1}{\sigma^2}\mathbf{x}'\mathbf{A}\mathbf{x} \sim \chi^2(r). \tag{5.10}$$

The two χ^2-distributions (5.9) and (5.10) will be used in the following sections of this chapter.

Test principles

Three types of test principles are distinguished in the statistical literature: 'Likelihood ratio tests', 'Wald-tests' and 'Lagrange multiplier tests'. These types will be encountered in following chapters. (See, for example, Section 4.6 in Stewart and Gill (1998), for a compact discussion on this topic.) For example, a frequently used test concerns the null hypothesis that an explanatory variable (X_{tk}) has no influence on the dependent variable (Y_t), in other words X_{tk} does not belong to the model, which is formulated as $H_0 : \beta_k = 0$. If this null hypothesis has not been rejected the model can be re-estimated without X_{tk}. Then we have an estimated unrestricted model and an estimated restricted model. The three test principles differ in which model is used to test the restriction. A summary of the test principle is given below.

■ **Likelihood ratio (LR)-tests**
The *LR*-test can be applied after both the unrestricted and restricted models have been estimated; the restricted model has to be 'nested' in the unrestricted model, which means that the restricted model is a special case of the unrestricted model. For example, suppose that g linear restrictions have been imposed. The maximum of the log-likelihood function of the unrestricted model is $L(\widetilde{\theta})$, and $L(\widetilde{\theta}_R)$ is the maximum of the log-likelihood function of the restricted model. The likelihood ratio λ is defined as $L(\widetilde{\theta}_R)/L(\widetilde{\theta})$, and the test statistic and its distribution (for large samples) under the null hypothesis are:

$$LR = -2ln\left(\lambda\right) = -2\left(ln\left(L(\widetilde{\theta}_R)\right) - ln\left(L(\widetilde{\theta})\right)\right) \overset{H_0}{\sim} \chi^2(g).$$

The *LR*-test statistic can easily be computed because the maximum value of the likelihood function is always printed in the regression output. In EViews an *LR*-test is also found, but this test can only be used to test the hypothesis that variables can be excluded from the model.

■ **Wald-tests**
  For the application of a Wald-type test for testing restrictions on parameters, only the unrestricted model has to be estimated. For example, the F- and t-test that are discussed in this chapter, are applied after the parameters of an unrestricted model have been estimated.

■ **Lagrange multiplier (LM)-tests**
  For the application of an *LM-test*, only the restricted model has to be estimated to test restrictions on parameters.

In the linear model it is possible that a null hypothesis that has been tested by an *LM-*, an *LR-* and a *Wald*-type test is rejected by, for example, the *Wald*-test and not by the *LM-* and/or the *LR-* test. This is often represented by the inequality:

$$LM \leq LR \leq W.$$

An underlying reason for different test results is that in small samples differences are caused by using either the unbiased estimator $\widehat{\sigma}_u^2$ or the biased but consistent ML estimator $\widetilde{\sigma}_u^2$ for the disturbance variance σ_u^2 in the various formulae. (See, for example, Greene (2000), Maddala (2001), or Stewart and Gill (1998) for more information on this property.)

5.5 Distribution of the residual variance estimator

In Section 4.4, a degenerated normal distribution was derived for the residual vector **e**. In this section, the χ^2-distribution of the squared residuals $\mathbf{e}'\mathbf{e}$ (or $\widehat{\sigma}_u^2$) is established, which will turn out to be a very useful distribution. The χ^2-distribution (5.10) from the previous section is applied to derive the distribution of $\widehat{\sigma}_u^2$, the estimator of the variance of the disturbance term σ_u^2, in the following way.

■ The disturbance term u_t is a normally independently distributed variable with variance σ_u^2:

$$\mathbf{u} \sim N\left(\mathbf{0}, \sigma_u^2 \mathbf{I}_n\right).$$

The matrix $\mathbf{M}_X$ is idempotent with rank $n - K$.
Then according to (5.10) we know that $(\mathbf{u}'\mathbf{M}_X\mathbf{u})/\sigma_u^2$ has the following χ^2-distribution:

$$\frac{1}{\sigma_u^2}\mathbf{u}'\mathbf{M}_X\mathbf{u} \sim \chi^2\left(n - K\right). \tag{5.11}$$

■ It is known that $\mathbf{e} = \mathbf{M}_X\mathbf{u}$ and that $\mathbf{e}'\mathbf{e} = \mathbf{u}'\mathbf{M}_X\mathbf{u}$. Substitution of this expression in (5.11) gives:

$$\frac{1}{\sigma_u^2}\mathbf{e}'\mathbf{e} \sim \chi^2\left(n - K\right). \tag{5.12}$$

However, because $\widehat{\sigma}_u^2 = \mathbf{e}'\mathbf{e}/\left(n - K\right)$, the statistic is written as:

$$(n - K)\frac{\widehat{\sigma}_u^2}{\sigma_u^2} \sim \chi^2\left(n - K\right). \tag{5.13}$$

The χ^2-distribution (5.13) will be used to eliminate the unknown parameter σ_u^2 from normal distributions that have σ_u^2 as a parameter, such as the normal distribution of the OLS estimator. It will be shown that the elimination of σ_u^2 results in t- or F-distributions with $\widehat{\sigma}_u^2$ in their expressions instead of the parameter σ_u^2. These distributions are used in practice to test hypotheses.

Also, observe that (5.13) implies that $\widehat{\sigma}_u^2$ is an unbiased estimator of σ_u^2. Making use of the property that the expectation of a χ^2-distributed variable is equal to its number of degrees of freedom:

$$E\left((n - K)\frac{\widehat{\sigma}_u^2}{\sigma_u^2}\right) = n - K$$

or

$$E\left(\widehat{\sigma}_u^2\right) = \sigma_u^2.$$

This is a more convenient way to prove its unbiasedness than the method given in Section 4.5.

5.6　Interval estimates and the t-test to test restrictions on parameters

The normal distribution of $\widehat{\beta}$:

$$\widehat{\beta} \sim N\left(\beta, \sigma_u^2\left(\mathbf{X}'\mathbf{X}\right)^{-1}\right)$$

contains the unknown parameter σ_u^2: therefore, this distribution can not be used directly to compute interval estimates for the unknown parameters. The parameter σ_u^2 can be eliminated by using the χ^2-distribution of $\widehat{\sigma}_u^2$ (5.13). This results in a Student's t-distribution for the standardised estimator $\widehat{\beta}_k$ of the parameter β_k. With the following steps the t-distribution of the $\widehat{\beta}_k$ is derived.

A first requirement is that the OLS estimator and the residuals are independently distributed. The notation as introduced in Section 4.7 is used by writing $\widehat{\beta}$ and $\mathbf{e}$ as linear functions in the same random vector with disturbances $\mathbf{u}$.

$$\widehat{\beta} = \beta + \left(\mathbf{X}'\mathbf{X}\right)^{-1}\mathbf{X}'\mathbf{u}$$
$$\mathbf{e} = \mathbf{M}_X\mathbf{u}.$$

Next, compute the covariance matrix $Cov\left(\widehat{\beta}, \mathbf{e}\right)$.

$$
\begin{aligned}
Cov\left(\widehat{\beta}, \mathbf{e}\right) &= (\mathbf{X}'\mathbf{X})^{-1}\mathbf{X}' \cdot Var(\mathbf{u}) \cdot \mathbf{M}'_X \\
&= (\mathbf{X}'\mathbf{X})^{-1}\mathbf{X}' \cdot \sigma_u^2 \mathbf{I}_n \cdot \mathbf{M}'_X \qquad \leftarrow \text{(Notice!)} \\
&= \sigma_u^2 (\mathbf{X}'\mathbf{X})^{-1}\mathbf{X}'\mathbf{M}'_X \\
&= \mathbf{0}.
\end{aligned}
$$

The covariance matrix equals a zero matrix as $\mathbf{M}_X\mathbf{X} = \mathbf{0}$. Notice that the assumptions of non-autocorrelated and homoskedastic disturbances have been substituted to obtain this result. So, it is established that $\widehat{\beta}$ and e are independently distributed.

On the basis of this result, a *t*-distribution is obtained according to its definition by dividing the standardised normally distributed OLS estimator (for one parameter) by the square root of the χ^2 distributed $\widehat{\sigma}_u^2$ (5.13) to eliminate the unknown σ_u^2. The distribution of an individual parameter estimator $\widehat{\beta}_k$ has been introduced in Section 4.7 as:

$$
\widehat{\beta}_k \sim N\left(\beta_k, \sigma_u^2 x^{kk}\right)
$$

where the earlier introduced notation has been used again: that x^{kk} is the *k*th diagonal element of $(\mathbf{X}'\mathbf{X})^{-1}$. Standardising $\widehat{\beta}_k$ gives:

$$
\frac{\widehat{\beta}_k - \beta_k}{\sigma_u \sqrt{x^{kk}}} \sim N(0, 1).
$$

The distribution (5.13) of $\widehat{\sigma}_u^2$ is:

$$
(n - K)\frac{\widehat{\sigma}_u^2}{\sigma_u^2} \sim \chi^2(n - K).
$$

Divide these two expressions, as done in (5.4), to yield the Student's *t*-distribution for the OLS estimator $\widehat{\beta}_k$:

$$
\left(\frac{\widehat{\beta}_k - \beta_k}{\sigma_u \sqrt{x^{kk}}} \cdot \sqrt{(n - K)}\right) \bigg/ \left(\sqrt{(n - K)}\frac{\widehat{\sigma}_u}{\sigma_u}\right) \sim t(n - K),
$$

or simplified:

$$
\frac{\widehat{\beta}_k - \beta_k}{\widehat{\sigma}_u \sqrt{x^{kk}}} \sim t(n - K).
$$

The expression $\widehat{\sigma}_u \sqrt{x^{kk}}$ in the denominator is the standard error, $se\left(\widehat{\beta}_k\right)$, of $\widehat{\beta}_k$. Next, the *t*-distribution of $\widehat{\beta}_k$ is written as:

$$
\frac{\widehat{\beta}_k - \beta_k}{se\left(\widehat{\beta}_k\right)} \sim t(n - K). \qquad (5.14)
$$

The result (5.14) is the well-known t-distribution for individual parameter estimators. Two things can be done with this distribution. Confidence intervals for the unknown parameters can be calculated and hypotheses about values of these parameters can be tested.

When α is the chosen significance level, a $(100 - \alpha)\%$ *confidence interval* for β_k is written as:

$$\widehat{\beta}_k \pm t_{\alpha/2}(n - K) \cdot se\left(\widehat{\beta}_k\right).$$

The value $t_{\alpha/2}(n - K)$ can be found in a table of the t-distribution. Hypotheses with respect to a particular value of β_k can be tested: for example, the null hypothesis

$$H_0 : \beta_k = c,$$

with c being any constant. The t-distribution is used under the null hypothesis by substituting the null hypothesis in the distribution (5.14):

$$\frac{\widehat{\beta}_k - c}{se\left(\widehat{\beta}_k\right)} \overset{H_0}{\sim} t(n - K).$$

Compute $\left(\widehat{\beta}_k - c\right)/se\left(\widehat{\beta}_k\right)$ and compare this value with the value of $t(n - K)$ in the table of the t-distribution for any significance level, or compute its matching p-value. The t-test is a Wald-type test because the restriction is tested by using the unrestrictedly estimated model.

The most common value for c is $c = 0$, to test for the significancy of the influence of X_{tk} on Y_t. The null hypothesis is that the variable X_{tk} has no influence on the dependent variable Y_t. All econometric software produces at least three columns in the output, a column with the *estimates*, the *standard errors* and the *t-statistics*. The third column with t-statistics is the quotient of the first two columns to test the null hypothesis

$$H_0 : \beta_k = 0$$

with

$$t_{\widehat{\beta}_k} = \frac{\widehat{\beta}_k}{se\left(\widehat{\beta}_k\right)}.$$

The t-statistics follow the Student's t-distribution under the null-hypothesis.

It is important to specify the alternative hypothesis H_1 accurately. The test can be used as a *one-* or *two-tailed test*, which depends on the formulation of the alternative hypothesis. There are three possibilities:

$$H_1 : \beta_k \neq 0, \text{ or } H_1 : \beta_k > 0, \text{ or } H_1 : \beta_k < 0.$$

In economic models, the researcher generally knows the signs of parameters of contemporaneous specified economic variables in time-series models. The signs of the parameters for most of the variables in a model for cross-section data will be known too. The null hypothesis is that the influence of X_{tk} on Y_t is absent, and the alternative hypothesis is that the influence of X_{tk} exists and can be either positive or negative. Then a one-tailed t-test is the obvious test. If lagged variables occur in time-series models then their signs are often less clear. Then a two-tailed test is needed. Examples are given below.

Remark 5.1 Testing the elasticity
When the variables have been transformed in logs, the parameters represent constant elasticities. Then it might also be appropriate to test the null hypothesis $H_0 : \beta_k = 1$. This hypothesis can simply be tested by the researcher by computing the *t*-statistic $\left(\widehat{\beta}_k - 1\right) / se \left(\widehat{\beta}_k\right)$, and comparing the value with the appropriate *t*-value in the table of the *t*-distribution. Such a *t*-statistic can be computed directly in EViews by using the procedure with 'scalar'. The value of the *k*th parameter estimate is also returned with @*coefs*(*k*) and the value of its standard error with @*stderrs*(*k*). For example, take the null hypothesis $H_0 : \beta_1 = 1$; or in EViews $c(2) = 1$. Then compute, for example, a *t*-statistic *tb1*:

$$scalar\ tb1 = (@coefs(2) - 1)/@stderrs(2).$$

Compare this value with an appropriate value in the table of the Student *t*-distribution.

Remark 5.2 Underlying assumptions
Be aware that *all the assumptions of the classical regression model have been used*! So, once again: in practice, first test the normality, the absence of autocorrelation and heteroskedasticity, before interpreting *t*-statistics in the regression output!

Remark 5.3 Probabilities, one- and two-tailed tests
EViews gives a fourth column with *p*-values for the *t*-statistics for the null hypothesis $H_0 : \beta_k = 0$ and the alternative $H_1 : \beta_k \neq 0$. So it is not necessary to use the table of the *t*-distribution. These *p*-values correspond to a two-tailed test. When in fact the test is one-sided, the *p*-values have to be halved. For example, look at the estimation result in Figure 4.4 where the *t*-statistic of the estimated coffee price parameter has a probability of 0.32%. That is 0.16% in the left-hand tail and 0.16% in the right-hand tail of the distribution. But as a positive influence from the coffee price is expected, the probability of its *t*-statistic is 0.16%. The difference is small in this example. For higher probabilities the difference can be more striking, and decisive for rejecting the null hypothesis or not. The sign of the parameter of P_{t-1}^{cof} is not known a priori, so the *t*-test is a two-sided test with a probability of 1.33%.

Remark 5.4 Lagged dependent variables
As discussed in Section 4.7, the estimation results can be judged asymptotically, for large samples, when a lagged dependent variable is included in the model. For the same reason this is true for the *t*-statistic that has an *asymptotic t*-distribution. With lagged dependent variables the standard errors and *t*-values have to be interpreted asymptotically. In your research papers you have to mention *asymptotic* standard errors and *asymptotic t*-values.

Example 5.1   A one-tailed *t*-test and a confidence interval

Suppose we have a model with four explanatory variables ($K = 4$, including the constant term). The parameters have been estimated from a sample with 44 observations. The null hypothesis will be tested, that the variable X_{t2} has no influence in the explanation of the dependent variable Y_t. A possible *positive* influence of X_2 is expected from the economic theory, so a one-tailed test will be performed:

$$H_0 : \beta_2 = 0,$$
$$H_1 : \beta_2 > 0.$$

Under the null hypothesis the following distribution of t_{β_2} is valid, with $\alpha = 5\%$ and $n - K = 40$:

$$t_{\beta_2} = \frac{\widehat{\beta}_2}{se\left(\widehat{\beta}_2\right)} \overset{H_0}{\sim} t(40).$$

In the table of the t-distribution we find that $t_{0.05}(40) = 1.68$. So H_0 (no influence of X_{t2}) is rejected in favour of H_1 (a positive influence of X_{t2}) at the 5% significance level if:

$$\frac{\widehat{\beta}_2}{se\left(\widehat{\beta}_2\right)} > 1.68.$$

This is shown in Figure 5.2.

If you want to report a 95% confidence interval for β_2 then you have to calculate:

$$\widehat{\beta}_2 \pm t_{0.025}(n - K) \cdot se(\widehat{\beta}_2).$$

As $t_{0.025}(40) = 2.02$, the interval in this example is:

$$\widehat{\beta}_2 \pm 2.02 \cdot se(\widehat{\beta}_2).$$

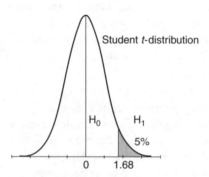

Figure 5.2:   Example of the one-tailed
t-test in Example 5.1

Example 5.2   A two-tailed *t*-test

Suppose that in the model of Example 5.1 the influence of X_{t3} is *unknown*. Then the null hypothesis, that X_{t3} has no influence, is tested with a two-tailed test. If the null hypothesis is rejected, we can judge whether the influence is positive or negative depending on the sign of $\widehat{\beta}_3$:

$$H_0 : \beta_3 = 0,$$
$$H_1 : \beta_3 \neq 0.$$

In the same table, we read again: $t_{0.025}(40) = 2.02$ ($2\frac{1}{2}\%$ of the left tail and $2\frac{1}{2}\%$ of the right tail). Then H_0 is rejected in favour of H_1 if:

$$\frac{\widehat{\beta}_3}{se\left(\widehat{\beta}_3\right)} > 2.02, \text{ or } \frac{\widehat{\beta}_3}{se\left(\widehat{\beta}_3\right)} < -2.02.$$

See Figure 5.3 as an illustration of this test.

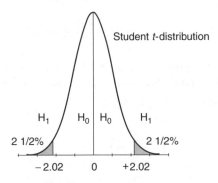

Figure 5.3:   Example of the two-tailed *t*-test in Example 5.2

Example 5.3   A different type of restriction

Consider the model:

$$Y_t = \beta_1 + \beta_2 X_t + \beta_3 X_{t-1} + \beta_4 Z_t + u_t.$$

Suppose the influence of X_t on Y_t is positive for economic theoretical reasons: $\beta_2 > 0$. The sign of β_3 can be positive or negative. If $\beta_3 > 0$, the model is called a distributed lag model: it takes more than one period before a change in the level of X_t has been completely effected in Y_t. Distributed lag models are extensively discussed in Chapter 14. On the other hand, it is possible that to observe that $\beta_3 < 0$, which can be seen as a correction for an over-reaction on the change of X_t in period t. However, it can also be an indication that more or less than just the change of X_t in period t is relevant for determining the level of Y_t. For example, if it looks that $\widehat{\beta}_2 \approx -\widehat{\beta}_3$, after a regression, then it might be relevant to test two-sided:

$$H_0 : \beta_2 = -\beta_3$$
$$H_1 : \beta_2 \neq -\beta_3,$$

or written as

$$H_0 : \beta_2 + \beta_3 = 0$$
$$H_1 : \beta_2 + \beta_3 \neq 0.$$

For example, this null hypothesis can be tested with a t-test, an F-test and a *Likelihood-ratio test (LR-test)*. Here the use of the t-test is shown. It is just an example because the t-test is not the most convenient method to test this restriction. If the null hypothesis is not rejected, the (restricted) model can be respecified with the first differences of X_t (∇X_t, see Remark 5.5 below), and estimated as:

$$Y_t = \beta_1 + \beta \nabla X_t + \beta_4 Z_t + u_t,$$

which gives one more degree of freedom and less multicollinearity (see Section 7.4). Write the null hypothesis as a homogeneous linear equation $H_0 : \beta_2 + \beta_3 = 0$, and the distribution of $\left(\widehat{\beta}_2 + \widehat{\beta}_3\right)$ becomes:

$$\frac{\left(\widehat{\beta}_2 + \widehat{\beta}_3\right) - (\beta_2 + \beta_3)}{\sqrt{var\left(\widehat{\beta}_2 + \widehat{\beta}_3\right)}} \sim t\,(n - K).$$

The t-statistic under the null hypothesis is:

$$t_{\left(\beta_2 + \beta_3\right)} = \frac{\left(\widehat{\beta}_2 + \widehat{\beta}_3\right)}{\sqrt{var\left(\widehat{\beta}_2\right) + var\left(\widehat{\beta}_3\right) + 2cov\left(\widehat{\beta}_2, \widehat{\beta}_3\right)}} \overset{H_0}{\sim} t\,(n - K).$$

To obtain the last component in the denominator, $cov\left(\widehat{\beta}_2, \widehat{\beta}_3\right)$, a printout of the co-variance matrix of $\widehat{\beta}$ is needed. This printout is obtained in EViews as follows. Click on 'View' in the 'Equation' window, after the equation has been estimated, and select 'Covariance Matrix'. Examples to test this null hypothesis in a more convenient way are given at the end of this chapter in Example 5.6.

Remark 5.5 Notation for a difference variable

Modelling variables in first differences will regularly occur in econometrics. Simple examples are found in this chapter, starting in the previous Example 5.3, and more extensive examples are found in Part IV. Two difference operators are distinguished, the nabla: ∇, and the delta: Δ. These operators are defined as follows:

$$\nabla X_t = X_t - X_{t-1},$$

and

$$\Delta X_t = X_{t+1} - X_t.$$

The ∇-operator will mainly be used in economic models, as differences with respect to a previous period in the past are more usual.

5.7 The Wald *F*-test to test restrictions on parameters

In Example 5.3, a hypothesis was tested about more than one parameter by using a *t*-test. Such a hypothesis can be tested more conveniently with a Wald *F*-test, which can directly be done in the EViews 'Equation' window. The example still concerns one restriction. However, with the *F*-test it is possible to test more than one restriction simultaneously. In general notation in this section, g linear restrictions on various parameters will be tested.

The null hypothesis concerning g linear restrictions on K parameters is written in matrix notation in the following way.

$$H_0 : \mathbf{R}\boldsymbol{\beta} = \mathbf{r}. \tag{5.15}$$

$\mathbf{R}$ is a $(g \times K)$ matrix, $\boldsymbol{\beta}$ is a $(K \times 1)$ vector and $\mathbf{r}$ is a $(g \times 1)$ vector. To illustrate this notation Example 5.3 from the previous section is used. The null hypothesis is:

$$H_0 : \beta_2 + \beta_3 = 0.$$

This is only one restriction, so $g = 1$ and the assumption was that $K = 4$. The restriction is written in the general notation as:

$$(0 \quad 1 \quad 1 \quad 0) \begin{pmatrix} \beta_1 \\ \beta_2 \\ \beta_3 \\ \beta_4 \end{pmatrix} = (0).$$

The test-statistic and its distribution will be derived as follows. The distribution of the OLS estimator $\widehat{\beta}$ is:

$$\widehat{\beta} \sim N\left(\beta, \sigma_u^2 \left(\mathbf{X}'\mathbf{X}\right)^{-1}\right),$$

assuming that all the classical assumptions have been satisfied. Next, write the distribution of $\mathbf{R}\widehat{\beta}$ by using the properties and notation discussed in Section 4.7:

$$\mathbf{R}\widehat{\beta} \sim N\left(\mathbf{R}\beta, \sigma_u^2 \mathbf{R}\left(\mathbf{X}'\mathbf{X}\right)^{-1}\mathbf{R}'\right)$$

$$\left(\mathbf{R}\widehat{\beta} - \mathbf{R}\beta\right) \sim N\left(0, \sigma_u^2 \mathbf{R}\left(\mathbf{X}'\mathbf{X}\right)^{-1}\mathbf{R}'\right).$$

The notation of the χ^2-distribution (5.9) from Section 5.4 is used to determine the distribution of the corresponding quadratic form:

$$\frac{1}{\sigma_u^2}\left(\mathbf{R}\widehat{\beta} - \mathbf{R}\beta\right)'\left(\mathbf{R}\left(\mathbf{X}'\mathbf{X}\right)^{-1}\mathbf{R}'\right)^{-1}\left(\mathbf{R}\widehat{\beta} - \mathbf{R}\beta\right) \sim \chi^2(g).$$

The variance σ_u^2 is an unknown parameter of this statistic. It can be eliminated by using the $\chi^2(n-K)$-distribution of $\widehat{\sigma}_u^2$. The OLS estimator $\widehat{\beta}$ and $\widehat{\sigma}_u^2$ are independently distributed. So, according to the definition of the F-distribution, the quotient of both χ^2-distributions is taken:

$$\frac{\left(\frac{1}{\sigma_u^2}\left(\mathbf{R}\widehat{\beta} - \mathbf{R}\beta\right)'\left(\mathbf{R}\left(\mathbf{X}'\mathbf{X}\right)^{-1}\mathbf{R}'\right)^{-1}\left(\mathbf{R}\widehat{\beta} - \mathbf{R}\beta\right)\right)/g}{(n-K)\left(\widehat{\sigma}_u^2/\sigma_u^2\right)/(n-K)} \sim F\left(g, n-K\right),$$

which is rewritten as:

$$\frac{1}{g\widehat{\sigma}_u^2}\left(\mathbf{R}\widehat{\beta} - \mathbf{R}\beta\right)'\left(\mathbf{R}\left(\mathbf{X}'\mathbf{X}\right)^{-1}\mathbf{R}'\right)^{-1}\left(\mathbf{R}\widehat{\beta} - \mathbf{R}\beta\right) \sim F\left(g, n-K\right). \qquad (5.16)$$

After substitution of the null hypothesis $\mathbf{R}\beta = \mathbf{r}$, the F-statistic can be computed and the null hypothesis can be tested:

$$\frac{1}{g\widehat{\sigma}_u^2}\left(\mathbf{R}\widehat{\beta} - \mathbf{r}\right)'\left(\mathbf{R}\left(\mathbf{X}'\mathbf{X}\right)^{-1}\mathbf{R}'\right)^{-1}\left(\mathbf{R}\widehat{\beta} - \mathbf{r}\right) \overset{H_0}{\sim} F\left(g, n-K\right). \qquad (5.17)$$

This is illustrated in Figure 5.4.

The F-statistic (5.17) is computed after only the unrestricted model has been estimated. For that reason the F-test is a Wald-test.

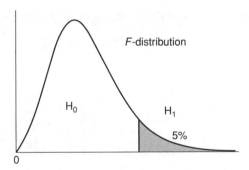

Figure 5.4:   Example of the use of the Wald
F-test

Example 5.4   Zero-slopes test

In the standard output of a least squares procedure, an F-statistic is always found; see
Figure 4.4. This F-statistic is used to test the null hypothesis of *zero slopes*:

$$H_0: \ \beta_2 = \beta_3 = \beta_4 = \ldots = \beta_K = 0,$$

which implies that no linear relationship exists between Y_t and the explanatory variables
$X_{t2}, \ldots, X_{tK}$. Using the standard formulation in (5.15), there are $K - 1$ restrictions on
$K - 1$ parameters: $g = K - 1$, $\mathbf{R}$ is a $((K - 1) \times K)$ matrix, and $\mathbf{r}$ is a $((K - 1) \times 1)$
vector with zeros.

Example 5.5   Testing a restriction with EViews

How can we use EViews to compute the F-test? In EViews, restrictions on parameters
are very simply tested with the Wald F-test. All the tests on parameters are found under
'View' in the 'Equation' window. After the equation has been estimated: click 'View',
'Coefficient Tests' and 'Wald Coefficient Restrictions...', next specify the restriction(s)
in the 'Wald Test' window. For example, consider again a model in general notation:

$$Y_t = \beta_1 + \beta_2 X_t + \beta_3 X_{t-1} + \beta_4 Z_t + u_t,$$

where the hypothesis will be tested:

$$H_0: \beta_2 = -\beta_3.$$

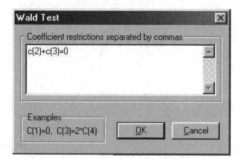

Figure 5.5: Application of the Wald F-test in EViews

The restriction $\beta_2 = -\beta_3$ or $\beta_2 + \beta_3 = 0$ is written in EViews as:

$$c\,(2) + c\,(3) = 0$$

in the 'Wald Test' window that has appeared (see Figure 5.5). That is all!

In the example below, a null hypothesis, as formulated above, is tested for the contemporaneous and lagged coffee price in our relationship between cocoa and coffee prices. If H_0 is not rejected then ∇P_t^{cof} can be specified instead of P_t^{cof} and P_{t-1}^{cof} individually. The output is given in the equation window (see Figure 5.6).

The F-statistic has a p-value of 7.85%, so the null hypothesis is not rejected at the 5% significance level, although it is not a very convincing result. The χ^2-statistic is explained at the end of Section 5.8 later. The output of the regression with the restriction is given in Figure 5.7.

The differences with the output of the unrestricted model in Figure 4.4 are rather small, so the restriction does not disturb the original unrestricted fit to the data. The

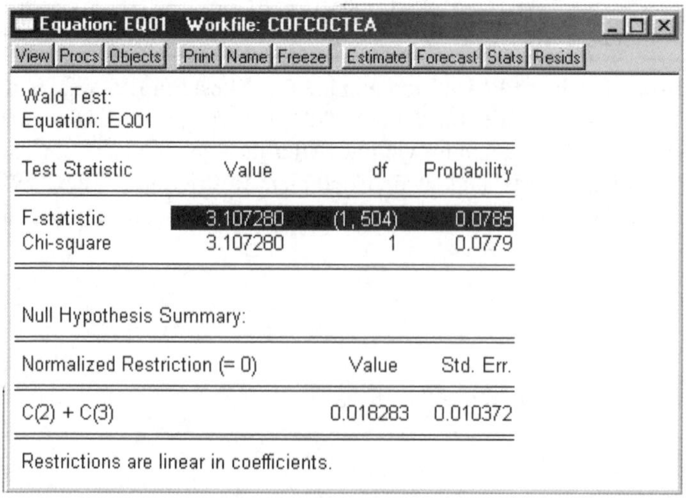

```
■ Equation: EQ01   Workfile: COFCOCTEA                          _□×
View Procs Objects  Print Name Freeze  Estimate Forecast Stats Resids

Wald Test:
Equation: EQ01

Test Statistic          Value         df      Probability

F-statistic           3.107280     (1, 504)     0.0785
Chi-square            3.107280        1         0.0779


Null Hypothesis Summary:

Normalized Restriction (= 0)          Value      Std. Err.

C(2) + C(3)                        0.018283    0.010372

Restrictions are linear in coefficients.
```

Figure 5.6: EViews output concerning the Wald F-test

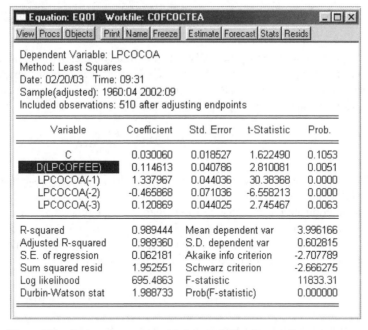

Figure 5.7: Regression output with the restriction $\beta_2 = -\beta_3$

Akaike and Schwartz information criteria are discussed in Section 14.7; these can also be used to judge the estimation results in this example.

Remark 5.6 Relationship between the *t*- and *F*-test in case of one restriction
From the statistical literature it is known that no difference exists between the F-test and the (two-sided) t-test if the null hypothesis concerns only one restriction. Look at the following two formulae. The first one is a repetition of the definition of the t-distribution (5.4).

$$\frac{x}{\sqrt{v^2/r}} \sim t(r).$$

The second relation is the definition of the F-distribution (5.5) applied to the variables $x^2 \sim \chi^2(1)$ and $v^2 \sim \chi^2(r)$:

$$\left(\frac{x}{\sqrt{v^2/r}}\right)^2 \sim F(1,r).$$

This implies, for example, the following identity:

$$F_{0.05}(1, n - K) = t^2_{0.025}(n - K).$$

5.8 Alternative expressions for the Wald *F*-test and the *LM*-test

It is possible to compute the statistic (5.17) in a completely different way, which can be convenient depending on the software used. First, estimate the unrestricted model and save the sum of squared residuals S. Then estimate the restricted model and save the sum of squared residuals S_R. It is now possible to prove that the F-statistic (5.17) is exactly equal to:

$$F = \frac{(S_R - S)/g}{S/(n-K)}. \tag{5.18}$$

This expression can be used to test very generally formulated restrictions, as will be seen in following chapters. The statistic is simply computed by hand. It is also a convenient way to compute the F-statistic (5.18) when software other than EViews is used, where it is less easy to test linear restrictions. Because expression (5.18) is frequently encountered in econometrics, it is useful to prove (5.18). In fact, the only thing that has to be proved is that the numerator of (5.18) is equal to the numerator of (5.17):

$$S_R - S = \left(\mathbf{R}\widehat{\beta} - \mathbf{r}\right)' \left(\mathbf{R}\left(\mathbf{X}'\mathbf{X}\right)^{-1}\mathbf{R}'\right)^{-1} \left(\mathbf{R}\widehat{\beta} - \mathbf{r}\right),$$

because for the denominator you immediately find:

$$gS/(n-K) = g\widehat{\sigma}_u^2.$$

Proof The result (5.18) is achieved after the following steps. The model with restrictions on the parameters is written as:

$$\mathbf{y} = \mathbf{X}\beta + \mathbf{u}$$

with g linear side conditions:

$$\mathbf{R}\beta = \mathbf{r}.$$

Next, compute the OLS estimator by minimising the sum of squared residuals subject to the g linear restrictions on the parameters. This is done by using the Lagrange function:

$$S\left(\widehat{\beta}_R, \lambda\right) = \left(\mathbf{y} - \mathbf{X}\widehat{\beta}_R\right)' \left(\mathbf{y} - \mathbf{X}\widehat{\beta}_R\right) - \lambda'\left(\mathbf{R}\widehat{\beta}_R - \mathbf{r}\right)$$

Differentiation of $S\left(\widehat{\beta}_R, \lambda\right)$ with respect to $\widehat{\beta}_R$ and λ results in the first-order conditions:

$$\frac{\partial S\left(\widehat{\beta}_R, \lambda\right)}{\partial \widehat{\beta}_R} = -2\mathbf{X}'\mathbf{y} + 2\mathbf{X}'\mathbf{X}\widehat{\beta}_R - \mathbf{R}'\lambda = 0$$

$$\frac{\partial S\left(\widehat{\beta}_R, \lambda\right)}{\partial \lambda} = -\left(\mathbf{R}\widehat{\beta}_R - \mathbf{r}\right) = 0.$$

Multiplying the first condition with $\mathbf{R}\,(\mathbf{X}'\mathbf{X})^{-1}$ and solving for $\boldsymbol{\lambda}$, yields:

$$\boldsymbol{\lambda} = -2\left(\mathbf{R}\,(\mathbf{X}'\mathbf{X})^{-1}\mathbf{R}'\right)^{-1}\left(\mathbf{R}\widehat{\beta} - \mathbf{r}\right),$$

with $\widehat{\beta} = (\mathbf{X}'\mathbf{X})^{-1}\mathbf{X}'\mathbf{y}$, as the expression for the unrestricted OLS estimator. Substituting for $\boldsymbol{\lambda}$ and solving for $\widehat{\beta}_R$, the restricted OLS estimator, gives:

$$\widehat{\beta}_R = \widehat{\beta} - (\mathbf{X}'\mathbf{X})^{-1}\mathbf{R}'\left(\mathbf{R}\,(\mathbf{X}'\mathbf{X})^{-1}\mathbf{R}'\right)^{-1}\left(\mathbf{R}\widehat{\beta} - \mathbf{r}\right).$$

With this formula restricted OLS estimates can be computed. It is not necessary to go on with determining the distribution of $\widehat{\beta}_R$, etc. because only (5.18) will be proved. Write the residuals from the estimated restricted model as:

$$\begin{aligned}
\mathbf{e}_R &= \mathbf{y} - \mathbf{X}\widehat{\beta}_R \\
&= \mathbf{y} - \mathbf{X}\widehat{\beta} + \mathbf{X}\,(\mathbf{X}'\mathbf{X})^{-1}\mathbf{R}'\left(\mathbf{R}\,(\mathbf{X}'\mathbf{X})^{-1}\mathbf{R}'\right)^{-1}\left(\mathbf{R}\widehat{\beta} - \mathbf{r}\right).
\end{aligned}$$

This is equal to the following expression.

$$\mathbf{e}_R = \mathbf{e} + \mathbf{X}\,(\mathbf{X}'\mathbf{X})^{-1}\mathbf{R}'\left(\mathbf{R}\,(\mathbf{X}'\mathbf{X})^{-1}\mathbf{R}'\right)^{-1}\left(\mathbf{R}\widehat{\beta} - \mathbf{r}\right). \tag{5.19}$$

Relation (5.19) shows the difference between the residuals of the restricted and unrestricted model. Next, compute the sum of squared residuals by multiplying with its transpose both sides of this equation. The cross-product vanishes because of the orthogonality property $\mathbf{X}'\mathbf{e} = \mathbf{0}$, which was derived in equation (5.1). The result is:

$$\mathbf{e}_R'\mathbf{e}_R = \mathbf{e}'\mathbf{e} + \left(\mathbf{R}\widehat{\beta} - \mathbf{r}\right)'\left(\mathbf{R}\,(\mathbf{X}'\mathbf{X})^{-1}\mathbf{R}'\right)^{-1}\left(\mathbf{R}\widehat{\beta} - \mathbf{r}\right), \tag{5.20}$$

or by writing $S_R = \mathbf{e}_R'\mathbf{e}_R$ and $S = \mathbf{e}'\mathbf{e}$:

$$S_R - S = \left(\mathbf{R}\widehat{\beta} - \mathbf{r}\right)'\left(\mathbf{R}\,(\mathbf{X}'\mathbf{X})^{-1}\mathbf{R}'\right)^{-1}\left(\mathbf{R}\widehat{\beta} - \mathbf{r}\right).$$

This is equal to the numerator of (5.17), which proves (5.18).

Remark 5.7 The coefficient of determination
Equation (5.20) has one more important consequence. The equation demonstrates that the residual sum of squares (RSS) decreases by adding variables! The equation

implies that $e'e < e'_R e_R$. This argues the statement made earlier that the coefficient of determination R^2, defined as:

$$R^2 = 1 - \frac{\sum\limits_{t=1}^{n} e_t^2}{\sum\limits_{t=1}^{n} (Y_t - \overline{Y})^2},$$

increases when any (correct or nonsense) variable is added to the model!

Example 5.6   Computational examples

In this example, some computational results are shown concerning statistics discussed in this chapter. All the results concern the null hypothesis of one restriction:

$$H_0 : \beta_2 + \beta_3 = 0,$$

in our example with cocoa and coffee prices.

- The result from Figure 5.6 was $F = 3.107280$ with a p-value of 0.0785.
- Next, compute the F statistic by using (5.18).
  In Figure 4.4 we read $S = 1.940586$.
  In Figure 5.7 we read $S_R = 1.952551$.
  Next, compute (5.18):

$$F = \frac{(S_R - S)/g}{S/(n - K)},$$

$$F = \frac{(1.952551 - 1.940586)/1}{1.940586/504} = 3.1075.$$

The small difference with the result from Figure 5.6 is due to rounding errors.
- The same hypothesis can also be tested with a likelihood-ratio test (see Section 5.4):

$$LR = -2ln(\lambda) = -2\left(ln\left(L(\widetilde{\theta}_R)\right) - ln\left(L(\widetilde{\theta})\right)\right) \overset{H_0}{\sim} \chi^2(g).$$

Read in Figure 4.4: $L(\widetilde{\theta}) = 697.0536$.
Read in Figure 5.7: $L(\widetilde{\theta}_R) = 695.4863$.

$$LR = -2ln(\lambda) = -2(695.4863 - 697.0536) = 3.1346.$$

This LR-statistic has a $\chi^2(1)$ distribution. The matching p-value is 0.0766.

Remark 5.8 Other expressions for the statistics

It is possible to obtain a *large sample test* for the Wald-test, which can be written as:

$$W = \frac{S_R - S}{S/n},$$

and for the Lagrange multiplier (LM) test:

$$LM = \frac{S_R - S}{S_R/n},$$

with S_R and S as the sums of squared residuals, as introduced above. Both test statistics have under the null hypothesis a $\chi^2(g)$ distribution, with g equal to the number of restrictions. In EViews, the value of this χ^2-test is also found in the output window of the F-test (see Figure 5.6).

The statistics can also be expressed in the coefficient of determination R^2, by using the equation:

$$TSS = ESS + RSS.$$

For example, the LM-test statistic is often computed as nR^2. It concerns the R^2 of the regression of the residuals from the restrictedly estimated model on the explanatory variables of the unrestricted model. The expression

$$LM = nR^2$$

for the LM test will regularly be encountered in Chapter 6. An expression of the F-test in terms of the R^2 does exist as well, but is not used in this book. Once again, see, for example, Greene(2000), Maddala (2001), or Stewart and Gill (1998) for more information about these test statistics.

Chapter 6

Testing the Stochastic Assumptions and Model Stability

6.1 Introduction

In this chapter, a number of statistical and econometric tests will be discussed so that all the disturbance-term assumptions, as formulated in Chapter 4, can be tested. The disturbance-term assumptions can be compactly written as:

$$\mathbf{u} \sim N\left(\mathbf{0}, \sigma_u^2 \mathbf{I}_n\right). \tag{6.1}$$

For individual disturbances this implies normality, no autocorrelation, and homoskedasticity. Before interval estimates, the t- and F-tests, as discussed in the previous chapter, can be used in practice, the validity of the stochastic assumptions about the disturbances has to be tested. If these assumptions are not rejected, then the t- and F-tests are carried out assuming (6.1). When a proper economic model is specified, any systematic process for the disturbance term should be absent. Errors made in the specification of the equation are found in the disturbance term. Therefore residual autocorrelation and/or heteroskedasticity are primarily considered as an indication of specification errors in the systematic part of the model. If these symptoms are found in the residuals, then the right way in general is to respecify the systematic part of the model to get well-behaved residuals. It makes no sense to test hypotheses about parameters in a wrongly specified model. In Chapter 8, we shall also see that heteroskedastic behaviour of the disturbance term is not always caused by specification errors but can belong to the model. If that is the case, the heteroskedasticity

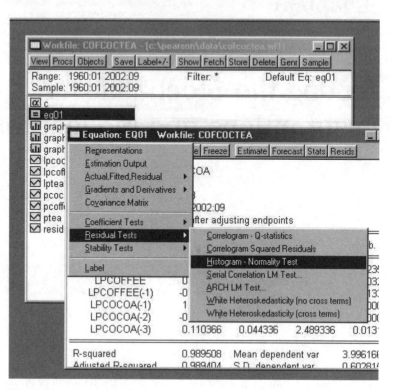

Figure 6.1: The options for residual tests in the 'Equation' window

can be modelled too. Autocorrelation in the disturbance term can arise by building a specific type of model, as is demonstrated with the SUR model (see Section 8.3).

In the 'Equation' window in Figure 6.1 the options under 'View' are shown. The window shows the different views of the regression result. 'Residual Tests' have been selected. Most of the items in 'Residual Tests' that are shown will be discussed in this chapter.

In this chapter, we will look at a variety of residual tests. In addition to using these statistical and econometric tests, it can be informative to look at a plot of the residuals. Cycles, outliers or other systematic behaviour can directly be observed in a picture of the residuals. Choose under 'View', 'Actual, Fitted, Residual', and select 'Graph' to get a picture like Figure 6.2. This is the plot of the residuals from the regression in Section 4.9. The same plot is obtained by clicking on the button 'RESIDS' in the equation window. The dotted lines around the residual graph are one standard error of regression: $0 \pm 1 \cdot \hat{\sigma}_u$. Some outliers are clearly observed and can be investigated.

In the following sections, a simple normality test and some tests for autocorrelation and for heteroskedasticity are introduced. At the end of the modelling process, when you are satisfied with the results of the tests with respect to the stochastic and deterministic assumptions, it is time to check the validity of the last assumption: model stability. How

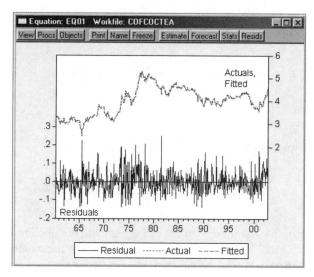

Figure 6.2: The actual and fitted observaions of $\ln\left(P_t^{coc}\right)$ and the residuals

to judge the model stability is discussed in Section 6.5. Always the use of the tests with EViews is discussed immediately after their theoretical introduction. In the last section of this chapter, the first research project is formulated in Case 2. For that reason, Case 2 is preceded by a section where some practical recommendations are given about writing a research paper and presenting estimation results.

6.2 A normality test

A standard normality test is the Jarque–Bera (JB) test. The test can be found in many statistical and econometric textbooks. This normality test goes back to its introduction by Fisher (1948), but nowadays the test is always referenced as the Jarque–Bera test (Jarque and Bera (1980)). See also the statistical literature for more detailed information. This normality test is included in EViews. The null hypothesis is H_0: the residuals are normally distributed. The JB-test statistic, which can be used for models with a constant term, is defined in the statistical literature as:

$$JB = n \left(\frac{S^2}{6} + \frac{(K - 3)^2}{24} \right),$$

and is $\chi^2\left(2\right)$ distributed under the null hypothesis. The JB-statistic is computed in EViews as:

$$JB = (n - K) \left(\frac{S^2}{6} + \frac{(K - 3)^2}{24} \right), \tag{6.2}$$

with S being the measure of skewness and K the measure of kurtosis. The JB-statistic is expressed in terms of the third and fourth moments of the disturbances:

$$S = \frac{\mu_3}{\sigma^3} = \frac{\mu_3}{(\mu_2)^{3/2}}$$

$$K = \frac{\mu_4}{\sigma^4} = \frac{\mu_4}{\mu_2^2}.$$

The moments can be estimated from the OLS residuals:

$$\widehat{\mu}_i = \frac{1}{n} \sum_{t=1}^{n} e_t^i, \text{ with } i = 2, 3, 4.$$

It is known that the third moment of a symmetric distribution is zero, so for a normally distributed variable we have $\mu_3 = 0$. With the help of the moment generating function for a variable from a normal distribution, you can derive that:

$$\mu_4 = 3\sigma^4 = 3\mu_2^2.$$

This implies the following values for K and S when the variable is standard normally distributed:

$$K = 3 \text{ and } S = 0.$$

These values of K and S imply that both components of the JB-statistic in (6.2) are zero under the null hypothesis of normality.

In EViews the JB-statistic (6.2) is computed by selecting 'Histogram - Normality Test' from the 'Residual Tests'. The test has a χ^2 (2)-distribution under the null hypothesis of normality. In Figure 6.3, the output with the histogram of the residuals and some statistics are shown. The figure concerns the residuals obtained from the regression example in Section 4.9 again. The null hypothesis is clearly rejected – the residuals are not normally distributed.

In Figure 6.4, the χ^2 (2) distribution has been drawn. The normality assumption is rejected at the 5% significance level if $JB > 5.99$.

The individual statistics K and S of the test are printed too, making it possible to observe which component causes possible rejection of the normality assumption. This normality test is a non-constructive test. If normality has been rejected, the test gives no clue about how to 'repair' this failure. A good tip, as mentioned in the introduction, is to look at a plot of the residuals. Deviations from normality can be caused by outliers in the residuals. When an outlier is observed, then try to find the reason for the outlier. If it is a typing error the observation can be corrected, but if the observation is right and a reason for the outlier can be found, you may eliminate that observation by specifying a dummy variable in the regression equation. (The use of dummy variables will be discussed in Section 7.5.) The p-value of the JB-test will increase in that way. In this example, the normality assumption has clearly been rejected, probably on account of some heavy outliers: see the plot of the residuals in Figure 6.2.

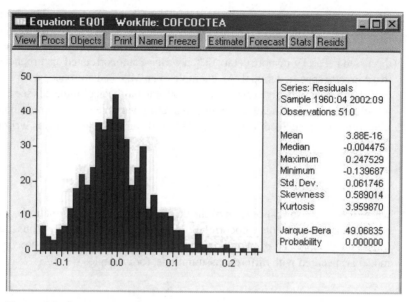

Figure 6.3:   The *JB* normality test

6.3   Tests for residual autocorrelation

It is obvious that autocorrelation is a phenomenon that can only occur in models for time-series data. When an economic model is specified from the economic theory you specify the systematic part of the model. After that has been done, the assumption is made that the difference ($\mathbf{u}$) between the dependent variable ($\mathbf{y}$) and the systematic part ($\mathbf{X}\beta$) is unsystematic.

In general, no economic reason exists to make an assumption that the disturbance term in an economic model is autocorrelated. However, two exceptions exist where systematic behaviour arises in the disturbance term. Models with autocorrelated disturbances because of theoretical reasons are discussed in Parts III and IV. One reason is the explicit specification of

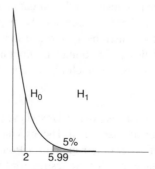

Figure   6.4: The $\chi^2 (2)$-distribution

autocorrelation, as happens in the SUR model in Chapter 8. A second theoretical reason that autocorrelated disturbances can arise is by a transformation of an original model, which can result in a moving-average or MA(1) disturbance term. (Some of these transformations are discussed in Part IV in more detail.) Then we have autocorrelated disturbances which belong to a correctly specified model. An example of an MA(1) disturbance term is, for example, a model where an (adaptive) expectations variable has been eliminated (see Section 13.4), or a distributed lag specification for an explanatory variable has been eliminated by Koyck's transformation (see Section 13.3). An MA(1) disturbance term (v_t) is written as:

$$v_t = u_t - \lambda u_{t-1} \qquad\qquad (6.3)$$

$$\text{with } u_t \sim NID\left(0, \sigma_u^2\right),$$

where u_t is the disturbance term of the original model. In both situations, you have knowledge about the form of the autocorrelation and/or heteroskedasticity. Thus it is not necessary to test for the absence of autocorrelation as it is known that v_t is autocorrelated. Such a model is specified with different assumptions, for example:

$$\mathbf{y} = \mathbf{X}\boldsymbol{\beta} + \mathbf{u}$$

$$\mathbf{u} \sim N\left(\mathbf{0}, \boldsymbol{\Omega}\right).$$

In theory, it is assumed that the covariance matrix $\boldsymbol{\Omega}$ is known. (See Section 8.5 for some explicit expressions of the matrix $\boldsymbol{\Omega}$ in case of autocorrelated disturbances and estimation procedures for the parameters of this model.)

In a standard situation, we know that residual autocorrelation means that the systematic part has been mis-specified. For example, the model had been specified with an insufficient number of lagged variables or not all the relevant explanatory variables have been specified in the model. In Section 7.2, the consequences of autocorrelation for the statistical properties of the OLS estimator are discussed. We will see that a lot is wrong with the estimates and the test statistics when the model has been mis-specified. The consequences of autocorrelation in the residuals are

- that standard errors are underestimated, so t-values are overestimated;
- that high values for the t-statistics and R^2 are observed in the output, leading to seriously misleading results if the output is not correctly interpreted. The Student's t-distribution of the t-statistic has been obtained on the basis of the NID-assumptions of the disturbance term. If these assumptions have been violated, the evaluation statistics in the computer output may not be interpreted in the usual way, as the critical values are much higher than the values as given in the table of the t-distribution.

Various autocorrelation tests exist. All tests have the same null hypothesis: the absence of autocorrelation in the disturbance term. The tests have different alternative hypotheses. The differences concern the order of the autocorrelation. When low frequency data is analysed, we do not expect strong dynamics. So testing for first or second order autocorrelation can be sufficient. When, for example, quarterly or monthly data is analysed, more dynamics can be expected and testing for higher order autocorrelation is relevant.

We will look at a number of tests with the null hypothesis:

$$H_0 : \text{no autorrelation in the disturbance term,}$$

and the alternative hypothesis

$$H_1 : u_t = \varphi_1 u_{t-1} + \varphi_2 u_{t-2} + \ldots \varphi_p u_{t-p} + v_t. \qquad (6.4)$$

The alternative hypothesis, in words: the disturbance term has autocorrelation of the pth order. Autocorrelation of the pth order is represented by an autoregressive model of order p as specified in (6.4). The process is called an AR(p) process for u_t:

$$u_t = \varphi_1 u_{t-1} + \varphi_2 u_{t-2} + \ldots \varphi_p u_{t-p} + v_t,$$

$$\text{with } v_t \sim NID\left(0, \sigma_v^2\right).$$

For example, when using quarterly or monthly data it is useful to look at seasonal frequencies in the residual autocorrelation function, such as four or 12, or a multiple of these orders, to check the presence or absence of seasonality in the residuals. So specification errors produce AR-processes in the disturbance term. In EViews two tests for pth order autocorrelation are found when selecting 'Residual tests': the *Breusch–Godfrey test* and *the Ljung–Box test*. They are discussed below.

The Breusch–Godfrey *LM*-test

Breusch (1978) and Godfrey (1978) have developed an autocorrelation test that is introduced here with an example. The idea behind the Breusch–Godfrey (BG) test is as follows. Suppose that the following linear model has been estimated with OLS:

$$Y_t = \beta_1 + \beta_2 X_t + \beta_3 Z_t + u_t.$$

Next, the residuals have been computed as e_t. The test is performed by estimating the following equation with OLS.

$$e_t = \varphi_1 e_{t-1} + \ldots + \varphi_p e_{t-p} + \beta_1^* + \beta_2^* X_t + \beta_3^* Z_t + \varepsilon_t. \qquad (6.5)$$

The null hypothesis is identical to the hypothesis that: $\varphi_1 = \varphi_2 = \ldots = \varphi_p = 0$. The test statistic of the BG-test is an LM-test that is denoted as $BG(p)$ when (6.4) is the alternative hypothesis. The statistic can be computed as nR^2, with the R^2 of equation (6.5). $BG(p)$ has an asymptotic $\chi^2(p)$ distribution under the null hypothesis of no autocorrelation:

$$BG\left(p\right) = nR^2 \overset{H_0}{\sim} \chi^2\left(p\right).$$

In EViews the $BG(p)$-test is called the *serial correlation LM test*. EViews also computes an F-statistic to test that all the φ_i are zero. Because the 'omitted' variables are residuals and not independent variables, the exact finite sample distribution of this F-statistic is not

Figure 6.5: Lag specification
BG-test

known. It is quite possible that the probabilities of the two statistics nR^2 and F differ considerably. The regression output of equation (4.12) is also given, so individual $\hat{\varphi}_i$s and their t-values are shown but, for the same reason as the F-statistic, the distribution of these t-statistics is unknown; therefore do not consider the t-values, or at best only in a possibly indicative way.

The example with the commodity prices is continued. Test the null hypothesis H_0: no residual autocorrelation, versus H_1: autocorrelation of the 3rd order. Select 'View', 'Residual Tests', 'Serial Correlation LM test ...', then the Breusch–Godfrey test will be computed after the order p has been given. The default value in EViews is $p = 2$. You have to type a relevant value for p yourself. The order is specified in the 'Lag Specification window', as shown in Figure 6.5.

A part of the output windows is given below. The output appears in the 'Equation' window, as shown in Figure 6.6.

Figure 6.6: Result of the $BG(3)$-test

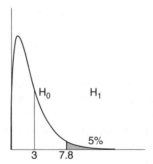

Figure 6.7: The χ^2 (3)-verdeling

The $BG(3)$-test has a p-value of 37.03%, so the null of non-autocorrelation is not rejected against the alternative of third-order autocorrelation. The χ^2 (3) distribution is plotted in Figure 6.7, with $\chi^2_{0.05}$ (3) = 7.815.

The Box–Pierce and the Ljung–Box tests

The Q^*-test of Box and Pierce (1970) is a useful test, or better formulated, as it yields a useful picture of the correlation behaviour of the residuals. The Box–Pierce test, or its modified version the Ljung–Box test, has an asymptotic χ^2 distribution, with p degrees of freedom under the null hypothesis of non-autocorrelation as well, when testing for pth-order autocorrelation. The Ljung–Box test will be discussed in more detail in Chapter 14 with respect to its use in estimating univariate time-series models. In EViews, the Ljung–Box test is called the Q-test, and therefore the Box–Pierce test will be shown as the Q^*-test in this book. These tests make use of autocorrelation coefficients of the residuals. The estimated autocorrelation coefficients are defined as $\widehat{\rho}_i$:

$$\widehat{\rho}_i = \frac{cov\left(e_t, e_{t-i}\right)}{\sqrt{var\left(e_t\right)} \cdot \sqrt{var\left(e_{t-i}\right)}}, \text{ for } i = 1, 2, 3, \ldots, p;$$

see Section 14.4 for more information. The theoretical autocorrelation coefficients ρ_i of the disturbances are zero under the null hypothesis of non-autocorrelation. So, in fact, we check whether the computed sample autocorrelation coefficients of the residuals $\left(\widehat{\rho}_i\right)$ are not significantly different from zero. It is interesting to look at a plot of the coefficients $\widehat{\rho}_i$, known as the autocorrelation function (ACF). The use of the ACF in a regression analysis is illustrated in this section.

The Q^*-test does not 'look' at the individual autocorrelation coefficients but considers the sum of a number of squared autocorrelation coefficients. The Box–Pierce Q^*-test is defined as:

$$Q^* = n \sum_{i=1}^{p} \widehat{\rho}_i^2,$$

and has a χ^2-distribution under the null hypothesis:

$$Q^* \overset{H_0}{\sim} \chi^2(p).$$

However, in the econometrics literature it is discussed that this test has low power in detecting autocorrelation. Therefore, in practice, it is more customary to use a significance level of 10% instead of 5% when using the Q^*-test.

The Q^*-test is not computed in EViews, but the Q-test of Ljung and Box (1978) is used. The Ljung–Box statistic is a modified Box–Pierce test that has the same asymptotic distribution but is closer to the $\chi^2(p)$-distribution in finite samples. The Q-statistic is defined as:

$$Q = n(n+2) \sum_{i=1}^{p} \frac{\widehat{\rho}_i^2}{n-i} \tag{6.6}$$

$$Q \overset{H_0}{\sim} \chi^2(p).$$

This test is widely used, but in the econometrics literature it is argued that the test is not an appropriate test in autoregressive models or models with lagged dependent variables. However, the pattern of the computed autocorrelation coefficients $\widehat{\rho}_i$ ($i = 1, 2, 3, \ldots$), or the probabilities of the Q-statistic give some information about possible residual autocorrelation. One more practical problem: if you wish to use the statistic as a test, you must choose the number of lags to use for the test. By choosing too small a number of lags you may not detect higher order serial correlation, whereas the test may have low power if too large a number of lags have been chosen.

In EViews, the Q-test (6.6) is found in the 'Equation' window under 'View', 'Residual Tests', 'Correlogram-Q-statistics'. It is also possible to double-click on RESID and to choose 'Correlogram'. In the standard linear regression model it makes no difference in which way the Q-test is computed. In Section 14.7 we will see that a difference between these two procedures exists when the null hypothesis is tested for the residuals of a univariate time-series model. Then the Q-test can only correctly be computed via the 'Equation' window.

In practice, it is convenient to keep (a part of) the residual correlogram in the corner of the screen because after each regression the correlogram is refreshed with the ACF of the residuals from the new regression. When modelling from general to specific you can see immediately when things go wrong.

The difference between the Q-test and the BG-test is that for the BG-test you have explicitly to choose one specific order of the autoregressive process specified under the alternative hypothesis. Report in your paper the result of the BG-test for one or two values of p.

In Figure 6.8, an example is given showing the correlogram of the cocoa residuals.

The first column is the autocorrelation function, ACF. The second column is the partial autocorrelation function (PACF): this function will be explained in Section 14.5. The third column gives the Q-values and in the fourth column the probabilities of the cumulating Q-values are found. Look at the pattern of the p-values; no significant autocorrelation coefficients are observed. Notice also the large difference in the p-value of the $BG(3)$ and

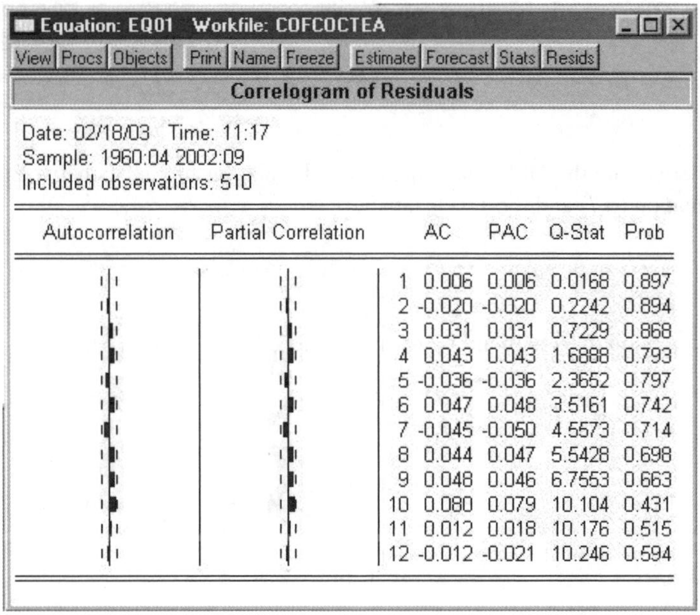

	AC	PAC	Q-Stat	Prob
1	0.006	0.006	0.0168	0.897
2	-0.020	-0.020	0.2242	0.894
3	0.031	0.031	0.7229	0.868
4	0.043	0.043	1.6888	0.793
5	-0.036	-0.036	2.3652	0.797
6	0.047	0.048	3.5161	0.742
7	-0.045	-0.050	4.5573	0.714
8	0.044	0.047	5.5428	0.698
9	0.048	0.046	6.7553	0.663
10	0.080	0.079	10.104	0.431
11	0.012	0.018	10.176	0.515
12	-0.012	-0.021	10.246	0.594

Figure 6.8: The Ljung–Box Q-test

the $Q(3)$-test, which could have been caused by the ineptitude of the Q-test as a statistical test in the dynamic regression model.

The Durbin–Watson test

Probably the Durbin–Watson (DW) test is the most well-known autocorrelation test. Durbin and Watson (1950) test the H_0: no autocorrelation, versus the H_1: first-order residual autocorrelation. However, the DW-test has the same limitations as the Q-statistic in dynamic regression models. The DW-statistic can be used if the explanatory variables are exogenous and a constant term has been included in the model. Its use is very limited because of these conditions. Therefore, it is a strange phenomenon that the DW-value is always printed in the regression output; see, for example, the examples with EViews regression output windows. The DW-test will be discussed here for that reason: it is always found in the output of a regression analysis, so you have to know the background of the test, but it is often not possible to apply it.

One more limitation is the alternative hypothesis of first-order autocorrelation. Higher-order autocorrelation is not detected. Therefore, you have to be sure that first-order autocorrelation is the only possible form of autocorrelation that is relevant for your model. But why would you limit yourself to test only for first-order autocorrelation as the previously discussed general autocorrelation test(s) can simply be used?

First-order autocorrelation in the disturbance term is represented by an AR(1) model:

$$u_t = \varphi_1 u_{t-1} + \varepsilon_t, \text{ with } |\varphi_1| < 1, \text{ and } \varepsilon_t \sim NID\left(0, \sigma_\varepsilon^2\right) \tag{6.7}$$

The DW-statistic has been defined as:

$$DW = \frac{\sum (e_t - e_{t-1})^2}{\sum e_t^2},$$ (6.8)

where e_t are the OLS residuals. A simple relationship exists between the parameter φ_1 in equation (6.7) and the DW-statistic:

$$DW \approx 2\,(1 - \varphi_1).$$ (6.9)

Expression (6.9) is found by rewriting the DW-statistic (6.8):

$$
\begin{aligned}
DW &= \frac{\sum (e_t - e_{t-1})^2}{\sum e_t^2} \\
&= \frac{\sum e_t^2}{\sum e_t^2} + \frac{\sum e_{t-1}^2}{\sum e_t^2} - 2\frac{\sum e_t e_{t-1}}{\sum e_t^2} \\
&\approx 1 + 1 - 2\varphi_1 \\
&= 2\,(1 - \varphi_1).
\end{aligned}
$$

From this relationship, we see the following properties of the DW-statistic.

- No residual autocorrelation: $\varphi_1 = 0 \Longrightarrow DW \approx 2$.
- Positive residual autocorrelation: $\varphi_1 > 0 \Longrightarrow DW < 2$.
- Negative residual autocorrelation: $\varphi_1 < 0 \Longrightarrow DW > 2$.

There is one more problem with this statistic. The distribution of (6.8) depends on the matrix $\mathbf{X}$ with observations on the explanatory variables. This means that the DW-statistic cannot be tabulated. However, it is possible to derive distributions of a lower and an upper bound for the DW-statistic, to obtain upper (d_U) and lower (d_L) bounds for the true critical values of the DW-statistic. The unknown distribution of (6.8) is between the distributions of the lower and upper bound. These two distributions depend only on the number of observations (n) and the number of explanatory variables (K). One can prove that the distribution is symmetric around 2; therefore, the DW-statistic is usually tabulated for values smaller than 2. The following conclusions are drawn (in case the DW-test is used).

- If $DW \geq d_U$: do not reject H_0.
- If $d_L < DW < d_U$: the test is inconclusive.
- If $DW \leq d_L$: reject the H_0 in favour of first-order residual autocorrelation.

In the econometrics literature, you regularly find the recommendation to use d_U as the true critical value because the inconclusive interval can be rather wide.

If $DW > 2$ because of possible negative autocorrelation, the same table can be used for the statistic $(4 - DW)$, as $(4 - DW) \approx 2\,(1 + \varphi_1)$ which is identical to $2\,(1 - \varphi_1)$ if $\varphi_1 < 0$.

As mentioned above, the test can only be used if the explanatory variables are exogenous and a constant term is included in the model. Do not use the DW-statistic if lagged dependent variables are present as explanatory variables in the model. It is not difficult to demonstrate that φ_1, and so the DW-statistic too, are clearly inconsistently estimated by using the autocorrelated OLS residuals (see, for example, Stewart and Wallis (1981)). The value of the DW-statistic can be very misleading in such a model. The test is consistent when $\varphi_1 = 0$, but that is a clear paradoxical situation. In this situation, you will frequently see that, for example, Durbin's h-test has been computed in empirical articles. This test is not found in EViews, but it can easily be computed if you wish to know its value; all the ingredients of the following expression are known. Its definition is:

$$h = \left(1 - \frac{1}{2}DW\right) \sqrt{\frac{n}{1 - var\left(\widehat{\beta}\right)}} \overset{H_0}{\sim} N(0,1),$$

where $\widehat{\beta}$ is the estimate of the parameter of Y_{t-1} in the model. If $\left(1 - var\left(\widehat{\beta}\right)\right)$ is negative, the h-test cannot be computed. For this situation, a second variant exists – the Durbin's alternative test – which has been introduced as a new test statistic. Durbin's alternative test is similar to the $BG(1)$-test. More variants around these tests can be found in the literature, like a DW_4-test for quarterly data, etc. In fact, all these tests around the DW-statistic have to be seen in a historical context. They have been discussed or mentioned in this section because you still find them in many articles and software. Take good note of the facts from this section and mention the DW-statistic in your paper only if all the conditions have been satisfied. However, it is more informative to publish the results of the Breusch–Godfrey test in your paper. In Chapter 12 we revert to the DW-statistic.

6.4   Tests for heteroskedasticity

The phenomenon of heteroskedasticity in the disturbances occurs mainly in models for cross-section data. Although heteroskedasticity can be an indication for specification errors too, it is quite possible that, contrary to autocorrelation, heteroskedasticity occurs in the model. In Chapter 8, models are discussed with an explicit specification of heteroskedastic disturbances.When heteroskedasticity occurs in the model it is possibly caused by a relationship between the disturbance variance and one or more variables, or their variances. But it can also be caused by the data. Therefore, heteroskedastic disturbances can also be found in models for time-series data. For example, when trends occur in the observations of time-series data, then they can induce trends in the variance of the variables. In such a situation, it can happen that a similar trend is found in the variance of the disturbance term as well. Analogous to the situation with autocorrelation, heteroskedasticity in the residuals causes underestimated standard errors, overestimated t-values, etc. For both mentioned forms of heteroskedasticity an alternative hypothesis can be formulated to test the null hypothesis of homoskedastic disturbances. In this section, we consider tests for the following three situations.

- A general heteroskedasticity test is White's test (White: 1980). It is the only heteroskedasticity test in EViews. It tests the homoskedasticity hypothesis against the alternative that heteroskedasticity is present, caused by the levels, squares and products of all the explanatory variables.
- With the Breusch–Pagan test (Breusch and Pagan: 1979) the null hypothesis is tested against the alternative that a concrete relationship between $\sigma^2_{u_i}$ and (the variance of) explanatory variables exists. This test is not a standard procedure in EViews, but it can be calculated simply in EViews.
- In the third situation, we look at possible monotonous trends in $\sigma^2_{u_i}$. Trends in the variance can occur in time-series and cross-section data. For example, in a cross-section the data will be organised according to the sequence of one of the variables (e.g. from low till high values). A time trend in $\sigma^2_{u_i}$ is also possible in models for time-series data, especially in series across a long period of time. The hypothesis that $\sigma^2_{u_i}$ has just an increasing or decreasing trend in the sample period can be tested with the Goldfeld and Quandt test (Goldfeld and Quandt: 1965). Also the Goldfeld and Quandt test statistic can be computed in a simple way by using regression results.

To conclude these introductory remarks: H_0 implies the disturbances are homoskedastic and H_1 will be different with respect to the form of the assumed heteroskedasticity. First, the White test is discussed, followed by the two other tests.

The White test

In the discussion of the tests the subscript i is used to indicate that these tests are more relevant for the analysis of cross-section data than time-series data. The null and alternative hypotheses for the White test are, in words:

- H_0: the variance of the disturbance term is constant;
- H_1: the variance of the disturbance term is heteroskedastic of unknown form.

Because of the generally formulated alternative hypothesis, the test is called a non-constructive test in the econometrics literature. The test is non-constructive because it gives little or no indication about the type of the heteroskedasticity in cases where the null hypothesis has been rejected. To make the test operational, one has to estimate such a relationship. This is done by using squared OLS residuals as the dependent variable, in a regression on linear and quadratic expressions of all the explanatory variables. The White test is actually an *LM*-test, so the nR^2 is used again as a test statistic.

In EViews, in 'Residual Tests', the White's heteroskedasticity test is found with two options: 'no cross terms' and with 'cross terms' (see Figure 6.1). The procedure is clarified with the next example. Suppose the specified model is:

$$Y_i = \beta_1 + \beta_2 X_i + \beta_3 Z_i + u_i.$$

Next the parameters are estimated with OLS and the residuals e_i are computed. For the test, one of the following regressions is calculated with OLS. Equation (6.10) is the equation without cross terms and equation (6.11) is with cross terms (in this example just one term).

$$e_i^2 = \gamma_1 + \gamma_2 X_i + \gamma_3 X_i^2 + \gamma_4 Z_i + \gamma_5 Z_i^2 + v_{t1}, \tag{6.10}$$

$$e_i^2 = \gamma_1 + \gamma_2 X_i + \gamma_3 X_i^2 + \gamma_4 Z_i + \gamma_5 Z_i^2 + \gamma_6 X_i Z_i + v_{t2}. \tag{6.11}$$

The null hypothesis is tested with the statistic nR^2, with n and R^2 from the regression (6.10) or (6.11):

$$nR^2 \overset{H_0}{\sim} \chi^2 (4) \text{ in equation (6.10)},$$

$$nR^2 \overset{H_0}{\sim} \chi^2 (5) \text{ in equation (6.11)}.$$

The statistic nR^2 is asymptotically χ^2-distributed under the null hypothesis. Similar to the BG-test, the distribution of the F-statistic, which is computed by EViews again, is not known and should not be used. Be aware that the number of degrees of freedom of regression (6.11) becomes very large when the model has many explanatory variables, which can reduce the power of the test.

We resume the example with the commodity prices. Part of the window with White's heteroskedasticity test without cross terms, applied on the cocoa residuals, is given in Figure 6.9.

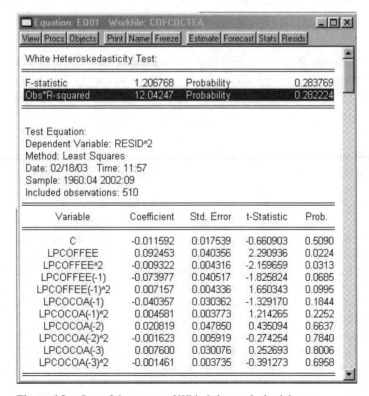

Figure 6.9: Part of the output of White's heteroskedasticity test

The null hypothesis of homoskedastic disturbances is not rejected with a p-value of 28.22%. As mentioned earlier, the White test is very general because after rejection of the null hypothesis, the test gives no clear indication as to what has been the cause of the heteroskedasticity, although the t-statistics give some indication. But be careful with the t-statistics as their distribution is not known as well. More information is obtained by using the next test, the Breusch–Pagan test, which requires, however, a specific alternative hypothesis.

The Breusch–Pagan test

If an idea exists as to which variable(s) may cause the heteroskedasticity in the disturbance term, then you can specify and estimate a test-equation yourself and perform the test. The variables for the test-equation can also be selected by looking at scatter diagrams between squared OLS residuals and explanatory variables. The regression of the residuals on the selected explanatory variables (or their squares) is the basis for the Breusch–Pagan test (BP-test). We continue with the simple previous example. Let us suppose that the variable X_i seems to be the source of the heteroskedasticity, then, for example, the following relationship can be postulated:

$$\sigma_{u_i}^2 = \gamma_1 + \gamma_2 X_i + \gamma_3 X_i^2 + v_t.$$

The original OLS residuals have been saved with a different name, for example:

$$genr\ res = resid,$$

or by using 'Procs', and selecting 'Make Residual Series . . .', which gives the suggested name $resid01$, when it is used the first time. Next, regress the squares of these residuals e_i^2 on X_i and X_i^2:

$$e_i^2 = \gamma_1 + \gamma_2 X_i + \gamma_3 X_i^2 + \varepsilon_i.$$

The Breusch–Pagan test is an LM-test too, so that the nR^2 is used as a test statistic, in fact to test the hypothesis $H_0 : \gamma_2 = \gamma_3 = 0$. In this example, nR^2 has the following distribution:

$$nR^2 \overset{H_0}{\sim} \chi^2\,(2)\,.$$

The number of degrees of freedom is equal to the number of parameters in the null hypothesis without the constant term. As an asymptotic equivalent test the zero-slopes F-test can be used, although some problems with the disturbance-term assumptions of ε_i can be expected (see, for example, Greene (2000)). Originally, Breusch and Pagan suggested regressing $e_i^2/\tilde{\sigma}_u^2$ on some variables and computing $\frac{1}{2}ESS$ of this regression as a test statistic. The proposed procedure given above is simpler and asymptotically equivalent to the original procedure. (See Johnston and DiNardo (1997) for more details and further references.)

To illustrate the use of the BP-test, the regression from Section 4.9 will be elaborated further. Although the distribution of the t-statistics in Figure 6.9 is unknown, the coffee prices have the highest t-values, which can be used as an indication of a possible source for heteroskedasticity. So assume that the (lagged) coffee prices possibly generate heteroskedasticity. After clicking 'Quick' and 'Estimate Equation', the following equation is

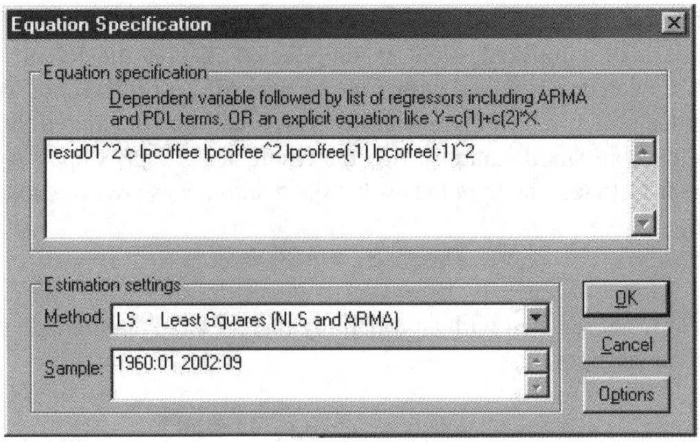

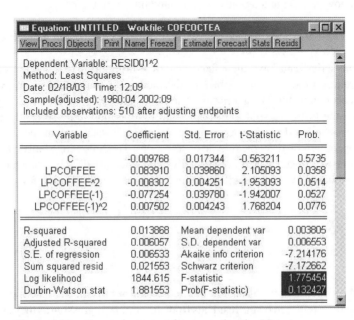

Figure 6.10: Specification of the equation for the *BP*-test

specified, without generating new variables beforehand:

$$resid01\hat{}2\ c\ lpcoffee\ lpcoffee\hat{}2\ lpcoffee(-1)\ lpcoffee(-1)\hat{}2.$$

See the 'Equation Specification' window in Figure 6.10.

Next, compute the value of nR^2 by using the results from the output window in Figure 6.11.

The calculated *BP*-test, with the p-value in parentheses, is:

$$\begin{aligned} nR^2 &= 510 \times 0.013868 \\ &= 7.0727\ (0.1321)\,. \end{aligned}$$

Equation: UNTITLED Workfile: COFCOCTEA

View | Procs | Objects | Print | Name | Freeze | Estimate | Forecast | Stats | Resids

Dependent Variable: RESID01^2
Method: Least Squares
Date: 02/18/03 Time: 12:09
Sample(adjusted): 1960:04 2002:09
Included observations: 510 after adjusting endpoints

Variable	Coefficient	Std. Error	t-Statistic	Prob.
C	-0.009768	0.017344	-0.563211	0.5735
LPCOFFEE	0.083910	0.039860	2.105093	0.0358
LPCOFFEE^2	-0.008302	0.004251	-1.953093	0.0514
LPCOFFEE(-1)	-0.077254	0.039780	-1.942007	0.0527
LPCOFFEE(-1)^2	0.007502	0.004243	1.768204	0.0776

R-squared	0.013868	Mean dependent var	0.003805
Adjusted R-squared	0.006057	S.D. dependent var	0.006553
S.E. of regression	0.006533	Akaike info criterion	-7.214176
Sum squared resid	0.021553	Schwarz criterion	-7.172662
Log likelihood	1844.615	F-statistic	1.775454
Durbin-Watson stat	1.881553	Prob(F-statistic)	0.132427

Figure 6.11: Regression output for computing the *BP*-test

The 5% and 10% critical values of the $\chi^2(4)$-distribution are: 9.4877 and 7.7794. The null hypothesis of homoskedasticity is not rejected again at the 5% or 10% level. The p-value of 0.1321 can be computed with, for example, Microsoft Excel or with any other statistical computer program. Alternatively, the F-test can be considered, although its distribution is not clear in small samples. See the result of the zero-slopes F-test in the window in Figure 6.11 to test the hypothesis that the disturbances are homoskedastic:

$$H_0 : c\,(2) = c\,(3) = c(4) = c(5) = 0.$$

The H_0 is not rejected with a probability of 13.24%. We conclude that the variance $\sigma^2_{u_t}$ is homoskedastic, or:

$$e^2_t = c(1) \text{ for all } t,$$

The probabilities of the χ^2- and F-tests are rather close because of the very large sample size.

The Goldfeld–Quandt test

Finally the Goldfeld–Quandt test (the GQ-test) is discussed as an alternative heteroskedasticity test. For cross-section data, first arrange the data in any logical order according to one of the variables. The GQ-test is used to test the null hypothesis of homoskedastic disturbances:

$$H_0 : \sigma^2_{u_i} = \sigma^2_u \text{ for all } i,$$

but now versus the alternative of a monotonous trend in $\sigma^2_{u_i}$:

$$H_1 : \text{the variance } \sigma^2_{u_i} \text{ has an increasing/decreasing monotonous trend.}$$

Time-series data have their fixed historical ordering. Cross-section data are ordered according to one of the variables of the model, the dependent or an explanatory variable. An economically relevant reason determines the choice of the ordering. Then the idea behind the test is to split the sample into two periods (time-series data) or into two parts (cross-section data) and to compare the residual variances in the two sub-samples (n is even, otherwise drop the middle observation). The following statistic has an F-distribution because the disturbances are normally, independently distributed, which are the conditions in the definition of the F-distribution as summarised in Section 5.1:

$$\mathbf{u} \sim N\left(\mathbf{0}, \sigma^2_u \mathbf{I}_n\right) \Longrightarrow$$

$$\frac{u^2_1 + u^2_2 + \ldots + u^2_{\frac{1}{2}n}}{u^2_{\frac{1}{2}n+1} + u^2_{\frac{1}{2}n+2} + \ldots + u^2_n} \sim F\left(\frac{1}{2}n, \frac{1}{2}n\right).$$

If the variances are constant, the quotient would be close to one. The unobserved disturbances cannot be replaced by the residuals from the original regression as they are not independently distributed; the numerator and the denominator will not be independent:

$$\mathbf{e} \sim N\left(\mathbf{0}, \sigma_u^2 \mathbf{M}_X\right) \Longrightarrow$$

$$\frac{e_1^2 + e_2^2 + \ldots + e_{\frac{1}{2}n}^2}{e_{\frac{1}{2}n+1}^2 + e_{\frac{1}{2}n+2}^2 + \ldots + e_n^2} \overset{H_0}{\approx} F\left(\frac{1}{2}n, \frac{1}{2}n\right).$$

For that reason, the sample is divided in two sub-samples. The model is estimated twice for the two sub-samples. Write the two regressions, with subscripts (1) and (2) corresponding to the two sub-samples, as:

$$\mathbf{y}_{(1)} = \mathbf{X}_{(1)}\boldsymbol{\beta} + \mathbf{u}_{(1)}; \ \mathbf{u}_{(1)} \sim N\left(\mathbf{0}, \sigma_{(1)u_i}^2 \mathbf{I}_{n/2}\right), \tag{6.12}$$

$$\mathbf{y}_{(2)} = \mathbf{X}_{(2)}\boldsymbol{\beta} + \mathbf{u}_{(2)}; \ \mathbf{u}_{(2)} \sim N\left(\mathbf{0}, \sigma_{(2)u_i}^2 \mathbf{I}_{n/2}\right). \tag{6.13}$$

The null hypothesis, H_0, can be written as:

$$H_0 : \sigma_{(1)u_i}^2 = \sigma_{(2)u_i}^2 = \sigma_u^2,$$

for all observations. So, estimate the parameters twice with OLS and compute the two residual vectors, $\mathbf{e}_{(1)}$ and $\mathbf{e}_{(2)}$. Under the null hypothesis, the two residual variables have the same parameter σ_u^2 in their distributions. This is written as follows:

$$\mathbf{e}_{(1)} \overset{H_0}{\sim} N\left(\mathbf{0}, \sigma_u^2 \mathbf{M}_{X_{(1)}}\right),$$

$$\mathbf{e}_{(2)} \overset{H_0}{\sim} N\left(\mathbf{0}, \sigma_u^2 \mathbf{M}_{X_{(2)}}\right).$$

The two residual vectors $\mathbf{e}_{(1)}$ and $\mathbf{e}_{(2)}$ are independently distributed. According to (5.12) in Section 5.5 we know that the two sums of squared residuals have the following independent χ^2-distributions:

$$\mathbf{e}_{(1)}'\mathbf{e}_{(1)} \overset{H_0}{\sim} \sigma_u^2 \chi^2\left(\frac{1}{2}n - K\right), \tag{6.14}$$

$$\mathbf{e}_{(2)}'\mathbf{e}_{(2)} \overset{H_0}{\sim} \sigma_u^2 \chi^2\left(\frac{1}{2}n - K\right). \tag{6.15}$$

The quotient of the statistics in (6.14) and (6.15) has, according to the definition of the Fisher F-distribution, the following F-distribution:

$$\frac{\mathbf{e}_{(1)}'\mathbf{e}_{(1)}}{\mathbf{e}_{(2)}'\mathbf{e}_{(2)}} \overset{H_0}{\sim} F\left(\frac{1}{2}n - K, \frac{1}{2}n - K\right).$$

To apply the test in practice with EViews, one has to do two additional regressions. The sums of squared residuals are given in the output. To compute the F-statistic of the GQ-test, you only have to divide these two values and determine the p-value. The two sub-samples can be separated more clearly by deleting more observations from the middle of the ranked data set, which makes the test more powerful. The number of observations that can be dropped from the middle is rather arbitrary and has to be done carefully because of the loss of degrees of freedom in the two regressions (6.12) and (6.13).

As an example, consider the unrestricted relationship between the cocoa and coffee price from Section 4.9. The date 1980(12) has been chosen to split the sample, because the period after 1980 was quieter for the coffee market than the preceding period with heavy price movements. For that reason, no observations have been deleted from the 'middle' of the sample. The equation has been re-estimated for the sample period 1960(1)–1980(12) and the period 1981(1)–2002(9). Period 1 has 261 observations ($n_1 = 261$) and the second period has 279 observation ($n_2 = 279$). The null hypothesis, H_0, is that the disturbances are homoskedastic and the alternative hypothesis, H_1, is that the variance in the first period is larger than in the second period. The resulting F-statistics, with the p-value in parentheses, and the matching 5% critical value are as follows:

$$e'_{(1)}e_{(1)} = 1.060631,$$

$$e'_{(2)}e_{(2)} = 0.824421,$$

$$F = \frac{e'_{(1)}e_{(1)}/(n_1-K)}{e'_{(2)}e_{(2)}/(n_2-K)} = \frac{1.060631/(261-6)}{0.824421/(279-6)} = 1.3773 \ (0.0047),$$

$$F_{0.05}(255, 273) = 1.2245.$$

This time, the null hypothesis of no heteroskedasticity is clearly rejected at the 5% level in favour of a decreasing variance of the disturbance term. This form of heteroskedasticity has not been found with the previously introduced heteroskedasticity tests. The estimation results are not given here, but the parameter estimates are quite different in the two sub-samples. This result is not unexpected for the reason given above and you can reproduce the results yourself by using the accompanying data set.

6.5   Checking the parameter stability

Finally, we return to the specification of the estimated model. The assumption has been made that the parameters of the explanatory variables are constant over time. An impression about the stability of the parameter estimates in the sample period can be obtained by computing *recursive coefficient estimates* and looking at their plots. This is not really a test, but the pictures of the recursively estimated coefficients are informative regarding the stability of the estimates. In the 'Equation' window click on 'View', 'Stability Tests', and select 'Recursive Estimates (OLS only)...', and mark 'Recursive Coefficients' in the obtained window, as shown in Figure 6.12. All the coefficients are shown in the list, but you can also select just a few parameters.

The idea behind recursively estimating the parameters of the equation is repeatedly adding one observation and subsequently re-estimating the parameters. If there are K coefficients to be estimated in the β vector, then first $K+1$ observations are used to estimate β. That is the smallest number of observations that can be used to estimate the

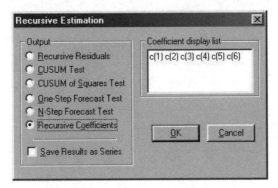

Figure 6.12: Specification of the coefficients that will be estimated recursively

parameters is $K + 1$, so we have only one degree of freedom. Then the next observation is added to the data set and $K + 2$ observations are used to compute the second estimate of β. This process is repeated until all the n sample data have been used, yielding $n - K$ estimates of the vector β. These estimates are plotted in separate graphs, as shown in Figure 6.13.

In this figure, only the coefficients C(2), C(3), C(4) and C(5) have been selected to present a clear Figure 6.13. The drawn 'zero lines' are not default, but can be made default via the 'Options' button. Together with the standard errors they are informative about the significance of the estimated parameters: for example, note that C(2) and C(3) become significantly different from zero at the end of the sample period.

Notice that recursive least squares is not an estimation method to estimate variable parameters – it produces estimates from a number of sub-periods. The last recursive estimate of β is equal to the OLS-estimate obtained earlier for the whole sample. It is normal that the first estimates behave in rather an unstable manner, because of the very low number of degrees of freedom at the beginning of this procedure. From these plots, you could conclude that the estimates are stable, as they hardly vary in the second half of the sample period. You can rescale the figures to show the estimates for only the second half or two-thirds of the sample period, for example, in your paper.

The window in Figure 6.12 shows that more output options concerning model stability can be chosen. For example, the 'CUSUM Test' and the 'CUSUM of Squares Test' can be selected. These tests, which will briefly be introduced here, also produce informative plots about the stability of the structure. The CUSUM statistic is based on cumulative sums of scaled recursive residuals and is plotted against time. The background of both the statistics will not be discussed here because their interpretation is straightforward. (See, for example, Johnston and DiNardo (1997) or Greene (2000) for more detailed theoretical information about the statistics.)

The expectations of the CUSUM statistics are zero under the null hypothesis of constant parameters. The CUSUM statistic is plotted in EViews with 5% significance confidence bounds. When the graph of the CUSUM statistics revolves around zero within its confidence bounds the null hypothesis of parameter constancy is not rejected.

The CUSUM of Squares statistic is a cumulative sum of squared residuals. The expectations of the CUSUM of Squares statistic run from zero at the first observation until the value

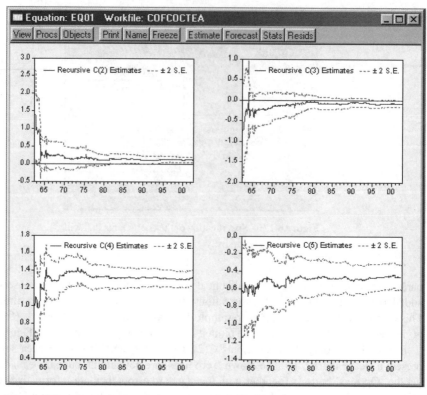

Figure 6.13: Plots of recursively estimated parameters

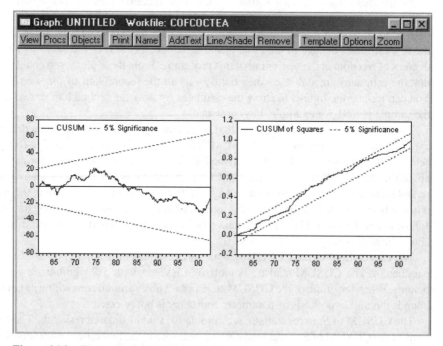

Figure 6.14: Example of the CUSUM and CUSUM of Squares Test

of one at the end of the sample period, under the null hypothesis of constant coefficients and variance. The CUSUM of Squares statistics are also plotted with 5% confidence bounds. In Figure 6.14, these plots are shown for our example with the regression of cocoa prices on coffee prices.

In Figure 6.14, we see that the price explosion of the commodity prices at the end of the 1970s caused some instability, as the graph of the CUSUM of Squares statistics hits the 5% significance bound.

6.6 Model estimation and presentation of estimation results

In this section, some practical aspects of the estimation procedure are discussed and suggestions provided for correctly publishing estimation results in an article. After the research problem has been introduced, the data have been described and analysed as indicated in Case 1, you next need to estimate an econometric model, as proposed in Case 2 in the next section.

In Section 4.9, the idea of modelling from general to specific was introduced as a structural method of modelling time-series data. First find a 'general model' like model (4.29). That is an estimated model, specified with a sufficient number of lags for the explanatory and dependent variables, such that residual autocorrelation is absent. Next, try to find a specific model by imposing zero and other restrictions on parameters. For example, look at the following situation, where a part of an estimated model is considered:

$$\widehat{Y}_t = \widehat{\beta}_1 + \widehat{\beta}_2 X_t + \widehat{\beta}_3 X_{t-1} + \widehat{\beta}_4 X_{t-2} + \ldots.$$

Suppose that the estimated parameters $\widehat{\beta}_2$ and $\widehat{\beta}_4$ are significantly different from zero whereas $\widehat{\beta}_3$ is not. Next, you may consider removing the variable X_{t-1} from the model for statistical reasons, but that is not correct because of economic reasons (see Remark 1.1). It is very irrational to suppose that an intervening period exists where the variable X_t does not influence the dependent variable Y_t. High correlation between the explanatory variables X_t, X_{t-1} and X_{t-2} causes multicollinearity. (This subject will be discussed in the next chapter.) Multicollinearity might have been the reason for the above-sketched problematic estimation result. The influence of X_t, X_{t-1} and X_{t-2} on Y_t cannot clearly be discriminated; all three variables behave in a similar way. Therefore, it is possible that a better result is obtained by deleting the 'significant' variable X_{t-2} because the variable X_{t-1} can take over the role of X_{t-2}. If re-estimation of the model without X_{t-2} still results in significant parameter estimates and absence of residual autocorrelation, then a good decision had been taken by deleting X_{t-2} from the model.

After a number of steps, the 'estimation and test' stage will be finished and the results have to be written and discussed in a research paper. Of course, do not include all the steps that have been done, only some of them will be interesting. It is clarifying for the reader to show some of the striking steps in the estimation procedure. This is well demonstrated by

Variables	Model 1	Model 2	Model 3	Model 4
Dependent variable: P_t^{coc}				
Explanatory variables:				
Constant	0.018 (0.020)	...	0.030 (0.019)	0.016 (0.020)
P_t^{cof}	0.114 (0.043)	...		0.121 (0.041)
P_{t-1}^{cof}	-0.106 (0.069)	...		-0.103 (0.041)
P_{t-2}^{cof}	0.070 (0.069)	...		1.328 (0.044)
P_{t-3}^{cof}	-0.062 (0.044)	...		
∇P_t^{cof}		...	0.115 (0.041)	
P_{t-1}^{coc}	1.328 (0.044)	...	1.338 (0.044)	1.328 (0.044)
P_{t-2}^{coc}	-0.467 (0.071)	...	-0.466 (0.071)	-0.462 (0.071)
P_{t-3}^{coc}	0.119 (0.045)	...	0.121 (0.044)	0.110 (0.044)
Sample period:				
1960(1)–2002(9)				
$BG\,(3)$	1.19(0.75)	...	4.36(0.23)	3.14(0.37)
JB	47.83(0.00)	...	50.14(0.00)	49.07(0.00)
$White$	14.79(0.39)	...	5.23(0.73)	12.04(0.28)
R^2	0.99	...	0.99	0.99

Table 6.1: Schematic example of a regression table

inserting a regression table in the paper, which is easier to survey than listing a number of estimated equations or regression outputs in the paper. An example is given in Table 6.1. The asymptotic standard errors of the estimated parameters have been given in parentheses. The prices are in logs.

In the first column in Table 6.1 all the explanatory variables used in the general model are included. Model 1 is the 'general model', Model 4 is the 'specific model', and Model 2 (no results have been given in this example) and Model 3 represent two interesting models to show the reader. Notice the change in the significance of the parameters by deleting P_{t-3}^{cof} from the model, which must have been caused by the multicollinearity problems, as described above.

The final estimation result will be repeated in the text and discussed as your proposed econometric model. The result has to be written in a mathematically and statistically correct way and concerns a couple of simple matters which are useful to restate. The correct way to present an estimation result is shown in the following two equations:

$$\widehat{Y}_t = \underset{(se(\beta_1))}{\widehat{\beta}_1} + \underset{(se(\beta_2))}{\widehat{\beta}_2} X_{t2} + \underset{(se(\beta_3))}{\widehat{\beta}_3} X_{t3} + \ldots + \underset{(se(\beta_K))}{\widehat{\beta}_K} X_{tK} \qquad (6.16)$$

or

$$Y_t = \underset{(se(\beta_1))}{\widehat{\beta}_1} + \underset{(se(\beta_2))}{\widehat{\beta}_2} X_{t2} + \underset{(se(\beta_3))}{\widehat{\beta}_3} X_{t3} + \ldots + \underset{(se(\beta_K))}{\widehat{\beta}_K} X_{tK} + e_t. \qquad (6.17)$$

Both equations are exact equations. If a hat (ˆ) has not been placed above the dependent variable or the residual variable e_t has not been included, the equation has not been written correctly. The notation of equation (6.16) is a standard method of writing an estimated model. The presentation of equation (6.17) is sometimes useful to show the estimation result for a specific situation, as will be seen in Chapter 12.

In the empirical literature you can see that standard errors or t-values are placed under the estimated coefficients in parentheses. In general, standard errors are better placed under the estimated coefficients. Then the null hypothesis $H_0 : \beta_k = c$, can be tested directly by the reader of the paper for any value of c, instead of zero only. Generally, write the standard errors rather than the t-values under the coefficients as t-values only test $H_0 : \beta_k = 0$.

Not only has the estimation stage to be done properly, the presentation of the estimation results also has to be correct. Under the estimated equation other statistics such as R^2 or $\overline{R}^2$, the JB statistic, some $BG(.)$ values, and possibly (if allowed) the DW-value, etc., are written. If possible, give p-values in parentheses behind the values of these statistics.

The final model for the cocoa prices can be written as follows (with variables in logs):

$$\widehat{P^{coc}_t} = \underset{(0.020)}{0.016} + \underset{(0.041)}{0.121} P^{cof}_t - \underset{(0.041)}{0.103} P^{cof}_{t-1} + \underset{(0.044)}{1.328} P^{coc}_{t-1} - \underset{(0.071)}{0.462} P^{coc}_{t-2} + \underset{(0.044)}{0.110} P^{coc}_{t-3},$$

$$R^2 : 0.99,\ JB : 49.07(0.00),\ BG(3) : 3.14(0.370),\ White : 12.04(0.28).$$

Sample period: 1960(1)–2002(9).

6.7 Case 2: an econometric model for time-series data

At this stage of the course, a sufficient number of tools have been introduced and discussed to start your first complete paper. From now on, models will be estimated and assumptions will be tested in a 'correct' way. However, probably not everything will be correct as only the OLS estimator has so far been used. No distinction will be made between exogenous and endogenous explanatory variables at this stage of the course. The consequences of that distinction for estimating the parameters of the model will be considered in Case 6, where you will re-estimate your model with the 2SLS estimator for obtaining consistent estimation results. Both the estimation results will be compared and evaluated in Case 6.

In Case 1, you have chosen one of the three offered 'research projects' with time-series data: one of the macroeconomic models, a model explaining the demand for vehicles in the USA or the retail gas price, or a model for the money demand in the USA. The same questions can be answered if you use your own data. A short introduction to the three subjects has been given in Chapter 2, followed by some directions for possible models that can be estimated with the data.

Preparations have been done in Case 1 with the analysis of the time-series data. Reconsider the results of that analysis and perform the estimation procedure in the correct order: model from *general to specific* according to the reference points given below.

■ Open in a corner of your screen the *correlogram* of the residuals 'RESID' to have 'continuous' information about the residual behaviour with respect to autocorrelation. Make a decision about modelling the original variables, deflated variables or the logs of the variables (parameters are constant elasticities). When not modelling the logs of the variables you can make a graph showing an interesting elasticity, as was demonstrated in Section 3.4, which gives you information about the stability of the elasticity in the sample period. You can do both and decide later on which model describes the economy in the best way. Specify in the 'Equation Specification' window an equation with an equal number of lags for all the variables and estimate the parameters with OLS.

■ Estimate a dynamic equation. Look at the correlogram of 'Resid' and the plot of the residuals. If autocorrelation is indicated, then respecify the equation with more lags for all the variables. Go on until a 'general' model without residual serial correlation has been found.

■ Start reducing the model by using t- and F-tests to test restrictions on parameters. Impose the restrictions, re-estimate the model and check the residual autocorrelation function. Restrictions can be zero restrictions (exclusion of variables), but sometimes a null hypothesis concerning first differenced variables can be relevant. In doing so, you are working in a structured way to find a good model. A good model is a parsimonious model that describes the economy according to the economic theory and that does not reject the stochastic assumptions.

■ Choose your final model and justify your choice.

■ Evaluate the estimation result by checking the stability of the parameter estimates by computing recursive parameter estimates and CUSUM statistics.

■ If you are content with the results, then also compute some interval estimates for parameters of interesting variables.

■ Test the normality assumption and the null hypothesis of homoskedastic disturbances for your final model (White, Goldfeld–Quandt or Breusch–Pagan). At this stage, you can only report the presence of heteroskedasticity in case the null hypothesis of homoskedastic disturbances has been rejected. After Chapter 8 has been studied, it will be possible to tackle this problem in Case 4.

■ The first two sections of your paper have been written in Case 1. Reconsider your text and decide which results have to be described in the paper and write, as far as possible, a complete paper.

Chapter 7

A Collection of Topics Around the Linear Model

7.1 Introduction

In this last chapter of Part II, the basic course is completed by discussing a number of subjects related to the reduced-form model. The chapter covers a variety of different subjects. We start with studying the consequences of specification errors in the linear model, in Section 7.2. It will become clear why it is a good idea to use Hendry's approach of 'general to specific modelling' to find a satisfactory econometric model. This approach to obtain a model by working in a structured way is obviously better than some 'trial and error' or data-mining procedure. A number of different subjects then follow. In Section 7.3, attention will be paid to prediction issues; in Section 7.4, effects of multicollinearity (correlation between explanatory variables) on estimation results are demonstrated; and in Section 7.5, the use of qualitative explanatory variables is illustrated. Qualitative explanatory variables can be used to specify a deterministic trend, seasonality and different regimes, and are sometimes employed to eliminate outliers.

7.2 Specification errors

In this section, the consequences of specification errors are discussed. It is a theoretical-oriented section, but with clear practical consequences. This section also demonstrates why the procedure of modelling 'from general to specific' is recommended to obtain a correctly specified parsimonious model (see also, for example, Hendry (1995) or Charemza and Deadman (1992) for discussions on this topic). Two types of specification errors can be considered. First, it is possible to have a model that is a number of variables short, and secondly it is possible that too many variables have been specified in the model. To examine the effects of these two types of errors, the following two models are considered:

$$y = X_1\beta_1 + u \tag{7.1}$$

and

$$y = X_1\beta_1 + X_2\beta_2 + u. \tag{7.2}$$

X_1 is an $(n \times K_1)$ matrix and X_2 is an $(n \times K_2)$ matrix. The following two situations are analysed:

- model (7.1) is 'true' but model (7.2) has been estimated,
- model (7.2) is 'true' but model (7.1) has been estimated.

The consequences of these two types of specification errors are elaborated in this section. The situation that the first model is true and the second model has been estimated can be compared with the start of 'general to specific modelling'.

Before these two situations are discussed the algebraic expressions (7.4) and (7.5) will be introduced, which are useful expressions for examining the properties of the OLS estimator in both the situations. Write model (7.2) in the partioned form:

$$y = \begin{pmatrix} X_1 & X_2 \end{pmatrix} \begin{pmatrix} \beta_1 \\ \beta_2 \end{pmatrix} + u.$$

Then the OLS estimator for all the parameters is written in partioned form as:

$$\begin{pmatrix} \widehat{\beta}_1 \\ \widehat{\beta}_2 \end{pmatrix} = \left(\begin{pmatrix} X_1 & X_2 \end{pmatrix}' \begin{pmatrix} X_1 & X_2 \end{pmatrix} \right)^{-1} \begin{pmatrix} X_1 & X_2 \end{pmatrix}' y. \tag{7.3}$$

It is possible to derive individual expressions for the subvectors $\widehat{\beta}_1$ and $\widehat{\beta}_2$ in equation (7.3). These expressions do not have any practical relevancy but are useful for the theoretical analysis. The expressions are:

$$\widehat{\beta}_1 = (X_1' M_{X_2} X_1)^{-1} X_1' M_{X_2} y, \tag{7.4}$$
$$\widehat{\beta}_2 = (X_2' M_{X_1} X_2)^{-1} X_2' M_{X_1} y. \tag{7.5}$$

Proof   If model (7.2) has been estimated with OLS, then the estimated model is written as:

$$y = X_1\widehat{\beta}_1 + X_2\widehat{\beta}_2 + e. \tag{7.6}$$

Define

$$\mathbf{M}_{X_1} = \mathbf{I}_n - \mathbf{X}_1 \left(\mathbf{X}_1'\mathbf{X}_1\right)^{-1} \mathbf{X}_1'$$

and multiply the estimated equation (7.6) with $\mathbf{M}_{X_1}$ on the left:

$$\mathbf{M}_{X_1}\mathbf{y} = \mathbf{M}_{X_1}\mathbf{X}_1\widehat{\beta}_1 + \mathbf{M}_{X_1}\mathbf{X}_2\widehat{\beta}_2 + \mathbf{M}_{X_1}\mathbf{e}.$$

Remember the property that $\mathbf{M}_{X_1}\mathbf{X}_1 = \mathbf{0}$, and observe that:

$$\begin{aligned}\mathbf{M}_{X_1}\mathbf{e} &= \left(\mathbf{I}_n - \mathbf{X}_1 \left(\mathbf{X}_1'\mathbf{X}_1\right)^{-1} \mathbf{X}_1'\right) \mathbf{e} \\ &= \mathbf{I}_n\mathbf{e} - \mathbf{0} \\ &= \mathbf{e}.\end{aligned}$$

Because the residuals and explanatory variables are orthogonal, $\mathbf{X}_1'\mathbf{e} = \mathbf{0}$. Using these properties gives the equation:

$$\mathbf{M}_{X_1}\mathbf{y} = \mathbf{M}_{X_1}\mathbf{X}_2\widehat{\beta}_2 + \mathbf{e}. \tag{7.7}$$

Multiply both sides of the equation with $\mathbf{X}_2'$ on the left:

$$\begin{aligned}\mathbf{X}_2'\mathbf{M}_{X_1}\mathbf{y} &= \mathbf{X}_2'\mathbf{M}_{X_1}\mathbf{X}_2\widehat{\beta}_2 + \mathbf{X}_2'\mathbf{e} \\ \mathbf{X}_2'\mathbf{M}_{X_1}\mathbf{y} &= \mathbf{X}_2'\mathbf{M}_{X_1}\mathbf{X}_2\widehat{\beta}_2,\end{aligned}$$

where the property is used that $\mathbf{X}_2'$ and $\mathbf{e}$ are orthogonal too. Provided that $\left(\mathbf{X}_2'\mathbf{M}_X\mathbf{X}_2\right)$ is a non-singular matrix, the expression (7.5) for the subvector $\widehat{\beta}_2$ is obtained:

$$\widehat{\beta}_2 = \left(\mathbf{X}_2'\mathbf{M}_{X_1}\mathbf{X}_2\right)^{-1} \mathbf{X}_2'\mathbf{M}_{X_1}\mathbf{y}.$$

By defining $\mathbf{M}_{X_2}$:

$$\mathbf{M}_{X_2} = \mathbf{I}_n - \mathbf{X}_2 \left(\mathbf{X}_2'\mathbf{X}_2\right)^{-1} \mathbf{X}_2',$$

the expression (7.4) for the subvector $\widehat{\beta}_1$ can be derived in a similar way:

$$\widehat{\beta}_1 = \left(\mathbf{X}_1'\mathbf{M}_{X_2}\mathbf{X}_1\right)^{-1} \mathbf{X}_1'\mathbf{M}_{X_2}\mathbf{y}.$$

So, the expressions (7.4) and (7.5) are the subvectors of expression (7.3).

Modelling from small to large; not a recommended procedure

First we look at the situation that model (7.2) is true but model (7.1) has been estimated. In other words, the model has been specified too small. It is easy to demonstrate that the OLS estimator for the parameter vector β_1 is biased and inconsistent. The parameter vector β_1 is estimated as:

$$\widehat{\beta}_1 = (\mathbf{X}_1'\mathbf{X}_1)^{-1}\mathbf{X}_1'\mathbf{y}$$
$$= (\mathbf{X}_1'\mathbf{X}_1)^{-1}\mathbf{X}_1'(\mathbf{X}_1\beta_1 + \mathbf{X}_2\beta_2 + \mathbf{u})$$
$$= \beta_1 + (\mathbf{X}_1'\mathbf{X}_1)^{-1}\mathbf{X}_1'\mathbf{X}_2\beta_2 + (\mathbf{X}_1'\mathbf{X}_1)^{-1}\mathbf{X}_1'\mathbf{u}.$$

The expectation of $\widehat{\beta}_1$ is (the explanatory variables are assumed to be exogenous):

$$E\widehat{\beta}_1 = \beta_1 + (\mathbf{X}_1'\mathbf{X}_1)^{-1}\mathbf{X}_1'\mathbf{X}_2\beta_2 + (\mathbf{X}_1'\mathbf{X}_1)^{-1}\mathbf{X}_1' \cdot E\mathbf{u}$$
$$= \beta_1 + (\mathbf{X}_1'\mathbf{X}_1)^{-1}\mathbf{X}_1'\mathbf{X}_2\beta_2$$
$$\neq \beta_1.$$

This proves that the OLS estimator is biased and inconsistent as the bias does not reduce to zero when the sample size increases. The residuals will be highly autocorrelated as the variables from $\mathbf{X}_2$ are included in the disturbance term. This implies that the Wald t- and F-tests cannot be used to find a correct model. An LM-test can be applied, but that test will not give specific information about the individual specified variables. No conclusion can be drawn from the OLS estimation result. Therefore, it is *not* a recommended procedure.

Modelling from large to small, a recommended procedure

With the notational result from (7.4) and (7.5) it is easy to prove that the parameter vector is unbiased and consistently estimated in a model which has been specified with too many variables. It can be proved that:

$$E\begin{pmatrix} \widehat{\beta}_1 \\ \widehat{\beta}_2 \end{pmatrix} = \begin{pmatrix} \beta_1 \\ 0 \end{pmatrix}, \tag{7.8}$$

when model (7.1) is true and model (7.2) has been estimated.

To show (7.8) we consider the two subvectors in (7.8) separately. First, look at the subvector $\widehat{\beta}_1$:

$$\widehat{\beta}_1 = (\mathbf{X}_1'\mathbf{M}_{X_2}\mathbf{X}_1)^{-1}\mathbf{X}_1'\mathbf{M}_{X_2}\mathbf{y}$$
$$= (\mathbf{X}_1'\mathbf{M}_{X_2}\mathbf{X}_1)^{-1}\mathbf{X}_1'\mathbf{M}_{X_2}(\mathbf{X}_1\beta_1 + \mathbf{u})$$
$$= \beta_1 + (\mathbf{X}_1'\mathbf{M}_{X_2}\mathbf{X}_1)^{-1}\mathbf{X}_1'\mathbf{M}_{X_2}\mathbf{u}.$$

This implies (with explanatory variables still assumed to be exogenous):

$$E\widehat{\beta}_1 = \beta_1.$$

Next, look at the second subvector $\widehat{\beta}_2$:

$$
\begin{aligned}
\widehat{\beta}_2 &= (\mathbf{X}_2'\mathbf{M}_{X_1}\mathbf{X}_2)^{-1}\mathbf{X}_2'\mathbf{M}_{X_1}\mathbf{y} \\
&= (\mathbf{X}_2'\mathbf{M}_{X_1}\mathbf{X}_2)^{-1}\mathbf{X}_2'\mathbf{M}_{X_1}(\mathbf{X}_1\beta_1+\mathbf{u}) \\
&= (\mathbf{X}_2'\mathbf{M}_{X_1}\mathbf{X}_2)^{-1}\mathbf{X}_2'\underbrace{\mathbf{M}_{X_1}\mathbf{X}_1}_{=\,0}\,\beta_1 + (\mathbf{X}_2'\mathbf{M}_{X_1}\mathbf{X}_2)^{-1}\mathbf{X}_2'\mathbf{M}_{X_1}\mathbf{u} \\
&= 0 + (\mathbf{X}_2'\mathbf{M}_{X_1}\mathbf{X}_2)^{-1}\mathbf{X}_2'\mathbf{M}_{X_1}\mathbf{u}.
\end{aligned}
$$

This implies (again the explanatory variables are assumed to be exogenous):

$$
E\widehat{\beta}_2 = 0.
$$

This result proves that in a model that has been specified with too many variables the OLS estimator remains unbiased and consistent. There is no reason for residual autocorrelation, so the Wald t- and F-tests may be used to find a correct model. One may expect that variables which do not belong to the model will have parameter estimates and t-values that are close to zero. This demonstrates that the 'general to specific modelling' strategy is a good one.

If lagged variables have been included in the model, the results obtained above are asymptotically valid. The estimates of the parameters β_1 in model (7.2) are less efficient when too many variables have been specified. In that situation we have:

$$
Var\left(\widehat{\beta}_1\right) = \sigma_u^2\left(\mathbf{X}_1'\mathbf{M}_{X_2}\mathbf{X}_1\right)^{-1}.
$$

It can be shown that the difference between the covariance matrix $\sigma_u^2\left(\mathbf{X}_1'\mathbf{M}_{X_2}\mathbf{X}_1\right)^{-1}$ and the actual covariance matrix $\sigma_u^2\left(\mathbf{X}'\mathbf{X}\right)^{-1}$ of the correct model is a positive definite matrix. The variance σ_u^2 has been biasedly estimated because the wrong number of degrees of freedom has been used $(n - K_1 - K_2)$ instead of $(n - K_1)$.

7.3 Prediction

Assumptions

One of the things that can be done with an estimated model is forecasting or policy simulation. In this section, the computation and properties of post-sample predictions are considered by using the estimated linear model. (See, for example, Clemens and Hendry (1998) for a detailed analysis of this subject.) The econometric model can be used for prediction purposes when the assumptions which have been made in the sample period remain unchanged in the prediction period. Although it makes no difference in computing predictions with an estimated model for time-series data or with a model for cross-section data, the terminology used in this section relates more to time-series models. In general notation, the model will be used to compute an $(n_1 \times 1)$ vector $\mathbf{y}_f$ with predictions of the dependent variable. This suggests that the $(n_1 \times K)$ matrix $\mathbf{X}_f$ with future observations of the explanatory variables is known. There are two possibilities to obtain these observations:

- If the model is used for a policy simulation, then the researcher provides the data on the explanatory variables.
- If the model is used for computing post-sample forecasts of the endogenous variable, then forecasts of future values of the explanatory variables have to be computed too; this can be done by using ARIMA-models for these variables (see Chapter 14).

It is clear that the predictions of $\mathbf{y}_f$ will be computed for given $\mathbf{X}_f$ by using the OLS estimates of the parameters from the sample period. Then the predictor $\widehat{\mathbf{y}}_f$ is defined as:

$$\widehat{\mathbf{y}}_f = \mathbf{X}_f \widehat{\boldsymbol{\beta}}.$$

First, it is necessary to check which additional assumptions have to be made to know that this is a correct procedure. Secondly, the properties of the predictor $\widehat{\mathbf{y}}_f$ have to be studied. The first aspect can be summarised by the following statement for time-series data.

The assumptions that have been made about the model for the sample period, have to be valid for the model in the prediction period too.

If the assumption is realistic that the economy, and so the structure of the model, will not change in the near future it makes sense to use the estimated model for forecasting. The assumptions are mathematically simply formulated as follows. The model for the n sample data is:

$$\mathbf{y} = \mathbf{X}\boldsymbol{\beta} + \mathbf{u}, \text{ with } \mathbf{u} \sim N\left(\mathbf{0}, \sigma_u^2 \mathbf{I}_n\right)$$

and the model for the n_1 future data is:

$$\mathbf{y}_f = \mathbf{X}_f \boldsymbol{\beta} + \mathbf{u}_f, \text{ with } \mathbf{u}_f \sim N\left(\mathbf{0}, \sigma_u^2 \mathbf{I}_{n_1}\right).$$

Both models are identical and the disturbances $\mathbf{u}$ and $\mathbf{u}_f$ are independent. The same parameter vector $\boldsymbol{\beta}$ and disturbance variance σ_u^2 have been specified, and identical statistical properties are assumed in the sample period and in the future period.

Prediction intervals

The presentation of only predicted values of the endogenous variable gives too little information. The quality of the result is clearer when the predictions are published with some confidence interval. However, that is not possible. You can estimate a parameter and compute, for example, a 95% confidence interval around the estimate. A forecast is not an estimate of a parameter, but a prediction of a stochastic variable. Therefore, a new terminology is introduced: *prediction intervals*. Prediction intervals give information about the accuracy of the computed forecasts a priori, and can be used a posteriori, when realisations of the forecasts are known, to test the assumption that the structure of the model has not changed in the prediction period.

The *prediction error* $\mathbf{f}$ is the basis for the derivation of the prediction interval. Define the $(n_1 \times 1)$ vector $\mathbf{f}$ with prediction errors as:

$$\mathbf{f} = \mathbf{y}_f - \widehat{\mathbf{y}}_f.$$

Rewrite the error as follows:

$$\begin{aligned}
\mathbf{f} &= \mathbf{X}_f \boldsymbol{\beta} + \mathbf{u}_f - \mathbf{X}_f \widehat{\boldsymbol{\beta}} \\
&= \mathbf{X}_f \left(\boldsymbol{\beta} - \widehat{\boldsymbol{\beta}} \right) + \mathbf{u}_f.
\end{aligned} \tag{7.9}$$

The prediction error consists of two components: the sampling error $\left(\boldsymbol{\beta} - \widehat{\boldsymbol{\beta}} \right)$ and the future disturbances $\mathbf{u}_f$. The distribution of the prediction error will be used for the computation of *prediction intervals*. Because $\mathbf{f}$ is a linear expression in $\widehat{\boldsymbol{\beta}}$ and $\mathbf{u}_f$, which are normally distributed variables, $\mathbf{f}$ is normally distributed too. Next we have to determine the expectation and variance of $\mathbf{f}$. First, it is shown that the two components of $\mathbf{f}$ are independent:

$$\begin{aligned}
\widehat{\boldsymbol{\beta}} &= \boldsymbol{\beta} + (\mathbf{X}'\mathbf{X})^{-1} \mathbf{X}'\mathbf{u} \Longrightarrow \\
\mathbf{X}_f \left(\boldsymbol{\beta} - \widehat{\boldsymbol{\beta}} \right) &= -\mathbf{X}_f (\mathbf{X}'\mathbf{X})^{-1} \mathbf{X}'\mathbf{u}.
\end{aligned}$$

The following $(n_1 \times n_1)$ covariance matrix is zero:

$$\begin{aligned}
Cov \left(\mathbf{X}_f \left(\boldsymbol{\beta} - \widehat{\boldsymbol{\beta}} \right), \mathbf{u}_f \right) &= -\mathbf{X}_f (\mathbf{X}'\mathbf{X})^{-1} \mathbf{X}' \cdot Cov(\mathbf{u}, \mathbf{u}_f) \\
&= \mathbf{0}, \text{ as } Cov(\mathbf{u}, \mathbf{u}_f) = \mathbf{0}.
\end{aligned}$$

Next determine the expectation and variance of $\mathbf{f}$.

$$\begin{aligned}
E(\mathbf{f}) &= E \left(\mathbf{X}_f (\boldsymbol{\beta} - \widehat{\boldsymbol{\beta}}) + \mathbf{u}_f \right) \\
&= \mathbf{X}_f \boldsymbol{\beta} - \mathbf{X}_f \boldsymbol{\beta} + \mathbf{0} \\
&= \mathbf{0}.
\end{aligned}$$

Because the two components are independent we get the following expression for the variance:

$$\begin{aligned}
Var(\mathbf{f}) &= Var \left(\mathbf{X}_f \left(\boldsymbol{\beta} - \widehat{\boldsymbol{\beta}} \right) \right) + Var(\mathbf{u}_f) \\
&= Var \left(-\mathbf{X}_f \widehat{\boldsymbol{\beta}} \right) + Var(\mathbf{u}_f) \\
&= -\mathbf{X}_f \cdot Var \left(\widehat{\boldsymbol{\beta}} \right) \cdot (-\mathbf{X}'_f) + Var(\mathbf{u}_f) \\
&= \mathbf{X}_f \cdot \sigma_u^2 (\mathbf{X}'\mathbf{X})^{-1} \cdot \mathbf{X}'_f + \sigma_u^2 \mathbf{I}_{n_1} \\
&= \sigma_u^2 \left(\mathbf{I}_{n_1} + \mathbf{X}_f (\mathbf{X}'\mathbf{X})^{-1} \mathbf{X}'_f \right).
\end{aligned} \tag{7.10}$$

This implies the following normal distribution for the prediction error $\mathbf{f}$:

$$\mathbf{f} \sim N\left(\mathbf{0}, \sigma_u^2 \left(\mathbf{I}_{n_1} + \mathbf{X}_f \left(\mathbf{X}'\mathbf{X}\right)^{-1} \mathbf{X}_f'\right)\right). \tag{7.11}$$

Notice that all the assumptions of the linear model have been used. The explanatory variables are assumed to be exogenous; with lagged-dependent variables the results are asymptotic in this section.

As before with the distribution of the OLS estimator, the unknown σ_u^2 has to be eliminated to make it possible to compute a prediction interval. Again, this will be done by using the definitions of the t- and F-distributions.

From (7.11) it follows that the χ^2-distribution for the quadratic form of the prediction error is:

$$\frac{\mathbf{f}' \left(\mathbf{I}_{n_1} + \mathbf{X}_f \left(\mathbf{X}'\mathbf{X}\right)^{-1} \mathbf{X}_f'\right)^{-1} \mathbf{f}}{\sigma_u^2} \sim \chi^2(n_1). \tag{7.12}$$

The disturbance variance σ_u^2 is eliminated by using the χ^2-distribution of the sum of squared residuals again:

$$(n - K) \frac{\widehat{\sigma}_u^2}{\sigma_u^2} \sim \chi^2(n - K). \tag{7.13}$$

This is possible, provided that the prediction error $\mathbf{f}$ and the residual vector $\mathbf{e}$ are independently distributed. This property is shown by using equation (7.9):

$$\mathbf{f} = \mathbf{X}_f \left(\boldsymbol{\beta} - \widehat{\boldsymbol{\beta}}\right) + \mathbf{u}_f$$
$$= -\mathbf{X}_f \left(\mathbf{X}'\mathbf{X}\right)^{-1} \mathbf{X}'\mathbf{u} + \mathbf{u}_f$$

and

$$\mathbf{e} = \mathbf{M}_x \mathbf{u}.$$

The covariance between $\mathbf{f}$ and $\mathbf{e}$ can be computed as:

$$Cov(\mathbf{f}, \mathbf{e}) = -\mathbf{X}_f \left(\mathbf{X}'\mathbf{X}\right)^{-1} \mathbf{X}' \cdot Var(\mathbf{u}) \cdot \mathbf{M}_X' + Cov\left(\mathbf{u}_f, \mathbf{u}\right) \cdot \mathbf{M}_X'$$
$$= -\mathbf{X}_f \left(\mathbf{X}'\mathbf{X}\right)^{-1} \mathbf{X}' \cdot Var(\mathbf{u}) \cdot \mathbf{M}_X'$$
$$= -\sigma_u^2 \mathbf{X}_f \left(\mathbf{X}'\mathbf{X}\right)^{-1} \mathbf{X}'\mathbf{M}_x'$$
$$= -\sigma_u^2 \mathbf{X}_f \left(\mathbf{X}'\mathbf{X}\right)^{-1} \cdot \mathbf{0}$$
$$= \mathbf{0}.$$

If an individual forecast has been computed, divide (7.11) expressed in one prediction error, by (7.13) to get, for example, a 95% *prediction interval* for the forecast by using the t-distribution.

If Y_{n+1} has been predicted by $\widehat{Y}_{n+1}$, we have a prediction error f_{n+1} that is distributed as:

$$f_{n+1} \sim N\left(0, \sigma_u^2\left(1 + \mathbf{x}'_{n+1}\left(\mathbf{X}'\mathbf{X}\right)^{-1}\mathbf{x}_{n+1}\right)\right).$$

The $(K \times 1)$ vector $\mathbf{x}_{n+1}$ is a vector with future values of the explanatory variables. Next standardise f_{n+1}:

$$\frac{f_{n+1}}{\sigma_u\sqrt{\left(1 + \mathbf{x}'_{n+1}\left(\mathbf{X}'\mathbf{X}\right)^{-1}\mathbf{x}_{n+1}\right)}} \sim N\left(0, 1\right).$$

Divide this distribution by the distribution 7.13 to get a Student t-distributed statistic:

$$\frac{f_{n+1}}{\widehat{\sigma}_u\sqrt{\left(1 + \mathbf{x}'_{n+1}\left(\mathbf{X}'\mathbf{X}\right)^{-1}\mathbf{x}_{n+1}\right)}} \sim t\left(n - K\right).$$

Define the standard error of f_{n+1} as $se\left(f_{n+1}\right)$ for notational convenience:

$$se\left(f_{n+1}\right) = \widehat{\sigma}_u\sqrt{\left(1 + \mathbf{x}'_{n+1}\left(\mathbf{X}'\mathbf{X}\right)^{-1}\mathbf{x}_{n+1}\right)}. \tag{7.14}$$

Then the 95% prediction interval for Y_{n+1} can be written as

$$\widehat{Y}_{n+1} - t_{0.025}\left(n - K\right)\cdot se\left(f_{n+1}\right) \leq Y_{n+1} \leq \widehat{Y}_{n+1} + t_{0.025}\left(n - K\right)\cdot se(f_{n+1}). \tag{7.15}$$

Notice once more that this interval is not a *confidence interval*. A confidence interval is computed for a parameter. The prediction interval is an interval for the variable Y_{n+1}, which is a stochastic variable. The standard errors (7.14) are computed in EViews. However the prediction interval (7.15) is not plotted by EViews, but instead the interval

$$\widehat{Y}_{n+1} - 2\cdot se\left(f_{n+1}\right) \leq Y_{n+1} \leq \widehat{Y}_{n+1} + 2\cdot se\left(f_{n+1}\right)$$

is plotted (see Figure 7.2 later).

In case an $(n_1 \times 1)$ vector $\widehat{\mathbf{y}}_f$ of predictions has been computed, a prediction interval for the vector $\mathbf{y}_f$ can be determined by dividing both χ^2-distributions (7.12) and (7.13), to get bounds with the following F-statistics:

$$\frac{\left(\mathbf{f}'\left(\mathbf{I}_{n_1} + \mathbf{X}_f\left(\mathbf{X}'\mathbf{X}\right)^{-1}\mathbf{X}'_f\right)^{-1}\mathbf{f}\right)/n_1}{\widehat{\sigma}_u^2} \overset{H_0}{\sim} F(n_1, n - K). \tag{7.16}$$

These F-values can also be used in retrospect when the observations Y_{n+i} have been realised and the prediction errors $\mathbf{f}$ can be computed. Then they are used as test statistics to test the null hypothesis that the model structure has not been changed in the forecasting period. The test is called a *forecast test*. The F-values are often computed in software packages. In EViews an alternative form of this test is computed that is called the *Chow forecast test* (see the end of this section for a discussion of this test).

Estimation of the mean of the dependent variable in the prediction period

Forecasting n_1 values of the stochastic variable Y with $\hat{\mathbf{y}}_f$ is equivalent to estimating the mean $E(\mathbf{y}_f)$, which is a parameter. For the forecast $\mathbf{y}_f$ a *forecasting interval* has been determined and for $E(\mathbf{y}_f)$ a *confidence interval* can be computed. In practice, the forecasting interval is mainly used. The predictor $\hat{\mathbf{y}}_f$ can be shown to be an unbiased estimator of $E(\mathbf{y}_f)$. We know already that it is an *unbiased predictor* (the new terminology) of $\mathbf{y}_f$ because the expectation of the prediction error is zero.

The distribution of $\hat{\mathbf{y}}_f$ has a smaller variance than the distribution of the prediction error $\mathbf{f}$. The first two moments of $\hat{\mathbf{y}}_f$ are:

$$E(\hat{\mathbf{y}}_f) = E\left(\mathbf{X}_f\hat{\boldsymbol{\beta}}\right)$$
$$= \mathbf{X}_f\boldsymbol{\beta}$$
$$Var(\hat{\mathbf{y}}_f) = Var\left(\mathbf{X}_f\hat{\boldsymbol{\beta}}\right)$$
$$= \mathbf{X}_f \cdot Var\left(\hat{\boldsymbol{\beta}}\right) \cdot \mathbf{X}_f'$$
$$= \sigma_u^2 \mathbf{X}_f (\mathbf{X}'\mathbf{X})^{-1} \mathbf{X}_f'. \tag{7.17}$$

Compare this expression (7.17) with the variance of $\mathbf{f}$ in (7.10)! So the distribution of $\hat{\mathbf{y}}_f$ is:

$$\hat{\mathbf{y}}_f \sim N\left(\mathbf{X}_f\boldsymbol{\beta}, \sigma_u^2 \mathbf{X}_f (\mathbf{X}'\mathbf{X})^{-1} \mathbf{X}_f'\right).$$

This distribution can be used, for example, when estimating the mean sales of any product in the next period with a 95% confidence interval.

Measures of accuracy of forecasts

Two things can be done when the observations of the prediction period have been realised. A forecast test can be computed to test that the structure of the model has not been changed, but also the forecast quality of the model can be analysed with measures of accuracy. For example, the forecast quality can already be analysed when the model has been estimated for a sub-sample and has been used to forecast the last observations in the sample. Various measures have been proposed for assessing the predictive accuracy of forecasting models. We look at a number of well-known inequality measures that are computed in EViews – the root mean squared error (*RMSE*), the mean absolute error (*MAE*) and the Theil inequality coefficient (U):

$$RMSE = \sqrt{\frac{1}{n_1} \sum_{t=n+1}^{n+n_1} \left(Y_t - \widehat{Y}_{f,t}\right)^2},$$

$$MAE = \frac{1}{n_1} \sum_{t=n+1}^{n+n_1} \left|Y_t - \widehat{Y}_{f,t}\right|,$$

$$U = \sqrt{\frac{\frac{1}{n_1} \sum_{t=n+1}^{n+n_1} \left(Y_t - \widehat{Y}_{f,t}\right)^2}{\frac{1}{n_1} \sum_{t=n+1}^{n+n_1} Y_t^2}}.$$

These measures will reflect the model's forecast accuracy: large values indicate a poor forecasting performance, whereas a value of zero implies a perfect forecast. These measures are not bounded and the values of the *RMSE* and *MAE* depend on the scale of the dependent variable. They can be used as relative measures to compare forecasts produced by different models for the same series. The *U*-coefficient is also called the standardised root mean squared forecasting error (*SRMSE*).

EViews computes two more statistics which are scale invariant: the mean absolute percentage error (*MAPE*) and another Theil inequality coefficient, *THEIL*.

$$MAPE = \frac{1}{n_1} \sum_{t=n+1}^{n+n_1} \left|\frac{Y_t - \widehat{Y}_{f,t}}{Y_t}\right|,$$

$$THEIL = \frac{\sqrt{\frac{1}{n_1} \sum_{t=n+1}^{n+n_1} \left(Y_t - \widehat{Y}_{f,t}\right)^2}}{\sqrt{\frac{1}{n_1} \sum_{t=n+1}^{n+n_1} Y_t^2} + \sqrt{\frac{1}{n_1} \sum_{t=n+1}^{n+n_1} \widehat{Y}_{f,t}^2}}.$$

The value of the *THEIL*-coefficient lies between zero and one. The square of the numerator can be written as:

$$\frac{1}{n_1} \sum_{t=n+1}^{n_1} \left(Y_t - \widehat{Y}_{f,t}\right)^2 = \frac{1}{n_1} \sum_{t=n+1}^{n_1} \left(\left(Y_t - \overline{Y}\right) - \left(\widehat{Y}_{f,t} - \overline{\widehat{Y}}_f\right) + \left(\overline{Y} - \overline{\widehat{Y}}_f\right)\right)^2.$$

Squaring the terms in brackets results, after some algebra, in:

$$\frac{1}{n_1} \sum_{t=n+1}^{n+n_1} \left(Y_t - \widehat{Y}_{f,t}\right)^2 = \left(\left(\overline{Y} - \overline{\widehat{Y}}_f\right)^2 + \left(s_Y - s_{\widehat{Y}}\right)^2 + 2\left(1 - r\right) s_Y . s_{\widehat{Y}}\right),$$

where s_Y and $s_{\widehat{Y}}$ are the (biased) standard deviations of Y_t and $\widehat{Y}_{f,t}$ respectively, and r is the correlation coefficient between Y_t and $\widehat{Y}_{f,t}$. So the square of U or the square of the *RMSE* is decomposed into three components: a *bias component*, a *variance component* and a *covariance component*, representing measures of unequal central tendencies, unequal variation, and imperfect covariation. In EViews the three components are defined as:

$$Bias : \frac{\left(\overline{Y} - \overline{\widehat{Y}}_f\right)^2}{\frac{1}{n_1} \sum\limits_{t=n+1}^{n+n_1} \left(Y_t - \widehat{Y}_{f,t}\right)^2}$$

$$Variance : \frac{\left(s_Y - s_{\widehat{Y}}\right)^2}{\frac{1}{n_1} \sum\limits_{t=n+1}^{n+n_1} \left(Y_t - \widehat{Y}_{f,t}\right)^2}$$

$$Covariance : \frac{2\left(1-r\right)s_Y . s_{\widehat{Y}}}{\frac{1}{n_1} \sum\limits_{t=n+1}^{n+n_1} \left(Y_t - \widehat{Y}_{f,t}\right)^2}.$$

Forecasting with EViews

In the 'Equation' window you will find the button 'Forecast'. Click on 'Forecast' and various options can be selected in the 'Forecast' window (see Figure 7.1 later). One option concerns the method of forecasting: indicate whether static or dynamic predictions have to be calculated. If a lagged dependent variable has been specified you have to choose between a *dynamic* or a *static* simulation. Of course both procedures are identical when the model is a static model. In a dynamic model you have to choose whether the forecasted or the observed (when they are known) values will be used for the computation of multi-period ahead forecasts. In the latter situation, the static procedure computes one-period ahead forecasts. For example, assume the following estimated model:

$$\widehat{Y}_t = \widehat{\beta}_1 + \widehat{\beta}_2 X_t + \widehat{\beta}_3 Y_{t-1}.$$

Predictions can be calculated in the following two ways. First, predict Y_{n+1}:

$$\widehat{Y}_{n+1} = \widehat{\beta}_1 + \widehat{\beta}_2 X_{n+1} + \widehat{\beta}_3 Y_n$$

where Y_n is the last observation of Y in the sample period. Further, Y_{n+2} can be predicted in two different ways, by using either Y_{n+1} (if known) or $\widehat{Y}_{n+1}$:

static: $\widehat{Y}_{n+2} = \widehat{\beta}_1 + \widehat{\beta}_2 X_{n+2} + \widehat{\beta}_3 Y_{n+1},$

or dynamic: $\widehat{Y}_{n+2} = \widehat{\beta}_1 + \widehat{\beta}_2 X_{n+2} + \widehat{\beta}_3 \widehat{Y}_{n+1},$

etc.

A problem with simulations is the prediction of turning points of the variables. When the model has no information about turning points, you can miss the change and are one period behind from then on (see Figure 7.4 later). Many studies can be found on this topic in the econometrics literature. To tackle this problem, you have to find informative *leading indicators* that can be included in the model (see, for example, Chapter 9 in Clemens and Hendry (1998)). This subject will not be discussed in this introductory course in econometrics.

A second option concerns the computation of standard errors of the predictions. Indicate whether they should be computed and saved in the workfile as a new series. The calculated standard errors are the square roots of the diagonal elements of the matrix (7.10):

$$\hat{\sigma}_u^2 \left(\left(\mathbf{I}_{n_1} + \mathbf{X}_f \left(\mathbf{X}'\mathbf{X} \right)^{-1} \mathbf{X}_f' \right) \right);$$

as written in (7.14):

$$se\left(f_{n+i}\right) = \hat{\sigma}_u \sqrt{\left(1 + \mathbf{x}_{n+i}' \left(\mathbf{X}'\mathbf{X} \right)^{-1} \mathbf{x}_{n+i}\right)}, \text{ with } i = 1, \ldots, n_1.$$

With these standard errors it is possible to compute the prediction interval(s) (7.15). You have to indicate whether the predictions and standard errors are to be plotted in a graph but such a graph is not very informative. A more informative plot is discussed later on in this section. This is a picture obtained by plotting both the actual and forecasted variables on one graph, together with $t_{\alpha/2}\left(n - K\right) \times$ the standard errors. You can also mark the 'Forecast evaluation' and the prediction period can be defined. Standard forecasts are stored in a variable that takes the name of the observed variable plus an 'f' added at the end. You can change that name to a more suitable one if you want.

Next, some examples of EViews output are given. The relationship between cocoa and coffee prices has been re-estimated for the period 1960(01)–2001(05) Next P_t^{coc} has been forecasted for the period 2001(06)–2002(09). This is specified in the 'Forecast' window shown in Figure 7.1. Indicate whether the simulation is dynamic or static when a lagged dependent variable has been included in the model. Give a name for the standard errors if you wish to see them in a plot of the predictions. The standard errors are stored in a new series in the workfile (here the name *sef* has been chosen).

Predictions are computed, inequality coefficients for the observed and the predicted variables are computed, and a plot of the forecasts and $\pm 2 \times$ the standard errors is made. This result is shown in Figure 7.2.

The graph in Figure 7.2 is not really very informative. It is more interesting to plot the actual and predicted prices together with the $t_{\alpha/2}\left(n - K\right) \times$ the standard errors in one figure. This can be done in the following manner. You generate two more series, for example in the following way:

$$genr\ se\_u = lpcocoaf + 1.96 * sef,$$

$$genr\ se\_l = lpcocoaf - 1.96 * sef,$$

$$\left(t_{0.025}\left(488\right) = 1.96\right),$$

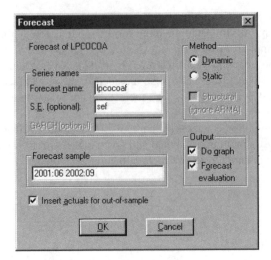

Figure 7.1: The 'Forecast' window

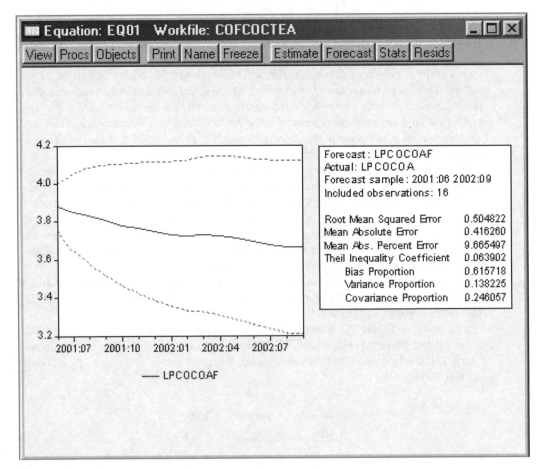

Figure 7.2: Forecast output in the 'Equation' window

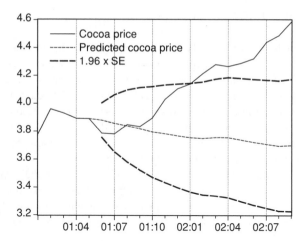

Figure 7.3: Actual and forecasted cocoa prices with $\pm 1.96 \times sef$

and make a group of *lpcocoa, lpcocoaf, se_u* and *se_l* to plot them all together. Change label names, etc. to get a nice plot of the actual (realised) and dynamic predictions, as given in Figure 7.3. The predictions from 2001(06)–2002(01) are within the bounds, but only the four short-run forecasts up to 2001(09) look acceptable.

The result of a static simulation (one-period ahead forecasting) is seen in Figure 7.4. The problem with forecasting turning points, as outlined before, is clearly seen in this figure.

From Figure 7.3 it is clear that the relationship between the cocoa and coffee prices is not very accurate in forecasting the cocoa prices. This is not strange, as the relationship does not concern a real economic model for the cocoa market, it concerns only a test for the hypothesis that the coffee market has influence on the price formation of the cocoa market.

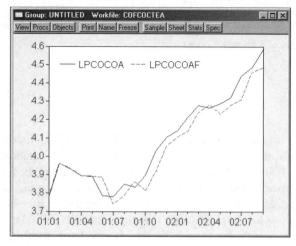

Figure 7.4: Static (one-period ahead) forecasting of $\ln\left(P_t^{coc}\right)$

The Chow forecast test

Besides the forecast test used to test the hypothesis of no structural change in the prediction period, as described above, you can use the *Chow forecast test* that has been programmed in EViews. We have n observations in the sample period and n_1 'realised' observations in the prediction period. So we have at our disposal a complete data set of $n + n_1$ observations, which is divided into n observations to be used for estimation and n_1 observations to be used for testing. In fact, the Chow test is considered as a test for *parameter constancy* but it is also a test of predictive accuracy. It is a similar test to the F-test (7.16), that is computed by estimating the parameters for the sample period with n observations and predicting the n_1 observations for the prediction period, after which the sampling distribution of the prediction errors is analysed under the null hypothesis of parameter constancy. Both tests can only be used ex-post. A second Chow test is the *Chow breakpoint test,* which tests a null hypothesis about structural breaks in the sample period; the breakpoint test is described in Section 7.5.

With the forecast test, the null hypothesis is tested that the vector β is identical both outside and within the sample period. The idea behind the Chow forecast test is as follows: do a restricted and an unrestricted regression and compute the well-known F-statistic:

$$F = \frac{(S_R - S)/g}{S/df},\qquad(7.18)$$

in the following way.

- ■ Estimate the parameters of the model for the sample with n observations, and obtain the *unrestricted* sum of squared residuals $S = \mathbf{e}_1'\mathbf{e}_1$. The number of degrees of freedom is $df = n - K$.
- ■ Next estimate the parameters of the same model with all $(n + n_1)$ observations and obtain the *restricted* sum of squared residuals $S_r = \mathbf{e}_r'\mathbf{e}_r$. The number of restrictions is $g = n_1$. The null hypothesis implies that the n_1 forecasts have been generated by the same structure.
- ■ Compute the F-statistic (7.18) that follows an F-distribution under the null hypothesis of parameter constancy:

$$F = \frac{(\mathbf{e}_r'\mathbf{e}_r - \mathbf{e}_1'\mathbf{e}_1)/n_1}{\mathbf{e}_1'\mathbf{e}_1/(n-K)} \overset{H_0}{\sim} F(n_1, n-K).\qquad(7.19)$$

However, it is not necessary to compute the regressions yourself, as in EViews the test (7.19) is found in the 'Equation' window under 'View', 'Stability Tests', 'Chow Forecast Test' (see Figure 7.5 for the opening window). The start of the forecasting period 2001(06) has been used to test the null hypothesis that the assumptions made in the sample period before June 2001 are still valid in the forecasting period after June 2001.

The Chow forecast test yields the output partially reproduced in Figure 7.6. The null hypothesis is not rejected at a 5% significance level, with a p-value of 9.10%. See the EViews User Guide for an explanation of the 'Log-likelihood ratio test' that is also reported in the output.

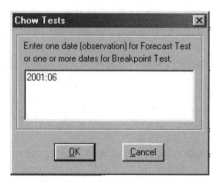

Figure 7.5:   Starting the Chow forecast test

Figure 7.6:   Output from the Chow forecast test

7.4   Multicollinearity

One more problem that you encounter when estimating the parameters of the linear model is the *multicollinearity* problem. Multicollinearity is a data problem, it has nothing to do with the violation of statistical assumptions. Multicollinearity influences the accuracy of the parameter estimates. Problems caused by multicollinearity are of a computational nature. For this introductory course it is sufficient to demonstrate the computational problem by giving some examples of the consequences. The explanatory variables are called multicollinear when they are highly correlated. In fact, they are always correlated, but serious correlation might give problems. The following problems will be highlighted.

- ■ The parameter estimates become inaccurate. The covariance matrix of the OLS estimator is:

$$Var\left(\hat{\beta}\right) = \sigma_u^2 \left(\mathbf{X}'\mathbf{X}\right)^{-1}.$$

If the correlation between some variables goes to 1, then the matrix $\mathbf{X}'\mathbf{X}$ is nearly singular and the determinant, $\det(\mathbf{X}'\mathbf{X})$, reduces to zero. The inverse matrix $\left(\mathbf{X}'\mathbf{X}\right)^{-1}$ can be written as:

$$\left(\mathbf{X}'\mathbf{X}\right)^{-1} = \frac{1}{\det\left(\mathbf{X}'\mathbf{X}\right)} \cdot adj\left(\mathbf{X}'\mathbf{X}\right),$$

where the last component is the adjugate or adjoint matrix. So the elements of the inverse matrix will increase as the correlation between explanatory variables increases, implying large standard errors of the parameter estimates.
- ■ Large standard errors result in small t-values; so be careful with the exclusion of variables because of low t-values only! Serious bias problems can be expected when the deleted variables belong to the model. When that is true, correlation exists between explanatory variables in the systematic part of the model and the disturbance term that contains the omitted variables.
- ■ The sample bias can become so large that the estimated coefficients get the incorrect sign.

In the second edition of Johnston (1972: pp.160–163), an example is found that very clearly clarifies the consequences of this problem. In the later editions (third and fourth) of Johnston this example is no longer found. The example starts with a model in deviation form $(x_{ti} = X_{ti} - \overline{X}_i)$:

$$y_t = \beta_2 x_{t2} + \beta_3 x_{t3} + (u_t - \overline{u}),$$

and suppose:

$$x_{t3} = \alpha x_{t2} + v_t,$$

and state for reasons of simplicity:

$$\sum x_{t2}^2 = \sum x_{t3}^2 = 1, \ \sum v_t = 0, \text{ and } \sum v_t x_{t2} = 0.$$

This makes the correlation coefficient r_{23} between x_{t2} and x_{t3} equal to α:

$$r_{23} = \frac{\sum x_{t2} x_{t3}}{\sqrt{\sum x_{t2}^2} \cdot \sqrt{\sum x_{t3}^2}} = \sum x_{t2}(\alpha x_{t2} + v_t) = \alpha.$$

Compute $(\mathbf{X'X})$ and its inverse matrix $(\mathbf{X'X})^{-1}$:

$$(\mathbf{X'X}) = \begin{pmatrix} \sum x_{t2}^2 & \sum x_{t2}x_{t3} \\ \sum x_{t2}x_{t3} & \sum x_{t3}^2 \end{pmatrix} = \begin{pmatrix} 1 & \alpha \\ \alpha & 1 \end{pmatrix},$$

$$(\mathbf{X'X})^{-1} = \frac{1}{1-\alpha^2} \begin{pmatrix} 1 & -\alpha \\ -\alpha & 1 \end{pmatrix}.$$

Next compute the variance-covariance matrix of the OLS estimator:

$$\widehat{Var(\beta)} = \hat{\sigma}_u^2 (\mathbf{X'X})^{-1} = \frac{\hat{\sigma}_u^2}{1-\alpha^2} \begin{pmatrix} 1 & -\alpha \\ -\alpha & 1 \end{pmatrix}.$$

The last expression shows that the variances of the estimates go to infinity when $\alpha \to 1$. It can be proved that $\hat{\sigma}_u^2$ is not affected by the multicollinearity. Compute the sample bias for the parameter estimates of this model:

$$\hat{\beta} = \beta + (\mathbf{X'X})^{-1} \mathbf{X'u},$$

$$\begin{pmatrix} \hat{\beta}_2 \\ \hat{\beta}_3 \end{pmatrix} = \begin{pmatrix} \beta_2 \\ \beta_3 \end{pmatrix} + \frac{1}{1-\alpha^2} \begin{pmatrix} 1 & -\alpha \\ -\alpha & 1 \end{pmatrix} \begin{pmatrix} \sum x_{t2}u_t \\ \sum x_{t3}u_t \end{pmatrix}.$$

Continue for $\hat{\beta}_2$ only:

$$\hat{\beta}_2 = \beta_2 + \frac{1}{1-\alpha^2} \left(\sum x_{t2}u_t - \alpha \sum x_{t3}u_t \right)$$

$$= \beta_2 + \frac{1}{1-\alpha^2} \left(\sum x_{t2}u_t - \alpha \sum (\alpha x_{t2} + v_t) u_t \right)$$

$$= \beta_2 + \frac{1}{1-\alpha^2} \sum x_{t2}u_t - \frac{\alpha^2}{1-\alpha^2} \sum x_{t2}u_t - \frac{\alpha}{1-\alpha^2} \sum v_t u_t$$

$$= \beta_2 + \sum x_{t2}u_t - \frac{\alpha^2}{1-\alpha^2} \sum v_t u_t.$$

Suppose that $\beta_2 > 0$, $\sum v_t u_t > 0$, then:

$$\frac{-\alpha^2}{1-\alpha^2} \sum v_t u_t \to -\infty \text{ if } \alpha \to 1.$$

So, it is quite possible that $\hat{\beta}_2 < 0$ for some α as the last term will dominate the other two terms. The same can be demonstrated for $\hat{\beta}_3$.

If, for example, $\beta_2 > 0$, and $\sum v_t u_t < 0$ then:

$$\frac{-\alpha^2}{1-\alpha^2} \sum v_t u_t \to +\infty \text{ if } \alpha \to 1.$$

Then the estimate $\widehat{\beta}_2$ gets high positive values, which is unrealistic from an economic point of view.

Two questions remain: how is multicollinearity detected? and what can we do about it? To detect multicollinearity problems in practice you can look at the following symptoms.

- High correlation coefficients in the correlation matrix of the variables that is computed as part of the data analysis.
- Unexpectedly large standard errors and so low t-values of the estimated parameters.
- Wrong signs or implausible magnitudes of parameter estimates for economic reasons.
- Very unstable parameter estimates. Compute recursive coefficients to observe this possible phenomenon. (See, for example, Greene (2000) p.257 for an empirical example.) One can use the included data file in Greene to compute recursive estimates for observing the effect of multicollinearity.

What can be done when the estimation results have been influenced by multicollinearity? Multicollinearity can be reduced by restricting parameters, for example, by giving a parameter of one of the multicollinear variables a value, based on knowledge from related publications published by other authors, or from the economic theory, and estimating the remaining parameters. In the case of lagged explanatory variables you can expect correlation between the lags, similar to our relationship between cocoa and coffee prices. Three lags of P_t^{coc} have been specified: for example, the first three autocorrelation coefficients of the cocoa prices are:

$$r\left(P_t^{coc}, P_{t-1}^{coc}\right) = 0.990$$

$$r\left(P_t^{coc}, P_{t-2}^{coc}\right) = 0.975$$

$$r\left(P_t^{coc}, P_{t-3}^{coc}\right) = 0.962.$$

One remedy can be the respecification of the equation with, for example, ∇X_t and X_{t-2} instead of X_t, X_{t-1} and X_{t-2} separately, if possible. For that reason, this hypothesis was tested with a Wald or LR-test in Sections 5.7 and 5.8. However be cautious, as the first-difference operator eliminates a linear trend in a variable (see Remark 7.1 below). If the linear trends in all the explanatory variables are eliminated by taking first differences, and the dependent variable also has a linear trend, then you get specification problems when that variable has not been adjusted. For more discussion see Chapter 12 and Remark 12.1 in particular.

7.5   Artificial explanatory variables

Artificial variables are variables which are not observed; their observations are deterministically determined values. The constant term, deterministic trends and dummy variables are examples of artificial explanatory variables (often called qualitative explanatory variables). It is also possible that the dependent variable is a dummy variable. That is the feature of *logit* and *probit* models. These models are introduced in Chapter 11. When an additive seasonal pattern of the dependent variable is not explained by one of the explanatory variables, dummy variables can be used to specify a seasonal pattern of the dependent variable. Dummy variables can be used to eliminate outliers, or to model different regimes, etc. In this section these variables are discussed in more detail.

The deterministic linear trend

If the dependent variable exhibits a linear trend and not one of the explanatory variables has such a pattern, then the estimation result will show a lot of residual autocorrelation. The model is not able to explain the trend. This problem is solved by including a deterministic linear trend variable in the equation as an additional explanatory variable. This yields a good fit of the equation to the sample data and possibly good short-term forecasts thereafter. The 'linear trend variable' t is defined as:

$$\mathbf{t}' = \begin{pmatrix} 1 & 2 & 3 & \dots & \dots & n \end{pmatrix}',$$

and a model specification as described above is, for example, specified as:

$$Y_t = \beta_1 + \beta_2 X_t + \beta_3 t + u_t. \tag{7.20}$$

In this example, the deterministic trend explains the trend in Y_t, whereas the economic variable X_t explains the variation of Y_t around the trend.

In EViews the linear trend is known as a variable with an @-sign: @TREND(d), with d being the start date that gets an 'observation' equal to zero. (EViews starts with zero instead of one.)

$$\mathbf{t}' = \begin{pmatrix} 0 & 1 & 2 & \dots & \dots & n-1 \end{pmatrix}',$$

this implies a different estimate for the constant term.

You then have the following options to specify a linear trend variable in the equation. If the trend variable is generated as a new series, then it is included in the workfile, for example:

$$genr\ [series\ name] = @TREND\,(d)$$
$$genr\ t = @trend(1960{:}01)$$

and specify equation (7.20) in the 'Equation Specification' window:

$$Y\ C\ X\ t.$$

But the trend variable can also be specified 'locally' in the 'Equation Specification' window. For example, equation (7.20) is specified as:

$$Y \; C \; X \; @TREND \, (1960{:}01) \, .$$

Remark 7.1

You have to be alert when specifying a deterministic trend variable in a model with differenced variables. See what happens in the following example:

$$Y_t = \beta_1 + \beta_2 X_t + \beta_3 t + u_t$$

$\downarrow$ take first differences

$$\nabla Y_t = \beta_2 \nabla X_t + \beta_3 + \nabla u_t$$

because

$$\nabla t = t - (t - 1) = 1.$$

So in a model with the variables in first differences, when the constant term (β_3) has been included explicitly, it is the coefficient of the linear trend term. The *real* constant term is present in the model in an implicit way and, as seen in Section 5.2, it can be computed as:

$$\widehat{\beta}_1 = \overline{Y} - \widehat{\beta}_2 \overline{X} - \widehat{\beta}_3 \overline{t}.$$

If an equation is estimated in first differences and a trend term does not belong to the model, no constant term should be specified in the 'Equation specification' window.

Remark 7.2

The specification with a deterministic linear trend term makes little or no economic sense in the long run. Realise that $Y_t \to \infty$ if $t \to \infty$, which is not really realistic behaviour for an economic variable. The specification of the trend yields a good fit of the model to the data in the sample period and can be used for short-run model forecasts only. This idea has an impact on the specification of the trend term. Other possibilities to model trend behaviour exist and are possibly more realistic from an economic point of view (see, for example, the discussion on deterministic and stochastic trends in Chapter 12).

What to do with outliers?

If the variable Y_t has an outlier which is not explained by one of the explanatory variables, this outlier is located back in the residuals. A dummy variable can be specified to eliminate that outlier. Be careful – this is only good practice if you know the reason for this outlier. If this is unknown, you have a problem, as it is not common sense to eliminate observations which you do not like! If an outlier is eliminated by a dummy variable, the reason why that observation is an outlier should be explained in the text of the paper. In fact, the dummy variable should have a name.

Suppose, for example, that the third observation of the dependent variable is an outlier, then specify the dummy variable D_t as:

$$\mathbf{D'} = \begin{pmatrix} 0 & 0 & 1 & 0 & \cdots & \cdots & 0 \end{pmatrix}'.$$

In EViews, generate a series equal to zero, and change the third observation in the series window. The equation is specified as:

$$Y_t = \beta_1 + \beta_2 X_t + \beta_3 D_t + u_t.$$

In this way, it is clearly visible that an observation has been eliminated. This means that the constant term is equal to β_1 for $t = 1, 2, 4, \ldots, n$ and is equal to $(\beta_1 + \beta_3)$ for $t = 3$. But, once more, only use such dummy variables if they have an economic interpretation. It does not make sense to eliminate every disturbing observation!

Seasonality

If the dependent variable exhibits a seasonal pattern and the explanatory variables do not exhibit a seasonal pattern, then the seasonal behaviour cannot be explained by these variables. When nothing is done, the seasonal pattern is found in the OLS residuals. You can choose either to model the seasonal pattern or to adjust the data for the seasonal pattern. EViews has a number of possibilities for seasonal adjustment. Double-click on the variable and click on 'Procs', 'Seasonal Adjustment' (see Figure 3.14). Next, an adjustment procedure has to be selected, such as *additive* or *multiplicative* adjustment under 'Moving Average Methods ...'. Multiplicative methods are appropriate if the series can be divided into a product of the trend component and a seasonal component, whereas additive methods are appropriate if the series can be divided into a sum of the trend component and a seasonal component. An additive seasonal pattern is rather restrictive, as it assumes that the seasonal effects in, for example, each quarter have the same magnitude. The multiplicative adjustment is probably the recommended choice in most cases. Other procedures are available in EViews such as the procedures X11 and X12 of the Census Bureau in Washington DC.

If you want to model an additive seasonal pattern, seasonal dummies can be specified. For example, in the case of quarterly data the model specification looks like:

$$Y_t = \beta_1 + \beta_2 X_t + \beta_3 D_{t1} + \beta_4 D_{t2} + \beta_5 D_{t3} + u_t.$$

The constant term β_1 is corrected in the first three quarters. The constant term is equal to $\beta_1 + \beta_3$ in quarter 1, to $\beta_1 + \beta_4$ in quarter 2, to $\beta_1 + \beta_5$ in quarter 3, and is just β_1 in quarter 4.

The matrix $\mathbf{X}$ looks like this:

$$\mathbf{X} = \begin{pmatrix} 1 & X_1 & 1 & 0 & 0 \\ 1 & X_2 & 0 & 1 & 0 \\ 1 & X_3 & 0 & 0 & 1 \\ 1 & X_4 & 0 & 0 & 0 \\ 1 & X_5 & 1 & 0 & 0 \\ 1 & X_6 & 0 & 1 & 0 \\ \vdots & \vdots & \vdots & 0 & 1 \\ \vdots & \vdots & \vdots & \vdots & 0 \\ \vdots & \vdots & \vdots & \vdots & \vdots \\ \vdots & \vdots & \vdots & \vdots & \vdots \\ \vdots & \vdots & \vdots & \vdots & \vdots \\ 1 & X_n & 0 & 0 & 0 \end{pmatrix}.$$

Observe that the rank of the matrix $\mathbf{X}$ is equal to $K - 1$ if four dummies and a constant term are included in the equation! Then $\mathbf{X}'\mathbf{X}$ is a singular matrix and OLS estimates cannot be computed.

In EViews, seasonal dummies can be generated to be included in the workfile, for example, by typing in the command line:

$$genr\ d1 = @seas\,(1)\,,\ genr\ d2 = @seas\,(2)\,,\ etc.$$

The figure d in @$seas(d)$ represents the dth season. But, just as with the trend, these dummies can also directly be specified in the 'Equation Specification' window. For example:

$$Y\ C\ X\ @seas\,(1)\ @seas\,(2)\ @seas\,(3)\,.$$

Then the workfile does not expand with more series.

Modelling different regimes

In the practice of econometric research, different regimes can be observed in a sample period. For example, when analysing the price formation on commodity markets that are ruled by an international commodity agreement (ICA), periods with an effective ICA and periods with a free-market situation can be distinguished. If the price of that particular commodity is below a certain level the agreement can become effective. A bufferstock manager can buy quantities of that commodity to stockpile during a period when the price is too low, or producers have to restrict their exports to quotas that are settled in the ICA, etc. So two different regimes ruling the market are observed in the sample. In fact, two different models are relevant to model the price formation for the different regimes. As an example, suppose that a simple model, in general notation, for the price of a commodity in periods without an effective agreement is:

$$Y_t = \beta_1 + \beta_2 X_t + u_{t1},$$

and that a model for periods with an effective agreement is:

$$Y_t = \beta_3 + \beta_4 X_t + u_{t2}.$$

The specifications of the equations are kept simple to illustrate clearly the problem and its solution. The two regimes can be specified in one equation by using a dummy variable D_t that has the value 0 if the ICA is not effective and the value 1 if the ICA is effective. For example:

$$\mathbf{d}' = \begin{pmatrix} 1 & 1 & 1 & 0 & 0 & 1 & 1 & 0 & \ldots & 1 \end{pmatrix}. \tag{7.21}$$

Then both the parameters, the intercept and the slope coefficient, have different values in the two regimes by specifying the model in the following way:

$$Y_t = \beta_1 + \beta_5 D_t + (\beta_2 + \beta_6 D_t) X_t + u_t. \tag{7.22}$$

Both the constant term and the regression coefficient are adjusted: $\beta_3 = \beta_1 + \beta_5$ and $\beta_4 = \beta_2 + \beta_6$. This equation is estimated as:

$$Y_t = \beta_1 + \beta_5 D_t + \beta_2 X_t + \beta_6 Z_t + u_t,$$

where $Z_t = D_t X_t$ is computed via a 'generate', or by specifying $D * X$ as a variable in the 'Equation specification' window. With a Wald F-test the null hypothesis:

$$H_0 : \beta_5 = \beta_6 = 0 \tag{7.23}$$

can be tested to verify that the data cannot be modelled with one model specification.

Realise that this is a restricted model, because in both regimes the variance of the disturbance term σ_u^2 is identical! If two separate regressions are performed then they will be different: σ_{u1}^2 and σ_{u2}^2.

As an example, from our own research, a picture of the residuals from an equation for the price formation of tin is given in Figure 7.7. An international tin agreement existed in the period 1976(01)–1985(06). After that period no market interventions took place.

The picture needs no comments! Modelling with the use of dummy variables is out of the question.

In EViews the dummy variable $\mathbf{d}'$ (7.21) can be created as follows.

- ∎ Genr $dummy = 0$ (or $= 1$, depending on what occurs the most) for the sample period.
- ∎ Double-click on $dummy$.

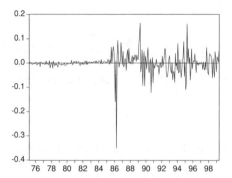

Figure 7.7:   Residuals from one model for a
sample period with two regimes

- Click in the 'Series window' the button 'Edit+/−'.
- Replace the zeros (or the ones) with ones (or zeros) for the dates that a different regime was effective.

The Chow breakpoint test

When different regimes are observed you may want to test whether they have to be modelled with different specifications or not. With the Chow breakpoint test the null hypothesis, of no structural break(s) in the sample period, will be tested. For a break at one date the test resembles the Chow forecast test, but a different null hypothesis is tested with a different test statistic (see the first example in Figure 7.8 later that can be compared with Figure 7.6 earlier). More dates can be specified for the breakpoint test. In fact it is an F-test, similar to the test in equation (7.23) $H_0 : \beta_5 = \beta_6 = 0$.

In general, suppose the sample has been divided into m sub-samples. If parameter constancy is tested, all the parameters are allowed to vary in each sub-sample. This would produce too many dummy variables for estimating the parameters of the equation. Instead of using dummies, the model is estimated for all m sub-samples. In sub-sample i we have m_i observations. So be sure that the sample size in every subset is sufficiently large so that it is possible to estimate the parameters $(m_i > K, i = 1, \ldots, m)$, otherwise the test breaks down. This results in m residual sums of squares.

Let S_R represent the RSS for the entire sample (the restricted sum of squares) and S_i the RSS in sub-sample i, then $\sum_{i=1}^{m} S_i$ is equal to the unrestricted sum of squares S in the

Equation: EQ01 Workfile: COFCOCTEA			
View Procs Objects Print Name Freeze Estimate Forecast Stats Resids			
Chow Breakpoint Test: 2001:06			
F-statistic	3.492378	Probability	0.002157
Log likelihood ratio	21.02003	Probability	0.001819

Figure 7.8:   Output of the Chow breakpoint test for one date

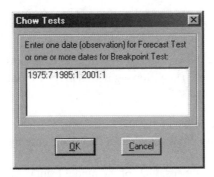

Figure 7.9: Specifying four sub-samples for the Chow breakpoint

well-known F-test:

$$F = \frac{(S_R - S)/g}{S/df},$$

with $g = (m-1)K$, and $df = n - mK$ as degrees of freedom. Test the null hypothesis H_0: no structural changes in the sample period at the specified dates, with the following F-statistic:

$$F = \frac{\left(S_R - \sum\limits_{i=1}^{m} S_i\right)/(m-1)\,K}{\left(\sum\limits_{i=1}^{m} S_i\right)/(n-mK)} \overset{H_0}{\sim} F\left((m-1)\,K, n-mK\right).$$

As usual, the F-distribution is valid if the disturbances are independently and identically normally distributed. The test is found in EViews in the equation window under 'View', 'Stability Tests', 'Chow Breakpoint Test . . .'. Two examples of the use of the test are shown in Figures 7.8 to 7.10. In the first example, the null of no structural break in June 2001 is tested (previously this date had been used as the start of the forecasting period).

The null hypothesis of no structural break is clearly rejected. Notice the different p-values in Figures 7.6 and 7.8. In the second example, the null hypothesis of identical model structures in four sub-samples of the entire sample is tested. This null hypothesis is clearly also rejected.

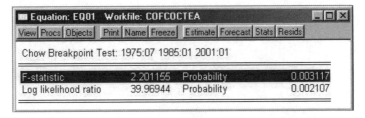

Figure 7.10:   Output of the Chow breakpoint test for more dates

7.6   Case 3: exercises with the estimated model

Case 3 concerns the various subjects that have been discussed in this chapter and is an extension of Case 2. The following points may be of interest relating to the model that has been estimated in Case 2.

- It is quite possible that the estimation result from Case 2 has suffered from multi-collinearity. Find out whether that is the case by applying the criteria mentioned in Section 7.4.
- Investigate the residuals of the model from Case 2 to ascertain whether outliers are present that can be *economically explained*. If such outliers are present then they can be eliminated by re-estimating the model by specifying one or more dummy variables. If you cannot explain an outlier, or if you do not find any outlier(s) with an interesting economic interpretation, then just report your results with supporting commentary.
- Is the structure of the model constant in the sample period? Reconsider the results of the CUSUM tests and the recursively-estimated coefficients. Look also at a graph of the residuals to search for any structural break at dates that can be explained by economic reasoning, and use the Chow breakpoint test to test the null hypothesis of no breaks.
- If non-seasonally adjusted data have been used, which is the case with Data set 4, then check whether the seasonal pattern can be considered as additive or not. Decide what to do: eliminating or modelling the seasonal variation are options. An additive seasonal pattern can be modelled by specifying quarterly dummy variables. For seasonally adjusted data, this point is not relevant.
- Re-estimate 'your model' without using the last four or eight quarters. Probably the same model specification will still satisfy, otherwise adapt the specification. With this model, compute static and dynamic forecasts for the omitted quarters and compare the predictions with the actual values according to the directions discussed in Section 7.3: graphically and by interpreting inequality coefficients. Apply the Chow forecast test.
- Append the results to your paper.

Specific Structural Models

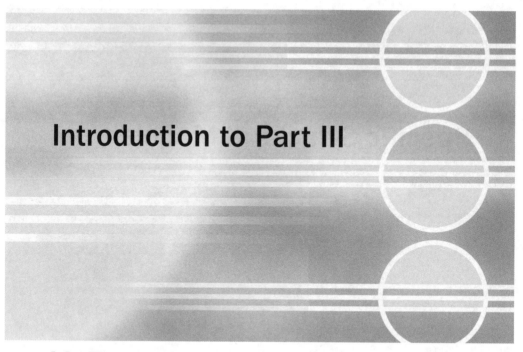

Introduction to Part III

In Part III, several special structural econometric models will be discussed. In Parts I and II sufficient subjects are discussed for a basic course in econometrics. With the subjects discussed in Part III, that basic course can be extended. Not all the subjects have to be discussed in a follow-up course; a selection can be made. Only if you choose to study the simultaneous equation model in Chapter 10 it is then also necessary to study the estimation problems in Chapter 9. In each chapter, a specific model will be introduced, after which we will show in what way its parameters can be estimated and what can be done with that model in practice.

In Chapter 8, a linear model will be introduced with different disturbance-term assumptions than have been made in Part II for the reduced-form model. The parameters of such a model can be estimated efficiently by the generalised least squares method (GLS). We also come across the first multiple equation model, the SUR (seemingly unrelated regression) model whose parameters can efficiently be estimated with GLS. The equations of a SUR model are treated as reduced-form equations in this chapter, but combining these equations in one system can improve the estimation results.

A third variant around the subject of different disturbance-term assumptions are the models with autoregressive conditional heteroskedastic disturbances, the ARCH and GARCH models.

In Chapter 9, the structural model is considered, where endogenous explanatory variables are introduced in the linear model. It is known that the OLS estimator is an inconsistent estimator for the parameters of such a model. Therefore, the two-stage least squares (2SLS) estimator will be introduced as a consistent estimator for this model. In Chapter 10, the simultaneous equation model (SEM) is introduced, which is a multiple structural equation model with endogenous and exogenous explanatory variables included in the equations.

In the last chapter of Part III, models are discussed that have a dummy variable as the dependent variable; these models have qualitative dependent variables. All the introduced models can be handled with procedures in EViews, which will be shown. Empirical cases are included in the chapters.

Chapter 8

Estimation with More General Disturbance-Term Assumptions

8.1 Introduction

In Part II, properties of the reduced-form model have been established under the assumption that the disturbances are independently and identically distributed. A number of auto-correlation and heteroskedasticity tests have been discussed to test this assumption. If autocorrelation and/or heteroskedasticity is detected, then this often has to be interpreted as the result of *specification errors* in the systematic part of the model. In Section 7.3, it was shown that the OLS estimator is biased and inconsistent in that case. There is one remedy to eliminate the violation of the disturbance-term assumptions, which is to respecify the systematic part of the model to get random residuals. It is not opportune to model the disturbance term, because the economic theory yields an economic model for the systematic part and not for the unsystematic part of the model. In Part II, it was also emphasised that the standard errors have been computed erroneously if the disturbances are autocorrelated and/or heteroskedastic. Remember that the expression

$$Var\left(\widehat{\beta}\right) = \sigma_u^2 \left(\mathbf{X'X}\right)^{-1}$$

has been obtained by making use of the assumption that

$$Var\left(\mathbf{u}\right) = \sigma_u^2 \mathbf{I}_n,$$

as was shown in Section 4.7. This substitution is not valid when autocorrelation or heteroskedasticity should belong to the data generating process (DGP), and it is certainly wrong when the model is mis-specified.

In this chapter, we will discuss models that have disturbances that are not random for obvious reasons. These reasons for systematic behaviour are of a theoretical or empirical nature. Another result from Chapter 7 is that the OLS estimator is an unbiased and/or consistent estimator when autocorrelation or heteroskedasticity is part of the DGP. The standard errors of the parameter estimates are wrong and the estimator is not efficient any more. In that situation, the generalised least squares estimator (GLS) is an estimation method that can be used to obtain efficient parameter estimates; this method also estimates parameters of a structure for the disturbance term. We will apply this method by modelling the disturbance term according to the indications from the theory or the empirical analysis. The linear model is now written as

$$y = X\beta + u, \text{ with } u \sim N\left(0, \Omega\right).$$

The $(n \times n)$ covariance matrix Ω may have unequal elements on the main diagonal (varying disturbance variances) and covariances unequal to zero. If this is a correct specification of the model then the parameters have to be estimated with the GLS estimator to get efficient estimates. Hypotheses about the form of the autocorrelation and/or the heteroskedasticity will be made to limit the number of parameters that has to be estimated.

In Section 8.2, the GLS estimator is introduced as a theoretical solution to the problem of estimating the parameters again in an efficient way. Next, a direct application of the GLS estimator is given in Section 8.3 for estimating the parameters of the Seemingly Unrelated Regression (SUR model). This is a multiple equation model where the matrix Ω is derived from the way this model has been specified. The SUR model is applied in Section 8.4 with Case 4.

Then we return to the linear single equation model. When the null hypothesis of no autocorrelation has been rejected, then we have to consider AR- or MA-disturbances. The meaning of these processes in the disturbance term for the specified model is discussed in Sections 8.5 and 8.6.

In the last section of this chapter, a brief introduction to ARCH and GARCH models is given.

8.2   The generalised least squares (GLS) estimator in theory

The GLS estimator will be derived to estimate the parameters of the following model:

$$y = X\beta + u, \text{ with } u \sim N\left(0, \Omega\right), \tag{8.1}$$

where Ω is assumed to be a known $(n \times n)$ positive definite variance-covariance matrix. Sometimes it is convenient to write the distribution of the disturbance term as follows:

$$N\left(0, \Omega\right) = N\left(0, \sigma^2\Lambda\right),$$

where σ^2 can be interpreted as a variance (u_t is autocorrelated but homoskedastic) or as a proportionality factor in the case of heteroskedasticity. The matrix Λ is assumed to be a known positive definite covariance matrix. Then its inverse matrix is positive definite also. That means that a Choleski decomposition can be applied to Λ^{-1}: it is possible to find an $(n \times n)$ non-singular lower triangular matrix C such that:

$$\Lambda^{-1} = C'C.$$

This equation can be rewritten to obtain the following property:

$$\Lambda = C^{-1}(C')^{-1}$$
$$C\Lambda C' = I_n.$$

The matrix C will be used to transform the model. Both sides of the equation are multiplied by the matrix C. The result will be a model with transformed disturbances Cu that are non-autocorrelated and homoskedastic:

$$Cy = CX\beta + Cu. \tag{8.2}$$

Derive the moments of the transformed disturbance term Cu to show the mentioned properties:

$$E(Cu) = CE(u) = 0$$
$$Var(Cu) = C \cdot Var(u) \cdot C'$$
$$= C \cdot \sigma^2 \Lambda \cdot C'$$
$$= \sigma^2 C\Lambda C'$$
$$= \sigma^2 I_n.$$

So model (8.2) satisfies the classical assumptions of no autocorrelation and no heteroskedasticity in the disturbance term. Then it follows that the OLS estimator applied to model (8.2) is an efficient estimator again. Apply OLS to equation (8.2) to get an expression for the GLS estimator.

$$\widehat{\beta}_{gls} = ((CX)'(CX))^{-1}(CX)'Cy$$
$$= (X'C'CX)^{-1}X'C'Cy$$
$$= (X'\Lambda^{-1}X)^{-1}X'\Lambda^{-1}y, \tag{8.3}$$

and analogous to OLS we get the following expression for the covariance matrix of β:

$$Var\left(\widehat{\beta}_{gls}\right) = \sigma^2\left((CX)'(CX)\right)^{-1}$$
$$= \sigma^2\left(X'\Lambda^{-1}X\right)^{-1}. \tag{8.4}$$

The sampling distribution of the GLS estimator is ($\mathbf{X}$ is exogenous):

$$\widehat{\beta}_{gls} \sim N\left(\beta, \sigma^2 \left(\mathbf{X}'\mathbf{\Lambda}^{-1}\mathbf{X}\right)^{-1}\right).$$

$Var\left(\widehat{\beta}_{gls}\right)$ can be estimated as:

$$\widehat{Var\left(\widehat{\beta}_{gls}\right)} = \widehat{\sigma}^2 \left(\mathbf{X}'\mathbf{\Lambda}^{-1}\mathbf{X}\right)^{-1}, \tag{8.5}$$

where $\widehat{\sigma}^2$, in case it is the disturbance variance, is computed from the GLS residuals:

$$\mathbf{e}_{gls} = \mathbf{y} - \mathbf{X}\widehat{\beta}_{gls} \tag{8.6}$$

$$\widehat{\sigma}^2 = \frac{1}{n-K}\mathbf{e}'_{gls}\mathbf{e}_{gls}.$$

The GLS estimator can be computed in two ways. Directly by computing the GLS estimators (8.3) and (8.5). Indirectly, the GLS estimates can be computed by estimating the transformed equation (8.2):

$$\mathbf{Cy} = \mathbf{CX}\beta + \mathbf{Cu}, \text{ with } \mathbf{Cu} \sim N\left(\mathbf{0}, \sigma^2\mathbf{I}_n\right). \tag{8.7}$$

Often $\mathbf{\Lambda}$ or $\mathbf{C}$ are unknown in practice, then it is recommended you estimate equation (8.7). In that situation, you can test, by using the tests for autocorrelation and heteroskedasticity from Chapter 6, whether the transformed disturbances $\mathbf{Cu}$ are indeed non-systematic. When the hypotheses of homoskedastic and non-autocorrelated disturbances are not rejected we consider the used matrix $\mathbf{C}$ as a feasible transformation.

8.3   The SUR model

The SUR model is a proper example of a model with autocorrelated disturbances caused by the model specification process. The disturbance term has a covariance matrix $\mathbf{\Omega}$ that originates in the manner in which the model is specified. This means that GLS is the appropriate method to efficiently estimate the parameters of the model. A SUR model is a multiple equation model with *seemingly unrelated regression equations*. It consists of equations explaining identical variables, but for different samples. For example, a number of coffee consumption equations can be estimated for various countries, or a number of production functions concerning the same product can be estimated for different companies, etc. The idea behind this model is that these equations are independent, but that correlation between the disturbance terms of the equations exists, representing identical unsystematic influences like world market developments or similar influences of economic cycles. These correlations do not influence the OLS-estimation results by equation, but a well-known statistical phenomenon is that the more information that is used, the more efficient the estimation results will be. The different equations are *seemingly unrelated*. To obtain an estimator for all the parameters of all the equations, the equations have to be written in a system as one model. To derive the specification of this model we consider m linear equations that are written as:

$$\mathbf{y}_1 = \mathbf{X}_1\boldsymbol{\beta}_1 + \mathbf{u}_1, \ \mathbf{u}_1 \sim N\left(\mathbf{0}, \sigma^2_{u_1}\mathbf{I}_n\right)$$
$$\mathbf{y}_2 = \mathbf{X}_2\boldsymbol{\beta}_2 + \mathbf{u}_2, \ \mathbf{u}_2 \sim N\left(\mathbf{0}, \sigma^2_{u_2}\mathbf{I}_n\right)$$
$$\vdots$$
$$\mathbf{y}_m = \mathbf{X}_m\boldsymbol{\beta}_m + \mathbf{u}_m, \ \mathbf{u}_m \sim N\left(\mathbf{0}, \sigma^2_{u_m}\mathbf{I}_n\right).$$

In general notation the ith equation is written as:

$$\mathbf{y}_i = \mathbf{X}_i\boldsymbol{\beta}_i + \mathbf{u}_i, \ \mathbf{u}_i \sim N\left(\mathbf{0}, \sigma^2_{u_i}\mathbf{I}_n\right), \ i = 1, \ldots, m.$$

The number of observations is equal to n in all the equations. The number of explanatory variables (K_i) may differ in each equation. This means that $\mathbf{y}_i$ and $\mathbf{u}_i$ are $(n \times 1)$ vectors, $\mathbf{X}_i$ is an $(n \times K_i)$ matrix and $\boldsymbol{\beta}_i$ is a $(K_i \times 1)$ vector. Each disturbance term is distributed as $NID\left(0, \sigma^2_{u_i}\right)$, implying that OLS, applied to each individual equation, is an (unbiased), consistent and efficient estimator, which can be written as:

$$\widehat{\boldsymbol{\beta}}_i = \left(\mathbf{X}'_i\mathbf{X}_i\right)^{-1}\mathbf{X}'_i\mathbf{y}_i$$

with variance-covariance matrix

$$Var\left(\widehat{\boldsymbol{\beta}}_i\right) = \sigma^2_{u_i}\left(\mathbf{X}'_i\mathbf{X}_i\right)^{-1}.$$

As written above, non-zero correlation between the different disturbance terms is expected. To limit the number of parameters, and not to make the model too intricate, it is usual to assume that the contemporaneous correlation is identical in each period; and that the correlation exists only contemporaneously. This is reflected in the following common notation for the variances and covariances of the disturbances, with: $\sigma_{11} = \sigma^2_{u_1}$, and $\sigma_{12} = \sigma_{u_1,u_2}$, etc.

$$cov\left(u_{ti}, u_{sj}\right) = \begin{cases} \sigma_{ij} & \text{if } t = s, \\ 0 & \text{if } t \neq s, \end{cases} \text{ with } t, s = 1, \ldots, n.$$

This can compactly be written in matrix notation as:

$$Cov\left(\mathbf{u}_i, \mathbf{u}_j\right) = \sigma_{ij}\mathbf{I}_n.$$

To combine all the equations in one model, the following vectors and matrices are defined.

$$\mathbf{y}_* = \begin{pmatrix} \mathbf{y}_1 \\ \mathbf{y}_2 \\ \vdots \\ \mathbf{y}_m \end{pmatrix}, \ \mathbf{X}_* = \begin{pmatrix} \mathbf{X}_1 & \mathbf{0} & \cdots & \mathbf{0} \\ \mathbf{0} & \mathbf{X}_2 & \cdots & \mathbf{0} \\ \vdots & \vdots & \ddots & \vdots \\ \mathbf{0} & \mathbf{0} & \cdots & \mathbf{X}_m \end{pmatrix}, \ \boldsymbol{\beta}_* = \begin{pmatrix} \boldsymbol{\beta}_1 \\ \boldsymbol{\beta}_2 \\ \vdots \\ \boldsymbol{\beta}_m \end{pmatrix}, \ \mathbf{u}_* = \begin{pmatrix} \mathbf{u}_1 \\ \mathbf{u}_2 \\ \vdots \\ \mathbf{u}_m \end{pmatrix}.$$

The vectors $\mathbf{y}_*$ and $\mathbf{u}_*$ are $(nm \times 1)$ vectors, the matrix $\mathbf{X}_*$ is an $\left(nm \times \sum_{i=1}^{m} K_i \right)$ matrix and $\boldsymbol{\beta}_*$ an $\left(\sum_{i=1}^{m} K_i \times 1 \right)$ vector. All the m equations are written in one system:

$$\mathbf{y}_* = \mathbf{X}_* \boldsymbol{\beta}_* + \mathbf{u}_*. \tag{8.8}$$

We have to know what the covariance matrix of the disturbance term $\mathbf{u}_*$ looks like. This knowledge is necessary for correctly choosing an estimator for all the parameters in the vector $\boldsymbol{\beta}_*$.

$$Var\left(\mathbf{u}_*\right) = \begin{pmatrix} Var\left(\mathbf{u}_1\right) & Cov\left(\mathbf{u}_1, \mathbf{u}_2\right) & \cdots & Cov\left(\mathbf{u}_1, \mathbf{u}_m\right) \\ Cov\left(\mathbf{u}_2, \mathbf{u}_1\right) & Var\left(\mathbf{u}_2\right) & \cdots & Cov\left(\mathbf{u}_2, \mathbf{u}_m\right) \\ \vdots & \vdots & \ddots & \vdots \\ Cov\left(\mathbf{u}_m, \mathbf{u}_1\right) & \cdots & \cdots & Var\left(\mathbf{u}_m\right) \end{pmatrix}$$

$$= \begin{pmatrix} \sigma_{11}\mathbf{I}_n & \sigma_{12}\mathbf{I}_n & \cdots & \sigma_{1m}\mathbf{I}_n \\ \sigma_{21}\mathbf{I}_n & \sigma_{22}\mathbf{I}_n & \cdots & \sigma_{2m}\mathbf{I}_n \\ \vdots & \vdots & \ddots & \vdots \\ \sigma_{m1}\mathbf{I}_n & \cdots & \cdots & \sigma_{mm}\mathbf{I}_n \end{pmatrix}$$

$$= \boldsymbol{\Omega}_*.$$

This is not a scalar matrix so the parameters of model (8.8) can be efficiently estimated with GLS. The use of the contemporaneous covariance σ_{ij} in estimating the parameters of the model will result in smaller standard errors and more efficient estimates compared to OLS by equation. The theoretical GLS estimator, according to (8.3), for this model is:

$$\widehat{\boldsymbol{\beta}}_* = \left(\mathbf{X}_*' \boldsymbol{\Omega}_*^{-1} \mathbf{X}_*\right)^{-1} \mathbf{X}_*' \boldsymbol{\Omega}_*^{-1} \mathbf{y}_*,$$

with covariance matrix according to (8.4):

$$Var\left(\widehat{\boldsymbol{\beta}}_*\right) = \left(\mathbf{X}_*' \boldsymbol{\Omega}_*^{-1} \mathbf{X}_*\right)^{-1}.$$

In practice, the matrix $\boldsymbol{\Omega}_*$ is unknown, so its parameters have to be estimated. The following feasible GLS procedure can be used to compute the SUR estimates.

- First, estimate the parameters of all the individual equations with OLS, that yields m residual vectors $\mathbf{e}_i$, with $i = 1, \ldots, m$.
- Estimate the unknown variances and covariances as follows:

$$\widehat{\sigma}_{ij} = \frac{1}{n}\mathbf{e}_i'\mathbf{e}_j = \frac{1}{n}\sum_{t=1}^{n} e_{ti}e_{tj}, \text{ with } i, j = 1, \ldots, m.$$

This is often done without making adjustments for degrees of freedom. In small samples, possible adjustments can be made by dividing through $\left(\sqrt{n-K_i}\right) \cdot \left(\sqrt{n-K_j}\right)$ instead of n.

■ Substitute these estimates into the matrix $\mathbf{\Omega}_*$ giving the matrix $\widehat{\mathbf{\Omega}}_*$, and compute the feasible GLS estimator:

$$\widehat{\beta}_* = \left(\mathbf{X}'_*\widehat{\mathbf{\Omega}}_*^{-1}\mathbf{X}_*\right)^{-1}\mathbf{X}'_*\widehat{\mathbf{\Omega}}_*^{-1}\mathbf{y}_*,$$

and covariance matrix, according to (8.5):

$$\widehat{Var\left(\widehat{\beta}_*\right)} = \left(\mathbf{X}'_*\widehat{\mathbf{\Omega}}_*^{-1}\mathbf{X}_*\right)^{-1}.$$

In the SUR model, the GLS estimator has been directly applied to estimate efficiently the parameters.

Remark 8.1
Check that the SUR estimates will be identical to the earlier obtained OLS estimates if the equations are 'really unrelated', that is when $\sigma_{ij} = 0$ for all $i \neq j$.

The SUR estimator can conveniently be computed in EViews. You have to define a system of equations (see the help function for all the information). In the EViews window click the buttons 'Objects', 'New Object', 'System', which results in the window in Figure 8.1.

Give the 'System' object a name and it is included in the workfile. Type in the 'System' window the equations according to the explicit form, and next click 'Estimate', then select 'Seemingly Unrelated Regression' as the estimation method. An example is given in Figure 8.2.

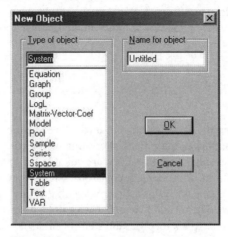

Figure 8.1: Creating the object 'system'

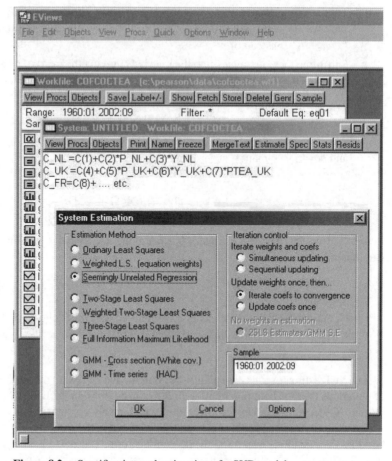

Figure 8.2:   Specification and estimation of a SUR model

Notice the other estimation procedures that are available in this window. For an example of a SUR model see, for example, Harvey (1990), where a SUR model is estimated that explains the attendance at various clubs in the English Football League.

8.4   Case 4: a SUR model for the macroeconomic data

The macroeconomic data of the five countries that accompany this book are used to estimate a SUR model in this exercise. It is interesting to compare the single-equation results with the full-model results. Two equations are suitable for this exercise: macroeconomic consumption equations or investment equations. Choose one of these equations for this case. Also, in this exercise, the OLS estimator is still the only estimator that has been discussed and will be used. The results from this case will be reconsidered in Case 6 after the model with endogenous explanatory variables has been discussed. Therefore keep the workfiles saved as you will need them again later.

The following checklist can be used to write a paper about this subject.

■ Estimate dynamic models for each of the five countries for identical sample periods in the same way as has been done in Case 2, and save the five residual variables. Of course, the residuals are not allowed to have significant autocorrelation. Re-estimate models with the White option if heteroskedasticity has been found in the residuals (see Section 8.6).

■ Compute the correlation matrix of the five residual variables to get an indication of whether or not the SUR model might improve the earlier-obtained single-equation results.

■ Open the new object 'System' and save it with any appropriate name.

■ Write the five consumption or investment equations in the explicit way in the 'System' window as shown in Figure 8.2. Use the specifications that have been found for the individual countries.

■ Estimate the parameters of all the equations with GLS by marking the SUR option. If the option OLS is selected then the single equation results are obtained again.

■ Under 'View', 'Residuals' the view option 'Correlation Matrix' (of all the residuals) is available. This can be an alternative for the procedure mentioned after the first bullet. White's estimation option is not available in the system window; neither are residual autocorrelation tests. But it is not expected that the SUR procedure generates autocorrelation in the residuals. You can look at graphs of the residuals. Under 'Procs' in the 'System' window the procedure 'Make Residuals' (for all the equations) is found. Thus it is always possible to look at the correlogram of the residuals.

■ Consider and compare all the obtained results. Are the SUR results more efficient in this case?

■ Write a clear and complete research paper.

8.5 Autocorrelated disturbances

Sometimes the GLS estimator can also be applied when the disturbance term is autocorrelated, but its use depends on the source of the autocorrelation. In case the autocorrelation exists because of a specific model specification, like the SUR model, or because of model transformations, it is a correct procedure to determine the covariance matrix Ω of the disturbances and to use GLS for getting efficient estimates of the parameters.

However, in many textbooks an AR(1) disturbance term is introduced, after an autocorrelation test (e.g. the DW-statistic) has rejected the null of no autocorrelation. That situation is utilised to show the use of GLS. Then an AR(1) model for the disturbance term is added to the model:

$$u_t = \varphi_1 u_{t-1} + v_t, \text{ with } v_t \sim NID\left(0, \sigma_v^2\right).$$

However, AR(1) residuals are often found after a mis-specified model has been estimated with OLS. Theoretical reasons for an AR(1) model are not present. So, as stated earlier: the systematic part of the model has to be respecified, and the use of the GLS estimator is not appropriate.

However, because AR(1) procedures are found in the econometrics literature and software, these procedures will briefly be mentioned here, so that you will recognise them and know not to use them.

If it is assumed that the disturbance term follows an AR(1) process, then the following matrix expressions can be derived.

$$\Omega = \sigma_u^2 \Lambda = \frac{\sigma_v^2}{1 - \varphi_1^2} \begin{pmatrix} 1 & \varphi_1 & \varphi_1^2 & \cdot & \cdot & \varphi_1^{n-1} \\ \varphi_1 & 1 & \varphi_1 & \cdot & \cdot & \varphi_1^{n-2} \\ \varphi_1^2 & \varphi_1 & 1 & \cdot & \cdot & \cdot \\ \cdot & \cdot & \cdot & \cdot & \cdot & \cdot \\ \cdot & \cdot & \cdot & \cdot & \cdot & \varphi_1 \\ \varphi_1^{n-1} & \varphi_1^{n-2} & \cdot & \cdot & \varphi_1 & 1 \end{pmatrix}, \tag{8.9}$$

and

$$C = \begin{pmatrix} \sqrt{1 - \varphi_1^2} & 0 & 0 & \cdot & \cdot & 0 \\ -\varphi_1 & 1 & 0 & \cdot & \cdot & 0 \\ 0 & -\varphi_1 & 1 & 0 & \cdot & 0 \\ \cdot & \cdot & \cdot & \cdot & \cdot & 0 \\ 0 & \cdot & \cdot & 0 & -\varphi_1 & 1 \end{pmatrix}.$$

For example, let us look at the bivariate linear model

$$Y_t = \beta_1 + \beta_2 X_{t2} + u_t,$$
$$u_t = \varphi_1 u_{t-1} + v_t. \tag{8.10}$$

Various methods exist to compute GLS estimates for the β_k and the φ_1 in this model. The procedures of Cochrane–Orcutt, Durbin, Hildreth–Lu, etc. are well-known. The objection against these procedures is that the model has been extended with a new parameter φ_1, the only interpretation being that the researcher has a mis-specified model! Therefore, once more: do not model the disturbance term when the systematic part of the model has to be modelled in a correct way. A second objection is that an AR(1) disturbance makes no sense with respect to the model specification from an economical-theoretical point of view. For example, the economic theory does not indicate specifying an AR(1) model for the disturbance term in some equation from a macroeconomic model.

In EViews the mis-specified bivariate model (8.10) can be estimated by specifying an AR(1) term in the 'Specification Equation window':

$$Y \ C \ X2 \ AR(1).$$

See the EViews User's Guide for a description of the non-linear estimation procedure to obtain estimates of the parameters of such a model, if you are interested.

When the first row of the matrix C (incorrectly) is deleted, then the following transformed model is obtained for the observations $t = 2, \ldots, n$:

$$(Y_t - \varphi_1 Y_{t-1}) = \beta_1(1 - \varphi_1) + \beta_2(X_{t2} - \varphi_1 X_{t-1,2}) + (u_t - \varphi_1 u_{t-1}),$$

with

$$(u_t - \varphi_1 u_{t-1}) = v_t.$$

Sometimes, this procedure is found in the (historical) literature. This procedure transforms the original static equation to a *restricted* dynamic equation. Respecification of the model by the researcher to eliminate the autocorrelation will result in a different, but correct, specification of a dynamic model. The transformation shows that the specification errors in the original model consist of a lack of dynamics, implying the model should be respecified in a dynamic direction.

A low DW-value is also found when the disturbance term follows, for example, an MA(1) process. An MA(1) process for the disturbance term can occur when this specification has arisen from a model transformation to solve other problems. Examples of autocorrelated disturbances caused by model transformations are found in Chapter 13. For this reason, it would be more sensible to derive 'MA(1)' procedures instead of 'AR(1)' procedures. For example, consider a bivariate model with an MA(1) disturbance term:

$$Y_t = \beta_1 + \beta_2 X_{t2} + v_t$$
$$v_t = u_t - \lambda u_{t-1}, \text{ with } u_t \sim NID\left(0, \sigma_u^2\right).$$

The random disturbance term u_t belongs to the originally specified model. Then the GLS estimator can be correctly used to obtain efficient estimates or asymptotic efficient estimates, depending on the specification of the transformed model.

The covariance matrix Ω of v_t is easily derived:

$$Cov\left(v_t, v_{t-i}\right) = E\left(u_t - \lambda u_{t-1}\right)\left(u_{t-i} - \lambda u_{t-i-1}\right).$$

Compute $Cov\left(v_t, v_{t-i}\right)$ for $i = 0, 1, 2, \ldots$:

$$
\begin{aligned}
i = 0: \quad & Cov\left(v_t^2\right) = \sigma_v^2 = \left(1 + \lambda^2\right)\sigma_u^2 \\
i = 1: \quad & Cov\left(v_t, v_{t-1}\right) = -\lambda\sigma_u^2 \\
i \geq 2: \quad & Cov\left(v_t, v_{t-i}\right) = 0.
\end{aligned}
$$

Next, the matrix Ω is written as:

$$
\Omega = \begin{pmatrix}
\left(1+\lambda^2\right)\sigma_u^2 & -\lambda\sigma_u^2 & 0 & \cdots & \cdots & 0 \\
-\lambda\sigma_u^2 & \left(1+\lambda^2\right)\sigma_u^2 & -\lambda\sigma_u^2 & 0 & \vdots & \vdots \\
0 & -\lambda\sigma_u^2 & \ddots & \ddots & \vdots & \vdots \\
\vdots & 0 & \ddots & \ddots & \ddots & 0 \\
\vdots & \vdots & \vdots & \ddots & \ddots & -\lambda\sigma_u^2 \\
0 & \cdots & \cdots & 0 & -\lambda\sigma_u^2 & \left(1+\lambda^2\right)\sigma_u^2
\end{pmatrix}.
$$

In EViews, the parameters of this model can be estimated by adding an MA(1) term to the equation in the 'Equation Specification' window:

$$Y \ C \ X2 \ MA(1)$$

See the EViews User's Guide for more information about the estimation procedure.

Summarising

- GLS is an estimation method that can be used to obtain a correctly specified and estimated econometric model, when theoretical reasons are known for some time-series model for the disturbance term, or an explicit expression for Ω has been derived for some structural model.
- GLS is an incorrectly used estimation method when no a priori reasons for autocorrelated disturbances exist, because in that case specification errors are the cause of the systematic behaviour of the disturbances. Then the systematic part of the model has to be respecified.

Of course, the same statements are true with respect to heteroskedasticity in the disturbance term. The heteroskedasticity problem is discussed in the next section.

8.6   Heteroskedastic disturbances

Heteroskedastic disturbances are mainly a problem in modelling with cross-section data, but the problem can also exist in causal models for time-series data. Heteroskedasticity can be part of the DGP for empirical and/or theoretical reasons, autocorrelation for theoretical reasons only. (See once more Section 6.4 for some possible causes of heteroskedasticity and the tests to detect these causes.) If heteroskedasticity belongs to the model then efficiently estimated parameters can be obtained by applying the GLS estimator.

The heteroskedasticity problem can be tackled in two ways. The first method is the application of the GLS procedure, as has been discussed in Section 8.2 concerning equation (8.7). The method is called *weighted least squares*. First, the source of the heteroskedasticity has to be found, then GLS estimates can be computed by estimating the parameters of a transformed equation like (8.7) with OLS. However, it is also possible that an economic reasoning exists for the existence of heteroskedasticity in the disturbance term of the model, but it is not interesting for economic reasons to determine a particular relationship for the variance $\sigma_{u_i}^2$. Then a second possibility exists to get asymptotically consistent estimates of the variance-covariance matrix of the parameter estimates. Estimates can be computed by using the *correction of White* when estimating the parameters with OLS. Both methods are discussed below.

Weighted least squares

The point of departure is that the heteroskedasticity belongs to the model, or has been caused by the sample data. In models for cross-section data, heteroskedasticity can be observed in the form of a relationship between $\sigma^2_{u_i}$ and explanatory variables. For example, in a model for cross-section data that explains personal consumption of some luxury article by personal income and some other economic variables, one can expect that the variance of the consumption is small for low income levels and large for high income levels. This pattern can also be found for the disturbance variance. In models for time-series data with many observations, variables can be observed with strong trends. Then it is also possible that a trend can be found in the residual variance. GLS can be applied to estimate the parameters of these models with heteroskedastic disturbances to obtain efficient estimates.

Then the question is: what does the covariance matrix $Var(\mathbf{u}) = \mathbf{\Omega}$ look like in these situations? We are more interested in the matrix $\mathbf{C}$, as we wish to transform the model to a model with a homoskedastic disturbance term. The covariance matrix of u_t when the disturbances are heteroskedastic but not autocorrelated can be written as:

$$\mathbf{\Omega} = \begin{pmatrix} \sigma^2_{u_1} & 0 & \cdots & \cdots & 0 \\ 0 & \sigma^2_{u_2} & 0 & \cdots & \vdots \\ \vdots & 0 & \ddots & \vdots & \vdots \\ \vdots & \vdots & \vdots & \ddots & 0 \\ 0 & \cdots & \cdots & 0 & \sigma^2_{u_n} \end{pmatrix}.$$

In the following steps, the transformation matrix $\mathbf{C}$ is derived. It is common to rewrite the matrix $\mathbf{\Omega}$ in the following way by introducing a constant σ^2 such that $\sigma^2_{u_i} = \sigma^2/\lambda_i$ for all i.

$$\mathbf{\Omega} = \begin{pmatrix} \frac{\sigma^2}{\lambda_1} & 0 & \cdots & \cdots & 0 \\ 0 & \frac{\sigma^2}{\lambda_2} & 0 & \cdots & \vdots \\ \vdots & 0 & \ddots & \ddots & \vdots \\ \vdots & \vdots & \ddots & \ddots & 0 \\ 0 & \cdots & \cdots & 0 & \frac{\sigma^2}{\lambda_n} \end{pmatrix} = \sigma^2 \begin{pmatrix} \frac{1}{\lambda_1} & 0 & \cdots & \cdots & 0 \\ 0 & \frac{1}{\lambda_2} & 0 & \cdots & \vdots \\ \vdots & 0 & \ddots & \ddots & \vdots \\ \vdots & \vdots & \ddots & \ddots & 0 \\ 0 & \cdots & \cdots & 0 & \frac{1}{\lambda_n} \end{pmatrix} = \sigma^2 \mathbf{\Lambda}.$$

In this situation, it is easy to derive the inverse matrix $\mathbf{\Lambda}^{-1}$ and the transformation matrix $\mathbf{C}$:

$$\mathbf{\Lambda}^{-1} = \begin{pmatrix} \lambda_1 & 0 & \cdots & \cdots & 0 \\ 0 & \lambda_2 & 0 & \cdots & \vdots \\ \vdots & 0 & \ddots & \ddots & \vdots \\ \vdots & \vdots & \ddots & \ddots & 0 \\ 0 & \cdots & \cdots & 0 & \lambda_n \end{pmatrix} \Rightarrow \mathbf{C} = \begin{pmatrix} \sqrt{\lambda_1} & 0 & \cdots & \cdots & 0 \\ 0 & \sqrt{\lambda_2} & 0 & \cdots & \vdots \\ \vdots & 0 & \ddots & \ddots & \vdots \\ \vdots & \vdots & \ddots & \ddots & 0 \\ 0 & \cdots & \cdots & 0 & \sqrt{\lambda_n} \end{pmatrix}.$$

Look at the transformation of, for example, the dependent variable **y**, to show the effect of this transformation matrix **C** on the variables of the model:

$$\mathbf{Cy} = \begin{pmatrix} \sqrt{\lambda_1} & 0 & \cdots & \cdots & 0 \\ 0 & \sqrt{\lambda_2} & 0 & \cdots & \vdots \\ \vdots & 0 & \ddots & \ddots & \vdots \\ \vdots & \vdots & \ddots & \ddots & 0 \\ 0 & \cdots & \cdots & 0 & \sqrt{\lambda_n} \end{pmatrix} \cdot \begin{pmatrix} Y_1 \\ Y_2 \\ \vdots \\ \vdots \\ Y_n \end{pmatrix} = \begin{pmatrix} \sqrt{\lambda_1} Y_1 \\ \sqrt{\lambda_2} Y_2 \\ \vdots \\ \vdots \\ \sqrt{\lambda_n} Y_n \end{pmatrix}.$$

All the observations are multiplied with $\sqrt{\lambda_i}$. This happens with the explanatory variables too. Suppose we have the following equation:

$$Y_i = \beta_1 + \beta_2 X_{i2} + \ldots + \beta_K X_{iK} + u_i.$$

Then the transformed equation is:

$$\sqrt{\lambda_i} Y_i = \beta_1 \sqrt{\lambda_i} + \beta_2 \sqrt{\lambda_i} X_{i2} + \ldots + \beta_K \sqrt{\lambda_i} X_{iK} + \sqrt{\lambda_i} u_i. \qquad (8.11)$$

In other words: the variables Y_i and X_{ik} are weighted with $\sqrt{\lambda_i}$. It is not a new model but a transformed equation for computational reasons only. This equation can be estimated with OLS to get efficient estimates of the β_k. The result (8.11) of the transformation explains the name *weighted least squares*. The transformed disturbance term $\sqrt{\lambda_i} u_i$ has a constant variance:

$$var\left(\sqrt{\lambda_i} u_i\right) = \lambda_i \sigma_{u_i}^2 = \lambda_i \frac{\sigma^2}{\lambda_i} = \sigma^2.$$

Relevant weights have to be established, for example the result of a Breusch–Pagan test (*BP*-test) can give a good indication. Suppose that the following form of the heteroskedasticity has been detected with a *BP*-test:

$$\sigma_{u_i}^2 = \sigma^2 X_{i2}^2.$$

Then the matching weights $\sqrt{\lambda_i}$ are found as follows:

$$\frac{1}{\lambda_i} = X_{i2}^2 \Longrightarrow$$

$$\sqrt{\lambda_i} = \frac{1}{X_{i2}}.$$

The parameters β_k can efficiently be calculated from the following regression:

$$\frac{Y_i}{X_{i2}} = \beta_1 \frac{1}{X_{i2}} + \beta_2 + \beta_3 \frac{X_{i3}}{X_{i2}} + \ldots + \beta_K \frac{X_{iK}}{X_{i2}} + \frac{u_i}{X_{i2}}.$$

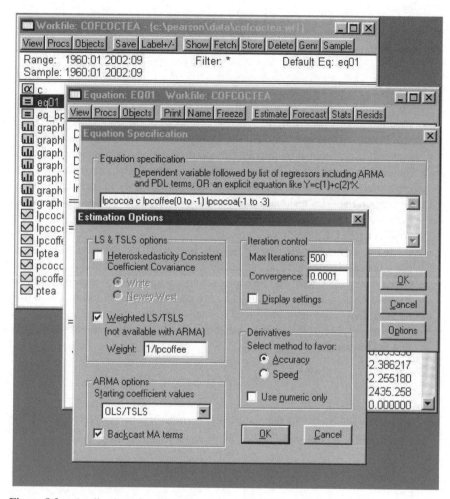

Figure 8.3: Application of weighted least squares in EViews

The transformed disturbance term u_i/X_{i2} is homoskedastic; β_2 is the constant term in the regression but remains the coefficient of X_{i2} in the economic model.

The weighted least squares estimator is found in EViews as one of the options in the 'Equation Specification' window. Click on 'Options', mark 'Weighted LS/TSLS', and type the name of the *weight*. See Figure 8.3 for an example concerning the relationship among cocoa and coffee prices.

In Chapter 6, we did not detect heteroskedasticity in the residuals of the equation for the cocoa price in the form of a relationship with one of the explanatory variables for the entire sample. Only a decreasing trend in the variance was found with the test of Goldfeld and Quandt. But suppose, only for the following schematic example, that we had detected the following form of heteroskedasticity:

$$\sigma_{u_t}^2 = \sigma^2 \left(P_t^{cof} \right)^2,$$

then the matching weights are:

$$\sqrt{\lambda_i} = \frac{1}{P_t^{cof}}.$$

This weight is shown, only as instructive example, in the 'Estimation Options' window in Figure 8.3. This procedure has one disadvantage: it means that the GLS estimator (8.3) is calculated, and we only get the GLS residuals (8.6). Of course the GLS residuals are heteroskedastic, as that is the model. So you do not have the possibility of checking whether the covariance matrix Ω has been sufficiently accurately approximated to reduce the heteroskedasticity. A White test will find heteroskedasticity in the GLS residuals, because it belongs in the GLS residuals. Therefore, good advice is do the procedure yourself by estimating an equation like equation (8.11) with OLS. Then a heteroskedasticity test can be applied to the OLS residuals.

So far, we have studied the GLS procedure with a straightforward proportionality of the disturbance variance with an explanatory variable. However, it is possible that the variance of the disturbance term can be expressed in a linear relationship of explanatory variables. In that situation, unknown parameters are part of that relationship. These parameters have to be estimated before the weighted least squares procedure can be applied. The theoretical procedure to obtain GLS estimates of the parameters can be summarised as follows. Suppose that in the model:

$$Y_i = \beta_1 + \beta_2 X_i + \beta_3 Z_i + u_i, \tag{8.12}$$

the homoskedasticity of the disturbance term u_i has been rejected with a Breusch–Pagan test, in favour of the alternative hypothesis that:

$$\sigma_{u_i}^2 = \alpha_1 + \alpha_2 X_i^2 + v_i.$$

Next, estimate, by using the OLS residuals e_i from equation (8.12), the equation:

$$\widehat{e^2}_i = \widehat{\alpha}_1 + \widehat{\alpha}_2 X_i^2.$$

Compute the predicted values $\widehat{e^2}_i$ of this relationship. Next, the weights can be computed as:

$$w_i = \frac{1}{\sqrt{\widehat{e^2}_i}}.$$

Generate the new variables, or specify the transformed variables in the 'Equation Specification' window, and estimate with OLS the equation:

$$(w_i Y_i) = \beta_1 w_i + \beta_2 (w_i X_i) + \beta_3 (w_i Z_i) + (w_i u_i).$$

Test whether the newly obtained residuals $\widehat{v}_i$ from this regression

$$\widehat{v}_i = (w_i Y_i) - \widehat{\beta}_1 w_i - \widehat{\beta}_2 (w_i X_i) - \widehat{\beta}_3 (w_i Z_i),$$

are homoskedastic. If this null is not rejected then efficient estimates have been obtained and the econometric model is written in the original specification by using these estimates:

$$\widehat{Y}_i = \widehat{\beta}_1 + \widehat{\beta}_2 X_i + \widehat{\beta}_3 Z_i.$$

In Example 8.1 an application of this procedure is given.

Example 8.1   Weighted least squares

We noticed in Part II that the relationship between cocoa and coffee prices was not very stable. So the relationship has been estimated once more but now for the sample period 1990(01)–2002(09). The estimation results are not reproduced here, but the result of the White test is $nR^2 = 19.76$ with a *p-value* of 0.03.

The null hypothesis of homoskedastic disturbances is rejected at a significance level of 3%. The regression output of the test suggested that almost all the variables contribute to the heteroskedasticity. Therefore, the decision has been taken to use the square roots of the predicted values, which is a linear combination of all the explanatory variables, as weights.

1. In the original equation, the OLS residuals have been saved – they got the name *RESID02*.

2. In the original equation the option 'Make Model' has been chosen under 'Procs'. The model is the estimated regression equation.

3. Choose in the 'Model' window: 'Solve'. Next the predicted values are calculated. They have been stored as *LPCOCOA_FIT.*

4. Next, the regression of the squared residuals *RESID02* has been performed on *LPCOCOA_FIT* (see Figure 8.4).

5. Finally, the predicted values are computed. This can be done in various ways. For example, remember the definition

$$\widehat{Y}_t = Y_t - e_t,$$

which can be used as a simple formula to compute these values:

$$GENR\ RES2F = (RESID02\hat{\ }2) - RESID.$$

The variable $RESID$ contains the residuals of the last regression from step 4. This is more convenient here than the procedure in steps 2 and 3. Now the predicted values of the regression from Figure 8.4 are in the series *RES2F*.

```
■ Equation: EQ_RESID02  Workfile: COFCOCTEA          _ □ x
View Procs Objects  Print Name Freeze  Estimate Forecast Stats Resids

Dependent Variable: RESID02^2
Method: Least Squares
Date: 02/27/03  Time: 16:05
Sample(adjusted): 1990:01 2002:09
Included observations: 153 after adjusting endpoints
```

Variable	Coefficient	Std. Error	t-Statistic	Prob.
C	0.023204	0.006888	3.368734	0.0010
LPCOCOA_FIT	-0.005007	0.001694	-2.955084	0.0036

R-squared	0.054670	Mean dependent var	0.002874
Adjusted R-squared	0.048409	S.D. dependent var	0.004328
S.E. of regression	0.004222	Akaike info criterion	-8.084115
Sum squared resid	0.002691	Schwarz criterion	-8.044502
Log likelihood	620.4348	F-statistic	8.732522
Durbin-Watson stat	1.994615	Prob(F-statistic)	0.003628

Figure 8.4:   Regression of squared residuals on the explanatory variables

Subsequently, the weighted regression equation is specified and estimated by dividing all the variables by $\sqrt{RES2F}$, as is shown in Figure 8.5. It is not necessary to generate the transformed variables and to include them in the workfile. They are specified in the 'Equation' window. The estimates in Figure 8.5 are the GLS estimates, or more specifically for this situation, the weighted least squares estimates.

```
■ Equation: EQ_GLS  Workfile: COFCOCTEA          _ □ x
View Procs Objects  Print Name Freeze  Estimate Forecast Stats Resids

Dependent Variable: LPCOCOA/(RES2F^0.5)
Method: Least Squares
Date: 02/27/03  Time: 15:55
Sample: 1990:01 2002:09
Included observations: 153
```

Variable	Coefficient	Std. Error	t-Statistic	Prob.
1/(RES2F^0.5)	0.079605	0.088428	0.900230	0.3695
LPCOFFEE/(RES2F...	0.130014	0.049352	2.634406	0.0093
LPCOFFEE(-1)/(RE...	-0.153164	0.049617	-3.086926	0.0024
LPCOCOA(-1)/(RES...	1.253655	0.078138	16.04421	0.0000
LPCOCOA(-2)/(RES...	-0.256884	0.123573	-2.078799	0.0394
LPCOCOA(-3)/(RES...	0.009660	0.081131	0.119065	0.9054

R-squared	0.997706	Mean dependent var	80.67009
Adjusted R-squared	0.997628	S.D. dependent var	20.99479
S.E. of regression	1.022452	Akaike info criterion	2.920711
Sum squared resid	153.6751	Schwarz criterion	3.039552
Log likelihood	-217.4344	Durbin-Watson stat	2.026790

Figure 8.5:   The weighted least squares regression

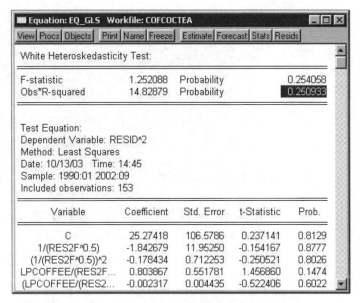

Figure 8.6: Result of the White test after the weighted least squares estimation

It is possible that 'missing values' are encountered in this regression as elements of the series *RES2F* might be negative, but that will be indicated in the heading of the window. Lastly, use the White test again to check whether our hypothesis concerning the source of the heteroskedasticity was a reasonable assumption. See the White test in the window in Figure 8.6. Indeed, the null hypothesis of no heteroskedasticity is not rejected at a significance level of 25.09%.

Heteroskedasticity (correction of White)

It is not always necessary to detect a particular relationship between the disturbance variance and explanatory variables in cases of heteroskedasticity. When it is known that we have heteroskedasticity, of an unknown form, in the disturbances in a particular model, owing to theoretical or empirical reasons, then asymptotic consistent estimates of the standard errors of the estimated parameters can be obtained in the following way. It is possible to estimate the parameters and standard errors consistently and asymptotic efficiently with OLS by using the EViews option 'Heteroskedasticity Consistent Coefficient Covariance' in the 'Equation Specification' window (White (1980)). This option is found under the 'Estimations Options' (see Figure 8.7).

Then the matrix Ω is estimated with the heteroskedasticity consistent covariance matrix estimator of White. With this option, the covariance matrix is estimated in a different but consistent way by making allowance for the heteroskedasticity. The 'White covariance matrix' can be chosen when the disturbances are only heteroskedastic. The option is used when the form or the source of the heteroskedasticity is unknown, or is irrelevant, and the systematic part of the model has been correctly specified.

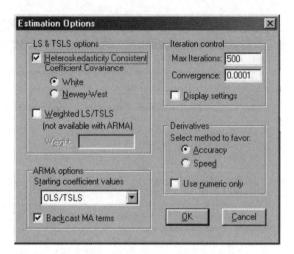

Figure 8.7: Specification of the White option

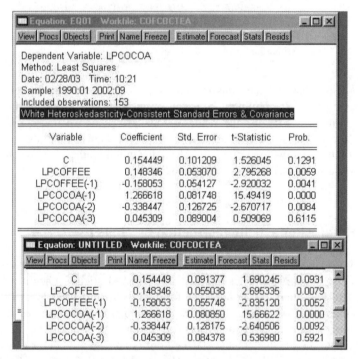

Figure 8.8: Comparison of the OLS output with and without the White correction

Another option is the *Newey–West option*. The Newey–West estimator of the disturbance covariance matrix is more general and is consistent in the presence of both heteroskedasticity and autocorrelation of an unknown form. But as in general residual autocorrelation is an indication of specification errors, it is advised only to use the White option. The point estimates of the parameters are not affected by the use of the White option, only the standard errors are estimated in a different way. See the EViews User's Guide for detailed information and the formulae. In Figure 8.8, the OLS output is given, with and without the use of the White option. The differences in the calculated standard errors are only small in this example.

In the econometrics literature sometimes it is suggested that heteroskedastic-consistent standard errors should always be computed because some residual heteroskedasticity will always be present. However, this is only good advice when you are sure that the heteroskedasticity is not the result of specification errors in the systematic part of the model.

8.7 Case 5: heteroskedastic disturbances

Cross-section data

In this case, you have to tackle the heteroskedasticity problem in a model for the cross-section data from Data set 5. The variables in the data set are described in Section 2.6. Find a correct model that explains the percentage of products that are new to the industry (*new_s_industry*), by using all or a selection of the other variables and by taking into account any possible heteroskedastic behaviour of the disturbances. The model will be estimated twice: (1) by using the option 'Heteroskedasticity Consistent Coefficient Covariances', and (2) by using the GLS estimator. A number of hints are given below.

- Estimate the model with OLS and test the assumption of homoskedastic disturbances with the White test. Also investigate the residuals for the presence of any particular regular behaviour or outliers by looking at a residual graph.
- Re-estimate the model with OLS by making corrections for heteroskedasticity and other problems. This can be done by using the White option for 'Heteroskedastic-ity Consistent Coefficient Covariances', and by specifying dummy variable(s) for possible outliers, etc.

That gives the first possibility for correctly estimating the standard errors of the estimated parameters of this model. A second possibility is the use of the GLS estimator, which is the weighted least squares estimator in this specific situation. Follow the procedure that has been discussed in Example 8.1 and compare the results with the previous results.

- Estimate the parameters with OLS.
- Test the homoskedasticity assumption with the test of Breusch–Pagan.
- Transform the model according to the outcomes of the test and estimate the parameters of that equation with OLS to obtain the GLS estimates.
- Test the homoskedasticity assumption of the disturbances of the transformed equation with the White test.
- Write a clear paper about the accomplishment of your estimated model, along similar lines as those in the first paper concerning the time-series data.

Time-series data

At the end of the first 'research paper' written in Case 2 the result of one or more heteroskedasticity tests had been reported. If you concluded that the residuals are heteroskedastic then try to find an explanation for the heteroskedasticity: could this be due to trends in the variance? Possibly, so apply the Goldfeld–Quandt test. Re-estimate the model twice: with GLS to get efficient estimates of the parameters, and with OLS and the White option for the standard errors. Compare the results and add the evaluation to your paper.

8.8   Introduction to ARCH and GARCH models

Heteroskedasticity is usually associated with models for cross-section data (with correlations between disturbances assumed to be zero), whereas models for time-series data are tested for autocorrelation usually with the assumption of homoskedastic disturbances. A form of heteroskedasticity that can be encountered in time-series models is the *(generalised) autoregressive conditional heteroskedasticity* (ARCH) or (GARCH). In this section, the ARCH and GARCH models are discussed at an introductory level. Testing and estimation procedures are available in EViews and are simple to apply, as will be seen later on. The concept of ARCH disturbances was introduced by Engle (1982). This concept may successfully be applied in models for volatile markets. In speculative markets like exchange rates and stock markets you can observe that large and small errors tend to occur in clusters. It looks something like 'autocorrelation in the heteroskedasticity'. Engle formulated the notion that information from the recent past might influence the conditional disturbance variance. Therefore, the conditional variance, or the volatility, of a variable will be modelled. Engle postulated the following relationship:

$$\sigma^2_{u_t} = \alpha_0 + \alpha_1 u^2_{t-1} + \ldots + \alpha_p u^2_{t-p}. \tag{8.13}$$

Volatility from the previous period is measured by the lags of the squared residuals. The conditional disturbance variance is the variance of u_t, conditional on information available up to time $t - 1$. This is written as follows:

$$\sigma^2_{u_t} = Var(u_t \mid u_{t-1}, \ldots, u_{t-p})$$
$$= E(u^2_t \mid u_{t-1}, \ldots, u_{t-p}).$$

Recent disturbances influence the variance of the current disturbance and thus the variance of the dependent variable. The process described above is called an ARCH(p) process. Notice that two distinct model specifications are considered: one for the conditional mean (of the dependent variable) and one for the conditional disturbance variance. The variance as modelled in equation (8.13) can arise from a disturbance term defined as:

$$u_t = \varepsilon_t \left(\alpha_0 + \alpha_1 u^2_{t-1} + \ldots + \alpha_p u^2_{t-p} \right)^{1/2},$$

where ε_t is a standard normally distributed variable. The unit variance is not a restriction as any other variance can be rescaled to unity by suitable adjustment of the other parameters. We go on, for reasons of simplicity, to study the properties of an ARCH(1) model. This model is written as:

$$Y_t = \beta_1 + \beta_2 X_{t2} + \ldots + \beta_K X_{tK} + u_t,$$

$$u_t = \varepsilon_t \sqrt{\alpha_0 + \alpha_1 u_{t-1}^2}.$$

Next, consider the unconditional and conditional moments of the disturbance term. The unconditional mean of the disturbance term u_t is zero and from the assumption that ε_t is standard normal it follows for the conditional mean that:

$$E\left(u_t \mid u_{t-1}\right) = 0.$$

The conditional variance of u_t is:

$$\begin{aligned}
Var\left(u_t \mid u_{t-1}\right) &= E\left(u_t^2 \mid u_{t-1}\right) \\
&= E\left(\varepsilon_t^2\right)\left(\alpha_0 + \alpha_1 u_{t-1}^2\right) \\
&= \alpha_0 + \alpha_1 u_{t-1}^2,
\end{aligned}$$

which is similar to equation (8.13). The disturbance term u_t is heteroskedastic conditional on u_{t-1}.

The unconditional variance of u_t can also be derived. In the first step of the derivation, a theorem about the decomposition of the variance of a variable from a joint distribution is used (see, for example, Greene (2000) p.81[*]):

$$\begin{aligned}
Var\left(u_t\right) &= E\left(Var\left(u_t \mid u_{t-1}\right)\right) \\
&= \alpha_0 + \alpha_1 E\left(u_{t-1}^2\right) \\
&= \alpha_0 + \alpha_1 Var\left(u_{t-1}\right) \\
&= \frac{\alpha_0}{1 - \alpha_1}.
\end{aligned}$$

This variance only exists if $\alpha_0 > 0$ and $|\alpha_1| < 1$. We see that the unconditional variance of u_t is constant, so u_t is homoskedastic.

---

[*] If x and y are bivariately distributed then:

$$Var(y) = Var_x\left(E\left(y \mid x\right)\right) + E_x\left(Var\left(y \mid x\right)\right).$$

Thus here:

$$\begin{aligned}
Var(u_t) &= Var\left(E\left(u_t \mid u_{t-1}\right)\right) + E\left(Var\left(u_t \mid u_{t-1}\right)\right) \\
&= 0 + E\left(Var\left(u_t \mid u_{t-1}\right)\right).
\end{aligned}$$

Also, it can be shown that the autocovariances of u_t are zero – the disturbances are not serially correlated. Altogether the unconditional distribution of u_t has been derived:

$$u_t \sim NID\left(0, \frac{\alpha_0}{1 - \alpha_1}\right) \text{ and } E\left(u_t u_{t-i}\right) = 0 \ \forall i \neq 0.$$

The implication of these properties of u_t is that OLS is still an efficient and consistent (linear) estimator. But a more efficient (non-linear) GLS estimator exists, which estimates all the parameters of the complete ARCH model (see, for example, Greene (2000) p.797).

Bollerslev (1986) has introduced the generalised autoregressive conditional hetero-skedasticity (GARCH) models. A GARCH(p, q) model is defined as:

$$\sigma_{u_t}^2 = \alpha_0 + \alpha_1 u_{t-1}^2 + \ldots + \alpha_p u_{t-p}^2 + \gamma_1 \sigma_{u_{t-1}}^2 + \ldots + \gamma_q \sigma_{u_{t-q}}^2.$$

Bollerslev has shown, with an example, that a GARCH model with a smaller number of terms can perform as well as or better than an ARCH model with many parameters.

The GARCH(1,1) model

$$\sigma_{u_t}^2 = \alpha_0 + \alpha_1 u_{t-1}^2 + \gamma_1 \sigma_{u_{t-1}}^2$$

is often used in quantitative financial research, where a trader predicts this period's variance by forming a weighted average of a long-term average (the constant term), from information about the volatility observed in the previous period (the ARCH term), and the forecasted variance from the last period (the GARCH term). This model is also consistent with the volatility clustering often seen in financial returns data, where large changes in returns are likely to be followed by further large changes.

More variations of the ARCH model exist. If it is, because of economical reasons, relevant to assume that downward movements in the market are less volatile than upward movements of the same magnitude (a kind of irreversibility) a TARCH model can be specified. The 'T' stands for threshold – a TARCH model is a GARCH model with a dummy variable which is equal to 0 or 1 depending on the sign of u_{t-1}. For example, a TARCH(1,1) model is specified as:

$$\sigma_{u_t}^2 = \alpha_0 + \alpha_1 u_{t-1}^2 + \delta u_{t-1}^2 D_t + \gamma_1 \sigma_{u_{t-1}}^2.$$

See the econometrics literature for a more extensive description of this type of model and for more ARCH-type models, for example, the examples given in Chapter 18 in Greene (2000). These models are not part of a basic course in econometrics.

Testing for ARCH effects and estimation with an ARCH disturbance in EViews

An example will be given that shows the use of an ARCH test and an estimation method to estimate all the parameters of an ARCH model. A straightforward method used to test for ARCH in the disturbance term is an *LM*-test performed in the following way. This is described as you would have to do it yourself if it were not a program in the software package.

- Regress y on the variables in **X** and save the residuals e.
- Perform with OLS the regression $\widehat{e^2}_t = \widehat{\alpha}_0 + \widehat{\alpha}_1 e_{t-1}^2 + \ldots + \widehat{\alpha}_p e_{t-p}^2$.
- Test the null hypothesis $H_0 : \widehat{\alpha}_1 = \widehat{\alpha}_2 = \ldots = \widehat{\alpha}_p = 0$, which is in agreement with the assumption that an ARCH(p) process is absent in the disturbances. Use the LM-test statistic nR^2.

Be aware of the fact that if specification errors in the systematic part of the model are the reason for ARCH residuals, then it makes no sense to estimate the model with ARCH disturbances. Just as before, when discussing autocorrelation and heteroskedasticity problems, the model has to be respecified if the disturbance-term problems have been caused by mis-specification. In EViews, the ARCH test is found in the 'Equation' window under 'View', 'Residual Tests'. See the example in Figure 8.9 where the null has been tested of no ARCH process against the alternative hypothesis that the disturbance term follows an ARCH(2) process. As before, it concerns the relationship between cocoa and coffee prices.

Both test statistics are reported: an F-test for the parameters of the lagged residuals (see the same outcome as the zero-slopes test) and the nR^2-statistic. Just as before with other residual tests, the distribution of this F-statistic is not known under the null hypothesis. The

```
Equation: EQ01_SHORT  Workfile: COFCOCTEA                    _ □ ×
View Procs Objects   Print Name Freeze   Estimate Forecast Stats Resids

ARCH Test:

F-statistic              5.938736   Probability              0.002823
Obs*R-squared            11.67347   Probability              0.002918


Test Equation:
Dependent Variable: RESID^2
Method: Least Squares
Date: 03/18/04  Time: 13:48
Sample(adjusted): 1960:06 2002:09
Included observations: 508 after adjusting endpoints
```

Variable	Coefficient	Std. Error	t-Statistic	Prob.
C	0.003095	0.000369	8.394770	0.0000
RESID^2(-1)	0.048953	0.044090	1.110311	0.2674
RESID^2(-2)	0.140761	0.044094	3.192309	0.0015

R-squared	0.022979	Mean dependent var	0.003816
Adjusted R-squared	0.019110	S.D. dependent var	0.006563
S.E. of regression	0.006500	Akaike info criterion	-7.228072
Sum squared resid	0.021338	Schwarz criterion	-7.203088
Log likelihood	1838.930	F-statistic	5.938736
Durbin-Watson stat	2.009302	Prob(F-statistic)	0.002823

Figure 8.9: The ARCH test

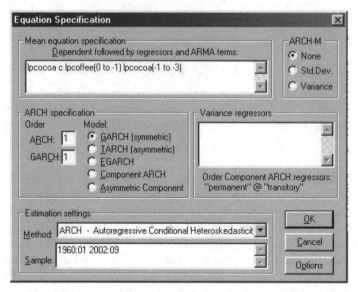

Figure 8.10: Specification of a GARCH(1,1) model

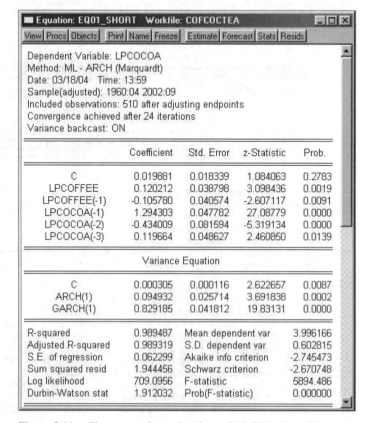

Figure 8.11: The output after estimating a GARCH(1,1) model

LM-test statistic nR^2 is asymptotically distributed as $\chi^2(p)$ under the null hypothesis of no ARCH(p) process.

The null hypothesis of no ARCH is clearly rejected at the 5% (even 0.5%) significance level. Economically, this means that the variance is influenced by the volatility of the two preceding months. Then you can choose ARCH as the estimation method in the 'Equation Specification' window, and the window shown in Figure 8.10 appears. A GARCH(1,1) model is estimated. It is a non-linear estimation procedure, see the EViews User's Guide for details about this procedure.

The value 1 is the default value for the order of the ARCH and GARCH model in EViews, because it is a popular alternative hypothesis in quantitative research in volatile markets. The output is given in Figure 8.11.

Compare this result with the original OLS output shown in Figure 4.4. The significance of the contemporaneous and one-month lagged coffee prices has clearly increased.

It is not a bad idea to use the ARCH test as one of the standard tests after estimating a regression equation, when it can be expected that volatile situations did occur in the sample period. Check your own estimation results.

Chapter 9

Models with Endogenous Explanatory Variables

9.1 Introduction

Brief introductory remarks about asymptotic behaviour of the OLS estimator have been given in Sections 4.3 and 4.8. In these sections, we have seen that the OLS estimator is no longer a consistent estimator when an endogenous explanatory variable has been specified. When is an economic variable an endogenous variable? In Section 1.4, a discussion and examples concerning this topic were given. To summarise that discussion: we consider an economic variable as endogenous if it can be explained in another equation which belongs to a complete simultaneous equation model (SEM) that can be specified for the research topic concerned. It is not necessary to specify a complete SEM if you are only interested in analysing how one economic phenomenon can be explained. For example, if you are interested in explaining money demand in a country, then it is not necessary to specify a complete monetary block as part of a macroeconomic model. Consider the explanatory variables in the money-demand equation and determine their nature, endogenous or exogenous, on the basis of your economic knowledge of the subject.

As it is not the intention to discuss asymptotic properties of estimators in detail, only some general aspects of asymptotic behaviour will be introduced and discussed to make results comprehensible and acceptable. It is important that the consequences for econometric practice are clear. Knowledge about asymptotic properties is necessary when the sampling distribution of an estimator cannot be derived. This happens with the OLS estimator when, for example, the classical assumptions of the classical regression model are relaxed. With endogenous explanatory variables in the model the consistency property of the OLS estimator is lost. Therefore, another but consistent estimator is introduced in this chapter: it is the two-stage least squares estimator (2SLS) or instrumental variable estimator (IV). The names of both estimators are of an historical nature so the estimators are introduced in an historical context to better understand how their names derived and the original procedures. The estimator can be derived directly in a very simple way by using GLS: this will be shown at the end of Section 9.3.

Before discussing the estimators, we look at the consistency property of the OLS estimator, as discussed in Section 4.7. This retrospect is a convenient introduction to the problems that are discussed in this chapter. As usual, the property is analysed by using the expression of the estimator in its sampling error:

$$\hat{\beta} = \beta + (\mathbf{X}'\mathbf{X})^{-1}\mathbf{X}'\mathbf{u}$$

$$= \beta + \left(\frac{1}{n}\mathbf{X}'\mathbf{X}\right)^{-1}\left(\frac{1}{n}\mathbf{X}'\mathbf{u}\right).$$

Remember the assumptions that have been made. It was assumed that the matrix $\frac{1}{n}\mathbf{X}'\mathbf{X}$ with sample moments of the explanatory variables converges to a non-singular matrix Ω_{XX} with population moments or with finite constants:

$$P\lim_{n\to\infty}\frac{1}{n}\mathbf{X}'\mathbf{X} = \Omega_{XX}.$$

The matrix Ω_{XX} is a non-singular matrix, so Ω_{XX}^{-1} exists. Secondly it was assumed that the explanatory variables and the disturbance term are independently distributed; then the following two expressions are valid:

$$P\lim_{n\to\infty}\left(\frac{1}{n}\mathbf{X}'\mathbf{X}\right)^{-1} = \Omega_{XX}^{-1}$$

$$P\lim_{n\to\infty}\left(\frac{1}{n}\mathbf{X}'\mathbf{u}\right) = 0.$$

The last expression is true if $\mathbf{X}$ contains exogenous and possibly lagged endogenous variables, but no contemporaneous endogenous variables. Considering the issues in the following sections, it is convenient to repeat the derivation of the probability limit for $\hat{\beta}$ here:

$$P\lim_{n\to\infty}\hat{\beta} = \beta + P\lim_{n\to\infty}\left((\mathbf{X}'\mathbf{X})^{-1}\mathbf{X}'\mathbf{u}\right)$$

$$= \beta + P\lim_{n\to\infty}\left(\left(\frac{1}{n}\mathbf{X}'\mathbf{X}\right)^{-1}\cdot\left(\frac{1}{n}\mathbf{X}'\mathbf{u}\right)\right)$$

$$= \beta + P\lim_{n\to\infty}\left(\frac{1}{n}\mathbf{X}'\mathbf{X}\right)^{-1}\cdot P\lim_{n\to\infty}\left(\frac{1}{n}\mathbf{X}'\mathbf{u}\right)$$

$$= \beta + \Omega_{XX}^{-1}\cdot 0$$

$$= \beta. \tag{9.1}$$

The independence of the explanatory variables $(\mathbf{X})$ and the disturbance term $(\mathbf{u})$ is crucial for the consistency property of the OLS estimator (β). In that case the $(K \times 1)$ vector $\underset{n \to \infty}{P \lim} \left(\frac{1}{n}\mathbf{X}'\mathbf{u} \right)$ is a vector with zeros only.

As the limiting distribution of $\widehat{\beta}$ collapses in β, the limiting distribution of the 'rescaled' $\widehat{\beta}, \sqrt{n}(\widehat{\beta} - \beta)$ can be derived:

$$\sqrt{n}(\widehat{\beta} - \beta) \overset{A}{\sim} N\left(\mathbf{0}, \sigma_u^2 \mathbf{\Omega}_{XX}^{-1} \right),$$

then the asymptotic distribution of $\widehat{\beta}$ is given by:

$$\widehat{\beta} \overset{A}{\sim} N\left(\beta, \sigma_u^2 \frac{1}{n} \mathbf{\Omega}_{XX}^{-1} \right).$$

The covariance matrix $\sigma_u^2 \frac{1}{n} \mathbf{\Omega}_{XX}^{-1}$ is approximated by $\widehat{\sigma}_u^2 (\mathbf{X}'\mathbf{X})^{-1}$ for the sample period. This result implies that for a model with lagged endogenous variables OLS is used in a similar way as before, but that the estimation results have to be interpreted as asymptotic results. Point this out in the text of the papers you write: standard errors, t- and F-values are asymptotic.

9.2   The instrumental-variable (IV) estimator

If endogenous explanatory variables are included in the model, the disturbance term and these endogenous variables are dependently distributed, as was shown in Example 4.4 in Section 4.7:

$$\underset{n \to \infty}{P \lim} \left(\frac{1}{n}\mathbf{X}'\mathbf{u} \right) \neq \mathbf{0}.$$

The OLS estimator is no longer a consistent estimator of the parameters. This is easily seen in formula (9.1) because $\underset{n \to \infty}{P \lim} \left(\frac{1}{n}\mathbf{X}'\mathbf{u} \right) \neq \mathbf{0}$. Notice that all the K parameter estimates have an inconsistency if only one of the explanatory variables and the disturbance term are dependently distributed.

A different estimator is necessary to obtain consistent estimation results. In this section the IV estimator is introduced as a consistent estimator. This estimator can always be used in situations when the OLS estimator is not consistent. First, the IV estimator is introduced in the classical historical way, then in the following section, its general form will be discussed which is called the 2SLS estimator. The IV and 2SLS estimator are similar estimation methods.

For the IV estimator, instrumental variables are necessary. The instruments are chosen in such a way that the instrumental variables and the disturbance term are independent. In the (classical) simple form, a matrix $\mathbf{Z}$ with instrumental variables is chosen of the same order as the matrix $\mathbf{X}$ with explanatory variables. The matrix $\mathbf{Z}$ is an $(n \times K)$ matrix with instrumental variables with the following properties. The instrumental variables and the disturbance term are independently distributed. This implies that the instruments are exogenous or predetermined variables. So:

$$P\lim_{n\to\infty} \left(\frac{1}{n}\mathbf{Z}'\mathbf{u}\right) = \mathbf{0}.$$

The sample moments of the instruments have to converge to finite constants for increasing n.

$$P\lim_{n\to\infty} \left(\frac{1}{n}\mathbf{Z}'\mathbf{Z}\right) = \mathbf{\Omega}_{ZZ}.$$

The $(K \times K)$ matrix $\mathbf{\Omega}_{ZZ}$ is a non-singular matrix. Finally, the instrumental variables and the explanatory variables are correlated.

$$P\lim_{n\to\infty} \left(\frac{1}{n}\mathbf{Z}'\mathbf{X}\right) = \mathbf{\Omega}_{ZX}.$$

The $(K \times K)$ matrix $\mathbf{\Omega}_{ZX}$ is also a non-singular matrix.
    Next consider the following linear estimator, expressed in $\mathbf{y}$:

$$\widehat{\boldsymbol{\beta}}_{IV} = (\mathbf{Z}'\mathbf{X})^{-1}\mathbf{Z}'\mathbf{y}. \tag{9.2}$$

In expression (9.2) the explanatory variables $(\mathbf{X})$ and the dependent variable $(\mathbf{y})$ are *weighted* with the matrix $\mathbf{Z}$. It is not difficult to see that $\widehat{\boldsymbol{\beta}}_{IV}$ is a consistent estimator of β. Rewrite this estimator in the expression with β and its sampling error.

$$\begin{aligned}
\widehat{\boldsymbol{\beta}}_{IV} &= (\mathbf{Z}'\mathbf{X})^{-1}\mathbf{Z}'\mathbf{y} \\
&= (\mathbf{Z}'\mathbf{X})^{-1}\mathbf{Z}'(\mathbf{X}\beta + \mathbf{u}) \\
&= \beta + (\mathbf{Z}'\mathbf{X})^{-1}\mathbf{Z}'\mathbf{u}.
\end{aligned}$$

Determine the probability limit for increasing n.

$$\begin{aligned}
P\lim_{n\to\infty}\widehat{\boldsymbol{\beta}}_{IV} &= \beta + P\lim_{n\to\infty}\left((\mathbf{Z}'\mathbf{X})^{-1}\mathbf{Z}'\mathbf{u}\right) \\
&= \beta + P\lim_{n\to\infty}\left(\left(\frac{1}{n}\mathbf{Z}'\mathbf{X}\right)^{-1}\cdot\left(\frac{1}{n}\mathbf{Z}'\mathbf{u}\right)\right) \\
&= \beta + P\lim_{n\to\infty}\left(\frac{1}{n}\mathbf{Z}'\mathbf{X}\right)^{-1}\cdot P\lim_{n\to\infty}\left(\frac{1}{n}\mathbf{Z}'\mathbf{u}\right) \\
&= \beta + \mathbf{\Omega}_{ZX}^{-1}\cdot\mathbf{0}. \\
&= \beta.
\end{aligned}$$

Thus the IV estimator $\widehat{\boldsymbol{\beta}}_{IV}$ of β is indeed a consistent estimator.

The asymptotic covariance matrix of $\widehat{\beta}_{IV}$ can be derived as

$$Var\left(\widehat{\beta}_{IV}\right) = \frac{1}{n}\sigma_u^2 \left(\Omega'_{ZX}\Omega_{ZZ}^{-1}\Omega_{ZX}\right)^{-1}.$$

In practice, this covariance matrix is estimated by

$$\widehat{Var\left(\widehat{\beta}_{IV}\right)} = \widehat{\sigma}_u^2 \left(\mathbf{Z'X}\right)^{-1}\left(\mathbf{Z'Z}\right)\left(\mathbf{X'Z}\right)^{-1}.$$

A difficult problem is finding variables to play the role of instrumental variables. You have to be sure that they are independent in the limit with the disturbances, but they should also be highly correlated with the explanatory variables. When correlation between the instruments and the explanatory variables decreases, it is simple to see that the standard errors of the estimates increase. This implies a high price for consistency. If the correlation is high, then a high sampling bias can still be expected because of the resemblance of the variables. That bias goes to zero when n increases because the estimator is consistent. However, in spite of this problem, the estimator can often successfully be applied.

An example is given below to illustrate the use of the IV estimator.

Example 9.1   A simple simultaneous equation model

The simplest Keynesian macro model that has been used frequently as an illustrative example in this book is:

$$C_t = \beta_1 + \beta_2 Y_t + u_t$$
$$Y_t = C_t + I_t.$$

The consumption (C_t) and income variables (Y_t) are considered as endogenous variables, and investments (I_t) is considered as an exogenous variable in this model. The reduced-form equation for Y_t is:

$$Y_t = \frac{\beta_1}{1 - \beta_2} + \frac{1}{1 - \beta_2}I_t + \frac{u_t}{1 - \beta_2}.$$

This equation shows that Y_t and u_t are dependently distributed. The covariance between Y_t and u_t was computed in Section 4.7 as:

$$Cov\left(Y_t, u_t\right) = E\left((Y_t - EY_t) \cdot u_t\right) = \frac{\sigma_u^2}{1 - \beta_2}.$$

The two parameters β_1 and β_2 of the consumption function are inconsistently estimated with OLS. However, the parameters of the consumption equation can be consistently estimated by using the instrumental variables method. The matrix $\mathbf{Z}$ is a $(n \times 2)$ matrix. In the first column we maintain the constant term. As an instrument variable we need a variable that correlates with income but is not endogenous. A possible choice is to use, for example, I_t as an instrumental variable for Y_t.

Then the matrices $\mathbf{X}$ and $\mathbf{Z}$ are:

$$
\mathbf{X} = \begin{pmatrix} 1 & Y_1 \\ 1 & Y_2 \\ 1 & Y_3 \\ \vdots & \vdots \\ & \\ \vdots & \vdots \\ 1 & Y_n \end{pmatrix}, \qquad \mathbf{Z} = \begin{pmatrix} 1 & I_1 \\ 1 & I_2 \\ 1 & I_3 \\ \vdots & \vdots \\ & \\ \vdots & \vdots \\ 1 & I_n \end{pmatrix},
$$

and then it follows for the IV estimator:

$$
\underset{n\to\infty}{P\lim} \begin{pmatrix} \widehat{\beta}_1 \\ \widehat{\beta}_2 \end{pmatrix}_{IV} = \begin{pmatrix} \beta_1 \\ \beta_2 \end{pmatrix} + \Omega_{ZX}^{-1} \cdot \underset{n\to\infty}{P\lim} \begin{pmatrix} \frac{1}{n}\sum_{t=1}^{n} u_t \\ \frac{1}{n}\sum_{t=1}^{n} I_t u_t \end{pmatrix}
$$

$$
= \begin{pmatrix} \beta_1 \\ \beta_2 \end{pmatrix} + \Omega_{ZX}^{-1} \cdot \begin{pmatrix} 0 \\ 0 \end{pmatrix}
$$

$$
= \begin{pmatrix} \beta_1 \\ \beta_2 \end{pmatrix}.
$$

So this choice of an instrument shows once again the consistency of the estimator.

A problem of using the IV method is that another computational result is obtained with every different choice of instrumental variables. In Example 9.1, we could also use, for example, Y_{t-1} as an instrument. This problem can be solved, to some extent, by using the two-stage least squares estimator.

9.3 The two-stage least squares (2SLS) estimator

The 2SLS estimator is discussed in two ways: first a historical but long description of the estimator is given, which explains the name two-stage least squares, and secondly a simple direct derivation of the estimator is given. If you are only interested in the mathematical expression and the consistency property of the estimator then you can skip the 'Historical introduction' and go immediately to the direct derivation.

Historical introduction

When more variables are available that can serve as instruments, then each choice of instruments yields different (consistent) parameter estimates. In such a situation, we can take a linear combination of these variables. The optimal linear combination is obtained by a regression of the endogenous explanatory variables on the possible instrumental variables;

that is a reduced-form regression. Historically, 2SLS was not one procedure for computing the estimates. Consistent estimates were computed with a two-step procedure, OLS was applied twice, which clarifies the name. This two-step procedure is presented first in this section. Later on, one formula is derived to compute 2SLS estimates, but the idea behind the 2SLS procedure and its name will become clearer by describing the two historical steps of the procedure.

The 2SLS estimator will be introduced by using the following example. Consider the following model, with endogenous variables Y_{t1} and Y_{t2}, and exogenous variables X_{t1} and X_{t2}:

$$Y_{t1} = \beta_1 + \beta_2 Y_{t2} + \gamma_1 X_{t1} + \gamma_2 X_{t2} + u_t, \tag{9.3}$$
$$u_t \sim NID\left(0, \sigma_u^2\right).$$

In the notation βs are used as parameters of endogenous variables and γs as parameters of exogenous variables. Assume that X_{t3} and X_{t4} are variables that can be used as instrumental variables, whereas only one instrumental variable is needed for Y_{t2}. Then in *the first stage* a reduced-form equation for the variable Y_{t2} is estimated with OLS:

$$\widehat{Y}_{t2} = \widehat{\pi}_1 + \widehat{\pi}_2 X_{t1} + \widehat{\pi}_3 X_{t2} + \widehat{\pi}_4 X_{t3} + \widehat{\pi}_5 X_{t4},$$

or written in the notation with the residual variable as:

$$Y_{t2} = \widehat{\pi}_1 + \widehat{\pi}_2 X_{t1} + \widehat{\pi}_3 X_{t2} + \widehat{\pi}_4 X_{t3} + \widehat{\pi}_5 X_{t4} + e_t$$
$$Y_{t2} = \widehat{Y}_{t2} + e_t. \tag{9.4}$$

In the *second stage*, substitute equation (9.4) into equation (9.3):

$$Y_{t1} = \beta_1 + \beta_2 \left(\widehat{Y}_{t2} + e_t\right) + \gamma_1 X_{t1} + \gamma_2 X_{t2} + u_t$$
$$Y_{t1} = \beta_1 + \beta_2 \widehat{Y}_{t2} + \gamma_1 X_{t1} + \gamma_2 X_{t2} + \left(u_t + \beta_2 e_t\right). \tag{9.5}$$

Next equation (9.5) can consistently be estimated with OLS as the disturbance term $(u_t + \beta_2 e_t)$ and the explanatory variables are independent. The variable $\widehat{Y}_{t2}$ and the residuals e_t are orthogonal (see Section 5.2), and the predicted values $\widehat{Y}_{t2}$ have nothing to do with the disturbances u_t. The variable $\widehat{Y}_{t2}$ is an exact linear expression in the exogenous variables. This means that consistent estimates of the parameters have been obtained in two stages, and all the instruments have been used by taking the optimal linear combination of them via the reduced-form equation.

However, these estimates can also be computed with one formula that can be programmed, as has been done in econometric software packages. This will be shown in two ways. First, the estimator will be derived according to the two steps that have been described above. Secondly, we shall see that we can forget the two steps, and the estimator will be derived in a direct way.

The first stage

The model is:

$$y = X\beta + u$$
$$u \sim N\left(0, \sigma_u^2 I\right).$$

with the $(n \times K)$ matrix X with explanatory variables consisting of exogenous, endogenous and/or lagged variables. Further we have an $(n \times p)$ matrix Z with instrumental variables, with $K < p < n$. The first step is to estimate K reduced-form equations for all the explanatory variables expressed in the p instrumental variables. If the X_{ti} is an endogenous explanatory variable the equation is a real reduced-form equation:

$$\widehat{X}_{ti} = \widehat{\alpha}_{1i} + \widehat{\alpha}_{2i} Z_{2t} + \widehat{\alpha}_{3i} Z_{3t} + \ldots + \widehat{\alpha}_{pi} Z_{pt},$$

and if X_{ti} is an exogenous or lagged explanatory variable, the 'reduced-form' equation is written as:

$$\widehat{X}_{ti} = 0 + 0 Z_{t2} + 0 Z_{t3} + \ldots + 1 Z_{ti} + \ldots + 0 Z_{tp} \text{ with}$$
$$Z_{ti} = X_{ti}.$$

After the explanatory variables have been regressed on the instrumental variables, predicted values are computed, and according to the equations above they are written in matrix notation as $(i = 1, \ldots, K)$:

$$\widehat{x}_i = Z\widehat{\alpha}_i,$$
$$= Z(Z'Z)^{-1} Z' x_i.$$

The vector x_i is an $(n \times 1)$ vector with observations of X_{ti}. Define the matrix $\widehat{X}$ as the $(n \times K)$ matrix whose columns are the vectors $\widehat{x}_i$ and rewrite that matrix in the following way:

$$\widehat{X} = (\widehat{x}_1, \widehat{x}_2, \ldots, \widehat{x}_K)$$
$$= (Z\widehat{\alpha}_1, Z\widehat{\alpha}_2, \ldots, Z\widehat{\alpha}_K)$$
$$= Z(\widehat{\alpha}_1, \widehat{\alpha}_2, \ldots, \widehat{\alpha}_K)$$
$$= Z\left((Z'Z)^{-1} Z' x_1, (Z'Z)^{-1} Z' x_2, \ldots, (Z'Z)^{-1} Z' x_K\right)$$
$$= Z(Z'Z)^{-1} Z' (x_1, x_2, \ldots, x_K)$$
$$= Z(Z'Z)^{-1} Z' X. \tag{9.6}$$

The regression coefficients $\widehat{\alpha}_i$ from the regressions of X_{ti} on the instrumental variables Z_{tj} are in the columns of the matrix $(Z'Z)^{-1} Z'X$. The matrix $\widehat{X}$ contains the predicted values from the estimated reduced-form equations, expressed in the originally observed variables in $\mathbf{X}$ and $\mathbf{Z}$. That makes it possible to write the 2SLS estimator in one formula that contains observed variables only, in the next stage.

The second stage

In the second stage, the regression of $\mathbf{y}$ on the predicted variables in $\widehat{\mathbf{X}}$ is performed, again with OLS. This has not changed the specification of the model, as the difference between the observed and predicted values of the variables, the reduced form residuals, is included in the disturbance term by the substitution, just as shown before in the simple example:

$$\mathbf{y} = \mathbf{X}\boldsymbol{\beta} + \mathbf{u},$$
$$\mathbf{X} = \widehat{\mathbf{X}} + \mathbf{E},$$

where $\mathbf{E}$ is the $(n \times K)$ matrix with OLS residuals in the columns from the K regressions in the first stage. Substitution of $\mathbf{X}$ in the model gives the following equation.

$$\mathbf{y} = \left(\widehat{\mathbf{X}} + \mathbf{E}\right)\boldsymbol{\beta} + \mathbf{u}$$
$$\mathbf{y} = \widehat{\mathbf{X}}\boldsymbol{\beta} + (\mathbf{E}\boldsymbol{\beta} + \mathbf{u}).$$

Then OLS yields consistent estimates because $\widehat{\mathbf{X}}$ is orthogonal with $\mathbf{E}$ and is independent of $\mathbf{u}$.

$$\widehat{\boldsymbol{\beta}}_{IV} = \left(\widehat{\mathbf{X}}'\widehat{\mathbf{X}}\right)^{-1}\widehat{\mathbf{X}}'\mathbf{y}, \tag{9.7}$$

or written in the originally observed variables by substituting expression (9.6):

$$\widehat{\boldsymbol{\beta}}_{IV} = \left(\mathbf{X}'\mathbf{Z}\left(\mathbf{Z}'\mathbf{Z}\right)^{-1}\mathbf{Z}'\mathbf{X}\right)^{-1}\mathbf{X}'\mathbf{Z}\left(\mathbf{Z}'\mathbf{Z}\right)^{-1}\mathbf{Z}'\mathbf{y}. \tag{9.8}$$

This expression (9.8) of the 2SLS estimator can simply be computed in one step, as is shown below.

The direct derivation of the 2SLS estimator

Alternatively, the expression (9.8) can conveniently be derived as an application of GLS. The original model is:

$$\mathbf{y} = \mathbf{X}\boldsymbol{\beta} + \mathbf{u}, \text{ with } \mathbf{u} \sim N\left(\mathbf{0}, \sigma_u^2 \mathbf{I}_n\right).$$

Multiplying this model with the $(p \times n)$ matrix $\mathbf{Z}'$ with instruments at both sides of the equation yields the 'weighted' model:

$$\mathbf{Z}'\mathbf{y} = \mathbf{Z}'\mathbf{X}\boldsymbol{\beta} + \mathbf{Z}'\mathbf{u}, \tag{9.9}$$

with the following covariance matrix of the transformed disturbance term $\mathbf{Z}'\mathbf{u}$:

$$\begin{aligned} Var\left(\mathbf{Z}'\mathbf{u}\right) &= \mathbf{Z}' \cdot Var\left(\mathbf{u}\right) \cdot \mathbf{Z} \\ &= \mathbf{Z}' \cdot \sigma_u^2 \mathbf{I}_n \cdot \mathbf{Z} \\ &= \sigma_u^2\left(\mathbf{Z}'\mathbf{Z}\right). \end{aligned}$$

So the transformed disturbance term $\mathbf{Z}'\mathbf{u}$ is distributed as:

$$\mathbf{Z}'\mathbf{u} \sim N\left(\mathbf{0}, \sigma_u^2\left(\mathbf{Z}'\mathbf{Z}\right)\right).$$

The parameters of equation (9.9) may be estimated with the GLS estimator which also results in expression (9.8):

$$\widehat{\beta}_{IV} = \left(\mathbf{X}'\mathbf{Z}\left(\mathbf{Z}'\mathbf{Z}\right)^{-1}\mathbf{Z}'\mathbf{X}\right)^{-1}\mathbf{X}'\mathbf{Z}\left(\mathbf{Z}'\mathbf{Z}\right)^{-1}\mathbf{Z}'\mathbf{y}.$$

In this way, the original two-step procedure is no longer recognisable. Perhaps, for simplicity, it would be better to forget the history of this estimation method. Then the estimator can be derived as above with the name IV estimator.

It is simple to see that $\widehat{\beta}_{IV}$ is a consistent estimator of β:

$$\begin{aligned} \widehat{\beta}_{IV} &= \beta + \left(\left(\frac{1}{n}\mathbf{X}'\mathbf{Z}\right)\left(\frac{1}{n}\mathbf{Z}'\mathbf{Z}\right)^{-1}\left(\frac{1}{n}\mathbf{Z}'\mathbf{X}\right)\right)^{-1} \\ &\quad \times \left(\frac{1}{n}\mathbf{X}'\mathbf{Z}\right)\left(\frac{1}{n}\mathbf{Z}'\mathbf{Z}\right)^{-1}\left(\frac{1}{n}\mathbf{Z}'\mathbf{u}\right) \end{aligned}$$

$$\begin{aligned} \underset{n\to\infty}{P\lim}\,\widehat{\beta}_{IV} &= \beta + \underset{n\to\infty}{P\lim}\left(\left(\frac{1}{n}\mathbf{X}'\mathbf{Z}\right)\left(\frac{1}{n}\mathbf{Z}'\mathbf{Z}\right)^{-1}\left(\frac{1}{n}\mathbf{Z}'\mathbf{X}\right)\right)^{-1} \\ &\quad \times \left(\frac{1}{n}\mathbf{X}'\mathbf{Z}\right)\left(\frac{1}{n}\mathbf{Z}'\mathbf{Z}\right)^{-1}\left(\frac{1}{n}\mathbf{Z}'\mathbf{u}\right) \\ &= \beta + \left(\Omega'_{ZX}\Omega_{ZZ}^{-1}\Omega_{ZX}\right)^{-1}\Omega'_{ZX}\Omega_{ZZ}^{-1} \cdot \mathbf{0} \\ &= \beta. \end{aligned}$$

Remark 9.1

If the number of instrumental variables is equal to the number of explanatory variables $(p = K)$ then $\mathbf{Z}$ is an $(n \times K)$ matrix, with rank K, and all the matrices in (9.8) are square non-singular matrices, and the 2SLS estimator (9.8) equals the IV estimator (9.2):

$$\begin{aligned} \widehat{\beta}_{IV} &= \left(\mathbf{Z}'\mathbf{X}\right)^{-1}\left(\mathbf{Z}'\mathbf{Z}\right)\left(\mathbf{X}'\mathbf{Z}\right)^{-1}\left(\mathbf{X}'\mathbf{Z}\right)\left(\mathbf{Z}'\mathbf{Z}\right)^{-1}\mathbf{Z}'\mathbf{y} \\ &= \left(\mathbf{Z}'\mathbf{X}\right)^{-1}\mathbf{Z}'\mathbf{y}. \end{aligned}$$

Asymptotic standard errors

The asymptotic distribution for $\sqrt{n}\left(\widehat{\boldsymbol{\beta}}_{IV} - \boldsymbol{\beta}\right)$ can be derived and looks like:

$$\sqrt{n}\left(\widehat{\boldsymbol{\beta}}_{IV} - \boldsymbol{\beta}\right) \sim N\left(\mathbf{0}, \sigma_u^2 \left(\boldsymbol{\Omega}'_{ZX}\boldsymbol{\Omega}_{ZZ}^{-1}\boldsymbol{\Omega}_{ZX}\right)^{-1}\right).$$

This gives the asymptotic distribution of $\widehat{\boldsymbol{\beta}}_{IV}$:

$$\widehat{\boldsymbol{\beta}}_{IV} \overset{A}{\sim} N\left(\boldsymbol{\beta}, \frac{1}{n}\sigma_u^2 \left(\boldsymbol{\Omega}'_{ZX}\boldsymbol{\Omega}_{ZZ}^{-1}\boldsymbol{\Omega}_{ZX}\right)^{-1}\right).$$

For the sample period, the variance-covariance matrix is approximated and computed as:

$$\widehat{\sigma}_u^2 \left(\mathbf{X}'\mathbf{Z}\left(\mathbf{Z}'\mathbf{Z}\right)^{-1}\mathbf{Z}'\mathbf{X}\right)^{-1}$$

with:

$$\widehat{\sigma}_u^2 = \frac{\left(\mathbf{y} - \mathbf{X}\widehat{\boldsymbol{\beta}}_{IV}\right)'\left(\mathbf{y} - \mathbf{X}\widehat{\boldsymbol{\beta}}_{IV}\right)}{n - K}$$

$$= \frac{1}{n - K}\sum_{t=1}^{n} e_{IV,t}^2,$$

and with the IV residuals denoted by $e_{IV,t}$ computed as:

$$\mathbf{e}_{IV} = \mathbf{y} - \mathbf{X}\widehat{\boldsymbol{\beta}}_{IV}. \tag{9.10}$$

Testing restrictions on parameters

After the parameters have been estimated with 2SLS restrictions on them they can be tested in an identical way as to when the parameters were estimated with OLS, as discussed in Section 5.7. However, problems exist when you want to use the Wald F-test, to test g restrictions on parameters, in its 'alternative form':

$$F = \frac{(S_R - S)/g}{S/(n - K)}. \tag{9.11}$$

The problems are caused by the fact that we have to deal with two residual variables, denoted by $e_{IV,t}$ and $e_{2,t}$. The residuals $e_{IV,t}$ are the correct residuals as defined in equation (9.10). These residuals have not been obtained after a regression and so they are not orthogonal to the explanatory variables. The residuals $e_{2,t}$ are obtained from the regression in the 'second round', so they are orthogonal to the explanatory variables. Look at the definitions of the residuals:

$$\mathbf{e}_{IV} = \mathbf{y} - \mathbf{X}\widehat{\boldsymbol{\beta}}_{IV},$$

$$\mathbf{e}_2 = \mathbf{y} - \widehat{\mathbf{X}}\widehat{\boldsymbol{\beta}}_{IV},$$

which imply that:

$$\mathbf{X}'\mathbf{e}_{IV} \neq \mathbf{0}$$
$$\widehat{\mathbf{X}}'\mathbf{e}_2 = \mathbf{0}.$$

The consequence is that we get different expressions for sums of squared residuals in the application of the F-test in its alternative form. See Section 5.8 for the derivation of the F-statistic, where the orthogonality property has been used. If we repeat that derivation here, then the residuals $\mathbf{e}_{IV,R}$ of the restricted equation:

$$\mathbf{e}_{IV,R} = \mathbf{y} - \mathbf{X}\widehat{\beta}_{IV,R}$$

have to be used. Similar to equation (5.19), the relationship between the residuals of the restricted and unrestricted model is written as:

$$\mathbf{e}_{IV,R} = \mathbf{e}_{IV} + \mathbf{X}(\widehat{\mathbf{X}}'\widehat{\mathbf{X}})^{-1}\mathbf{R}'\left(\mathbf{R}(\widehat{\mathbf{X}}'\widehat{\mathbf{X}})^{-1}\mathbf{R}'\right)^{-1}\left(\mathbf{R}\widehat{\beta}_{IV} - \mathbf{r}\right).$$

In equation 5.19 it was possible to square the equation without getting the cross product on the right-hand side of the equation because the orthogonality condition $\mathbf{X}'\mathbf{e} = \mathbf{0}$ is valid. However, this is not valid with the IV residuals $\mathbf{e}_{IV}$, so it is not possible to proceed with the equation above.

Therefore, we cannot compute (9.11). In more advanced textbooks one finds alternative expressions of quadratic forms of the residuals that can be used in a similar way as (9.11), but that is beyond the scope of this book. In EViews we test restrictions on parameters in the same way as before: select in the 'Equation' window: 'View', 'Coefficient Tests' and 'Wald Coefficient Restrictions . . . ', and specify the restriction(s) in the 'Wald Test' window, after which the test is performed. See the EViews User's Guide for more details.

9.4 IV and 2SLS estimation in EViews

In EViews, an estimation method is selected after the model has been specified in the 'Equation Specification' window. The name for 2SLS is TSLS in EViews. If TSLS has been selected, the list of instrumental variables has to be specified (the matrix $\mathbf{Z}$). 2SLS estimates are computed if the list of instrumental variables is longer than the number of explanatory variables. As an example a data set is used from Johnston and DiNardo (1997). It concerns the following quarterly data, for the period 1959(01)–1990(04):

Y_t : log per capita real expenditure on gasoline and oil,
X_{t2} : log of real price of gasoline and oil,
X_{t3} : log per capita real disposable income,
X_{t4} : log of miles per gallon.

```
Equation: EQ01   Workfile: AUTO2                                    _ □ ×
View Procs Objects   Print Name Freeze   Estimate Forecast Stats Resids

Dependent Variable: Y
Method: Least Squares
Date: 03/06/03   Time: 13:26
Sample(adjusted): 1959:2 1990:4
Included observations: 127 after adjusting endpoints
```

Variable	Coefficient	Std. Error	t-Statistic	Prob.
C	-0.505971	0.126580	-3.997258	0.0001
X2	-0.227326	0.031209	-7.283992	0.0000
X2(-1)	0.173076	0.032494	5.326367	0.0000
X3	0.346865	0.063183	5.489836	0.0000
X4	-0.187604	0.034149	-5.493674	0.0000
Y(-1)	0.648618	0.061427	10.55913	0.0000

R-squared	0.985789	Mean dependent var	-7.761041
Adjusted R-squared	0.985202	S.D. dependent var	0.118535
S.E. of regression	0.014419	Akaike info criterion	-5.594380
Sum squared resid	0.025159	Schwarz criterion	-5.460009
Log likelihood	361.2431	F-statistic	1678.724
Durbin-Watson stat	2.063660	Prob(F-statistic)	0.000000

Figure 9.1:   OLS estimates

An acceptable (concerning absence of autocorrelation) model estimated with OLS is given in Figure 9.1.

However, the price variable is an endogenous variable, whereas some doubts exist concerning 'logs of miles per gallon'. Next the equation is re-estimated with 2SLS. The window to specify the model and the matrix $\mathbf{Z}$ are given in Figure 9.2. The variables $X_{t-2,2}$ and $X_{t-3,2}$ have been used as instruments for X_{t2}, and $X_{t-1,4}$ as an instrument for $X_{t,4}$.

The output of this 2SLS estimation is shown in Figure 9.3. The price elasticity has clearly reduced, the influence of the lagged price has disappeared, whereas the other parameter estimates have hardly changed. So the endogeneity of the price variable has apparently influenced the OLS estimates. The model can be refined further as the lagged price is not significantly different from zero.

In the output window the IV residuals are used to compute the sum of squared residuals SSR and the standard error of regression $\widehat{\sigma}_u$:

$$SSR = \sum_{t=1}^{n} e_{IV,t}^2$$

and

$$\widehat{\sigma}_u = \sqrt{\frac{1}{n-K} \sum_{t=1}^{n} e_{IV,t}^2}.$$

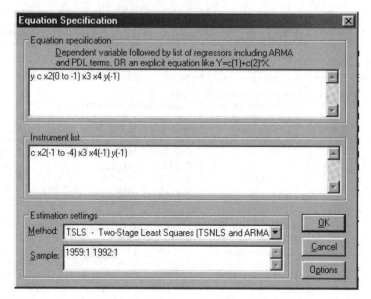

Figure 9.2: Specification of the model and the matrix **Z** with instruments

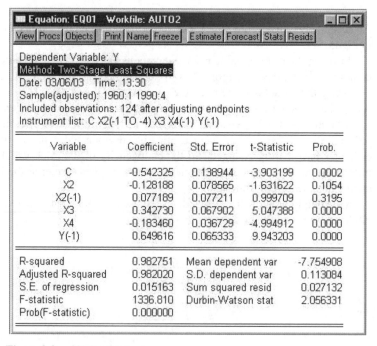

Figure 9.3: 2SLS output

9.5 Case 6: consistent estimation of structural models

In Case 2, a model has been established with OLS as an estimator for the parameters. In this exercise, the results are reconsidered. Use the following reference points to adjust your paper once more.

- Determine the nature of the explanatory variables of your econometric model. Are they all predetermined? So was it correct to use the OLS estimator?
- In case you find that endogenous explanatory variables are part of the model, estimate the parameters of your model in a consistent way by using the 2SLS estimator and check whether the specification of the model can be maintained. If no new economic variables are available to serve as instrumental variables, then lagged (predetermined) variables can be used as instruments.
- Compare the OLS and 2SLS estimation results in an economical and statistical way. Do you consider the new (consistent) estimated elasticities are more realistic, etc.?
- In Case 5, the parameters of a SUR model have been estimated with OLS. Re-estimate these parameters with 2SLS also and compare the results with the early obtained results.
- Write a comment on your previous paper using the results from this case.

Chapter 10

Simultaneous Equation Models

10.1 Introduction

A second multiple equation model, called the *simultaneous equation model* (SEM), is the subject of this chapter. A SEM is a structural model formulated from the economic theory. It is a multiple equation model, where explanatory variables from one equation can be dependent variables in other equations. So in a SEM we have to deal with endogenous explanatory variables that are explicitly specified in a structural equation. We know that endogenous explanatory variables are correlated with the disturbance terms in all the structural equations of the SEM, which results in inconsistent OLS estimates. Therefore, other but consistent estimation methods will be considered when estimating the parameters of the structural form of the model. These concern single-equation methods, such as 2SLS, and full-system (full-information) methods. Using all the information from the entire model results in more efficient estimates. The estimation methods are described in Section 10.5 and applied in Case 8 in Section 10.6.

With an estimation method such as IV, we are able to consistently estimate the parameters equation by equation. But do we know what we are estimating? Is the specification of each equation unique in the system? This is an important aspect of the SEM: the identification of its equations. The identification problem is discussed in Section 10.3. An equation is identified if no linear combination of other equations exists that produces an identical equation. Each equation has to be unique in the model, otherwise you do not know what kind of equation you are trying to estimate. After the problem has been illustrated, methods will be discussed to check the identifiability of the equations in a straightforward way. Homogeneous linear restrictions on the parameters will be necessary for the identifiability of the equations, sometimes together with restrictions on the covariance matrix of the disturbances. This last aspect is shown in Section 10.7 where the recursive models are discussed. The criteria for identification are conveniently applied when the SEM is written in matrix notation, which is introduced in Section 10.2. These identification criteria are applied in Case 7 in Section 10.4.

10.2 Mathematical notation of the SEM

A clear mathematical notation of the model is helpful to define criteria for determining the identifiability of its equations. The notation is presented in this section, then the identification of the equations is discussed in the next section.

A SEM has a *structural form*, a *reduced form* and a *final form*. The structural form contains the behavioural equations stemming from the economic theory. The standard notation of the structural form of a SEM is as follows.

■ The structural model has G endogenous variables, both dependent and explanatory variables, denoted as: Y_{tj}, $j = 1, \ldots, G$, observed for $t = 1, \ldots, n$, specified with parameters β_{ij}. The subscript i corresponds with the equation number and the subscript j refers to the jth variable.
■ The structural form has K exogenous explanatory variables X_{tk}, with $t = 1, \ldots, n$ and $k = 1, \ldots, K$, with parameters γ_{ik}.
■ Because the reduced form is the solution of the structural form for the endogenous variables Y_{tj}, we need G structural equations. So both i and j run from 1 till G. Then the model is said to be complete. For a description of the final form, see later in this section.

The structural model without any restrictions on the parameters can be written like:

$$Y_{t1} = \gamma_{11} + \beta_{12}Y_{t2} + \ldots + \beta_{1G}Y_{tG} + \gamma_{12}X_{t2} + \ldots + \gamma_{1K}X_{tK} + u_{t1}$$
$$Y_{t2} = \gamma_{21} + \beta_{21}Y_{t1} + \ldots + \beta_{2G}Y_{tG} + \gamma_{22}X_{t2} + \ldots + \gamma_{2K}X_{tK} + u_{t2}$$
$$\ldots \tag{10.1}$$
$$Y_{tG} = \gamma_{G1} + \beta_{G1}Y_{t1} + \ldots + \beta_{GG-1}Y_{tG-1} + \gamma_{G2}X_{t2} + \ldots + \gamma_{GK}X_{tK} + u_{tG}.$$

It is clear that the equations are not identified as every equation looks like the other equations, and every linear combination of equations results in an identical equation. This implies that for identifiability of an equation not all the variables can occur in the equation, or the other way round: that in each equation some variables have to be *excluded*. We will need a number of *exclusion (or zero) restrictions* on the parameters. Criteria for the number of these restrictions are derived in Section 10.3.

A matrix notation for the SEM is convenient, because that notation will be used to establish criteria as to whether or not an equation is identified. In matrix notation, eliminating the time subscript, model (10.1) is written as:

$$\mathbf{y}_1 = \mathbf{Z}_1\boldsymbol{\alpha}_1 + \mathbf{u}_1$$

$$\mathbf{y}_2 = \mathbf{Z}_2\boldsymbol{\alpha}_2 + \mathbf{u}_2$$

$$\ldots$$

$$\mathbf{y}_G = \mathbf{Z}_G\boldsymbol{\alpha}_G + \mathbf{u}_G.$$

In equation i the matrix with explanatory variables $\mathbf{Z}_i$ consists of G_i endogenous variables and K_i exogenous variables. Each disturbance term has the usual stochastic assumptions:

$$\mathbf{u}_i \sim N\left(\mathbf{0}, \sigma_{u_i}^2 \mathbf{I}_n\right), \; cov(u_{ti}, u_{tj}) = \sigma_{ij} \text{ for all } t; \text{ and } i, j = 1, \ldots, G.$$

This notation will not be used for the model as it is more convenient to use a different vector notation. The vectors are defined across the variables instead of across time. Define the vectors $\mathbf{y}_t$, $\mathbf{x}_t$ and $\mathbf{u}_t$ as follows:

$$\mathbf{y}_t \atop (G\times1) = \begin{pmatrix} Y_{t1} \\ Y_{t2} \\ \vdots \\ \vdots \\ Y_{tG} \end{pmatrix}, \quad \mathbf{x}_t \atop (K\times1) = \begin{pmatrix} 1 \\ X_{t2} \\ \vdots \\ \vdots \\ \vdots \\ X_{tK} \end{pmatrix}, \quad \mathbf{u}_t \atop (G\times1) = \begin{pmatrix} u_{t1} \\ u_{t2} \\ \vdots \\ \vdots \\ u_{tG} \end{pmatrix}.$$

The vector $\mathbf{y}_t$ is the vector (now eliminating the variable subscript) with all the endogenous variables, observed at time t; $\mathbf{x}_t$ is the vector with all the exogenous variables at time t; and $\mathbf{u}_t$ the vector with all the disturbance terms of the model, or has a zero when an equation is an identity. Bring all the variables to the left-hand side of the equation. Then the model is written as one equation:

$$\mathbf{B}\mathbf{y}_t + \mathbf{\Gamma}\mathbf{x}_t = \mathbf{u}_t, \tag{10.2}$$

The disturbance terms are assumed to be identically contemporaneously correlated in each period, which is identical to the assumptions made for the SUR model. The contemporaneous correlation between the disturbance terms is visible in the notation:

$$\mathbf{u}_t \sim NID(\mathbf{0}, \mathbf{\Omega}), \; t = 1, \ldots, n \tag{10.3}$$

with:

$$\underset{(G \times G)}{\Omega} = \begin{pmatrix} \sigma_{11} & \sigma_{12} & \cdots & \sigma_{1G} \\ \sigma_{21} & \sigma_{22} & \cdots & \sigma_{2G} \\ \vdots & \vdots & \vdots & \vdots \\ \vdots & \vdots & \vdots & \vdots \\ \sigma_{G1} & \sigma_{G2} & \cdots & \sigma_{GG} \end{pmatrix}.$$

The diagonal elements have the same notation as introduced for the SUR model in Section 8.3: $\sigma_{ii} = \sigma_{u_i}^2$. The $(G \times G)$ matrix $\mathbf{B}$ and $(G \times K)$ matrix $\mathbf{\Gamma}$ with the parameters are:

$$\underset{(G \times G)}{\mathbf{B}} = \begin{pmatrix} 1 & -\beta_{12} & \cdots & -\beta_{1G} \\ -\beta_{21} & 1 & \cdots & -\beta_{2G} \\ \vdots & \vdots & \vdots & \vdots \\ \vdots & \vdots & \vdots & \vdots \\ -\beta_{G1} & -\beta_{G2} & \cdots & 1 \end{pmatrix},$$

$$\underset{(G \times K)}{\mathbf{\Gamma}} = \begin{pmatrix} -\gamma_{11} & -\gamma_{12} & \cdots & \cdots & -\gamma_{1K} \\ -\gamma_{21} & -\gamma_{21} & \cdots & \cdots & -\gamma_{2K} \\ \vdots & \vdots & \ddots & \vdots & \vdots \\ \vdots & \vdots & \vdots & \ddots & \vdots \\ -\gamma_{G1} & -\gamma_{G2} & \cdots & \cdots & -\gamma_{GK} \end{pmatrix}.$$

In the ith row of each matrix are the parameters of the ith equation.

If $\mathbf{B}$ is not a singular matrix, then the model can be solved for the endogenous variables, which gives the *reduced-form* model:

$$\mathbf{y}_t = -\mathbf{B}^{-1}\mathbf{\Gamma}\mathbf{x}_t + \mathbf{B}^{-1}\mathbf{u}_t,$$

or in general matrix notation, with

$$\mathbf{\Pi} = -\mathbf{B}^{-1}\mathbf{\Gamma}, \text{ and } \mathbf{v}_t = \mathbf{B}^{-1}\mathbf{u}_t :$$
$$\mathbf{y}_t = \mathbf{\Pi}\mathbf{x}_t + \mathbf{v}_t.$$

This is a similar notation for the individual reduced-form equations as that introduced in Section 1.5:

$$Y_{t1} = \pi_{11} + \pi_{12}X_{t2} + \pi_{13}X_{t3} + \ldots \pi_{1K}X_{tK} + v_{t1}$$
$$Y_{t2} = \pi_{21} + \pi_{22}X_{t2} + \pi_{23}X_{t3} + \ldots \pi_{2K}X_{tK} + v_{t2}$$

$$\ldots$$

$$Y_{tG} = \pi_{G1} + \pi_{G2}X_{t2} + \pi_{G3}X_{t3} + \ldots \pi_{GK}X_{tK} + v_{tG}.$$

The reduced-form parameters (π_{ij}) are non-linear functions of all the structural parameters, and the reduced-form disturbances are functions of all the structural disturbances, which shows the dependency of all the structural disturbances and all the endogenous variables. If the model is dynamic then lagged endogenous variables are among the variables X_{ti}, implying that some of the reduced-form equations are difference equations. Solving these difference equations results in the *final form* of the model.

The reduced-form equations are written in matrix notation (identical to the general linear model) as:

$$\mathbf{y}_1 = \mathbf{X}\boldsymbol{\pi}_1 + \mathbf{v}_1$$
$$\mathbf{y}_2 = \mathbf{X}\boldsymbol{\pi}_2 + \mathbf{v}_2$$
$$\vdots$$
$$\mathbf{y}_G = \mathbf{X}\boldsymbol{\pi}_G + \mathbf{v}_G,$$

with $\mathbf{X} = \begin{pmatrix} \boldsymbol{\iota} & \mathbf{x}_2 & \mathbf{x}_3 & \cdots & \mathbf{x}_K \end{pmatrix}$, and $\boldsymbol{\iota}$ a vector with elements equal to 1 (the constant term), or more usually the entire reduced-form model as introduced above is:

$$\mathbf{y}_t = \mathbf{\Pi}\mathbf{x}_t + \mathbf{v}_t \tag{10.4}$$

The parameters of the reduced-form model can consistently be estimated with OLS, as always. The notation, as introduced in this section, is a standard notation in most of the existing econometrics literature. An example of this matrix notation applied to the equations of a simple macroeconomic model is given in Example 10.1.

Example 10.1 A macroeconomic model

This example is based on an example in Intrilligator, Bodkin and Hsiao (1996). Consider a simple macro model with the following three structural equations:

$$C_t = \gamma_{11} + \beta_{11}Y_t + u_{t1}$$
$$I_t = \gamma_{21} + \beta_{21}Y_t + \gamma_{22}Y_{t-1} + u_{t2}$$
$$Y_t = C_t + I_t + G_t.$$

The endogenous variables C_t, I_t, and Y_t represent consumption, investment and national income respectively. There is one exogenous variable G_t for government spending, and one predetermined variable, the lagged income variable Y_{t-1}. In matrix notation the structural form of the model is written as follows.

$$\begin{pmatrix} 1 & 0 & -\beta_{11} \\ 0 & 1 & -\beta_{21} \\ -1 & -1 & 1 \end{pmatrix} \begin{pmatrix} C_t \\ I_t \\ Y_t \end{pmatrix} + \begin{pmatrix} -\gamma_{11} & 0 & 0 \\ -\gamma_{21} & -\gamma_{22} & 0 \\ 0 & 0 & -1 \end{pmatrix} \begin{pmatrix} 1 \\ Y_{t-1} \\ G_t \end{pmatrix} = \begin{pmatrix} u_{t1} \\ u_{t2} \\ 0 \end{pmatrix}.$$

The reduced-form equations, as solutions of the structural model are:

$$C_t = \frac{\gamma_{11}(1-\beta_{21}) + \beta_{11}\gamma_{21}}{1-\beta_{11}-\beta_{21}} + \frac{\beta_{11}}{1-\beta_{11}-\beta_{21}}G_t + \frac{\beta_{11}\gamma_{22}}{1-\beta_{11}-\beta_{21}}Y_{t-1}$$
$$+ \frac{(1-\beta_{21})u_{t1} + \beta_{11}u_{t2}}{1-\beta_{11}-\beta_{21}}$$

$$I_t = \frac{\gamma_{21}(1-\beta_{11})}{1-\beta_{11}-\beta_{21}} + \frac{\beta_{21}}{1-\beta_{11}-\beta_{21}}G_t + \frac{\gamma_{22}(1-\beta_{11})}{1-\beta_{11}-\beta_{21}}Y_{t-1}$$
$$+ \frac{\beta_{21}u_{t1} + (1-\beta_{11})u_{t2}}{1-\beta_{11}-\beta_{21}}$$

$$Y_t = \frac{\gamma_{11}+\gamma_{21}}{1-\beta_{11}-\beta_{21}} + \frac{1}{1-\beta_{11}-\beta_{21}}G_t + \frac{\gamma_{22}}{1-\beta_{11}-\beta_{21}}Y_{t-1} + \frac{u_{t1}+u_{t2}}{1-\beta_{11}-\beta_{21}}.$$

In these equations, we clearly see that all the three endogenous variables are influenced by all the disturbance terms of the structural form, illustrating the dependence of the disturbance terms and the endogenous variables. In general notation, the reduced-form equations are more simply written as

$$C_t = \pi_{11} + \pi_{12}G_t + \pi_{13}Y_{t-1} + v_{t1} \tag{10.5}$$

$$I_t = \pi_{31} + \pi_{32}G_t + \pi_{33}Y_{t-1} + v_{t3} \tag{10.6}$$

$$Y_t = \pi_{21} + \pi_{22}G_t + \pi_{23}Y_{t-1} + v_{t2}. \tag{10.7}$$

Notice that the reduced-form equation of Y_t is a difference equation. The equations (10.5) and (10.6) are final-form equations already, whereas equation (10.7) has to be solved to know the influence of the exogenous variable G_t through time. Recursively substituting back to $t = 0$, yields

$$Y_t = \pi_{21}\left(1 + \pi_{23} + \pi_{23}^2 + \pi_{23}^3 + \ldots + \pi_{23}^{t-1}\right)$$
$$+ \pi_{23}^t Y_0 + \pi_{22}\left(G_t + \pi_{23}G_{t-1} + \pi_{23}^2 G_{t-2} + \pi_{23}^3 G_{t-3} + \ldots + \pi_{23}^{t-1}G_1\right)$$
$$+ \left(v_{t2} + \pi_{23}v_{t-1,2} + \pi_{23}^2 v_{t-2,2} + \pi_{23}^3 v_{t-3,2} + \ldots + \pi_{23}^{t-1}v_{1,2}\right). \tag{10.8}$$

This equation is the final-form equation for income. From this equation all the multipliers for income, both short-run and long-run, can be calculated. Thus the impact multiplier, giving the effect on current income of a change in current government expenditure, is obtained from equation (10.8) as:

$$\frac{\partial Y_t}{\partial G_t} = \pi_{22} = \frac{1}{1-\beta_{11}-\beta_{21}}. \tag{10.9}$$

The effect on current income of a change in government spending in the previous period is:

$$\frac{\partial Y_t}{\partial G_{t-1}} = \pi_{22}\pi_{23}. \tag{10.10}$$

Adding (10.9) and (10.10) gives the effect of a change in government spending over both the current and the previous period. The result is the two-period cumulative multiplier:

$$\pi_{22}\left(1 + \pi_{23}\right).$$

Similarly the three-period cumulative multiplier is:

$$\pi_{22}\left(1 + \pi_{23} + \pi_{23}^2\right),$$

etc.

Finally the long-run multiplier is ($\pi_{23} < 1$):

$$\pi_{22}\left(1 + \pi_{23} + \pi_{23}^2 + \ldots\right) = \frac{\pi_{22}}{1 - \pi_{23}}.$$

In Chapter 12, long-run and short-run effects are discussed in more detail.

10.3 Identification

From the economic theory, unique equations have to be specified in a simultaneous equation model, otherwise you do not know what you are working on. It is necessary to check whether each equation in the model is identified. A structural equation is identified if the equation is unique in the model or, in other words, an equation is identified if no linear combination of structural equations exists that is identical to that particular equation. Then the reduced-form model is the solution of only one structural form model. Or, again in other words, *the structural equations of the model are identified if the reduced form has exactly one structural form.*

To demonstrate this concept multiply the structural form:

$$\mathbf{B}\mathbf{y}_t + \mathbf{\Gamma}\mathbf{x}_t = \mathbf{u}_t \tag{10.11}$$

with a $(G \times G)$ non-singular transformation matrix $\mathbf{C}$. The transformed structural model

$$\mathbf{C}\mathbf{B}\mathbf{y}_t + \mathbf{C}\mathbf{\Gamma}\mathbf{x}_t = \mathbf{C}\mathbf{u}_t \tag{10.12}$$

has exactly the same reduced form as the original model (10.11), as is shown below by solving model (10.12):

$$\begin{aligned}
\mathbf{y}_t &= -\left(\mathbf{C}\mathbf{B}\right)^{-1}\mathbf{C}\mathbf{\Gamma}\mathbf{x}_t + \left(\mathbf{C}\mathbf{B}\right)^{-1}\mathbf{C}\mathbf{u}_t \\
&= -\mathbf{B}^{-1}\mathbf{C}^{-1}\mathbf{C}\mathbf{\Gamma}\mathbf{x}_t + \mathbf{B}^{-1}\mathbf{C}^{-1}\mathbf{C}\mathbf{u}_t \\
&= -\mathbf{B}^{-1}\mathbf{\Gamma}\mathbf{x}_t + \mathbf{B}^{-1}\mathbf{u}_t.
\end{aligned}$$

This reduced form belongs to an infinite number of structural forms as every choice of a non-singular matrix $\mathbf{C}$ yields another structural form with the same reduced form. However, the restrictions on the parameters of the original structural model (10.11) (exclusion of variables and normalisation) must also be imposed on the parameters of the transformed model (10.12). If these restrictions result in the situation that the only allowed transformation matrix C is the identity matrix I_G, then the model is identified. Thus the reduced form belongs to just one structural form, so the structural model is unique and therefore identified.

As an example, the identification of the structural equations of the macro model of the previous section is checked. First, we look at the consumption equation. If it is possible to show that the first row of the matrix C is the first row of the identity matrix, then the consumption equation is identified. The transformed parameters of the consumption equation are:

$$\begin{pmatrix} c_{11} & c_{12} & c_{13} \end{pmatrix} \begin{pmatrix} 1 & 0 & -\beta_{11} \\ 0 & 1 & -\beta_{21} \\ -1 & -1 & 1 \end{pmatrix} \text{ and } \begin{pmatrix} c_{11} & c_{12} & c_{13} \end{pmatrix} \begin{pmatrix} -\gamma_{11} & 0 & 0 \\ -\gamma_{21} & -\gamma_{22} & 0 \\ 0 & 0 & -1 \end{pmatrix}.$$

That now results in the following transformed consumption equation:

$$(c_{11} - c_{13}) C_t = (c_{11}\gamma_{11} + c_{12}\gamma_{21}) + (-c_{12} + c_{13}) I_t + (c_{11}\beta_{11} + c_{12}\beta_{21} - c_{13}) Y_t$$
$$+ c_{12}\gamma_{22} Y_{t-1} + c_{13} G_t + (c_{11} u_{t1} + c_{12} u_{t2}).$$

Identical restrictions with respect to normalisation and exclusion of variables have to be imposed on this transformed equation. The coefficient of C_t is equal to 1. The variables I_t, G_t and Y_{t-1} do not occur in the consumption equation; their coefficients are zero. These conditions are required for the transformed parameters too. Next, the elements of the first row of the matrix C can be determined, to ensure that the first equation is a consumption function as originally specified.

$$c_{11} - c_{13} = 1$$
$$-c_{12} + c_{13} = 0$$
$$-c_{12}\gamma_{22} = 0$$
$$-c_{13} = 0 \qquad\qquad (10.13)$$
$$\implies \begin{pmatrix} c_{11} & c_{12} & c_{13} \end{pmatrix} = \begin{pmatrix} 1 & 0 & 0 \end{pmatrix}.$$

This is the first row of the identity matrix I_3. Notice that the constant, the parameter of Y_t and the disturbance term are identical to the original ones.

In a similar way, the investment equation can be checked to see whether or not it is identified. The transformed coefficients are computed from the multiplication given below.

$$\begin{pmatrix} c_{21} & c_{22} & c_{23} \end{pmatrix} \begin{pmatrix} 1 & 0 & -\beta_{11} \\ 0 & 1 & -\beta_{21} \\ -1 & -1 & 1 \end{pmatrix} \text{ and } \begin{pmatrix} c_{21} & c_{22} & c_{23} \end{pmatrix} \begin{pmatrix} -\gamma_{11} & 0 & 0 \\ -\gamma_{21} & -\gamma_{22} & 0 \\ 0 & 0 & -1 \end{pmatrix}.$$

The transformed investment equation is:

$$(c_{22} - c_{23}) I_t = (c_{21}\gamma_{11} + c_{22}\gamma_{21}) + (-c_{21} + c_{23}) C_t + (c_{21}\beta_{11} + c_{22}\beta_{21} - c_{23}) Y_t$$
$$+ c_{22}\gamma_{22}Y_{t-1} + c_{23}G_t + (c_{11}u_{t1} + c_{12}u_{t2}).$$

Next, derive the conditions so that the equation is again an investment equation as originally specified.

$$c_{22} - c_{23} = 1$$
$$-c_{21} + c_{23} = 0$$
$$c_{23} = 0 \qquad\qquad (10.14)$$
$$\Longrightarrow \begin{pmatrix} c_{21} & c_{22} & c_{23} \end{pmatrix} = \begin{pmatrix} 0 & 1 & 0 \end{pmatrix}.$$

This is the second row of the identity matrix I_3.

The third equation is an identity and is always identified because no parameters have to be estimated.

What do we observe when we look at equations (10.13) and (10.14) that specify the identifiability conditions? The number of exclusion restrictions are sufficient to establish that both behavioural equations are identified. The number of equations for the conditions (10.14) is three for the three unknown coefficients c_{2j} $(j = 1, 2, 3)$, which is exactly the necessary number of equations to solve for c_{2j}. The number of equations for the conditions (10.13) is four for the three unknown coefficients c_{1j} $(j = 1, 2, 3)$, which is one equation too much. For that reason, we call the consumption equation *over-identified* and the investment equation *exactly identified*. We observe that two variables have been excluded to obtain an exactly identified investment equation. Three variables have been excluded to get an over-identified consumption equation. So, in this example with three endogenous variables and three equations we need at least *two excluding restrictions* for identifiability of each of the equations. This result can be generalised and formalised in two conditions which are called: *the order condition* and *the rank condition*.

The order condition

From the above example it is clear that a necessary condition for an equation from a G-equation SEM to be identified is that it has at least $G - 1$ exclusion restrictions. An exclusion restriction is a linear homogeneous restriction. This condition can be generalised by extending the excluding restrictions to linear homogeneous restrictions in general: a necessary condition for an equation from a G-equation SEM to be identified is that it has at least $G - 1$ *linear homogeneous restrictions*. A restriction like $\beta_2 = -\beta_3$, or written as $\beta_2 + \beta_3 = 0$, also contributes to making an equation unique in a model.

This order condition is a necessary condition but is not sufficient because identical restrictions can occur in different equations. A necessary and sufficient condition is the rank condition. The reason is that restrictions in more than one equation can be 'dependent', for example, when two equations should have identical restrictions, whereas the number of restrictions in each equation is sufficient for identification. Then the equations are not identified.

The rank condition

A necessary and sufficient condition for an equation from a G-equation SEM to be identified is that the rank of the matrix with parameters formed by the restrictions in the equation under study has rank $G - 1$. If this condition is fulfilled, then dependencies, as mentioned above, do not occur.

To summarise the conditions for identifiability we see that three situations are possible. Denote the number of linear homogeneous restrictions in equation i with R_i, and the matrix with columns that represent these restrictions with $\mathbf{A}_i$, then the following proposition has been made plausible.

$$
\begin{aligned}
R_i &< G - 1 & \Longrightarrow & \quad \text{equation } i \text{ is not identified,} \\
R_i &= G - 1, \text{ and } r(\mathbf{A}_i) = G - 1 & \Longrightarrow & \quad \text{equation } i \text{ is exactly identified,} \\
R_i &> G - 1, \text{ and } r(\mathbf{A}_i) = G - 1 & \Longrightarrow & \quad \text{equation } i \text{ is over-identified.}
\end{aligned}
$$

The order condition can be rewritten in an interesting way. The order condition says that equation i is identified if:

$$
R_i \geq G - 1.
$$

The number R_i is the number of excluded variables, so as $(K - K_i)$ and $(G - G_i)$ are the number of excluded exogenous and excluded endogenous variables in equation i respectively, the inequality becomes:

$$
\begin{aligned}
R_i = (K - K_i) + (G - G_i) &\geq G - 1, \\
\Longrightarrow K - K_i &\geq G_i - 1. \tag{10.15}
\end{aligned}
$$

On the left-hand side of (10.15) the number of *possible* instrumental variables that is needed to estimate equation i is found, whereas on the right-hand side of the inequality the number of *necessary* instrumental variables appears because $(G_i - 1)$ is the number of endogenous explanatory variables in equation i. So if the (in)equality holds, the parameters can be estimated by IV or 2SLS. The distinction between exact and over identification is, in fact, historical too. In the past, we stated that the parameters of an exactly identified equation had to be estimated with IV, and the parameters of an over-identified equation with 2SLS. Those were two different methods, viewed computationally. Nowadays, this distinction is not really relevant, as computational limitations no longer exist.

Example 10.2   Order and rank condition

These conditions will be applied to the macro model again. For reasons of convenience the model in matrix notation is shown again:

$$
\begin{pmatrix} 1 & 0 & -\beta_{11} \\ 0 & 1 & -\beta_{21} \\ -1 & -1 & 1 \end{pmatrix} \begin{pmatrix} C_t \\ I_t \\ Y_t \end{pmatrix} + \begin{pmatrix} -\gamma_{11} & 0 & 0 \\ -\gamma_{21} & -\gamma_{22} & 0 \\ 0 & 0 & -1 \end{pmatrix} \begin{pmatrix} 1 \\ Y_{t-1} \\ G_t \end{pmatrix} = \begin{pmatrix} u_{t1} \\ u_{t2} \\ 0 \end{pmatrix}.
$$

Count the restrictions: $R_1 = 3$, $R_2 = 2$, whereas $G = 3$. So according to the order condition it is possible that the first equation is over-identified ($R_1 = 3 > 2 = G - 1$) and the second equation is exactly identified ($R_2 = 2 = G - 1$). So check the rank condition for the consumption and investment equation:

$$\mathbf{A}_1 = \begin{pmatrix} 0 & 0 & 0 \\ 1 & -\gamma_{22} & 0 \\ -1 & 0 & -1 \end{pmatrix}, \quad \mathbf{A}_2 = \begin{pmatrix} 1 & 0 \\ 0 & 0 \\ -1 & -1 \end{pmatrix}.$$

Here it is not difficult to recognise that $r(\mathbf{A}_1) = 2$, and that $r(\mathbf{A}_2) = 2$, so the first equation is over-identified and the second equation is exactly identified. Both structural equations can be consistently estimated by 2SLS (or IV).

If an equation is not identified it can become identified by imposing more restrictions on its parameters or by adding variables in other equations of the model. Although the investment equation is identified, this equation will be used to present an example of how a restriction can be added to its parameters. Suppose that the following null hypothesis is not rejected: $H_0 : \beta_{21} + \gamma_{22} = 0$, after the parameters of the investment equation have been estimated. Then the investment equation has one more linear homogeneous restriction and can be written as:

$$I_t = \gamma_{21} + \beta \nabla Y_t + u_{t2}.$$

This equation only makes sense if I_t does not show a linear trend, because the transformation ∇Y_t eliminates a possible linear trend in Y_t. A model that has a dependent variable with a linear trend and explanatory variables without trends has not been correctly specified because the trend in the dependent variable is not explained. These aspects concerning trend characteristics of an economic variable will be elaborated and formalised in Chapter 12. The concept of *order of integration* of a variable will be introduced, which is useful to check the trend behaviour of all the specified variables. It is important to mention this point here. The restriction is a linear homogeneous restriction, so $R_2 = 3 > 2 = G - 1$, and the matrix $\mathbf{A}_2$ becomes a (3×3) matrix, because a third column is added for this extra linear homogeneous restriction:

$$
\begin{array}{ccc}
C_t & G_t & \nabla Y_t \\
excluded & excluded & \downarrow \\
\searrow & \downarrow & \beta_{i1}+\gamma_{i2}=0 \\
& & \swarrow
\end{array}
$$

$$\mathbf{A}_2 = \begin{pmatrix} 1 & 0 & -\beta_{11} \\ 0 & 0 & 0 \\ -1 & -1 & 1 \end{pmatrix}.$$

The rank of $\mathbf{A}_2$ is still equal to 2, $r(\mathbf{A}_2) = 2$, but in this situation the equation is called over-identified. In the original specification the equation was exactly identified.

10.4   Case 7: identification of the equations of a SEM

This case is an exercise to practise the conditions for identifiability on the equations of a simple macroeconomic model. Consider the following dynamic macro model with a behavioural equation for consumption and investments, and an identity defining income:

$$C_t = \gamma_{11} + \beta_{11}Y_t + \gamma_{12}Y_{t-1} + u_{t1}$$
$$I_t = \gamma_{21} + \beta_{21}Y_t + \gamma_{22}Y_{t-1} + \gamma_{24}I_{t-1} + u_{t2}$$
$$Y_t = C_t + I_t + G_t.$$

The variables C_t, I_t, Y_t are considered as endogenous variables, and the variable G_t for government spending is considered as an exogenous variable. Then consider the following:

■   Check the identifiability of the equations of this macroeconomic model.
■   Suppose that the government spending was constant in the sample period:

$$G_t = \overline{G}.$$

   Check again the identifiability of the equations of the macroeconomic model with this assumption.
■   Next assume that the government spending G_t is also an endogenous variable, so one more behavioural equation is added to the model, for example:

$$G_t = \gamma_{31} + \gamma_{32}Y_{t-1} + \gamma_{34}I_{t-1} + u_{t3}.$$

   What can be said about the identification of the three behavioural equations of the new model?
■   The new model of the previous question is maintained. After the parameters have consistently been estimated, the null hypothesis

$$H_0 : \beta_{21} = -\gamma_{22}$$

   was tested and was not rejected. What is the impact of this result on the identifiability of the equations?

10.5   Estimation methods

Two types of estimation methods are distinguished for a SEM: *single-equation methods* and *full-model* (or *full-information*) *methods*. Single-equation methods do not use the information that contemporaneous correlation exists between the disturbance terms of the complete model. They are not asymptotically efficient, but only consistent. Some well-known, single-equation estimation methods are IV, 2SLS and LIML (*limited-information maximum likelihood*). The first two methods have been discussed before. LIML is the maximum likelihood estimator applied to one equation, and is called 'limited' for that reason.

Complete system methods are, for example, FIML (*full-information maximum likelihood*) and 3SLS (*three-stage least squares*), which are consistent and asymptotically efficient estimation methods. These two methods are asymptotically equivalent (see, for example, Greene (2000) Section 16.6 and included references). The principle of 3SLS is identical to that of the SUR model. One mathematical expression for the 3SLS estimator can be derived, but historically the three stages were considered separately. For didactical reasons, to understand in a clear way what is done, these three steps are illustrated here in an example. The method is applied to a two-equation system:

$$Y_{t1} = \gamma_{11} + \beta_{12}Y_{t2} + \gamma_{12}X_{t2} + u_{t1}$$
$$Y_{t2} = \gamma_{21} + \beta_{21}Y_{t1} + \gamma_{23}X_{t3} + u_{t2}.$$

Remember the disturbance-term assumptions (10.3) for all the disturbance terms of the model:

$$\mathbf{u}_t \sim NID(\mathbf{0}, \mathbf{\Omega}), \; t = 1, \ldots, n.$$

This can be written in this example as:

$$\begin{pmatrix} u_{t1} \\ u_{t2} \end{pmatrix} \sim NID \left(\begin{pmatrix} 0 \\ 0 \end{pmatrix}, \begin{pmatrix} \sigma_{u_1}^2 & \sigma_{u_1 u_2} \\ \sigma_{u_1 u_2} & \sigma_{u_2}^2 \end{pmatrix} \right).$$

The first two stages consist of the computation of the parameter estimates of the individual equations with 2SLS. Similar to the SUR estimator, the variances and covariances of all the (2SLS) residual vectors of the model are computed in the third stage, which gives an estimated covariance matrix $\widehat{\mathbf{\Omega}}$, after which GLS estimates can be computed. Both equations are exactly identified as each equation has one exclusion restriction. A summary of the 'three stages' is given in the following scheme.

- In the first stage, OLS is applied to each of the reduced-form equations and the predicted values $\widehat{Y}_{t1}$ and $\widehat{Y}_{t2}$ are calculated.
- Secondly, substitute $Y_{t1} = \widehat{Y}_{t1} + e_{t1}$, and $Y_{t2} = \widehat{Y}_{t2} + e_{t2}$ in the structural equations and estimate the structural parameters with OLS to obtain consistent 2SLS estimates of the parameters:

$$Y_{t1} = \gamma_{11} + \beta_{12}\widehat{Y}_{t2} + \gamma_{12}X_{t2} + (u_{t1} + \beta_{12}e_{t1})$$
$$Y_{t2} = \gamma_{21} + \beta_{21}\widehat{Y}_{t1} + \gamma_{23}X_{t3} + (u_{t2} + \beta_{21}e_{t2}).$$

Save the 2SLS residuals $e_{IV,t1}$ and $e_{IV,t2}$.

■ Next, in the third stage, estimate the variances and covariances of the disturbance terms:

$$\widehat{\sigma}^2_{u_1} = \frac{1}{n} \sum_{t=1}^{n} e^2_{IV,t1}$$

$$\widehat{\sigma}^2_{u_2} = \frac{1}{n} \sum_{t=1}^{n} e^2_{IV,t2}$$

$$\widehat{\sigma}_{u_1 u_2} = \frac{1}{n} \sum_{t=1}^{n} e_{IV,t1} e_{IV,t2}.$$

This gives an estimate of the covariance matrix $\boldsymbol{\Omega}$:

$$\widehat{\boldsymbol{\Omega}} = \begin{pmatrix} \widehat{\sigma}^2_{u_1} & \widehat{\sigma}_{u_1 u_2} \\ \widehat{\sigma}_{u_1 u_2} & \widehat{\sigma}^2_{u_2} \end{pmatrix}.$$

The two equations are combined in one model in an identical way as in the SUR model, with identical notation: $\mathbf{X}_i$ being the matrix with the explanatory variables and $\boldsymbol{\alpha}_i$ the vector with parameters of the ith equation:

$$\begin{pmatrix} \mathbf{y}_1 \\ \mathbf{y}_2 \end{pmatrix} = \begin{pmatrix} \mathbf{X}_1 & \mathbf{0} \\ \mathbf{0} & \mathbf{X}_2 \end{pmatrix} \begin{pmatrix} \boldsymbol{\alpha}_1 \\ \boldsymbol{\alpha}_2 \end{pmatrix} + \begin{pmatrix} \mathbf{u}_1 \\ \mathbf{u}_2 \end{pmatrix} \implies$$

$$\mathbf{y}_* = \mathbf{X}_* \boldsymbol{\alpha}_* + \mathbf{u}_*, \text{ with}$$

$$\mathbf{u}_* \sim N(\mathbf{0}, \boldsymbol{\Omega}).$$

For this model, the feasible GLS estimator $\widehat{\boldsymbol{\alpha}}_*$ is calculated:

$$\widehat{\boldsymbol{\alpha}}_* = \left(\mathbf{X}'_* \widehat{\boldsymbol{\Omega}}^{-1} \mathbf{X}_* \right)^{-1} \mathbf{X}'_* \widehat{\boldsymbol{\Omega}}^{-1} \mathbf{y}_*.$$

The elements of the vector $\widehat{\boldsymbol{\alpha}}_*$ are the 3SLS estimates of all the parameters of the SEM.

The procedures in EViews to compute 3SLS and FIML estimates are similar to the procedure to estimate the parameters of the SUR model. The following must be done: select 'New Object', 'System', and type the structural equations in the 'System' window. However, be aware that identities are not allowed in the 'System' window! A list with instrumental variables has to be included in the system. These IV variables can be specified for the entire system or by equation (see the examples below). Identities should be substituted in the other equations and these equations can be specified in the system.

For example, the macroeconomic model from Case 7 can be written as:

$$C_t = \gamma_{11} + \beta_{11} (C_t + I_t + G_t) + \gamma_{12} Y_{t-1} + u_{t1}$$
$$I_t = \gamma_{21} + \beta_{21} Y_t + \gamma_{22} Y_{t-1} + \gamma_{24} I_{t-1} + u_{t2}.$$

When, for example, the variables G_t and $Y_{t-1}, \ldots, Y_{t-4}$ and $I_{t-1}, \ldots, I_{t-4}$ are chosen as instrumental variables for the entire system, the 'System' window looks as follows:

```
CONS = C(1) + C(2) * (CONS + INV + GOV) + C(3) * Y(-1)
INV = C(4) + C(5) * Y + C(6) * Y(-1) + C(7) * INV(-1)

INST GOV Y(-1 to -4) INV(-1 to -4)
```

It is possible to stay closer to each equation by specifying IV variables by equation, by separating each equation and its IV variables with the @ sign, for example in the following way:

```
CONS = C(1) + C(2) * (CONS + INV + GOV) + C(3) * Y(-1)
@ CONS(-1 to -2) INV(-1 to -2) GOV Y(-1)
INV = C(4) + C(5) * Y + C(6) * Y(-1) + C(7) * INV(-1)
@ Y(-1 to -3) INV(-1)
```

Next, select the estimation method 3SLS or FIML under the 'Estimate' button (see Figure 8.2 for an example of that window). More information and advanced information about the use of a system is found in the EViews User's Guide.

10.6 Case 8: simultaneous estimation of a macroeconomic model

With the knowledge obtained in this chapter, we are able to estimate the parameters of the structural equations of one of the macroeconomic models simultaneously. Some suggestions are given as follows:

- Choose one of the countries from Data set 2 with macroeconomic data.
- Specify a dynamic consumption and investment equation and check the identifiability of the two structural equations.
- Add a discrepancy variable to the identity to make the identity balanced before substituting the identity in one of the structural equations (see Section 2.3).
- Estimate the parameters of the two equations with 2SLS. If Data set 2 had been used in Case 2, one of the equations has already been estimated.
- Open a new object 'System' and specify both equations in the system window, in the first instance according to the previous individual results. Specify the instrumental variables according to one of the two mentioned possibilities in the previous section. Alternatively, estimate the parameters twice in both manners to see the effects of this choice on the results.
- Click the button 'Estimate' and select 3SLS as the estimation method.

■ Check the results in an economical and statistical way, just as was done with the SUR model in Case 5. Are the estimation results realistic and do the residuals obey the underlying assumptions? Compare the full-system results with the single-equation results.

■ Finally, write a paper about the estimation results and all other relevant findings.

10.7 Two specific multiple-equation models

In this section, some attention is given to recursive models. Two forms of recursivity in a SEM can be distinguished: *simple-recursive* models and *block-recursive* models. These are models with specific restrictions on parameters and covariances of disturbance terms. The simple-recursive model is more restrictive than the block-recursive model. These two models also play a role in the history of econometrics. The simple-recursive model is, in fact, a historical model. In the past, when the computational possibilities were limited by lack of computers, the simple-recursive model was an interesting structure for a SEM. Everyone was happy when OLS could be used by equation, instead of full SEM methods. Nowadays, these computational restrictions no longer exist, and many have doubts about the reliability of the assumptions underlying this model and its practical usefulness. The block-recursive model is still useful, as in large SEMs the number of predetermined variables can become too large, larger than the number of observations. Then computational problems arise when estimating the parameters of reduced-form equations in the first step of the 2SLS procedure. Or, in other words, when only talking about the mathematical expression (9.8) for the 2SLS estimator, singular matrices appear in that expression. This problem is overcome by splitting the model into a number of simultaneous blocks. The two models will be described briefly in this section. As these models can still be encountered in the literature it is good to know their features.

The simple-recursive model

The SEM is called a *simple-recursive model* if in the simultaneous-equation model:

$$\mathbf{B}\mathbf{y}_t + \mathbf{\Gamma}\mathbf{x}_t = \mathbf{u}_t$$

$$\mathbf{u}_t \sim NID(\mathbf{0}, \mathbf{\Omega}), \ t = 1, \ldots, n,$$

the matrices $\mathbf{B}$ and $\mathbf{\Omega}$ can be restricted in the following way:

$$
\mathbf{B}_{(G \times G)} =
\begin{pmatrix}
1 & 0 & \cdots & \cdots & 0 \\
-\beta_{21} & 1 & \cdots & \cdots & 0 \\
\vdots & \vdots & \ddots & \vdots & \vdots \\
\vdots & \vdots & \vdots & \ddots & 0 \\
-\beta_{G1} & -\beta_{G2} & \cdots & \cdots & 1
\end{pmatrix},
\quad
\mathbf{\Omega}_{(G \times G)} =
\begin{pmatrix}
\sigma_{11} & 0 & \cdots & \cdots & 0 \\
0 & \sigma_{22} & \cdots & \cdots & 0 \\
\vdots & \vdots & \ddots & \vdots & \vdots \\
\vdots & \vdots & \vdots & \ddots & 0 \\
0 & 0 & \cdots & \cdots & \sigma_{GG}
\end{pmatrix}.
$$

The matrix $\mathbf{B}$ is triangular and Ω is a diagonal. The disturbance terms of the SEM are assumed to be independent. When checking the identifiability of the equations we see that only the first equation is identified according to the order and rank condition: $R_1 = G - 1$, $R_i < G - 1$ for $i = 2, \ldots, G$. If the model is transformed by using a transformation matrix $\mathbf{C}$ as before, it is possible to show that the equations are identified, which is caused by the extra restrictions on the covariance matrix Ω of the disturbance terms. This can be made clear with the following example based on an example in Johnston (1984). Consider the model:

$$y_{t1} - \gamma_{11} x_{t1} = u_{t1}$$

$$y_{t2} - \beta_{21} y_{t1} - \gamma_{21} x_{t1} = u_{t2},$$

with $u_{ti} \sim NID(0, \sigma_{ii})$ and $\sigma_{12} = 0$. The model is written in matrix notation as:

$$\begin{pmatrix} 1 & 0 \\ -\beta_{21} & 1 \end{pmatrix} \begin{pmatrix} y_{t1} \\ y_{t2} \end{pmatrix} - \begin{pmatrix} \gamma_{11} \\ \gamma_{21} \end{pmatrix} (x_{t1}) = \begin{pmatrix} u_{t1} \\ u_{t2} \end{pmatrix},$$

with

$$\begin{pmatrix} u_{t1} \\ u_{t2} \end{pmatrix} \sim N \left(\begin{pmatrix} 0 \\ 0 \end{pmatrix}, \begin{pmatrix} \sigma_{11} & 0 \\ 0 & \sigma_{22} \end{pmatrix} \right).$$

The first equation of this model is identifiable and the second is not, according to the order and rank condition. Using the matrix:

$$\mathbf{C} = \begin{pmatrix} c_{11} & c_{12} \\ c_{21} & c_{22} \end{pmatrix}$$

as a transformation matrix and using the additional restriction on the covariance matrix Ω, it is possible to show that the second equation is also identified. The transformed equations become:

$$(c_{11} - c_{12}\beta_{21})y_{t1} + c_{12}y_{t2} - (c_{11}\gamma_{11} + c_{12}\gamma_{21})x_{t1} = c_{11}u_{t1} + c_{12}u_{t1},$$

$$(c_{21} - c_{22}\beta_{21})y_{t1} + c_{22}y_{t2} - (c_{21}\gamma_{11} + c_{22}\gamma_{21})x_{t1} = c_{21}u_{t1} + c_{22}u_{t2}.$$

The transformed coefficients have to obey the same restrictions as those of the original equations, so this gives the following conditions on the transformed parameters:

$$c_{11} - c_{12}\beta_{21} = 1$$

$$c_{12} = 0$$

$$c_{22} = 1$$

which implies: $c_{11} = 1$ and $c_{12} = 0$ and $c_{22} = 1$. Then the matrix $\mathbf{C}$ looks like:

$$\mathbf{C} = \begin{pmatrix} 1 & 0 \\ c_{21} & 1 \end{pmatrix}.$$

The second row is not the second row from the identity matrix I_2. But there are more restrictions:

$$\Omega = \begin{pmatrix} \sigma_{11} & 0 \\ 0 & \sigma_{22} \end{pmatrix}.$$

Of course, the restriction of the zero covariance must also be valid in the transformed model. The covariance matrix of the transformed disturbances is $Var\,(\mathbf{Cu}_t)$, then:

$$Var\,(\mathbf{Cu}_t) = \mathbf{C} \cdot Var\,(\mathbf{u}_t) \cdot \mathbf{C}'$$
$$= \mathbf{C\Omega C}'.$$

This matrix must obey the restriction that the non-diagonal elements are zero, that is:

$$\mathbf{c}_1 \Omega \mathbf{c}_2' = 0,$$

or

$$\begin{pmatrix} 1 & 0 \end{pmatrix} \begin{pmatrix} \sigma_{11} & 0 \\ 0 & \sigma_{22} \end{pmatrix} \begin{pmatrix} c_{21} \\ 1 \end{pmatrix} = 0,$$

or:

$$c_{21}\sigma_{11} = 0.$$

This implies that:

$$c_{21} = 0, \text{ as } \sigma_{11} \neq 0.$$

Thus the only admissible transformation matrix is the identity matrix:

$$\mathbf{C} = \begin{pmatrix} 1 & 0 \\ 0 & 1 \end{pmatrix} = \mathbf{I}_2,$$

which means that both the equations are identified. Identification has been achieved by restrictions on the structural parameters and the covariance matrix of the disturbances of the model.

The parameters of the equations can be consistently estimated by OLS. The first equation is a reduced-form equation and, in the second equation, the disturbance term u_{t2} and the explanatory endogenous variable y_{t1} are independently distributed:

$$cov\,(u_{t2}, y_{t1}) = cov\,(u_{t2}, (\gamma_{11}x_{t1} + u_{t1})) = 0,$$

because $cov\,(u_{t2}, x_{t1}) = 0$, and $cov\,(u_{t2}, u_{t1}) = 0$.

If you really want to use the properties of this simple recursive model you should be convinced that the strong restrictions on the parameters of this model are realistic. Estimation of the parameters with a simultaneous estimation method is more obvious.

The block-recursive model

The simple-recursive model can be modified to a less-restrictive model, the *block-recursive model,* when not all the elements in the right-upper part of **B** are zero. The model consists of independent blocks of simultaneous equations. This model produces 'blocks' around the main diagonal. The order of the blocks around the diagonal of Ω is assumed to be identical to those of the blocks around the diagonal of **B**. Let us look at an example to clarify this model. Suppose that we have a SEM with five endogenous variables and equations, and the following restrictions on its parameters are given:

$$
\underset{(5\times5)}{\mathbf{B}} =
\begin{pmatrix}
1 & -\beta_{12} & 0 & 0 & 0 \\
-\beta_{21} & 1 & 0 & 0 & 0 \\
-\beta_{31} & -\beta_{32} & 1 & 0 & 0 \\
-\beta_{41} & -\beta_{42} & 0 & 1 & -\beta_{45} \\
0 & -\beta_{52} & -\beta_{53} & 0 & 1
\end{pmatrix},
\quad
\underset{(5\times5)}{\Omega} =
\begin{pmatrix}
\sigma_{11} & \sigma_{12} & 0 & 0 & 0 \\
\sigma_{21} & \sigma_{22} & 0 & 0 & 0 \\
0 & 0 & \sigma_{33} & 0 & 0 \\
0 & 0 & 0 & \sigma_{44} & \sigma_{45} \\
0 & 0 & 0 & \sigma_{54} & \sigma_{55}
\end{pmatrix}.
$$

The model has been divided into three blocks. Equations 1 and 2 are a simultaneous block, equation 3 is statistically independent of the system, and equations 4 and 5 form a simultaneous block too. If these restrictions are valid, then the identification of the equations is checked by block and the parameters of the equations are estimated by block. Identification is not checked in this example as no matrix Γ is considered. It is just an example to illustrate the properties of this model. Suppose that all the equations are (over)-identified, then the parameters of the first two equations are estimated with, for example, 2SLS, the parameters of the 3rd equation are estimated with OLS, and the parameters of equations 4 and 5 are estimated again with 2SLS.

The advantage of this model is that when a SEM is very large, it can be convenient to handle it as a block-recursive model, as the number of predetermined variables of each block will be smaller than the number of predetermined variables in the entire model. This overcomes possible estimation problems when the number of observations is smaller than the number of predetermined variables in the entire model. In practice, it is not impossible that the restrictions of the block-recursive model are acceptable and can be applied in very large models.

Chapter 11

Qualitative Dependent Variables

11.1 Introduction

The last specific structural model to be discussed in Part III is the model with a qualitative dependent variable. The dependent variable is a dummy variable. This subject can be discussed very extensively, for example, Maddala (1983) provides a very complete text. Maddala (2001) also considers this subject in his *Introduction to Econometrics*, 'This is a complete area by itself, so we give only an elementary introduction,' and this is done, in an even more elementary fashion, in this chapter.

The dependent variable is often a binary variable. However, that depends on the formulation of the research problem. The dummy variable can take more than two values, but that is not a topic in this book. Dummy variables which have more than two values complicate this subject more than those taking only two values. In this introductory course, only binary dummies that take zero or one as values are considered. Such a dependent variable is called a *dichotomous* or *binary* variable.

The necessary data for estimating the parameters of such a relationship clearly concern a cross-section. For example, look at a dichotomous variable that a person possesses a personal computer or not (PC_i), which is related to a number of relevant variables like income (Y_i), education (E_i), age (A_i), etc.:

$$PC_i = \beta_1 + \beta_2 Y_i + \beta_3 E_i + \beta_4 A_i + u_i. \tag{11.1}$$

$$PC_i = \begin{cases} 1 \text{ if person } i \text{ has a PC,} \\ 0 \text{ if person } i \text{ has no PC.} \end{cases}$$

The (cross-section) data necessary to estimate the parameters of the model are collected by asking a group of people whether or not they have a PC ($PC_i = 0$ or 1) and what their age, income and education is. Education will be a qualitative variable too, for example, ranked from 0 (no education) to 10 (highest level of education). If such a relationship has been estimated, then it will be possible to predict whether a person owns a PC given his or her income, education and age.

It will be clear that the variable PC_i does not have a normal distribution, to mention just one of the problems. Model (11.1) is also known as a *discrete regression model*. More types of these models exist, even for time-series data. In cases where the parameters are estimated with OLS the model is called the *linear probability model*. The *linear discriminant function* is an example of another model which is related to the linear probability model. These models will be explained to a certain extent in Section 11.2. One more option is to say that there is a 'latent variable' Y_i^* underlying the process that is not observed. Only a dummy variable Y_i is observed in the following way:

$$Y_i = \begin{cases} 1, & \text{if } Y_i^* > 0, \\ 0, & \text{otherwise.} \end{cases}$$

This idea results in what is known in the econometrics literature as the *probit* and *logit* models. These models are discussed in Section 11.3. Sufficient introductory knowledge about a number of these models will be obtained from this chapter, to make it possible to apply them at an elementary level. Applications are presented in Section 11.4, where the use of EViews is described to estimate the parameters of a discrete regression model.

11.2   The linear probability model

The linear probability model, mentioned in the previous section, model (11.1), denotes a model with a dichotomous dependent variable (PC_i) which takes the values 1 or 0 (yes or no):

$$PC_i = \beta_1 + \beta_2 Y_i + \beta_3 E_i + \beta_4 A_i + u_i$$

with $E(u_i) = 0$. This implies that:

$$E(PC_i) = \beta_1 + \beta_2 Y_i + \beta_3 E_i + \beta_4 A_i.$$

For notational convenience we consider one explanatory variable X_{i2} in this chapter to explain the models:

$$PC_i = \beta_1 + \beta_2 X_{i2} + u_i$$
$$E(PC_i) = \beta_1 + \beta_2 X_{i2}.$$

The expected value of a qualitative variable like $E\left(PC_i\right)$ has an interesting interpretation with respect to probabilities. Define the probability P_i as the chance that person i has a PC:

$$P_i = \text{Prob}\left(PC_i = 1\right).$$

But realise that PC_i can only take the value 0 or 1 which means that:

$$\text{Prob}\left(PC_i = 0\right) = 1 - P_i.$$

Next, compute the expected value of the binary variable:

$$\begin{aligned} E\left(PC_i\right) &= 1 \cdot \text{Prob}\left(PC_i = 1\right) + 0 \cdot \text{Prob}\left(PC_i = 0\right) \\ &= 1 \cdot P_i + 0 \cdot \left(1 - P_i\right) \\ &= P_i. \end{aligned}$$

The expectation of the binary variable $E\left(PC_i\right)$ is simply the probability that person i has a PC given the values of the exogenous variables:

$$P_i = \beta_1 + \beta_2 X_{i2}.$$

This model is called the *linear probability model*. The equation can be estimated by using OLS. With the econometric model, predictions of the probabilities can be computed given particular values of the explanatory variables. However, this model has a number of problems. It is clear that the value of a probability is in the interval $(0, 1)$. That can go wrong with the predicted values $\widehat{PC_i}$. $\widehat{PC_i}$ is the estimated probability that the event of the ownership of a PC occurs. But it is clear that these predicted values can lie outside the interval $(0, 1)$. Further, we have a problem with the distribution of the disturbance term. The disturbances of this model cannot be normally distributed. They must have a binomial distribution.

Because PC_i is equal to 0 or 1, the disturbance term u_i can also take only two values: $1 - \beta_1 - \beta_2 X_{i2}$ and $-\beta_1 - \beta_2 X_{i2}$, with probabilities $P_i = \beta_1 + \beta_2 X_{i2}$ and $(1 - P_i) = 1 - \beta_1 - \beta_2 X_{i2}$. Recall the statistical expression for the variance of a random variable:

$$\begin{aligned} var(u_i) &= E\left(\left(u_i - \mu\right)^2\right) \\ &= \sum_{u_i} \left(u_i - \mu\right)^2 f\left(u_i\right) \\ &= \sum_{u_i} \left(u_i\right)^2 f\left(u_i\right), \end{aligned}$$

as $\mu = 0$. Then compute the variance of u_i from the linear probability model:

$$\begin{aligned} \sigma_{u_i}^2 &= \left(1 - \left(\beta_1 + \beta_2 X_{i2}\right)\right)^2 \left(\beta_1 + \beta_2 X_{i2}\right) + \left(- \left(\beta_1 + \beta_2 X_{i2}\right)\right)^2 \left(1 - \left(\beta_1 + \beta_2 X_{i2}\right)\right) \\ &= \left(\beta_1 + \beta_2 X_{i2}\right)\left(1 - \left(\beta_1 + \beta_2 X_{i2}\right)\right) \\ &= E\left(PC_i\right)\left(1 - E\left(PC_i\right)\right). \end{aligned}$$

This means that the disturbance term of the linear probability model is heteroskedastic and that OLS estimation produces non-efficient estimates. Efficient estimates can be computed by using a weighted least squares estimator (GLS) as discussed in Section 8.6, because the form of the heteroskedasticity is known in this model. This is done by first estimating the equation with OLS, after which the predicted values $\widehat{PC}_i$ are computed. With these predictions the weights w_i are calculated:

$$w_i = \frac{1}{\sqrt{\widehat{PC}_i(1 - \widehat{PC}_i)}},$$

and the weighted least squares estimates can be computed. To keep it simple, it is also possible to use White's 'heteroskedastic consistent covariance matrix estimator' to obtain consistent estimates of the standard errors.

More problems can be mentioned such as standard test statistics that cannot be used in a straight manner as the disturbance term is not normally distributed: and, more importantly, as mentioned before, the computed probabilities can lie outside the interval (0,1) in many cases. Figure 11.1 shows an illustration of this problem. The variable X_{i2} is any explanatory variable to serve as an example for the scatter diagram.

Since PC_i can take the values 0 or 1 only, a scatter diagram will consist of just two horizontal rows of points. OLS will fit a line through these points similar to the one drawn in Figure 11.1. From this figure it is also seen that the coefficient of determination R^2 is likely to be low, as no straight line could fit the scatter. R^2 is not a good measure for

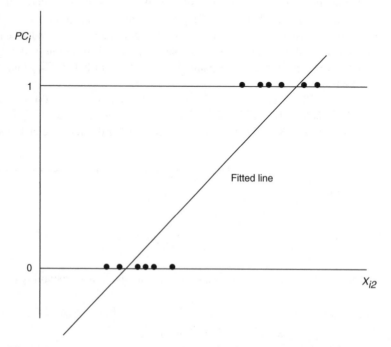

Figure 11.1:   A scatter diagram of data for the linear probability model

the quality of the performance of the model when the dependent variable is a qualitative dummy variable. This problem is discussed in more detail in Section 11.3. For a more detailed discussion on the models in this chapter see, for example, the above mentioned books of Maddala or Chapter 19 in Greene (2000).

> **Remark 11.1 The linear discriminant function**
> As mentioned in the introduction, the 'linear discriminant function' is another model which is related to the linear probability model. This function will not be discussed in this book, only the idea behind this function is mentioned here. For example, n observations on an economic variable have been collected. The economic phenomenon is explained by K explanatory variables. Next, suppose that the n observations can be split into two groups, such that n_1 of them belong to one group and n_2 belong to a second group, with $n = n_1 + n_2$. If a linear function of the K variables can be found that separates the two groups in an optimal way, then this function is called the linear discriminant function. The discriminant function makes it possible to predict whether new observations belong to group one or group two. The linear discriminant function is the best discriminator between the two groups according well-defined criteria. The statistical analysis used to find this function is called discriminant analysis, but is beyond the scope of this book.

11.3 Probit and logit models

Because of the problems that we have established with the linear probability model different models will be used. One of the possible approaches that has been developed in the econometrics literature is to model a *latent variable* Y_i^* and to specify the model as follows. The bivariate model is used again in general notation. The model is:

$$Y_i^* = \beta_1 + \beta_2 X_{i2} + u_i,$$

where Y_i^* is an unobservable variable. For example Y_i^* represents the amount of money that person i has spent on buying a PC. What we observe is a dummy variable Y_i defined by:

$$Y_i = \begin{cases} 1, & \text{if } Y_i^* > 0, \\ 0, & \text{otherwise.} \end{cases}$$

Denote by P_i the probability that the event $Y_i^* > 0$ occurs:

$$
\begin{aligned}
P_i &= \text{Prob}\,(Y_i = 1) \\
&= \text{Prob}\,(Y_i^* > 0) \\
&= \text{Prob}\,(\beta_1 + \beta_2 X_{i2} + u_i > 0) \\
&= \text{Prob}\,(u_i > -(\beta_1 + \beta_2 X_{i2})).
\end{aligned}
$$

If we use a symmetric distribution of the disturbance term u_i that is symmetrical around its zero mean then the following equation applies:

$$\text{Prob}\left(u_i > -(\beta_1 + \beta_2 X_{i2})\right) = \text{Prob}\left(u_i < \beta_1 + \beta_2 X_{i2}\right).$$

This means for the probability P_i:

$$P_i = \text{Prob}\left(Y_i = 1\right)$$
$$= \text{Prob}\left(u_i < \beta_1 + \beta_2 X_{i2}\right).$$

The probability P_i depends on the distribution of the disturbance term u_i. Two distributions are considered in this context: the normal distribution and the logistic distribution. If the u_i are assumed to be normally distributed, then we get a model that is known as the *probit model*. However, in that case it appears that the above-derived probability is rather complicated to work out and therefore researchers prefer to use the logistic distribution. The cumulative logistic distribution is used for u_t. Thus we have the following distribution function:

$$F(\beta_1 + \beta_2 X_{i2}) = \frac{e^{\beta_1 + \beta_2 X_{i2}}}{1 + e^{\beta_1 + \beta_2 X_{i2}}}$$
$$= \frac{1}{1 + e^{-\beta_1 - \beta_2 X_{i2}}}$$
$$= \frac{1}{1 + \exp\left(-\beta_1 - \beta_2 X_{i2}\right)}.$$

A convenient notation is introduced in the last expression. The resulting model is called the *logit model*. The logistic function can be drawn as an S-shaped curve that is bounded between 0 and 1, as shown in Figure 11.2.

With the logistic function, we have the following logit model for P_i:

$$P_i = \frac{1}{1 + \exp\left(-Y_i^*\right)}$$
$$= \frac{1}{1 + \exp\left(-(\beta_1 + \beta_2 X_{i2} + u_i)\right)}. \tag{11.2}$$

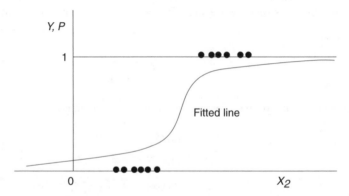

Figure 11.2:   The logistic function

This equation ensures that P_i lies between the values 0 and 1. This property is clear from Figure 11.2 and is also easily established by looking at the following limits:

If $X_{i2} \to \infty$ with $\beta_2 > 0$, then it follows that $P_i \to 1$, and
if $X_{i2} \to -\infty$ with $\beta_2 > 0$, then it follows that $P_i \to 0$.

Rewrite the expression (11.2) for $1 - P_i$:

$$1 - P_i = \frac{\exp\left(-\left(\beta_1 + \beta_2 X_{i2} + u_i\right)\right)}{1 + \exp\left(-\left(\beta_1 + \beta_2 X_{i2} + u_i\right)\right)}, \tag{11.3}$$

from which it follows that:

$$\ln\left(\frac{P_i}{1 - P_i}\right) = \beta_1 + \beta_2 X_{i2} + u_i. \tag{11.4}$$

This result is easily verified:

$$\ln\left(\frac{P_i}{1 - P_i}\right) = \ln\left(\frac{1}{1 + \exp\left(-Y_i^*\right)} \times \frac{1 + \exp\left(-Y_i^*\right)}{\exp\left(-Y_i^*\right)}\right)$$

$$= \ln\left(\frac{1}{\exp\left(-Y_i^*\right)}\right)$$

$$= Y_i^*$$

$$= \beta_1 + \beta_2 X_{i2} + u_i.$$

The logit model (11.4) is a non-linear model; its parameters have to be estimated by a non-linear estimation method. The cumulative normal and the cumulative logistic curve are very close to each other except at the tails; a similar property when comparing the normal and the Student's t-distribution.

The results of the logit and probit models will not differ very much. However, the estimates of the parameters are not directly comparable. The variance of the logistic distribution is $\pi^2/3$ and the variance of the standard normal distribution is of course equal to 1. Therefore, the estimates of the parameters obtained from the logit model have to be multiplied by $\sqrt{3}/\pi$ (≈ 0.551) to be comparable to the estimates obtained from the probit model. Amemiya (1981) proposes to multiply the logit estimates by $1/1.6 = 0.625$ as this transformation produces a closer approximation between the logistic and the standard normal distribution. To compare the parameter estimates of the linear probability model and the logit model, Amemiya suggests multiplying all the parameters of the logit model with 0.25 and further adding 0.5 to the constant term.

The coefficient of determination R^2 is an inappropriate measure of goodness of fit, as was the case with the linear probability model. To test the specification of the model an LR-test can be used to test the null hypothesis that the parameters are zero. The standard OLS zero-slopes F-test is not used due to its relationship to R^2. This null hypothesis is tested with a likelihood ratio test. Let L_U be the value of the log-likelihood function of the unrestrictedly estimated model and let L_R be the value of the log-likelihood function of the restrictedly estimated equation that has only the intercept as regressor. Then the LR-test statistic is the well-known statistic:

$$LR = -2 \left(\ln \left(L_R \right) - \ln \left(L_U \right) \right),$$

that has an asymptotic $\chi^2(K-1)$ distribution under the null hypothesis of zero-slopes coefficients. This LR-test statistic is always printed in the EViews output when a logit or probit model has been estimated with a constant term. Pseudo-$R^2 s$ are found in the literature, but they are not often used. In the EViews procedure that estimates logit and probit models, the McFadden pseudo-R^2 is computed and printed in the output. The McFadden pseudo-R^2 is defined as:

$$\text{Pseudo-}R^2 = 1 - \frac{L_U}{L_R}.$$

It is a pseudo-R^2 because this coefficient does not have the interpretation of a ratio between unexplained and total variation of the dependent variable Y_i, so it has nothing to do with the coefficient of determination as discussed in Section 5.3. More information about these subjects can be found in the earlier mentioned references and other econometrics literature.

11.4 Estimation of binary dependent variable models with EViews

Estimation of the parameters of models with qualitative dependent variables with EViews is just as simple as all the discussed estimation methods from previous chapters. For estimating a *linear probability model* just specify the equation and estimate with least squares, but remember all the mentioned problems with respect to the estimation result. In the EViews User's Guide, an extensive description of the procedures can be found. Below an example is given, where artificial data have been used. The sample contains 60 observations. The variables that have been simulated are:

$$PC_i = \begin{cases} 0 & \text{person } i \text{ has no PC,} \\ 1 & \text{person } i \text{ has a PC;} \end{cases}$$

$EDUC_i$: number of years of schooling after primary school, ranking in the interval 0–15;

$$INC_i = \begin{cases} 0 & \text{income of person i: } \leq \$10,000 \\ 1 & \$10,000 < \text{income of person i: } \leq \$20,000 \\ 2 & \$20,000 < \text{income of person i: } \leq \$30,000 \\ 3 & \$30,000 < \text{income of person i: } \leq \$40,000 \\ 4 & \$40,000 < \text{income of person i: } \leq \$50,000 \\ 5 & \text{income of person i: } > \$50,000; \end{cases}$$

AGE_i : age of person i, ranking in the interval 18–81.

These artificial data are available at the website in the file *pcdata.xls*, so it is possible to reproduce the exercise in this section.

```
■ Equation: EQ_PC  Workfile: CSDATA                        _ □ ×
View Procs Objects   Print Name Freeze   Estimate Forecast Stats Resids

Dependent Variable: PC
Method: Least Squares
Date: 07/31/03   Time: 12:43
Sample(adjusted): 1 59
Included observations: 59 after adjusting endpoints
White Heteroskedasticity-Consistent Standard Errors & Covariance

      Variable      Coefficient   Std. Error   t-Statistic    Prob.

         C           0.687309     0.183892     3.737575     0.0004
        AGE         -0.020856     0.006281    -3.320461     0.0016
        EDUC         0.023636     0.016393     1.441843     0.1550
        INC          0.249640     0.054552     4.576157     0.0000

R-squared            0.440981   Mean dependent var      0.525424
Adjusted R-squared   0.410489   S.D. dependent var      0.503640
S.E. of regression   0.386693   Akaike info criterion   1.003015
Sum squared resid    8.224211   Schwarz criterion       1.143865
Log likelihood      -25.58895   F-statistic             14.46222
Durbin-Watson stat   1.932844   Prob(F-statistic)       0.000000
```

Figure 11.3:   An estimated linear probability model

In Figure 11.3, the least squares output is shown, but not all results are relevant. The option 'Heteroskedasticity Consistent Coefficient Covariance' has been used to work with the heteroskedastic disturbance term, although the source of the heteroskedasticity is not unknown here.

In Figure 11.4, where the residuals, actual and fitted values have been plotted, you can observe that several predicted probabilities are outside the interval $(0, 1)$, with two extreme negative values of -0.54.

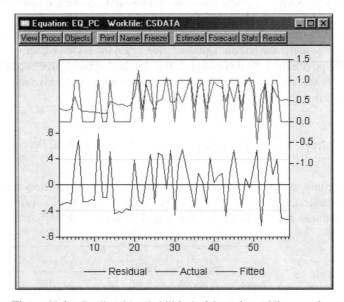

Figure 11.4:   Predicted 'probabilities' of the estimated linear probability model

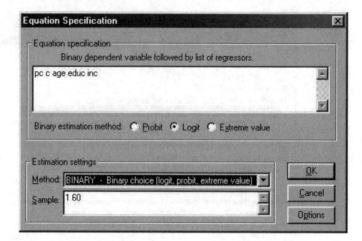

Figure 11.5:   Example of the selection of the logit estimation procedure

The estimated model is written as:

$$\widehat{PC}_i = \underset{(0.184)}{0.687} - \underset{(0.006)}{0.021}\ AGE_i + \underset{(0.016)}{0.024}\ EDUC_i + \underset{(0.055)}{0.250}\ INC_i,$$

The model can be used to predict the chance that a person has a PC given the *not exceptional* values of the explanatory variables age, education and income. The model cannot predict correct probabilities for extreme values of the explanatory variables.

To estimate a *logit* or *probit model* the equation is specified again in the 'Equation' window. The specification of a binary model may never be entered as an 'explicit' equation. Select 'BINARY' as the estimation method and choose the method: *logit* or *probit*. The third possible method (extreme value) is not discussed here. See Figures 11.5 and 11.6 as examples of estimating a logit model for the PC-equation. Various estimation options are available under the button 'Options'. See again the EViews User's Guide for a description of the possibilities. In this example, the standard options have been used.

EViews maximises the likelihood function with an iterative method. It is important to realise that the output has to be read as follows:

$$\ln\left(\frac{\widehat{PC}_i}{1-PC_i}\right) = \underset{(2.868)}{7.620} - \underset{(0.139)}{0.453}\ AGE_i + \underset{(0.244)}{0.246}\ EDUC_i + \underset{(1.478)}{4.728}\ INC_i.$$

According to the arithmetical rules of Amemiya the parameters are multiplied with 0.25 and subsequently the intercept term is increased with 0.5 to make them comparable with the estimated parameters of the linear probability model:

	β_1	β_2	β_3	β_4
Logit:	2.405	−0.113	0.061	1.182
OLS:	0.687	−0.021	0.024	0.250

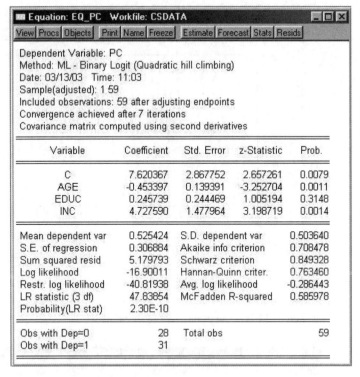

Figure 11.6: The estimated logit model

All the logit estimates are clearly larger than the OLS estimates.

As explained in the previous section, the McFadden pseudo-R^2 and the LR-test are found in the output. The value of the LR-test is 47.83 (0.00), so the null hypothesis of zero slopes is clearly rejected. See the EViews User's Guide for an explanation of other printed statistics. Finally, the residuals, actual and fitted values are given again, where now all the predicted values are within the range $(0, 1)$ (see Figure 11.7).

Next probabilities $\widehat{PC}_i$ can be computed for given values of the explanatory variables. For given values of age, education and income it is convenient to compute a probability by using expression (11.3). This is illustrated in Figure 11.8 and explained below.

The following steps have been done after the logit model has been estimated as given in Figure 11.6 earlier:

■ Under the button 'View' in the 'Equation' window select 'Representations'; then the 'Equation' window looks like the window shown in Figure 11.8.

■ Copy the 'Substituted Coefficients', as marked in the figure, in the command window. The formula is based on equation (11.3). In the figure, this has been done twice, both to show the formula and to show the formula with the substituted values of the explanatory variables in the figure.

■ As an example, the probability (p) has been computed that a person aged 35 with little education ($educ = 1$), but high income ($inc = 5$) possesses a PC. Change 'PC'

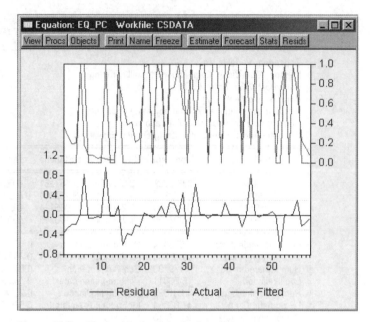

Figure 11.7:   The residuals of the logit model

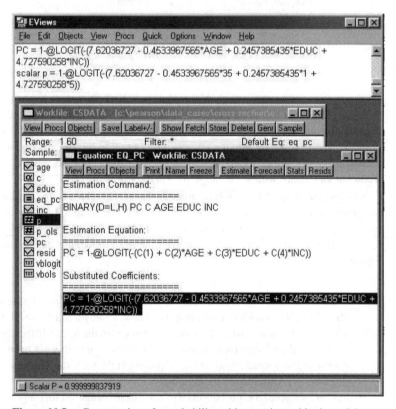

Figure 11.8:   Computation of a probability with an estimated logit model

in 'scalar p' and substitute the values for age, $educ$ and inc. After double-clicking on p the probability is shown at the bottom of the EViews window: $p = 0.99$.

When the probability is computed with the linear probability model, the outcome is $p = 1.23$, which is a useless result.

11.5   Case 9: modelling a qualitative dependent variable

Data set 5 with the cross-section data on many Dutch companies is used to estimate a model for a binary dependent variable. For example, we can consider the variable *extech*, which is a dummy variable that indicates whether a firm needs to acquire external technological knowledge, as an interesting variable that is dependent on other variables. Then the probability can be computed that a firm wishes to have external help given values of the other variables. Let us look at a linear probability model and a logit model for this qualitative variable. A number of reference points are given below:

■   Look at the description of the available variables in Data set 5. Determine which of these variables are candidates that influence the need for external technological knowledge by a firm, and determine the signs of their parameters. Analyse the data.
■   Estimate a linear probability model and a logit model. The linear probability model can be estimated with weighted least squares or with White's correction for heteroskedasticity to compute the standard errors. Look at the residual behaviour. For the logit model, use the LR-test as a goodness-of-fit test.
■   Compare both the estimation results by using the arithmetical rules of Amemiya.
■   Estimate probabilities that a firm needs external technological knowledge with both models, by using plausible and extreme values of the explanatory variables. This can conveniently be done by looking at the descriptive statistics of the involved series, where the minimum, mean and maximum value of the variables are shown. In EViews use the procedure 'scalar' to compute these probabilities in a neat way.

Time-series Models

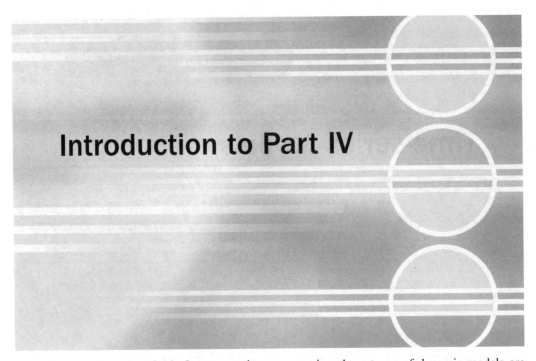

Introduction to Part IV

In the last part of this first course in econometrics, three types of dynamic models are discussed in its three chapters. These are error-correction models, distributed-lag models and univariate time-series models. Before discussing these models, some general aspects of causal dynamic economic models are discussed in more detail in the first three sections of Chapter 12. An interesting question is: what are the long-run properties of an unrestrictedly estimated, dynamic short-run model? It is possible that these properties are unrealistic from an economic point of view, like improbable values of long-run parameters or elasticities. This is not necessarily a bad property of the model, as in fact the model is only valid for the sample period that has been used to establish it. But if a long-run relationship is expected to exist for theoretical economic reasons, then a possible solution for the improper long-run behaviour of the model is restricting the long-run parameters. The restricted long-run model is imposed as a solution of a matching dynamic short-run model. That restricted short-run model is called an *error-correction model*. The central topic in Chapter 12 is an integrated discussion of modelling the short and the long run of the economy. Error-correction models, unit-root tests and the concept of cointegration are introduced and extensively discussed.

In Chapters 13 and 14, different dynamic models are discussed. In Chapter 13 we study a model with many lags of one or more explanatory variables. Such a specification results in estimation problems, such as a very few degrees of freedom, and inaccurate estimates because of severe multicollinearity. The problem is solved by using a *distributed lag specification* for those explanatory variables. At the end of that chapter, explicit attention will be paid to the specification of a lagged dependent variable. The question – What is the economic interpretation of a lagged dependent variable and what is the interpretation of the magnitude of its coefficient? – is discussed in more detail.

Finally, in Chapter 14, the univariate time-series models, the ARIMA models, are introduced. Univariate ARIMA models are statistical models for one variable. The variable is explained by its behaviour in the past and by lagged disturbances. These models have the ability to produce accurate short-run forecasts. The procedures to determine an ARIMA model and to compute forecasts are called the *Box–Jenkins methods*, which are extensively discussed with many examples.

Chapter 12

Dynamic Models, Unit Roots and Cointegration

12.1 Introduction

Before the dynamic models are discussed, a new notation for representing dynamic models is introduced in Section 12.2. That concerns the introduction of the lag operator. The use of the lag operator will turn out to be rather useful in the analysis of dynamic time-series models. In Section 12.3, the lag operator will be applied to analyse the long-run properties of a dynamic short-run model. Of course, this is only done if there are economic reasons for studying a possible long-run equilibrium model. When that is not the case, the project ends with the estimated short-run model that can be used for several other targets. An unrestricted short-run model is, mathematically seen, a difference equation. The solution of this difference equation is a static equation that perhaps can be interpreted as the unrestricted long-run model. It is possible that an acceptable equilibrium relationship is found, but it can also happen that such a solution results in a nonsense model from an economic point of view. Examples of this type of quantitative economic analysis are given in Section 12.3.

To overcome the problem of an unrealistic long-run model you can examine whether restricting the parameters of the long-run equation yields economically realistic results. Restricting the long-run parameters can be done in two ways:

■ the researcher sets a long-run parameter to a value that is plausible from the theory based on his or her economic knowledge; or
■ the researcher tries to estimate a static long-run model.

When a long-run model has been imposed as a given solution of the short-run model by the researcher, then it causes restrictions on the parameters of the dynamic short-run model. This restricted short-run model is called an *error-correction model*. The error-correction model will be introduced and detailed in Section 12.4. The solution of an error-correction model is known a priori as it has been imposed: the model converges to the restricted or to the estimated long-run model. An error-correction model is a dynamic model for the short run that has a special explanatory variable – the *error-correction term* – which represents the equilibrium equation. By means of this term, the restricted dynamic short-run model converges to the imposed long-run model. Restricting a long-run parameter requires economic knowledge about the long run. When the economic theory is not clear about the exact specification of an equilibrium relationship, it is perhaps possible to estimate the equilibrium relationship. That is the second mentioned method: estimation of an equilibrium model. Such an estimated long-run model is a static equation.

In Part I we saw that estimated static equations usually have autocorrelated residuals, which is an indication for model mis-specification. That is true because the static model is a mis-specified model for the short run. However, in Section 12.6 we investigate conditions on which an estimated static equation can be considered to be a long-run relationship among the economic variables. If those conditions are not satisfied, then the static equation is a mis-specified model and the regression is called a *spurious regression*. The conditions for a static equation to represent a long-run model are based on the trend behaviour of the involved variables. If the variables have comparable trends then it is possible that the static model is a long-run model. The tools for this analysis consist of unit-root tests, applied on the variables and on the residuals of the static regression. The unit-root tests are discussed in Section 12.5. The procedures to model long-run and short-run models are explained in Section 12.6. For more detailed information see e.g. Hamilton (1994), Hendry (1995) and Maddala and Kim (1998), books that extensively deal with these topics.

So summarising, two situations will be examined in this chapter:

■ model and estimate the short-run and check the long-run properties of the model, as discussed in Section 12.3; and
■ estimate or restrict a static equation, representing the long run, and estimate a matching corresponding dynamic short-run model, which is discussed in detail in Sections 12.4 and 12.6.

12.2 Lag operators, notation and examples

This section is a preparatory section concerned with the use of a different notation: the lag operator L is introduced. This notation is convenient in studying theoretical aspects of dynamic models. But, in addition, long-run multipliers can easily be computed by using lag operators in the model specification. Some specific models, which will be studied in the next two chapters, serve as examples with respect to this notation. The lag operator is useful for notational and algebraic convenience only. Define the operator L as follows:

$$LX_t = X_{t-1}.$$

Then the following use of the lag operator will be clear:

$$L^2 X_t = L(LX_t) = LX_{t-1} = X_{t-2}.$$

In some books and journals the B (backward-shift operator) is used instead of L. Although L is an operator, it is sometimes convenient to use it as a variable to perform some simple algebraic operations. Mathematically seen, it looks fishy using operators like variables. Some authors, like Stewart (1991), define the lag polynomials in a variable μ, and after the desired computations have been done the μ is replaced by the operator L. However, the result is identical to the result when just the L had been used for the computations. In fact, the result of a computation with the operator L is defined as a new operator; this is illustrated with examples in this and following sections.

We start by looking at the specification of a dynamic model of two variables, with p lags of the dependent variable and s lags of the explanatory exogenous variable. That is written as:

$$Y_t = \beta_0 + \beta_1 Y_{t-1} + \beta_2 Y_{t-2} + \ldots + \beta_p Y_{t-p}$$
$$+\gamma_0 X_t + \gamma_1 X_{t-1} + \gamma_2 X_{t-2} + \ldots + \gamma_s X_{t-s} + u_t. \tag{12.1}$$

Bring the lags of the endogenous variable to the left-hand side of the equation:

$$Y_t - \beta_1 Y_{t-1} - \beta_2 Y_{t-2} - \ldots - \beta_p Y_{t-p}$$
$$= \beta_0 + \gamma_0 X_t + \gamma_1 X_{t-1} + \gamma_2 X_{t-2} + \ldots + \gamma_s X_{t-s} + u_t.$$

Then apply the lag operator for the lagged variables and rewrite the equation:

$$Y_t - \beta_1 L Y_t - \ldots - \beta_p L^p Y_t = \beta_0 + \gamma_0 X_t + \gamma_1 L X_t + \ldots + \gamma_s L^s X_t + u_t$$
$$(1 - \beta_1 L - \ldots - \beta_p L^p) Y_t = \beta_0 + (\gamma_0 + \gamma_1 L + \ldots + \gamma_s L^s) X_t + u_t.$$

Next define the lag polynomials $\beta(L)$ of order p and $\gamma(L)$ of order s:

$$\beta(L) = 1 - \beta_1 L - \beta_2 L^2 - \ldots - \beta_p L^p,$$

$$\gamma(L) = \gamma_0 + \gamma_1 L + \gamma_2 L^2 + \ldots + \gamma_s L^s.$$

Now the general dynamic model (12.1) is written in a simple notation as:

$$\beta(L) Y_t = \beta_0 + \gamma(L) X_t + u_t. \tag{12.2}$$

Model (12.1), or written as model (12.2), is a difference equation. To check the stability of this model, the lag polynomials $\beta(L)$ and $\gamma(L)$ are considered as polynomials in the 'complex plane' $\mathbb{C}$, where they have p and s complex roots respectively. A necessary and sufficient condition for stability is that all the roots of $\beta(L)$ lie outside the unit circle in $\mathbb{C}$.

This will be made clear by looking at a simple AR(1) model (AutoRegressive model of order 1) for Y_t:

$$Y_t = \beta_0 + \beta_1 Y_{t-1} + u_t,$$

or written as:

$$(1 - \beta_1 L) Y_t = \beta_0 + u_t.$$

In this case $\beta(L)$ is a first-order lag polynomial:

$$\beta(L) = 1 - \beta_1 L.$$

Solve this polynomial for L:

$$\beta(L) = 0$$
$$(1 - \beta_1 L) = 0$$
$$L = \frac{1}{\beta_1}.$$

The condition $|L| > 1$ implies that $|\beta_1| < 1$. This condition is the well-known condition for the AR(1) model to be stable. In general, the polynomial $\beta(L)$ can be factored as:

$$\beta(L) = (1 - b_1 L)(1 - b_2 L) \ldots (1 - b_p L),$$

then the roots $1/b_i$ must be such that $|L| > 1$, all the p roots have to lie outside the unit circle, implying that $|b_i| < 1$ for $i = 1, \ldots, p$. These stability conditions yield restrictions on the parameters β_i of the original model (12.1).

Special expressions with the lag operator will be defined as new operators. For example, two *sum operators* will now be introduced. The only reason to introduce these algebraic operations is that the result is convenient in analysing the properties of dynamic models. Applications of the mathematical results on econometric models obtained in this section, are given in the next section.

The sum operator, that sums the observations of a variable from 'the Big Bang' up till now is defined as the operator

$$\frac{1}{1 - L}.$$

$$\sum_{i=0}^{\infty} X_{t-i} = X_t + X_{t-1} + X_{t-2} + \ldots$$
$$= X_t + L X_t + L^2 X_t + \ldots$$
$$= (I + L + L^2 + \ldots) X_t$$
$$= \frac{1}{1 - L} X_t,$$

so:

$$\frac{1}{1 - L} X_t = \frac{X_t}{1 - L} = \sum_{i=0}^{\infty} X_{t-i}. \tag{12.3}$$

Another useful sum operator is the operator with parameter λ:

$$\frac{1}{1 - \lambda L},$$

with $0 < \lambda < 1$. This operator will be used for the sum of the geometrically declining influence of lags of a variable. It is a weighted infinite sum where the influence of the past fades away, as seen below:

$$\sum_{i=0}^{\infty} \lambda^i X_{t-i} = X_t + \lambda X_{t-1} + \lambda^2 X_{t-2} + \lambda^3 X_{t-3} + \ldots$$

$$= X_t + \lambda L X_t + \lambda^2 L^2 X_t + \lambda^3 L^3 X_t + \ldots$$

$$= \left(1 + \lambda L + \lambda^2 L^2 + \lambda^3 L^3 + \ldots \right) X_t$$

$$= \frac{1}{1 - \lambda L} X_t.$$

If the observations of the series $\{X_t\}$ are 'normal' economic observations, in the sense that their values are bounded and not all zero, we can expect that the variance of $X_t / (1 - L)$ is infinite, and the variance of $X_t / (1 - \lambda L)$ is finite. These are important features of the two sum operators. The essential difference between the two operators is that one operator has a parameter that is less than one, whereas the other operator has a parameter that is equal to one. More details about these sum operators, and related aspects are discussed in Section 12.5. One more feature of the new notation has become clear: when the lag operator appears in the denominator of an operator then we have an infinite (weighted) sum of past values of the involved variable. It is useful to remember this property from now on.

Expressions like $X_t / (1 - \lambda L)$ will frequently be encountered in the econometric time-series literature. An example where this notation is used is the following (distributed lag) model with an infinite number of lags of one explanatory variable:

$$Y_t = \beta_0 + \gamma_0 X_t + \gamma_1 X_{t-1} + \gamma_2 X_{t-2} + \gamma_3 X_{t-3} + \ldots + u_t.$$

The parameters of this model cannot be estimated without making further assumptions. The distributed lag model is discussed in the next chapter in more detail. A solution to the problem of the infinite number of parameters is to assume that the influence of the variable X_t declines geometrically in time; originally introduced by Koyck (1954). The assumption of a decreasing explanatory influence in time is not unrealistic from an economic point of view. The assumption is written as:

$$\gamma_i = \lambda \gamma_{i-1}, \text{ with } |\lambda| < 1.$$

Substitute this in the equation and use the lag operator:

$$Y_t = \beta_0 + \gamma_0 X_t + \gamma_0 \lambda L X_t + \gamma_0 \lambda^2 L^2 X_t + \gamma_0 \lambda^3 L^3 X_t + \ldots + u_t$$
$$Y_t = \beta_0 + \gamma_0 \left(1 + \lambda L + \lambda^2 L^2 + \lambda^3 L^3 + \ldots\right) X_t + u_t$$
$$Y_t = \beta_0 + \gamma_0 \frac{1}{1 - \lambda L} X_t + u_t.$$

In the last non-linear equation, with a sum operator, only three parameters have to be estimated.

The last example in this section of the use of lag operators concerns *difference operators*. As introduced in Section 5.6, the first-difference operator ∇ is defined as:

$$\nabla X_t = X_t - X_{t-1}$$
$$= (1 - L) X_t.$$

This implies the following relationship between the operators ∇ and L:

$$\nabla = 1 - L.$$

Then the inverse of the operator $\nabla : \nabla^{-1}$ has the following expressions:

$$\nabla^{-1} = \frac{1}{1 - L} = \sum.$$

We see that *summing is the inverse of differencing*. This is the 'discrete analogy' of differentiating and integrating of continuous functions. The definitions were given in Section 5.6 but once more the names are mentioned: ∇ is called nabla and Δ is called delta. The definition of Δ is:

$$\Delta X_t = X_{t+1} - X_t.$$

Both operators are simply related to each other:

$$\Delta X_t = X_{t+1} - X_t = (1 - L) X_{t+1} = \nabla X_{t+1}.$$

In economic research, the 'nabla' is mainly used, as it is more useful to look at changes with respect to the previous period in the past. The first difference operator eliminates a linear trend in a variable, as was shown in Remark 7.1 in Section 7.5:

$$\nabla t = t - (t - 1) = 1.$$

Of course, we can difference a differenced variable once more, resulting in a twicely differenced variable. Second differences are written as $\nabla^2 X_t$:

$$\nabla^2 X_t = \nabla X_t - \nabla X_{t-1}.$$

The second difference operator eliminates a trend in the growth rate of a variable.

Sometimes, when it is relevant, seasonal differences of a series can be taken as one more method to adjust for seasonal movements in a variable. The seasonal difference operator ∇_s, with period s, is defined as:

$$\nabla_s = 1 - L^s.$$

An example of the use of a seasonal difference operator in a sample with quarterly data is the operator ∇_4 that is defined as:

$$\nabla_4 Y_t = \left(1 - L^4\right) Y_t$$
$$= Y_t - Y_{t-4}.$$

The difference operators are also defined in EViews. Therefore, it is not necessary to generate difference variables in EViews. The workfile grows with every new 'generate'. Instead of generating a new variable like dY:

$$\text{genr } dY = Y - Y\left(-1\right),$$

the difference operators can be used. The difference operator is defined and used in the following way:

- $d\left(Y\right)$ or $d\left(Y, 1, 0\right)$ or $d\left(Y, 0, 0\right)$ for the first difference: ∇Y_t;
- $d\left(Y, 2\right)$ or $d\left(Y, 2, 0\right)$ for the second difference: $\nabla^2 Y_t$;
- $d\left(Y, 0, 4\right)$ for the seasonal difference in case of quarterly data: $\nabla_4 Y_t$;
- $d\left(Y, 1, 4\right)$ for the first difference of a seasonal difference: $\nabla \nabla_4 Y_t$.

The transformation $\nabla \nabla_s$ is not unusual in the empirical econometrics literature. In EViews, the operator $dlog$ is also defined. The operator $dlog\left(Y, n, s\right)$ is identically defined as $d\left(Y, n, s\right)$, but it returns differences of the logs of the variable. (See also Chapter 14 for the use of this notation in ARIMA models.)

The use of difference operators in EViews is very convenient for forecasting the level of a variable, in the situation that the model is specified in the differences of the variables. Mostly you will be interested in predicting the level and not the change of the variable. In that situation, it is possible to choose whether forecasts for the level or for the first differences of the variable have to be computed, after the 'Forecast' button has been selected. See Figure 12.1 for an example.

Figure 12.1 relates to a relationship between the commodity prices (in logs) that have been estimated in first differences. Because we would like to predict future cocoa prices, the difference operator was used as shown in Figure 12.1. The same is true for other transformations with the difference operator.

12.3 Long-run effects of short-run dynamic models

The main topic in this chapter is a discussion about estimating and solving dynamic short-run models for economic variables to obtain long-run models. For example, if a dynamic short-run model is used for simulation experiments, then we are interested in knowing the

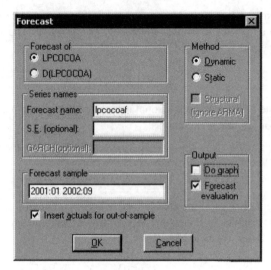

Figure 12.1: Forecasting P_t^{coc} in a model that explains ∇P_t^{coc} (in logs)

properties of the model with respect to its long-run behaviour. A short-run dynamic model can explode or converge in a straight or in a cyclical way, which are the properties of difference equations. Look at the following example with two different dynamic models, as an illustration of dynamic short-run models and matching long-run models. Model (12.4) has a lagged exogenous variable and the other model (12.5) has a lagged dependent variable.

$$Y_t = \beta_0 + \gamma_0 X_t + \gamma_1 X_{t-1} + u_t \tag{12.4}$$

$$Y_t = \beta_0 + \gamma_0 X_t + \beta_1 Y_{t-1} + u_t \tag{12.5}$$

In model (12.5) the *stability condition*: $|\beta_1| < 1$ is required. Next, look in Table 12.1 at the short-run, intermediate, and long-run response to Y_t of a unit change in X_t in consecutive periods.

The solution of a dynamic model can result in a satisfactory long-run model, but there is also a possibility that the values of the long-run parameters are economically unrealistic. The long-run multiplier $\gamma_0/(1 - \beta_1)$ in model (12.5) – see Table 12.1 – depends on the

Period	Model (12.4)	Model (12.5)
$t = 1$	γ_0	γ_0
$t = 2$	$\gamma_0 + \gamma_1$	$\gamma_0 + \gamma_0\beta_1 = \gamma_0(1 + \beta_1)$
$t = 3$	$\gamma_0 + \gamma_1$	$\gamma_0 + \gamma_0\beta_1 + \gamma_0\beta_1^2 = \gamma_0(1 + \beta_1 + \beta_1^2)$
$\vdots$	$\vdots$	$\vdots$
long-run:	$\gamma_0 + \gamma_1$	$\gamma_0/(1 - \beta_1)$, because: $|\beta_1| < 1$

Table 12.1: Short- and long-run responses

values of the sample estimates of γ_0 and β_1. But the other way around, if $\widehat{\gamma}_0/(1 - \widehat{\beta}_1)$ has an economic unrealistic value, it is possible to restrict this parameter to an acceptable value that is known from the theory or from other research, for example, $\gamma_0/(1 - \beta_1) = c$. Next a short-run model can be estimated with this restriction on the long run, by substituting the restriction in the short-run model. The restricted short-run model can be maintained when the restriction does not generate residual autocorrelation. Restrictions on parameters will not be imposed in this way but by specifying an *error-correction model* for the short run. In Section 12.4 the error-correction model is introduced. The short-run model has been respecified in such a way that the long-run restriction is clearly visible in the specification. The error-correction model converges to the long-run model with the imposed parameter value(s).

However, first we look at the corresponding long-run models of models (12.4) and (12.5) by using the lag operator. Consider model (12.4) and rewrite the model with the lag operator:

$$Y_t = \beta_0 + \gamma_0 X_t + \gamma_1 L X_t + u_t$$
$$Y_t = \beta_0 + (\gamma_0 + \gamma_1 L) X_t + u_t.$$

The 'parameter' of the variable X_t is:

$$(\gamma_0 + \gamma_1 L). \tag{12.6}$$

Remember that we had established that the long-run response of Y_t to a unit change in X_t is $\gamma_0 + \gamma_1$. Observe that this value of the long-run response is found by substituting $L = 1$ in the expression (12.6):

$$\gamma_0 + \gamma_1.$$

Then the static equation

$$Y = \beta_0 + (\gamma_0 + \gamma_1) X$$

represents the long-run equilibrium equation between Y and X.

Next, rewrite model (12.5) with the lag operator and solve the equation for Y_t:

$$Y_t = \beta_0 + \gamma_0 X_t + \beta_1 L Y_t + u_t$$
$$(1 - \beta_1 L) Y_t = \beta_0 + \gamma_0 X_t + u_t$$
$$Y_t = \frac{\beta_0}{(1 - \beta_1)} + \frac{\gamma_0}{(1 - \beta_1 L)} X_t + \frac{u_t}{(1 - \beta_1 L)}. \tag{12.7}$$

Notice that:

$$\frac{\beta_0}{(1 - \beta_1 L)} = \frac{\beta_0}{(1 - \beta_1)},$$

as a constant term cannot be lagged. In model (12.5) we had established that the long-run response of Y_t to a unit change in X_t is $\gamma_0/(1-\beta_1)$. In equation (12.7) we observe again that this long-run response is found by substituting $L=1$ in the operator

$$\frac{\gamma_0}{(1-\beta_1 L)}$$

of X_t. Substitute $L=1$ and the long-run multiplier is:

$$\frac{\gamma_0}{1-\beta_1}.$$

The static equation

$$Y = \frac{\beta_0}{1-\beta_1} + \frac{\gamma_0}{1-\beta_1}X$$

represents the long-run equilibrium equation between Y and X as a result of the short-run model (12.5). As a side effect, equation (12.7) shows why an estimated mis-specified static equation suffers from serious residual autocorrelation: the disturbance term is specified with a distributed lag.

With these examples it has become clear that the use of the lag operator is convenient in computing long-run multipliers. Now look at the general dynamic model (12.2). The long-run response to Y_t of a unit change in X_t is computed in the following way. First rewrite the model:

$$\beta(L) Y_t = \beta_0 + \gamma(L) X_t + u_t,$$

$$Y_t = \frac{\beta_0}{\beta(L)} + \frac{\gamma(L)}{\beta(L)}X_t + \frac{u_t}{\beta(L)},$$

then compute the long-run response by substituting $L=1$:

$$\frac{\gamma(1)}{\beta(1)} = \frac{\gamma_0 + \gamma_1 + \gamma_2 + \ldots + \gamma_s}{1 - \beta_1 - \beta_2 - \ldots - \beta_p}.$$

By substituting $L=1$ all the parameters are summed. The long-run equilibrium equation is

$$Y = \frac{\beta_0}{1 - \beta_1 - \beta_2 - \ldots - \beta_p} + \frac{\gamma_0 + \gamma_1 + \gamma_2 + \ldots + \gamma_s}{1 - \beta_1 - \beta_2 - \ldots - \beta_p}X.$$

Example 12.1   A macroeconomic model

In the macro model from Example 10.1 in Section 10.1, the long-run multiplier for income with respect to government expenditures was recursively computed as $\pi_{22}/(1-\pi_{23})$. This can be obtained more conveniently by using the lag operator in the reduced-form equation (10.7). Rewrite the equation as before:

$$Y_t = \pi_{21} + \pi_{22}G_t + \pi_{23}Y_{t-1} + v_{t2}$$

$$Y_t = \pi_{21} + \pi_{22}G_t + \pi_{23}LY_t + v_{t2}$$

$$(1 - \pi_{23}L)\, Y_t = \pi_{21} + \pi_{22}G_t + v_{t2} \tag{12.8}$$

$$Y_t = \frac{\pi_{21}}{1-\pi_{23}} + \frac{\pi_{22}}{1-\pi_{23}L}G_t + \frac{v_{t2}}{1-\pi_{23}L}. \tag{12.9}$$

Equation (12.9) is identical to equation (10.8), so notice the notational simplicity achieved by using the lag operator! The long-run multiplier is obtained for $L = 1$, which is of course equal to $\pi_{22}/(1-\pi_{23})$ as before.

In empirical econometrics we frequently observe that the transformation $\nabla log\,(X_t)$ is applied as an approximation for the relative changes of X_t. For instance in the next example, Example 12.2, inflation is approximated by the first differences of the logs of the consumer price index: $\nabla \ln(CPI_t)$. Such a transformation can be used as a proxy for the relative change of the variable up to a maximum of about 15%. This can be seen by means of the following algebraic exercise.

$$\nabla log\,(X_t) = log\,(X_t) - log\,(X_{t-1})$$

$$= log\left(\frac{X_t}{X_{t-1}}\right)$$

$$= log\left(1 + \frac{X_t - X_{t-1}}{X_{t-1}}\right)$$

$$\approx \frac{X_t - X_{t-1}}{X_{t-1}}.$$

In the last step, the fact has been used that for x close to zero, $log(1 + x) \approx x$. This result can be verified graphically, but it can also be shown by using a Taylor series. In general, the value of $f(x)$ at $x = c + \varepsilon$ is:

$$f(c+\varepsilon) = f(c) + \left.\frac{df(x)}{dx}\right|_{x=c} \cdot \varepsilon + \frac{1}{2!}\left.\frac{d^2 f(x)}{dx^2}\right|_{x=c} \cdot \varepsilon^2 + \ldots.$$

The approximation for $log(1 + x)$ is obtained when computing a first-order Taylor series for $f(x) = log(x)$ with $x = c + \varepsilon$ around $c = 1$. Then we see the approximation shows up:

$$log\,(1+\varepsilon) \approx log\,(1) + \left.\frac{d\,(log\,(x))}{dx}\right|_{x=1} \cdot \varepsilon$$

$$= 0 + 1 \cdot \varepsilon$$

$$= \varepsilon.$$

For example, use your calculator and see that $ln(1.05) = 0.049$, but $ln(1.15) = 0.140$, so that the approximation has already deviated by 1 percentage point, Because of this property, $\nabla \ln(CPI_t)$ is frequently used as a proxy for the inflation in applied econometric work, as is the case in the next example.

Example 12.2   A macroeconomic consumption function

The long-run implications of dynamic short-run models are illustrated with this example, based on an example in Stewart (1991: p.196), concerning a model for UK consumption (C_t). The variables are in logs. Explanatory variables are real personal disposable income (Y_t) and inflation (∇CPI_t), approximated by the first differences of the logarithm of the consumer price index. By using annual data for the sample period 1960–1984, the following estimation results have been obtained, where only the Breusch–Godfrey $BG(1)$-statistic, with p-value in parentheses, is reported to give an indication about the quality of the estimated result: absence of first-order autocorrelation.

$$1 : \widehat{C}_t = 0.25 + 0.93Y_t - 0.14\nabla CPI_t$$
$$BG(1) = 4.53 \ (0.033)$$

$$2a : \widehat{C}_t = 0.25 + 0.88Y_t - 0.16\nabla CPI_t + 0.06Y_{t-1} \text{ or}$$
$$2b : \widehat{C}_t = 0.25 + (0.88 + 0.06L)Y_t - 0.16\nabla CPI_t$$
$$BG(1) = 9.74 \ (0.002)$$

$$3a : \widehat{C}_t = 0.16 + 0.71Y_t - 0.18\nabla CPI_t + 0.24C_{t-1} \text{ or}$$
$$3b : \widehat{C}_t = \frac{0.16}{1 - 0.24} + \frac{0.71}{1 - 0.24L}Y_t - \frac{0.18}{1 - 0.24L}\nabla CPI_t$$
$$BG(1) = 5.98 \ (0.014)$$

$$4a : \widehat{C}_t = -0.01 + 0.68Y_t - 0.15\nabla CPI_t - 0.40Y_{t-1} + 0.72C_{t-1} \text{ or}$$
$$4b : \widehat{C}_t = -\frac{0.01}{1 - 0.72} + \frac{0.68 - 0.40L}{1 - 0.72L}Y_t - \frac{0.15}{1 - 0.72L}\nabla CPI_t$$
$$BG(1) = 0.36 \ (0.549)$$

The Breusch–Godfrey test shows that only model 4 is acceptable. The estimated contemporaneous and long-run elasticities, by substituting $L = 1$, of these equations are given in Table 12.2.

The estimated long-run elasticity of model 4 is as expected from economic theory; this result looks even too good! The computed long-run equation of model (4) is obtained by the substitution of $L = 1$ in equation (4b):

$$\widehat{C} = -0.04 + 1.00Y - 0.54\nabla CPI.$$

Model	Short run	Long run
Model 1:	0.93	0.93
Model 2:	0.88	$0.88 + 0.06 = 0.94$
Model 3:	0.71	$0.71/(1 - 0.24) = 0.94$
Model 4:	0.68	$(0.68 - 0.40)/(1 - 0.72) = 1.00.$

Table 12.2: Short-run and long-run income elasticities

So far, the description of an econometric analysis is based on an unrestrictedly estimated model for the short run with a solution for the long run. In Sections 12.4 and 12.6 matching econometric models for the short and the long run are discussed, starting with restricting the long-run equation.

12.4 Error-correction models

When we are convinced that a long-run model exists, and the unrestrictedly determined long-run model is an unrealistic model, we may try to impose restrictions on the parameters of the long-run model. These restrictions work through in the accompanying short-run model. This restricted accompanying short-run model is called an *error-correction model* (ECM).

The plan for the rest of this chapter is as follows. The general idea of ECMs is introduced in this section. The long-run equilibrium relationship has parameters that have been fixed at values known from some economic source. The ECM converges to this relationship. Then, in Section 12.5 the concept of unit roots and of unit-root tests is introduced as tools to analyse trends in the data. This knowledge is used in the study of the nature of an estimated static equation, which will be discussed in Section 12.6. An estimated static equation can be either a spurious regression or an estimated equilibrium equation. An estimated long-run model has also a matching ECM. However, in this section, we start with a long-run model that is a given model, based on the economic theory or known from empirical observations.

Some historical remarks

It is interesting to see how this modelling concept has evolved in the econometrics literature over time. Granger and Newbold (1974) show that in most cases high t-values, high R^2s are found, together with low values of the DW-statistic when a static regression of two independent random walks is computed. Such a regression result is called a *spurious regression*. So the other way around, when your (static) result shows high t-values, a high R^2 and a low DW-value, then be aware of spurious results.

In the well-known article of Davidson, Hendry, Srba and Yeo (1978) the error-correction model was introduced. It is a new way of modelling a short-run dynamic model with a given long-run relationship. Their approach will be shown in this section.

Granger (1981) combines the concept of the error-correction model with his previous work by showing that a static estimation result is not necessarily a spurious regression. The static regression is either spurious or conditions can be established that the static equation can be interpreted as a long-run equilibrium relationship. Important in this context is analysing whether the time-series have common trends or if they behave according to their own individual trends. This makes the distinction between a spurious relationship or not.

The trends will be analysed by looking at the 'order of integration' of the variables, which will be explained in Section 12.5. The order of integration of economic variables will be determined by testing whether the lag polynomials, which have been introduced in Section 12.2, have a root equal to one. If the polynomial has a unit root then the variable has a linear trend. This is tested with a *unit-root test*. The unit-root tests were introduced by Dickey and Fuller (1979) and many unit-root tests were later established, such as the tests of Phillips (1987), and Phillips and Perron (1988). These tests (and some more) can be applied with EViews, but the discussion in this book will be limited to the Dickey–Fuller tests.

The static relationship will not be a spurious regression if the variables have common trends and the residuals are stationary. Then the variables are integrated in a similar way and for that reason they are called *cointegrated*. The concept of cointegration will be introduced and discussed in Section 12.6. Then finally, we look at the Engle and Granger (1987) formal two-step procedure to test for, and estimate, long-run and matching short-run error-correction models.

A sufficient discussion on these topics along the lines as outlined above, to make this methodology operational, is given in this and the following sections. In this section, the error-correction model is introduced; in Section 12.5 the unit-root tests are discussed; and in Section 12.6 the tests around the cointegration analysis are described.

Restricting the long run

The concept of error-correction models will now be introduced and discussed in general, after which we will look at some examples. An unrestricted dynamic model between two variables Y_t and X_t has been specified in Section 12.2 as:

$$\beta(L) Y_t = \beta_0 + \gamma(L) X_t + u_t, \tag{12.10}$$
$$u_t \sim NID\left(0, \sigma_u^2\right),$$

with the lag polynomials $\beta(L)$ and $\gamma(L)$:

$$\beta(L) = 1 - \beta_1 L - \beta_2 L^2 - \ldots - \beta_p L^p,$$
$$\gamma(L) = \gamma_0 + \gamma_1 L + \gamma_2 L^2 + \ldots + \gamma_s L^s.$$

To obtain the long-run relationship, equation (12.10) has been rewritten as:

$$Y_t = \frac{\beta_0}{\beta(L)} + \frac{\gamma(L)}{\beta(L)} X_t + \frac{1}{\beta(L)} u_t. \tag{12.11}$$

Rewrite the constant term and define β_0^*, $\gamma^*(L)$ and u_t^*:

$$\beta_0^* = \frac{\beta_0}{\beta(L)} = \frac{\beta_0}{1 - \sum\limits_{i=1}^{p} \beta_i},$$

$$\gamma^*(L) = \frac{\gamma(L)}{\beta(L)},$$

$$u_t^* = \frac{1}{\beta(L)} u_t,$$

and substitute them in equation (12.11):

$$Y_t = \beta_0^* + \gamma^*(L) X_t + u_t^*.$$

The long-run response of Y_t to a unit change in X_t is $\gamma^*(1)$:

$$\gamma^*(1) = \frac{\gamma(1)}{\beta(1)} = \frac{\gamma_0 + \gamma_1 + \gamma_2 + \ldots + \gamma_s}{1 - \beta_1 - \beta_2 - \ldots - \beta_p}.$$

The long-run relationship between Y_t and X_t is:

$$Y_t = \beta_0^* + \gamma^*(1) X_t + u_t^*.$$

The parameter $\gamma^*(1)$ is the unrestricted long-run response of Y_t to a unit change in X_t. Suppose that a long-run equilibrium between the variables Y_t and X_t is imposed according to some economic theory; in particular assume that the theory states that Y and X are in equilibrium in the long run:

$$Y = X. \tag{12.12}$$

Imposing (12.12) as the equilibrium relationship (12.12) implies restrictions on the parameters of the short-run model (12.10):

$$\gamma^*(1) = 1.$$

This restriction will be found again in the short-run model. Because of this restriction we have assured ourselves that the dynamic short-run model (12.10) converges to the long-run model (12.12). This concept is elaborated in this section for two models.

An error-correction model for two variables with first-order lag polynomials

Let us first look at a dynamic model for two variables that are represented by AR(1) processes: both the lag polynomials $\beta(L)$ and $\gamma(L)$ are of first order. This is the most simple example to start with:

$$\beta(L) = 1 - \beta_1 L,$$
$$\gamma(L) = \gamma_0 + \gamma_1 L.$$

Then, with these polynomials the unrestricted model (12.10),

$$\beta(L) Y_t = \beta_0 + \gamma(L) X_t + u_t,$$

is written as,

$$Y_t = \beta_0 + \gamma_0 X_t + \gamma_1 X_{t-1} + \beta_1 Y_{t-1} + u_t, \tag{12.13}$$
$$u_t \sim NID\left(0, \sigma_u^2\right); \ |\beta_1| < 1.$$

Rewrite the model using the lag operator and the notation introduced above.

$$Y_t = \frac{\beta_0}{1 - \beta_1} + \frac{\gamma_0 + \gamma_1 L}{1 - \beta_1 L} X_t + \frac{u_t}{1 - \beta_1 L}; \tag{12.14}$$

$$\beta_0^* = \frac{\beta_0}{1 - \beta_1}$$

$$\gamma^*(L) = \frac{\gamma_0 + \gamma_1 L}{1 - \beta_1 L}$$

$$u_t^* = \frac{u_t}{1 - \beta_1 L}$$

Then equation (12.14) is written as:

$$Y_t = \beta_0^* + \gamma^*(L) X_t + u_t^*.$$

The unrestricted long-run response is $\gamma^*(1)$:

$$\gamma^*(1) = \frac{\gamma_0 + \gamma_1}{1 - \beta_1}. \tag{12.15}$$

If the parameters of equation (12.13) have been estimated and a long-run relationship exists, you have to check whether the estimated model converges to an economically realistic long-run equation. Calculate and evaluate (12.15): $(\widehat{\gamma}_0 + \widehat{\gamma}_1) / \left(1 - \widehat{\beta}_1\right)$.

If this value of the long-run parameter is not in accordance with what is expected from an economic point of view, then the parameter can be restricted. The restriction can conveniently be imposed when the model has been rewritten in the following way. Write model (12.13) in first differences and correct for the newly introduced lags (the equation remains unchanged):

$$Y_t = \beta_0 + \gamma_0 X_t + \gamma_1 X_{t-1} + \beta_1 Y_{t-1} + u_t,$$
$$\nabla Y_t + Y_{t-1} = \beta_0 + \gamma_0 \nabla X_t + \gamma_0 X_{t-1} + \gamma_1 X_{t-1} + \beta_1 Y_{t-1} + u_t,$$
$$\nabla Y_t = \beta_0 + \gamma_0 \nabla X_t + \gamma_0 X_{t-1} + \gamma_1 X_{t-1} + \beta_1 Y_{t-1} - Y_{t-1} + u_t,$$
$$\nabla Y_t = \beta_0 + \gamma_0 \nabla X_t + (\gamma_0 + \gamma_1) X_{t-1} + (\beta_1 - 1) Y_{t-1} + u_t,$$
$$\nabla Y_t = \beta_0 + \gamma_0 \nabla X_t + (\beta_1 - 1) \left(Y_{t-1} + \frac{\gamma_0 + \gamma_1}{\beta_1 - 1} X_{t-1} \right) + u_t,$$

or

$$\nabla Y_t = \beta_0 + \gamma_0 \nabla X_t + (\beta_1 - 1) \left(Y_{t-1} - \frac{\gamma_0 + \gamma_1}{1 - \beta_1} X_{t-1} \right) + u_t. \qquad (12.16)$$

The parameter in parentheses for X_{t-1} is exactly equal to the long-run parameter (12.15) and can easily be restricted.

As a simple example the following long-run relationship is imposed:

$$Y = X.$$

This gives a restriction on the parameter of the long-run response $\gamma^*(1)$:

$$\gamma^*(1) = \frac{\gamma_0 + \gamma_1}{1 - \beta_1} = 1.$$

Substitute this value in the short-run model (12.16), which results in the restricted short-run model:

$$\nabla Y_t = \beta_0 + \gamma_0 \nabla X_t + (\beta_1 - 1)(Y_{t-1} - X_{t-1}) + u_t. \qquad (12.17)$$

Model (12.17) is the *error-correction model*. The last term $(Y_{t-1} - X_{t-1})$ is called *the error-correction term*, which is exactly the long-run relationship written with subscript $t-1$. An error-correction model is an equation specified with variables in first differences and with an error-correction term. The model shows the long-run relationship and the short-run deviations from the equilibrium relationship. Notice that the disturbance-term u_t has remained unaltered after rewriting the equation, so the original disturbance-term assumptions are unaltered! The parameters can consistently be estimated with OLS. When residual autocorrelation is absent, the restriction and the specification can be maintained. The coefficient of the error-correction term is negative as $|\beta_1| < 1$. It can be shown that a value close to one implies a fast convergence to the equilibrium relationship and a value close to zero a slow convergence. This will be explained in Section 13.4.

It is also possible and interesting to compute the parameters γ_i^* from the infinite polynomial $\gamma^*(L)$:

$$\gamma^*(L) = \gamma_0^* + \gamma_1^* L + \gamma_2^* L^2 + \dots.$$

The coefficients γ_i^* show the pattern and the speed of convergence to the equilibrium relationship:

$$\gamma_0^*, \ (\gamma_0^* + \gamma_1^*), \ (\gamma_0^* + \gamma_1^* + \gamma_2^*), \dots, \ \sum_{i=1}^{\infty} \gamma_i^*.$$

In this example, the last coefficient is equal to one:

$$\sum_{i=1}^{\infty} \gamma_i^* = 1.$$

The series of coefficients is called the *step-response function*. These steps show the convergence rate to the equilibrium relation: $Y = X$. For example, these coefficients can be computed in the following way by evaluating $\gamma^*(L) X_t$.

$$\gamma^*(L) X_t = \frac{\gamma_0 + \gamma_1 L}{1 - \beta_1 L} X_t$$

$$= \frac{1}{1 - \beta_1 L} (\gamma_0 + \gamma_1 L) X_t$$

$$= \left(1 + \beta_1 L + \beta_1^2 L^2 + \beta_1^3 L^3 + \dots\right) (\gamma_0 + \gamma_1 L) X_t.$$

Next compute, term by term:

$$\gamma^*(L) X_t = \gamma_0 X_t + (\gamma_1 + \beta_1 \gamma_0) X_{t-1} + \beta_1 (\gamma_1 + \beta_1 \gamma_0) X_{t-2}$$
$$+ \beta_1^2 (\gamma_1 + \beta_1 \gamma_0) X_{t-3} + \dots.$$

Then we have found the polynomial $\gamma^*(L)$:

$$\gamma^*(L) = \gamma_0 + (\gamma_1 + \beta_1 \gamma_0) L + \beta_1 (\gamma_1 + \beta_1 \gamma_0) L^2$$
$$+ \beta_1^2 (\gamma_1 + \beta_1 \gamma_0) L^3 + \dots. \tag{12.18}$$

The coefficients in the polynomial (12.18) form the step-response function. When the parameters of the error-correction model (12.17) have been estimated, then it is easy to compute some coefficients of the lag polynomial $\gamma^*(L)$. See the elaborated example at the end of this section for an application with a relationship between coffee prices on the world market and in importing countries.

An error-correction model for two variables with second-order lag polynomials

The exercise will be done once more for a model where the two variables are AR(2) processes. It is an identical exercise as before, but the example illustrates how things look for higher-order lag polynomials. Both the lag polynomials are of second order. Just as before, the assumed equilibrium relationship is:

$$Y = X.$$

The second-order lag polynomials $\beta(L)$ and $\gamma(L)$ are:

$$\beta(L) = 1 - \beta_1 L - \beta_2 L^2,$$
$$\gamma(L) = \gamma_0 + \gamma_1 L + \gamma_2 L^2.$$

The unrestricted short-run model (12.10) is:

$$Y_t = \beta_0 + \gamma_0 X_t + \gamma_1 X_{t-1} + \gamma_2 X_{t-2} + \beta_1 Y_{t-1} + \beta_2 Y_{t-2} + u_t,$$
$$u_t \sim NID\left(0, \sigma_u^2\right).$$

Substitution of the lag operator and solving the equation for Y_t gives:

$$Y_t - \beta_1 L Y_t - \beta_2 L^2 Y_t = \beta_0 + \gamma_0 X_t + \gamma_1 L X_t + \gamma_2 L^2 X_t + u_t$$
$$\left(1 - \beta_1 L - \beta_2 L^2\right) Y_t = \beta_0 + \left(\gamma_0 + \gamma_1 L + \gamma_2 L^2\right) X_t + u_t$$
$$Y_t = \frac{\beta_0}{1 - \beta_1 - \beta_2} + \frac{\gamma_0 + \gamma_1 L + \gamma_2 L^2}{1 - \beta_1 L - \beta_2 L^2} X_t + \frac{u_t}{1 - \beta_1 L - \beta_2 L^2}.$$

This corresponds to our general notation of the unrestricted short-run model:

$$Y_t = \beta_0^* + \gamma^*(L) X_t + u_t^*.$$

The unrestricted long-run model is obtained by substituting $L = 1$:

$$Y_t = \beta_0^* + \gamma^*(1) X_t + u_t^*.$$

The long-run response $\gamma^*(1)$ is:

$$\gamma^*(1) = \frac{\gamma_0 + \gamma_1 + \gamma_2}{1 - \beta_1 - \beta_2}. \tag{12.19}$$

The given equilibrium relationship $Y = X$ implies restrictions on the parameters by restricting the long-run response $\gamma^*(1)$, as seen before:

$$\gamma^*(1) = 1,$$

implying the restriction for the parameters of the short-run model too:

$$\frac{\gamma_0 + \gamma_1 + \gamma_2}{1 - \beta_1 - \beta_2} = 1. \tag{12.20}$$

Again, rewrite the model in first differences and correct for the newly introduced lags.

$$Y_t = \beta_0 + \gamma_0 X_t + \gamma_1 X_{t-1} + \gamma_2 X_{t-2} + \beta_1 Y_{t-1} + \beta_2 Y_{t-2} + u_t,$$

$$\nabla Y_t + Y_{t-1} = \beta_0 + \gamma_0 \nabla X_t + \gamma_0 X_{t-1} + \gamma_1 X_{t-1} - \gamma_2 \nabla X_{t-1} + \gamma_2 X_{t-1}$$
$$+ \beta_1 Y_{t-1} + \beta_2 Y_{t-2} + u_t,$$

$$\nabla Y_t = \beta_0 + \gamma_0 \nabla X_t - \gamma_2 \nabla X_{t-1} + \gamma_0 X_{t-1} + \gamma_1 X_{t-1} + \gamma_2 X_{t-1}$$
$$+ \beta_1 Y_{t-1} + \beta_2 Y_{t-2} - Y_{t-1} + u_t,$$

$$\nabla Y_t = \beta_0 + \gamma_0 \nabla X_t - \gamma_2 \nabla X_{t-1} + (\gamma_0 + \gamma_1 + \gamma_2) X_{t-1}$$
$$+ (\beta_1 + \beta_2 - 1) Y_{t-1} + u_t.$$

This results in the following unrestricted equation for the short run:

$$\nabla Y_t = \beta_0 + \gamma_0 \nabla X_t - \gamma_2 \nabla X_{t-1} - \beta_2 \nabla Y_{t-1}$$
$$+ (\beta_1 + \beta_2 - 1) \left(Y_{t-1} - \frac{\gamma_0 + \gamma_1 + \gamma_2}{1 - \beta_1 - \beta_2} X_{t-1} \right) + u_t. \qquad (12.21)$$

Just as in the first example, the coefficient of X_{t-1} in parentheses in model (12.21) is equal to the long-run response (12.19), and can easily be restricted. Substitution of the long-run restriction (12.20) in the short-run model gives the error-correction model:

$$\nabla Y_t = \beta_0 + \gamma_0 \nabla X_t - \gamma_2 \nabla X_{t-1} - \beta_2 \nabla Y_{t-1} + (\beta_1 + \beta_2 - 1)(Y_{t-1} - X_{t-1}) + u_t.$$
$$(12.22)$$

Because the variables Y_t and X_t are AR(2) processes, we observe that ∇X_{t-1} and ∇Y_{t-1} have entered the unrestricted model (12.21) and the error-correction model (12.22). In practice, the orders of the processes are unknown, so by modelling the ECM from 'general to specific' the orders will be empirically determined, as shown later on.

For this model, the step-response function can also be computed. This can be done in the following way. Rewrite $\gamma^*(L) X_t$:

$$\gamma^*(L) X_t = \frac{\gamma(L)}{\beta(L)} X_t$$
$$= \frac{\gamma_0 + \gamma_1 L + \gamma_2 L^2}{1 - \beta_1 L - \beta_2 L^2} X_t$$
$$= \frac{1}{1 - \beta_1 L - \beta_2 L^2} (\gamma_0 + \gamma_1 L + \gamma_2 L^2) X_t.$$

The coefficients of $\gamma^*(L)$ can be computed in the following way:

$$\gamma^*(L) = \beta^{-1}(L) \gamma(L)$$

or:

$$\beta(L)\gamma^*(L) = \gamma(L)$$

$$(1 - \beta_1 L - \beta_2 L^2)(\gamma_0^* + \gamma_1^* L + \gamma_2^* L^2 + \gamma_3^* L^3 + \ldots) - (\gamma_0 + \gamma_1 L + \gamma_2 L^2) = 0.$$

Then, collect the parameters for the identical powers of L and compute the coefficients recursively:

$$
\begin{aligned}
1: \quad & \gamma_0^* - \gamma_0 = 0 && \Rightarrow && \gamma_0^* = \gamma_0 \\
L: \quad & \gamma_1^* - \beta_1 \gamma_0^* - \gamma_1 = 0 && \Rightarrow && \gamma_1^* = \beta_1 \gamma_0 + \gamma_1 \\
L^2: \quad & \gamma_2^* - \beta_1 \gamma_1^* - \beta_2 \gamma_0^* - \gamma_2 = 0 && \Rightarrow && \gamma_2^* = \beta_1(\beta_1\gamma_0 + \gamma_1) + \beta_2\gamma_0 + \gamma_2 \\
& && \text{or:} && \gamma_2^* = \beta_1\gamma_1^* + \beta_2\gamma_0^* + \gamma_2 \\
L^3: \quad & \gamma_3^* - \beta_1\gamma_2^* - \beta_2\gamma_1^* = 0 && \Rightarrow && \gamma_3^* = \beta_1\gamma_2^* + \beta_2\gamma_1^* \\
\ldots \quad & \ldots && && \ldots \quad \ldots \\
L^i \quad & \gamma_i^* - \beta_1\gamma_{i-1}^* - \beta_2\gamma_{i-2}^* = 0 && \Rightarrow && \gamma_i^* = \beta_1\gamma_{i-1}^* + \beta_2\gamma_{i-2}^* ; \text{ for } i \geq 3.
\end{aligned}
$$

The coefficients γ_i^* of the polynomial $\gamma^*(L)$ form the step response function as before and can be computed after the parameters of the error-correction model (12.22) have been estimated. It is possible that the first values of the γ_i^* become larger than the restricted equilibrium value, and after that converge to the equilibrium value, which is an overshooting effect (see the elaborated example at the end of this section).

Error-correction models in practice and irreversible behaviour of explanatory variables

A practical aspect when estimating an error-correction model, is that no a priori knowledge is available about the order of the lag polynomials. Therefore, Hendry's principle of 'modelling from general to specific' will be used again. Start with a specification that has sufficient lagged-endogenous, lagged-exogenous variables (both in first differences), and an error-correction term as explanatory variables. For example, when we have a bivariate model and the long-run equilibrium relationship is assumed to be $Y = X$, we can start with the assumption of p lags for Y_t and X_t as a general dynamic model without residual autocorrelation.

$$
\begin{aligned}
\nabla Y_t &= \beta_0 + \beta_1 \nabla Y_{t-1} + \ldots + \beta_{p-1}\nabla Y_{t-p+1} + \gamma_0 \nabla X_t + \ldots + \gamma_{p-1}\nabla X_{t-p+1} \\
&\quad + \gamma(Y_{t-1} - X_{t-1}) + u_t, \\
u_t &\sim NID(0, \sigma_u^2).
\end{aligned}
$$

Test whether the specification can be narrowed after the parameters have been estimated with OLS. This happens in the usual way by checking the residuals for absence of serial correlation and by testing the significancy of the parameters.

When changes of variables are modelled, an interesting question arises: has a positive unit change of an explanatory variable an identical influence on the dependent variable as a negative unit change of that explanatory variable? The relationship as given above is called a *reversible model* because this specification shows an identical change of the dependent variable for a positive or a negative unit change of the explanatory variable. In fact, that is a restriction! If this restriction is not valid, the estimation results can be improved by specifying increases $(\nabla^+ X_t)$ and decreases $(\nabla^- X_t)$ of the explanatory variable as separate variables. A model specified with such variables is called an *irreversible model*. Define the new variables as follows:

$$\nabla^+ X_t = \begin{cases} \nabla X_t & \text{if } \nabla X_t > 0 \\ 0 & \text{if } \nabla X_t \leq 0 \end{cases} \quad \text{and} \quad \nabla^- X_t = \begin{cases} \nabla X_t & \text{if } \nabla X_t < 0 \\ 0 & \text{if } \nabla X_t \geq 0 \end{cases}.$$

For example, a simple bivariate reversible ECM is:

$$\nabla Y_t = \beta_0 + \gamma_0 \nabla X_t + (\beta_1 - 1)(Y_{t-1} - X_{t-1}) + u_t, \tag{12.23}$$

which is respecified as an irreversible model:

$$\nabla Y_t = \beta_0 + \gamma_0^+ \nabla^+ X_t + \gamma_0^- \nabla^- X_t + (\beta_1 - 1)(Y_{t-1} - X_{t-1}) + u_t. \tag{12.24}$$

The practice of estimating an irreversible model with EViews is not difficult. The variables $\nabla^+ X_t$ and $\nabla^- X_t$ can easily be generated in EViews by using dummy variables. These dummies are created as follows. Generate the variable DX as the first differences of the variable X:

$$DX = X - X(-1).$$

Next, generate two dummy variables that have, for example, the names DXP and DXN. Write the 'generate' in EViews exactly as written below (see also Figure 12.2):

$$DXP = DX > 0$$
$$DXN = DX <= 0.$$

DXP and DXN are dummy variables with values 0 and 1 that have been assigned as follows:

$$DXP = \begin{cases} 1 & \text{if } \nabla X_t > 0 \\ 0 & \text{if } \nabla X_t \leq 0 \end{cases} \quad \text{and} \quad DXN = \begin{cases} 1 & \text{if } \nabla X_t < 0 \\ 0 & \text{if } \nabla X_t \geq 0 \end{cases}.$$

The variables DXP and DXN obtain the real values of the positive and negative changes by multiplying the two dummies with the first differences in DX:

$$DXP = DX * DXP$$
$$DXN = DX * DXN.$$

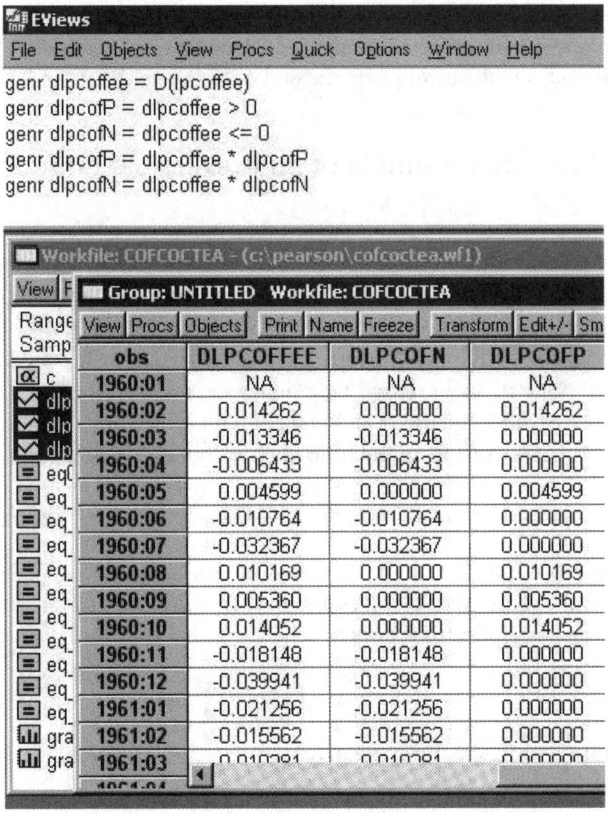

Figure 12.2: Creation of $\nabla^+ P_t^{cof}$ and $\nabla^- P_t^{cof}$ (in logs), and the result shown in a group

The resulting irreversible variables DXP and DXN are equal to the above-defined variables $\nabla^+ X_t$ and $\nabla^- X_t$:

$$\nabla^+ X_t = DXP$$

$$\nabla^- X_t = DXN.$$

With an irreversible model, different time paths to the equilibrium level can be computed for responses to positive and negative changes of the explanatory variables. In Figure 12.2, the creation of $\nabla^+ P_t^{cof}$ and $\nabla^- P_t^{cof}$ in the EViews workfile is shown. These variables will be used as explanatory variables in an elaborated example of an ECM for coffee prices at the end of this section.

The hypothesis that the influence of a differenced variable is reversible can be tested in various ways. For example, test in the estimated equation (12.24) the null hypothesis:

$$H_0 : \gamma_0^+ = \gamma_0^-$$

with the Wald F-test, or the likelihood-ratio test (LR-test) when both the restricted model (12.23) and the unrestricted model (12.24) have been estimated. For an example using the Wald F-test, see the example at the end of Section 12.6.

An elaborated example of an irreversible error-correction model

In an econometric study about the price formation of coffee, Vogelvang (1988) has shown that the response of retail prices of coffee in importing countries to coffee price changes on the world coffee market is an irreversible matter for many countries. We could expect that this property will be valid for more commodities than coffee only. The quarterly model explaining the coffee retail prices has been derived in the following manner. Assume that the retail price p_t^r in an importing country depends on the costs to purchase coffee on the world market p_t^w in quarter t and preceding quarters, and on the costs of roasting coffee k_t in quarter t. This results in the following economic model:

$$p_t^r = (1 + \eta)\,(k_t + \gamma\,(L)\,p_t^w) + u_t,$$

where η represents the 'mark-up'. As no observations exist on k_t some assumption has to be made about this variable. It is assumed that the costs of roasting coffee are proportional to the consumer price index cpi_t:

$$k_t = \alpha \cdot cpi_t.$$

Substitution of this assumption gives:

$$p_t^r = \alpha(1 + \eta)cpi_t + (1 + \eta)\gamma\,(L)\,p_t^w + u_t.$$

Divide the two sides of the equation by cpi_t:

$$\frac{p_t^r}{cpi_t} = \alpha(1 + \eta) + (1 + \eta)\gamma\,(L)\,\frac{p_t^w}{cpi_t} + \frac{u_t}{cpi_t}. \qquad (12.25)$$

In this way, the prices have become real prices, and equation (12.25) is written in real prices as:

$$p_t^r = \alpha^* + \gamma^*\,(L)\,p_t^w + u_t^*,$$

with

$$\alpha^* = \alpha\,(1 + \eta)$$
$$\gamma^*\,(L) = (1 + \eta)\gamma\,(L)$$
$$u_t^* = \frac{u_t}{cpi_t}.$$

The long-run coefficient is $\gamma^*\,(1) = 1 + \eta$. If u_t^* is homoskedastic then it implies that the original disturbance term is heteroskedastic. Information from the coffee branch suggested a mark-up of 30%, so the restricted equilibrium equation is:

$$p^r = 1.3p^w.$$

This long-run restriction was necessary because no realistic values for the mark-up had been obtained by estimating and solving unrestrictedly short-run dynamic equations.

The model has been estimated for various countries for the sample period 1976(01)–1981(03). As an example, the irreversible results for France and the Netherlands are given successively (with asymptotic t-values in parentheses):

$$\widehat{\nabla p^r_{Fr,t}} = \underset{(3.50)}{5.82} + \underset{(1.70)}{0.19} \nabla^+ p^w_t + \underset{(2.97)}{0.60} \nabla^+ p^w_{t-1}$$
$$+ \underset{(0.68)}{0.07} \nabla^- p^w_t + \underset{(0.75)}{0.14} \nabla^- p^w_{t-1} - \underset{(4.24)}{0.57} \left(p^r_{Fr,t-1} - 1.3p^w_{t-1} \right),$$

$$\widehat{\nabla p^r_{Nl,t}} = \underset{(2.10)}{1.14} - \underset{(0.05)}{0.006} \nabla^+ p^w_t + \underset{(3.96)}{0.79} \nabla^+ p^w_{t-1}$$
$$+ \underset{(3.38)}{0.52} \nabla^- p^w_t + \underset{(2.82)}{0.47} \nabla^- p^w_{t-1} - \underset{(2.42)}{0.26} \left(p^r_{Nl,t-1} - 1.3p^w_{t-1} \right).$$

Contemporaneous price increases on the world market have a more significant influence on the retail price than world-market price decreases. The error-correction terms are clearly significantly different from zero (it is a one-sided t-test). The accumulated step responses have been computed to increases and decreases of the world market price. For France, the step-response function clearly exhibits asymmetric behaviour in response to changing world market prices, and also an overshooting effect for price increases is observed (see Table 12.3).

			Lag		
Change of p^w_t	0	1	2	3	4
+	0.19	1.42	1.35	1.32	1.31
−	0.07	0.63	1.01	1.17	1.25

Table 12.3: Step-response function for the coffee retail price in France

The estimation results for the Netherlands are quite different, as shown in Table 12.4. In the Netherlands, a strong governmental price regulation was effective during the estimation period. The step-response function shows that the regulation really worked out.

			Lag		
Change of p^w_t	0	1	2	3	4
+	0.01	1.12	1.17	1.20	1.23
−	0.52	1.19	1.22	1.24	1.25

Table 12.4: Step-response function for the coffee retail price in the Netherlands

Hardly any differences exist between the response function for price increases and for price decreases.

12.5 Trends and unit-root tests

To obtain a satisfactory econometric model with respect to economical and statistical assumptions, it is important to have knowledge about the trend behaviour of the economic variables that are modelled. Are trends present or absent in the variables? If a trend is present then what type of trend is it, is it deterministic or stochastic? These are the topics addressed in this section.

A time-series will be considered as a stochastic process and some aspects of a stochastic process will be investigated for the involved variables. Because of the choice for an empirically oriented 'first course in econometrics' as presented in this book, there is no place for a theoretical introduction into the subject of stochastic processes. Only introductory remarks are given here concerning some elementary aspects of a *stochastic process*. More discussion on this subject can be found in the statistical literature.

A stochastic process for n observations is a time-ordered sequence of n random variables with their own probability distribution. These random variables are not independently distributed, they have an n-variate distribution. A time-series can be seen as a realisation (or a draw) from a joint density function $p(Y_1, Y_2, \ldots, Y_n)$. A time-series is, in fact, a 'time slice'. We will look at time-series that have a joint distribution that is independent of time, so the distribution of $Y_1, Y_2, \ldots, Y_n$ is identical to the distribution of $Y_{1+s}, Y_{2+s}, \ldots, Y_{n+s}$, where s can be either positive or negative. It does not matter where the time slice has been made. If this is true, then the process is called a *strong-stationary process*. If the distributions are not equal with respect to all the moments of the distributions, for example, only the first two moments are independent of time, then the process is called a *weak-stationary process*.

In this chapter, stochastic processes that are normally distributed are considered and entitled *Gaussian* processes. This implies that weak stationarity of the second order is a sufficient condition for strong stationarity, because the normal distribution is completely determined when the first two moments of the distribution are known. The means, variances and covariances will be examined whether or not they are independent of time. Economic time-series often behave with a trend and in such a case the process is not stationary with respect to the mean.

If the trend behaves linearly in time then a simple transformation, such as taking the first differences of the observations, makes the process stationary. If the graph of the variable shows heteroskedastic behaviour of the variable, then the process is probably not stationary with respect to the variance. Often, in that case, the *log* transformation is useful in obtaining more stationary behaviour. A combination of transformations such as the ∇log transformation is frequently encountered in the literature. The ∇log transformation is a proxy for the relative change of the variable, as shown in Section 12.3. Thus if the logs of a variable are specified and if the variable has a trend, then the assumption is made that the growth rate of the series is a stationary stochastic process. In this section, attention will be given to the analysis of the trend behaviour of an economic variable; after that relationships between non-stationary variables will be analysed in more detail in the next section.

Trends

Let us look at various possible trends in an economic variable. Usually, many economic time-series will behave like a trended variable, which is the reason why the variables are non-stationary processes with respect to the mean.

A linear deterministic trend in a time-series variable Y_t has been introduced earlier in Section 7.5. Such a variable can be written as:

$$Y_t = \alpha_0 + \alpha_1 t + u_t,$$
$$u_t \sim NID\left(0, \sigma_u^2\right).$$

The process $\{Y_t\}$ is clearly a non-stationary process. This process can be made stationary by correcting Y_t for the trend:

$$(Y_t - \alpha_0 - \alpha_1 t) = u_t. \tag{12.26}$$

The process (12.26) is called a *trend-stationary process* (TSP process).

Next, a random walk can be considered as a process that moves in all directions:

$$Y_t = Y_{t-1} + u_t \tag{12.27}$$
$$u_t \sim NID\left(0, \sigma_u^2\right).$$

This process is stationary with respect to the mean but not with respect to the variance, as shown below. Write (12.27) with the lag operator conveniently showing these two characteristics.

$$Y_t = \frac{1}{1 - L} u_t$$
$$= u_t + u_{t-1} + u_{t-2} + u_{t-3} + \ldots.$$

The mean and the variance are:

$$E(Y_t) = E(u_t) + E(u_{t-1}) + E(u_{t-2}) + \ldots$$
$$= 0 + 0 + 0 + \ldots$$
$$= 0,$$
$$Var(Y_t) = Var(u_t) + Var(u_{t-1}) + Var(u_{t-2}) + \ldots$$
$$= \sigma_u^2 + \sigma_u^2 + \sigma_u^2 + \ldots$$
$$= \infty.$$

The variance of a random walk process does not exist.

The random walk process can be extended with a constant term. Then the process is called a *random walk with drift*. The drift parameter (constant) pushes the process in one direction, increasing or decreasing. This process will appear to be a process that can frequently be used to describe a stochastic trend in a non-stationary economic variable:

$$Y_t = \beta_0 + Y_{t-1} + u_t.$$

Taking first differences of the observations of Y_t makes the random-walk processes stationary, possibly with a drift parameter:

$$(Y_t - Y_{t-1}) = u_t$$
$$(1 - L) Y_t = u_t.$$

This process of Y_t is a *difference-stationary process* (DSP process); it is also called a *unit-root process*, as the process written as $\beta(L) Y_t$ has a specific lag polynomial:

$$\beta(L) = 1 - L.$$

That polynomial has a root equal to one, or in other words the polynomial has a *unit root*, which explains its name.

For economic reasons, it is important to distinguish between a stationary and a non-stationary process. For that purpose, compare the non-stationary random walk model:

$$Y_t = Y_{t-1} + u_t, \qquad\qquad\qquad (12.28)$$
$$u_t \sim NID\left(0, \sigma_u^2\right),$$

with the stationary AR(1) process:

$$Y_t = \beta_1 Y_{t-1} + u_t, \text{ with } |\beta_1| < 1 \qquad\qquad\qquad (12.29)$$
$$u_t \sim NID\left(0, \sigma_u^2\right).$$

Use the lag operator to rewrite model (12.29) and to compute the mean and variance to see that the process is stationary:

$$Y_t = \beta_1 Y_{t-1} + u_t$$
$$Y_t = \frac{1}{1 - \beta_1 L} u_t$$
$$Y_t = u_t + \beta_1 u_{t-1} + \beta_1^2 u_{t-2} + \beta_1^3 u_{t-3} + \cdots$$
$$E\left(Y_t\right) = 0 + 0 + 0 \ldots = 0$$
$$var(Y_t) = \sigma_u^2 \left(1 + \beta_1^2 + \beta_1^4 + \beta_1^6 + \cdots\right) = \frac{\sigma_u^2}{1 - \beta_1^2}.$$

In a similar way, one can verify that the covariances $cov\left(Y_t, Y_{t-i}\right)$, with $i = 1, 2, 3, \ldots$ are constant. In fact this has been done before in Section 8.5 when determining the elements of the covariance matrix Ω of an AR(1) disturbance term in (8.9). The process $\{Y_t\}$ is Gaussian, and the first and second moments are constant, so independent of time, which proves that the process is strong stationary. An important economic difference between the non-stationary random walk and the stationary AR(1) process is that a shock in u_t has a permanent influence on Y_t in model (12.28), whereas in model (12.29) the influence of the shock on Y_t fades away over time.

Compare the two models by using a lag polynomial to see the difference more clearly:

$$(1 - L)\,Y_t = u_t, \text{ for model (12.28), and}$$
$$(1 - \beta_1 L)\,Y_t = u_t, \text{ for model (12.29).}$$

In the random walk model, the polynomial $\beta\,(L)$ has one solution, $L = 1$, and for the AR(1) model the polynomial $\beta\,(L)$ has one solution, $L = 1/\beta_1$. In other words, the polynomial of the non-stationary process has a *unit root* and the polynomial of the stationary process has a root larger than one. This property had been established earlier, but has been repeated here because a test for non-stationarity will be formalised in terms of the roots of the polynomial $\beta\,(L)$. The null hypothesis will be tested that $\beta\,(L)$ has a unit root against the alternative that $\beta\,(L)$ has a root larger than one, which means that we will test the null hypothesis that Y_t is non-stationary against the alternative that Y_t is stationary. The null and alternative hypotheses with respect to equation (12.29) are:

$$H_0 : \beta_1 = 1 \qquad\qquad (12.30)$$
$$H_1 : |\beta_1| < 1.$$

For economic reasons, it will generally be more relevant to test the alternative

$$H_1 : 0 < \beta_1 < 1.$$

Notation

A new notation and terminology will be introduced that is convenient in the context of unit roots. If the process $\{Y_t\}$ is non-stationary and the process $\{\nabla Y_t\}$ is stationary then the lag polynomial $\beta\,(L)$ of Y_t has a *unit root* and the variable is known to be *integrated of first order*. This is written with the following notation:

$$Y_t \sim I\,(1)\,.$$

This concept is in accordance with the analogy around 'summing'/'integrating' and 'differencing'/'differentiating' that was introduced in Section 12.2. An $I\,(1)$-variable is stationary after transforming the variable into first differences:

$$(1 - L)Y_t = u_t, \quad \text{or} \quad \nabla Y_t = u_t$$
$$\nabla Y_t \sim I\,(0)\,.$$

If the polynomial $\beta\,(L)$ has two unit roots (see later on in this section) then the variable is *integrated of second order*, in notation:

$$Y_t \sim I\,(2)\,.$$

An $I\,(2)$ variable will be stationary after transforming the variable in second differences:

$$(1 - L)^2 Y_t = \nabla Y_t - \nabla Y_{t-1}$$
$$= (1 - L)\nabla Y_t$$
$$= \nabla^2 Y_t$$
$$\nabla^2 Y_t \sim I\,(0)\,.$$

This implies for the model

$$\beta(L)Y_t = u_t,$$

that if $\beta(L)$ is of the second degree, that the polynomial is a specific second-degree polynomial:

$$\beta(L) = (1 - L)^2$$

$$\beta(L)Y_t = u_t$$

$$(1 - L)^2 Y_t = u_t$$

$$\nabla^2 Y_t = u_t.$$

See also the following notational sequence if $Y_t \sim I(2)$:

$$Y_t \sim I(2) \Rightarrow \nabla Y_t \sim I(1) \Rightarrow \nabla^2 Y_t \sim I(0).$$

The economic interpretation is that Y_t has a trend in the growth rate, ∇Y_t has a linear trend, and $\nabla^2 Y_t$ is stationary.

Which behaviour can be expected of economic variables? Economic variables will be: $I(0)$, stationary; $I(1)$, linear trend in the data; or $I(2)$, trend in the growth rate. Time-series that are $I(3)$ (exponential trend in the growth rate) or higher are very unusual from an economic point of view, but do exist sometimes. Many economic variables are trended and will behave like an $I(1)$ process. Examples of $I(2)$ variables are prices and wages in some inflationary periods, for example, the 1970s. Greene (2000) mentions money stocks and price levels in hyper-inflationary economies such as those of interwar Germany or Hungary after World War II as examples of $I(3)$ series, which imply exponential trends in the growth rates.

Later in this section, we will look at general lag polynomials $\beta(L)$ other than only first- or second-order polynomials. The lag polynomial $\beta(L)$ is a polynomial of degree p, and has at most one or two roots equal to one, whereas the remaining roots are larger than one.

Dickey–Fuller unit-root tests

To test the null hypothesis of a unit root you have to estimate the β_1 in equation (12.29) with OLS. However, it is not possible to use a standard Student's t-test to test the null hypothesis:

$$H_0 : \beta_1 = 1$$

$$H_1 : 0 < \beta_1 < 1,$$

in the equation:

$$\widehat{Y}_t = \widehat{\beta}_1 Y_{t-1},$$

with the t-statistic $t_{\hat{\beta}_1} = \hat{\beta}_1 / se\left(\hat{\beta}_1\right)$. The t-statistic $t_{\hat{\beta}_1}$ does not follow a Student's t-distribution as is demonstrated below. The asymptotic distribution of the OLS estimator $\hat{\beta}_1$ of β_1 under H_1 looks like:

$$\sqrt{n}\left(\hat{\beta}_1 - \beta_1\right) \overset{A}{\sim} N\left(0, \left(1 - \beta_1^2\right)\right) \text{ for } |\beta_1| < 1.$$

The distribution makes no sense for $\beta_1 = 1$ because of a zero variance. This distribution can be determined as follows. In Section 9.2, an expression for the asymptotic distribution of the OLS estimator in the K-variate model was given:

$$\sqrt{n}\left(\hat{\boldsymbol{\beta}} - \boldsymbol{\beta}\right) \overset{A}{\sim} N\left(\mathbf{0}, \sigma_u^2 \Omega_{XX}^{-1}\right).$$

In the model

$$Y_t = \beta_1 Y_{t-1} + u_t, \text{ with } |\beta_1| < 1, \tag{12.31}$$

the variance of Y_t is equal to:

$$var(Y_t) = \frac{\sigma_u^2}{1 - \beta_1^2}.$$

Then, use these expressions for the OLS estimator $\hat{\beta}_1$ of β_1 in model (12.31), so:

$$\hat{\beta}_1 = \frac{\sum Y_t Y_{t-1}}{\sum Y_{t-1}^2},$$

$$var(\hat{\beta}_1) = \frac{\sigma_u^2}{\sum Y_{t-1}^2}.$$

It follows that:

$$\sqrt{n}(\hat{\beta}_1 - \beta_1) \overset{A}{\sim} N\left(0, \sigma_u^2 \left(\frac{\sigma_u^2}{1 - \beta_1^2}\right)^{-1}\right),$$

$$\sqrt{n}(\hat{\beta}_1 - \beta_1) \overset{A}{\sim} N\left(0, \left(1 - \beta_1^2\right)\right) \text{ with } |\beta_1| < 1.$$

This distribution is valid under H_1 for $|\beta_1| < 1$. We do not have a distribution of $\hat{\beta}_1$ under $H_0 : \beta_1 = 1$. The same is valid for the Student's t-distribution of the t-statistic $t_{\hat{\beta}_1}$:

$$t_{\hat{\beta}_1} = \frac{\hat{\beta}_1}{s.e\left(\hat{\beta}_1\right)} \overset{H_0}{\approx} t\left(n - 1\right).$$

The t-statistic t_{β_1} does not follow the Student's t-distribution as was shown by Dickey and Fuller (1979). Thus we cannot test the null hypothesis that $\beta_1 = 1$. Dickey and Fuller have found that a non-degenerated distribution of $n\left(\widehat{\beta}_1 - 1\right)$ exists, but that distribution has no analytical expression. In the 1970s, Dickey and Fuller, and others afterwards, computed critical values for this distribution by simulation (see, for example, Fuller (1976)). Therefore, the test is called a Dickey–Fuller t-test (DF-t-test). Tables with critical values for this non-standard distribution can be found in Hamilton (1994), for example, with references to the work of Dickey and Fuller. Because the distribution of $n\left(\widehat{\beta}_1 - 1\right)$ exists instead of $\sqrt{n}\left(\widehat{\beta}_1 - 1\right)$, the OLS estimator of β_1 is called *super consistent*.

To apply the test, called a *unit-root test*, it is not necessary to specify the regression equation yourself in most of the well-known econometric software. Unit-root tests are included in EViews. Critical values and probabilities are computed by EViews when performing a unit-root test and printed in the output. Three different situations are distinguished with three distributions for the test statistic, and statistical tables are available for these three different situations. The situations are described below[*]. In the description of the three situations the most simple assumption is made that the variable Y_t follows a first-order autoregressive process. Hereafter, a more general AR(p) process will be used for the application of the test.

Situation 1: no constant term and no linear trend in the model

The equation that will be estimated for performing the test is:

$$Y_t = \beta_1 Y_{t-1} + u_t. \tag{12.32}$$

We want to test the null hypothesis,

$$H_0 : Y_t \sim I\left(1\right), \text{ or } H_0 : \beta_1 = 1,$$

against

$$H_1 : Y_t \sim I\left(0\right), \text{ or } H_1 : 0 < \beta_1 < 1.$$

It is convenient to subtract Y_{t-1} from both sides of equation (12.32) and to estimate the parameter in the equation:

$$\nabla Y_t = \left(\beta_1 - 1\right) Y_{t-1} + u_t.$$

Write the model with $\theta = \left(\beta_1 - 1\right)$,

$$\nabla Y_t = \theta Y_{t-1} + u_t,$$

---

[*] A fourth situation can be distinguished. In that situation the Student's t-distribution can be used. This case is not considered here, see, for example, Hamilton (1994) for details.

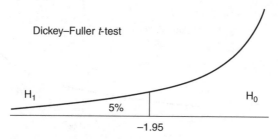

Figure 12.3: Testing for a unit root in
$Y_t = \beta_1 Y_{t-1} + u_t$

estimate θ with OLS and compute the t-statistic $t_{\hat{\theta}}$:

$$t_{\hat{\theta}} = \frac{\hat{\theta}}{s.e\left(\hat{\theta}\right)}.$$

This t-statistic is directly given in the computer output of the unit-root test. Then the null
and alternative hypotheses are identical to:

$$H_0 : \theta = 0$$
$$H_1 : \theta < 0.$$

When using EViews, go to the 'Series' window and find the option 'Unit-root test' under
'View'. In the output, EViews gives the critical values and probabilities belonging to the
computed t-statistic $t_{\hat{\theta}}$. This t-statistic follows a DF-t-distribution under the null hypothesis
of a unit root. For example, suppose we have a series with 100 observations, then the critical
value is -1.95 at the 5% significance level. The testing of the null hypothesis has been
illustrated in Figure 12.3.

Situation 2: a constant term but not a linear trend in the model

The omission of the constant term in the equation (12.32) can be rather restrictive. With a
constant term the equation that will be estimated is:

$$Y_t = \beta_0 + \beta_1 Y_{t-1} + u_t.$$

Again this equation is rewritten to make it more suitable to test directly the null hypothesis
$H_0 : Y_t \sim I(1)$ versus $H_1 : Y_t \sim I(0)$:

$$\nabla Y_t = \beta_0 + (\beta_1 - 1) Y_{t-1} + u_t,$$

and with $\theta = \beta_1 - 1$ the equation is:

$$\nabla Y_t = \beta_0 + \theta Y_{t-1} + u_t.$$

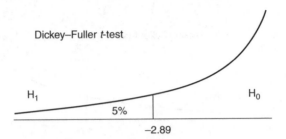

Figure 12.4: Testing for a unit root in
$Y_t = \beta_0 + \beta_1 Y_{t-1} + u_t$

Estimate the parameters and compute the t-statistic $t_{\hat\theta}$:

$$t_{\hat\theta} = \frac{\hat\theta}{s.e\left(\hat\theta\right)}.$$

This t-statistic follows a DF-t-distribution under the null hypothesis of a unit root. In EViews, the critical values for the test are computed. Using the same example as in the first situation of a time-series with 100 observations, the 5% critical value is -2.89. The picture that illustrates the test is given in Figure 12.4.

The critical value of -2.89 clearly deviates from the 5% critical value of the Student's t-distribution: $t_{0.05}(100) = -1.66$.

Situation 3: a constant term and a deterministic linear trend in the model

The last situation that we consider is a situation that a linear deterministic trend has also to be included in the equation. Then the equation is:

$$Y_t = \beta_0 + \beta_1 Y_{t-1} + \gamma t + u_t.$$

The null hypothesis of a unit root will be tested in the rewritten equation:

$$\nabla Y_t = \beta_0 + (\beta_1 - 1) Y_{t-1} + \gamma t + u_t,$$
$$\nabla Y_t = \beta_0 + \theta Y_{t-1} + \gamma t + u_t.$$

Just as before, estimate the θ with OLS and test $H_0 : Y_t \sim I(1)$ versus $H_1 : Y_t \sim I(0)$, with the t-statistic $t_{\hat\theta}$:

$$t_{\hat\theta} = \frac{\hat\theta}{s.e\left(\hat\theta\right)},$$

by using a DF-t-distribution. For example, the 5% critical value for $n = 100$ is -3.45.

The use of the *DF*-test in practice

In the econometric practice, you have to choose one of the DF-t-tests. For an economic variable, situation 2 will be the most appropriate because a constant term will be necessary and an additional trend term is generally superfluous. Later on, the test will also be applied on regression residuals where the first situation can often be used as the residuals have a zero mean. In the description of the DF-t-test, a first-order autoregressive process for the variable had been assumed. In practice, we do not know the order of the process and so the order has to be determined empirically. In general, an AR(p)-process will be assumed and the order p will be determined by 'modelling from general to specific'. The general model is:

$$\beta(L) Y_t = \beta_0 + u_t$$
$$Y_t = \beta_0 + \beta_1 Y_{t-1} + \beta_2 Y_{t-2} + \ldots + \beta_p Y_{t-p} + u_t.$$

The equation, in rewritten form (using α_i as notation for the transformed β_i) is:

$$\nabla Y_t = \beta_0 + (\beta_1 - 1) Y_{t-1} + \sum_{i=1}^{p-1} \alpha_i \nabla Y_{t-i} + u_t, \tag{12.33}$$

or

$$\nabla Y_t = \beta_0 + \theta Y_{t-1} + \sum_{i=1}^{p-1} \alpha_i \nabla Y_{t-i} + u_t.$$

In practice, choose p in such a way that the residuals are not autocorrelated. Under the null hypothesis of a unit root we have the following properties of the 'explanatory variables': Y_{t-1} is non-stationary but the first differenced lagged variables ∇Y_{t-i} are stationary. This means that $t_{\hat{\alpha}_i} = \hat{\alpha}_i / se(\hat{\alpha}_i)$ is Student's t-distributed and $t_{\hat{\theta}} = \hat{\theta}/se\left(\hat{\theta}\right)$ is DF-t-distributed. This implies that the number of lags ∇Y_{t-i} can be determined by using the Student's t-distribution by testing that α_i is significantly different from zero. A linear trend term can also be included in equation (12.33). Of course, do not use the DW-statistic to test for residual autocorrelation, but look at the correlogram (Q-test) of the residuals. When a specific specification has been accepted, test the null hypothesis $H_0 : \theta = 0$. This 'variant' of the unit-root test has got its own name, the *Augmented Dickey–Fuller test* (ADF-test). Other well-known unit-root tests are the Phillips and Phillips–Perron tests. These tests assume any ARMA process for Y_t.

If the unit-root hypothesis has not been rejected, the conclusion is drawn that *at least* one unit root exists in the process, as it is possible that a second unit root exists. Rejection of the null hypothesis implies stationarity of the process. When the null hypothesis has not been rejected, we have to test for a second unit root by testing the null hypothesis $H_0 : Y_t \sim I(2)$, which can be done by testing $H_0 : \nabla Y_t \sim I(1)$. That is done with equation (12.33) specified for ∇Y_t:

$$\nabla^2 Y_t = \tilde{\beta}_0 + \tilde{\theta} \nabla Y_{t-1} + \sum_{i=1}^{p-1} \tilde{\alpha}_i \nabla^2 Y_{t-i} + \tilde{u}_t.$$

$H_0 : Y_t \sim I(1)$
$H_1 : Y_t \sim I(0)$
H_0 rejected: $Y_t \sim I(0)$
H_0 not rejected $\Longrightarrow$ $H_0 : Y_t \sim I(2)$
                                        or $H_0 : \nabla Y_t \sim I(1)$
                                        $H_1 : Y_t \sim I(1)$
                                        H_0 rejected: $Y_t \sim I(1)$
                                        H_0 not rejected $\Longrightarrow$ $H_0 : Y_t \sim I(3)$
                                                                                or $H_0 : \nabla^2 Y_t \sim I(1)$
                                                                                $H_1 : Y_t \sim I(2)$
                                                                                H_0 rejected: $Y_t \sim I(2)$
                                                                                H_0 not rejected: problems

Table 12.5: A scheme for testing for the order of integration of an economic variable

The notation with the tilde above the parameters has been used to discern the parameters from the parameters in equation (12.33); also the disturbance term is different. A procedure for testing for the order of integration of an economic variable is shown in Table 12.5.

If $\beta(L)$ is a lag polynomial of degree p and the polynomial has one unit root, then the process is not stationary and the polynomial can be factored as follows:

$$\beta(L) = 1 - \beta_1 L - \beta_2 L^2 - \ldots - \beta_p L^p$$
$$\beta(L) = (1 - L)\left(1 - \beta_1^* L - \beta_2^* L^2 - \ldots - \beta_{p-1}^* L^{p-1}\right)$$
$$\beta(L) = (1 - L)\beta^*(L),$$

so that:

$$\beta(L) Y_t = u_t$$
$$\beta^*(L)(1 - L) Y_t = u_t$$
$$\beta^*(L) \nabla Y_t = u_t,$$

where ∇Y_t is a stationary process and $\beta^*(L)$ is a lag polynomial of degree $p - 1$.
The same is valid for two unit roots:

$$\beta(L) Y_t = u_t$$
$$\beta^{**}(L)(1 - L)^2 Y_t = u_t$$
$$\beta^{**}(L) \nabla^2 Y_t = u_t,$$

where $\nabla^2 Y_t$ is a stationary process and $\beta^{**}(L)$ is a lag polynomial of degree $p - 2$.

To perform a unit-root test in EViews, the relevant variable is selected by double-clicking on its name: the 'Unit Root Test' is found under 'View' in the 'Series' window. Besides the $(A)DF$-test you find other unit-root tests that are not discussed in this book. To apply the $(A)DF$-test, you have to specify whether a constant term (situation 2), an intercept and a

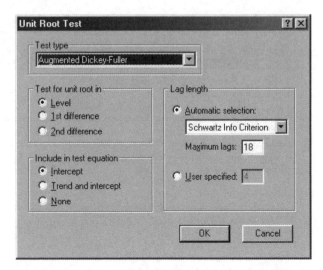

Figure 12.5: Selection and specification of a unit-root test

linear trend term (situation 3), or nothing (situation 1), has to be included. To test for unit roots in economic variables situation 2 will mainly be used, whereas situation 1 can be the appropriate situation for a differenced variable (and later on, for regression residuals).

Then you have to specify the degree of the polynomial (p) by indicating the number of lagged differences $(p-1)$. This selection can be done by yourself but also with the help of any of the available information criteria. You also have to select the level, first or second differences, of the variable to perform the test. EViews makes it easy to perform these unit-root tests and deciding the order of integration of an economic variable. After this procedure has been done, first double-click on RESID to look at the Q-test and the sample residual autocorrelations. Without significant autocorrelation it is possible to use the t-test to test for the degree of the lag polynomial. When a correct specification has been found, the null hypothesis of a unit root can be tested by using the t-statistic of the estimated parameter of Y_{t-1}.

In Figures 12.5 and 12.6, some EViews examples are given of the windows and output concerning the Dickey–Fuller test to test the null hypothesis that the cocoa price is first-order integrated (in logs). In Figure 12.5 you can see the start of the test. Six tests can be found under 'Test type', but we consider the ADF-test only. The three discussed 'situations' can be recognised: 'Intercept' is Situation 2, 'Trend and intercept' is Situation 3, and 'None' is Situation 1. Level and Situation 2 have been selected as shown. For specifying (or searching) for the order p of the polynomial you can choose whether the computer or yourself selects the lag length. For the automatic selection, EViews uses an information criterion. The Schwartz Information Criterion (SIC) appears by default in the window, but five other criteria, like the Akaike Information Criterion (AIC), are available. These two criteria are discussed in Section 14.7. A priori it is not obvious what is the best choice. If the automatic selection has been chosen one has still to check the results, such as absence of residual autocorrelation and the significance of the parameters. In the given example, the automatic selection yielded an acceptable result; the lowest value of the SIC has been chosen for a regression with a maximum of 18 lags.

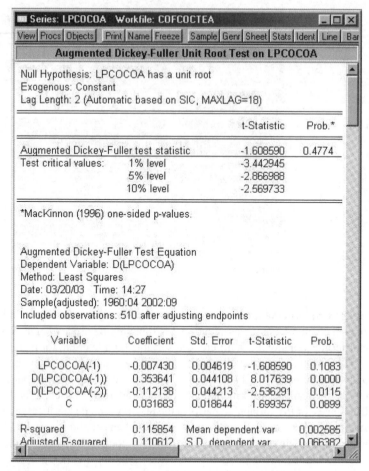

Figure 12.6: Output from the ADF t-test applied on ln (P_t^{coc})

The null hypothesis of a unit root in ln (P_t^{coc}) is not rejected. An AR(3) process has been assumed for the cocoa price $((p - 1) = 2)$. Next proceed with testing for a second unit root, by testing for a unit root in the first differences of the cocoa price ∇ ln (P_t^{coc}):

$$H_0 : \ln (P_t^{coc}) \sim I(2)$$
$$H_0 : \nabla \ln (P_t^{coc}) \sim I(1).$$

After a first regression it was obvious that the constant term could be dropped from the regression (a zero coefficient and t-value), so the final result for situation 1 is shown in Figures 12.7 and 12.8.

The null hypothesis of a unit root in $\nabla (\ln (P_t^{coc}))$ is clearly rejected, so the cocoa price is integrated of first order:

$$\ln (P_t^{coc}) \sim I(1).$$

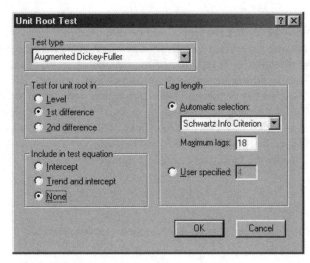

Figure 12.7: Selection and specification of a unit-root test for
$\nabla \ln \left(P_t^{coc} \right)$

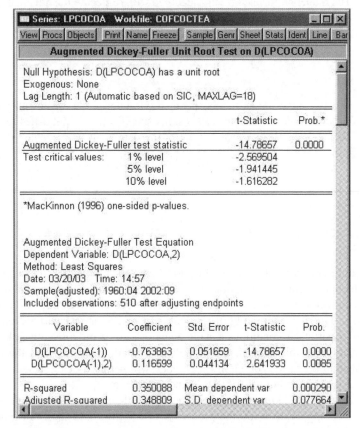

Figure 12.8:   Output from the ADF t-test for $\nabla \ln \left(P_t^{coc} \right)$

Remark 12.1 Unit-root tests and causal models

For obtaining a correct specification of a causal economic model, it is important to know the order of integration of the dependent and all the explanatory variables. Look at the following situation: the dependent variable Y_t has a trend $(Y_t \sim I(1))$ and none of the explanatory variables has a trend (they are $I(0)$). Then a lot of autocorrelation will be found in the residuals, or the other way around. The trend is found in the residuals, as the trend in the dependent variable is not explained by any of the specified variables.

Consider the following example. Suppose the model is:

$$Y_t = \beta_1 + \beta_2 X_t + \beta_3 Z_t + u_t,$$

with the following orders of integration (varying between 0–2) of the explanatory variables:

$$X_t \sim I(d_x), \; Z_t \sim I(d_z) \text{ and } u_t \sim I(0).$$

The model has been correctly specified with respect to the orders of integration if the order of integration of the dependent variable (Y_t) is equal to the maximum order of integration that occurs at the right-hand side of the equation:

$$Y_t \sim I(\max(d_x, d_z)).$$

Otherwise the model is mis-specified. Granger (1981) writes that, in practice, it is not uncommon to see this type of mis-specification in published research. This also means that unit-root tests belong to the data analysis preceding the model estimation.

12.6   Relationships between non-stationary variables

A different approach for modelling an ECM is the use of an estimated long-run equation as the imposed long-run solution of a dynamic short-run model, instead of the assumed static relationships that were used in the previous section. Up to now, we considered estimated static equations, with a lot of residual autocorrelation, as spurious regressions. However, under particular conditions a static equation can be interpreted as a long-run equilibrium equation. In this section, the properties of static equations and the conditions that the equation is spurious or a long-run model, will be discussed in detail. This is done using a clear and consistent way of testing and modelling.

The obtained knowledge about trends and the unit-root tests from the previous section will be applied to study the properties of long-run and short-run relationships between non-stationary variables.

We start by looking at a spurious regression of two variables, to keep the discussion simple. In Section 12.4, the study of Granger and Newbold (1974) was mentioned. They demonstrated that static regressions between two *independent* unit-root processes, Y_t and X_t, as in the following equation:

$$Y_t = \beta_1 + \beta_2 X_t + u_t \tag{12.34}$$

will frequently have high t-values and high $R^2 s$, together with low values of the DW-statistic, representing specification errors with respect to the dynamics of the model. For the static model (12.34), it can be shown that the t-statistic does not have an (asymptotic) t-distribution and that t-values rise for $n \rightarrow \infty$, and further that the DW-statistic reduces to zero. In other words, the residuals have a unit root:

$$u_t = \varphi_1 u_{t-1} + \varepsilon_t,$$
$$(1 - \varphi_1 L) u_t = \varepsilon_t,$$
$$DW \approx 2(1 - \varphi_1),$$
$$DW = 0 \Longrightarrow \varphi_1 = 1,$$
$$u_t \sim I(1).$$

These are properties of a spurious regression. However, perhaps something different is going on. It is possible that a low value of the DW-statistic is found, but the DW-statistic is not equal to zero. In that case $|\varphi_1| < 1$ and u_t is stationary: $u_t \sim I(0)$. This difference in the behaviour of the disturbance term is decisive in the conclusion about the nature of the static relationship of non-stationary variables: a spurious equation or a long-run equation. So the nature of the relationship depends on the properties of the processes in the variables and in the residuals from the static regression. In the beginning of this chapter, the distinction was introduced between variables that are DSP and those that are TSP. Which property the variables has is of importance in judging the static relationship of the variables. If the variables are TSP then the regression will be spurious as the variables follow their own deterministic trends. But if the non-stationary variables are DSP, they can have similar trends that cancel in a linear combination of the variables: the static regression. This means that a static regression between non-stationary variables is a long-run equilibrium relationship when the variables are integrated of first order and the OLS residuals are stationary. So the variables are non-stationary, but a stationary linear combination of the variables exists. When this occurs, the integrated variables are called *cointegrated*. Both variables have a similar stochastic trend, whereas the linear combination of the two variables e_t, written as

$$e_t = Y_t - \widehat{\beta}_1 - \widehat{\beta}_2 X_t,$$

is stationary. The variables may not drive apart from each other when they form part of an equilibrium relationship. They drive apart when they have their own specific trend.

The discussion of the concept of cointegration in this 'first course in econometrics' will be limited to the investigation of the existence of one long-run relationship among a number of economic variables. Mathematically seen, it is possible that a maximum number of $(K - 1)$ static relationships exist between K variables. In a multivariate model, one can test for the number of cointegrating relationships by using the maximum likelihood methodology of Johansen. Extensive econometrics literature exists about this subject, starting with the articles of Johansen (1988) and Johansen and Juselius (1990). Johansen and Juselius' approach is beyond the scope of this introductory course, but the interested reader can find good descriptions in many textbooks such as Hamilton (1994), Cuthbertson, Hall and Taylor (1992) or Verbeek (2000). Various applications of this methodology can be found in the econometics literature; for example, see Vogelvang (1992) where a cointegration analysis of spot prices of various types of coffee is presented. The procedures of Johansen are included in EViews with the option 'Cointegration Test' under 'View' in the 'Group' window (see the EViews User's Guide for a description).

We will limit ourselves to the Engle Granger two-step procedure (EG procedure) as mentioned earlier. In step 1 the existence of a cointegrating relationship between two or more variables, as specified from the economic theory, will be tested. If such a cointegrating relationship exists then a corresponding error-correction model exists for the short run and will be estimated in step 2. The two-step procedure will be discussed together with its application in EViews. For the formal discussion of the cointegration concept, given below, we consider the static relationship:

$$Y_t = \beta_1 + \beta_2 X_{t2} + \ldots + \beta_K X_{tK} + u_t. \tag{12.35}$$

A condition for the existence of cointegration of the variables $Y_t, X_{t2}, \ldots, X_{tK}$ is that these variables have similar stochastic trends. A second condition is that the residuals of equation (12.35) are stationary. Then equation (12.35) concerns a cointegrating relationship and can be considered as a long-run equilibrium relationship. First, the null hypothesis that the variables are $I(1)$ is tested:

$$H_0 : Y_t \sim I(1), \ X_{t2} \sim I(1), \ldots, X_{tK} \sim I(1)$$
$$H_1 : Y_t \sim I(0), \ X_{t2} \sim I(0), \ldots, X_{tK} \sim I(0),$$

by using the ADF test. Choose the number of lags of the dependent variable or choose the 'Automatic selection', in such a way that residual autocorrelation is absent. If H_0 is not rejected, then the next step is to test the hypothesis that the differenced variables have a unit root:

$$H_0 : \nabla Y_t \sim I(1), \ \nabla X_{t2} \sim I(1), \ldots, \nabla X_{tK} \sim I(1)$$
$$H_1 : \nabla Y_t \sim I(0), \ \nabla X_{t2} \sim I(0), \ldots, \nabla X_{tK} \sim I(0).$$

Because only $I(1)$ variables are considered as candidates for a possible cointegrating relationship, $I(2)$ series are not considered here.[†] After the unit-root hypotheses for the variables have been tested and not rejected, the null hypothesis that the variables follow a difference stationary process is tested. In EViews an equation like equation (12.36) has to be specified in an 'Equation Specification' window and estimated with OLS to perform the F-test, to test the null hypothesis that the process is a DSP (or a unit-root process). For

---

[†] See, for example, Haldrup's contribution in McAleer and Oxley (1999) for a survey of the literature on $I(2)$ processes.

| | Critical values | | |
Sample size n	0.10	0.05	0.025
25	5.91	7.24	8.65
50	5.61	6.73	7.81
100	5.47	6.49	7.44
250	5.39	6.34	7.25
500	5.36	6.30	7.20
∞	5.34	6.25	7.16

Table 12.6: Critical values for the DF F-test

Source: Part of Table B.7 in Hamilton (1994), based on the source Dickey and Fuller (1981).

example, for the variable Y_t the following equation is specified:

$$\nabla Y_t = \beta_0 + (\beta_1 - 1)Y_{t-1} + \gamma t + \sum_{i=1}^{p-1} \alpha_i \nabla Y_{t-i} + u_t. \tag{12.36}$$

The variable Y_t is DSP if the null hypothesis

$$H_0 : \beta_1 = 1 \text{ and } \gamma = 0,$$

has not been rejected. After the parameters have been estimated, the F-test is computed via 'View', 'Coefficient Tests', 'Wald Coefficient Restrictions' to test the null hypothesis: $C(2) = C(3) = 0$. But do not use the standard F-distribution, as this F-statistic is not Fisher F-distributed, instead use Table 12.6 for the Dickey–Fuller F-statistic. So do *not* look at the printed p-value in the EViews output!

For example, again for a series with about 100 observations, the test of the null hypothesis that the variable follows a DSP process is illustrated in Figure 12.9, where the hypothesis is tested at the 5% significance level.

In the following example, the null hypothesis is tested that the cocoa price follows a unit-root process. First, specify the equation in the 'Equation Specification' window, as shown in Figure 12.10.

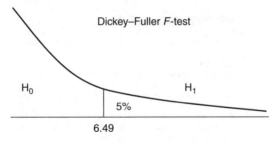

Figure 12.9: Example of a DF-F distribution to test the hypothesis that the process is DSP

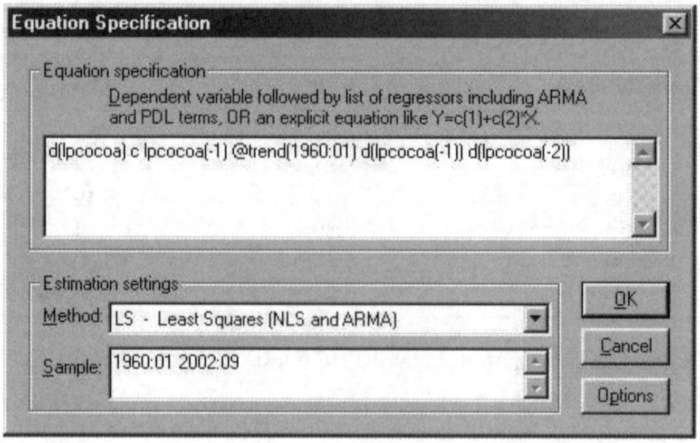

Figure 12.10: Specification for the Dickey–Fuller F-test

The number of two lagged dependent variables was sufficient to have a specification with non-autocorrelated residuals, $LB(36) = 30.74$ (0.72), as was checked beforehand. The OLS output is not given. The test statistic has been computed with the result shown in Figure 12.11.

The Fisher F-test indicates a probability of 19.4%, but this value comes from a Fisher-F distribution: we are concerned in this case with a Dickey–Fuller F-distribution. The regression concerns 510 observations, therefore we use the row entry for $\mathrm{n} = 500$ in Table 12.6, which shows a 5% critical value of 6.30. The null hypothesis that the coffee price follows a difference stationary process is clearly not rejected at the 5% (or 10%) significance level.

Of course, the F-test can also be computed as:

$$F = \frac{(S_R - S)/g}{S/(n-K)}. \tag{12.37}$$

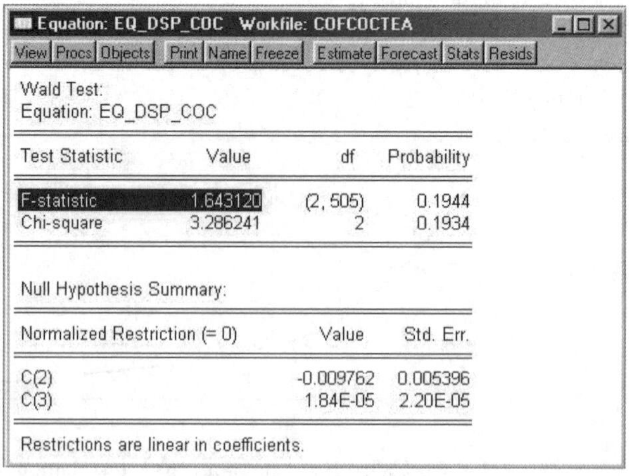
Equation: EQ_DSP_COC Workfile: COFCOCTEA

View | Procs | Objects | Print | Name | Freeze | Estimate | Forecast | Stats | Resids

Wald Test:
Equation: EQ_DSP_COC

Test Statistic	Value	df	Probability
F-statistic	1.643120	(2, 505)	0.1944
Chi-square	3.286241	2	0.1934

Null Hypothesis Summary:

Normalized Restriction (= 0)	Value	Std. Err.
C(2)	-0.009762	0.005396
C(3)	1.84E-05	2.20E-05

Restrictions are linear in coefficients.

Figure 12.11: Result of the F-test

Estimate (12.36) and equation (12.38)

$$\nabla Y_t = \beta_0 + \sum_{i=1}^{p-1} \alpha_i \nabla Y_{t-i} + u_t, \tag{12.38}$$

and compute (12.37) with the residual sums of squares (S_R) of the restricted (12.38) and the residual sums of squares (S) of the unrestricted equation (12.36). Then of course use the table of the DF-F-distribution. The same procedure is applied on the explanatory variables $X_{t2}, \ldots, X_{tK}$.

After we have not rejected that all the variables are unit-root processes the static relationship is estimated:

$$Y_t = \beta_1 + \beta_2 X_{t2} + \beta_3 X_{t3} + \ldots + \beta_K X_{tK} + u_t$$

with OLS. This equation is a long-run equilibrium relationship if the OLS residuals e_t are stationary, with e_t:

$$e_t = Y_t - \widehat{\beta}_1 - \widehat{\beta}_2 X_{t2} - \ldots - \widehat{\beta}_K X_{tK}.$$

The last condition is checked by testing the null hypothesis that the OLS residuals have a unit root, which implies that they are *not* stationary, and that the variables are *not cointegrated*.

$$H_0 : e_t \sim I(1)$$
$$H_1 : e_t \sim I(0).$$

Other critical values than before need to be used, because the residuals have been obtained conditional on the estimated model. Use Table 12.7 when the ADF-test will be used to test H_0. The critical values of the standard DF t-test in EViews are not valid for the OLS residuals.

If this null hypothesis has not been rejected, the static relationship is a spurious regression. In case the hypothesis has been rejected, the variables are assumed to be cointegrated and the static relationship is an estimated long-run equilibrium relationship. The DW-statistic will be low, but not equal to zero. Then the linear combination of K non-stationary variables is stationary. This procedure yields an *estimated* long-run relationship, in contrast with the

		Situation 1			Situation 2			Situation 3		
n	K	2.5%	5%	10%	2.5%	5%	10%	2.5%	5%	10%
500	1	−3.05	−2.76	−2.45	−3.64	−3.37	−3.07	−3.68	−3.42	−3.13
500	2	−3.55	−3.27	−2.99	−4.02	−3.77	−3.45	−4.07	−3.80	−3.52
500	3	−3.99	−3.74	−3.44	−4.37	−4.11	−3.83	−4.39	−4.16	−3.84
500	4	−4.38	−4.13	−3.81	−4.71	−4.45	−4.16	−4.77	−4.49	−4.20
500	5	−4.67	−4.40	−4.14	−4.98	−4.71	−4.43	−5.02	−4.74	−4.46

Table 12.7: *DF* t-distributions for unit-root tests for the residuals of the static equation

Source: Part of Table B.9 in Hamilton (1994), based on Fuller (1976).

given long-run relationships in Section 12.4. The parameters β_k ($k = 1, \ldots, K$) of the static equation have been *super consistently* estimated with OLS, because the rate of convergence is n instead of $\sqrt{n}$ (see the previous section). A side-effect of this property is that the bias and inconsistency of the OLS estimator, caused by endogenous explanatory variables, are cancelled out. It is not necessary to use the 2SLS estimator.

By using the residuals (e_t) from the long-run equation (12.35) a short-run error correction model is estimated, according to step 2 in Engle and Granger (1987). For notational convenience only, a bivariate model for the variables Y_t and X_t is used here as example. The ECM is of the form as equation (12.39), a specification in first differences (possibly in irreversible form) and an error-correction term (e_{t-1}).

$$\nabla Y_t = \beta_0 + \sum_{i=0}^{s-1} \gamma_i \nabla X_{t-i} + \sum_{j=1}^{p-1} \beta_j \nabla Y_{t-j} + \gamma e_{t-1} + u_t \tag{12.39}$$

The lag polynomials of Y_t and X_t are assumed to be of order p and s, as usual. In equation (12.39), the lagged residual variable e_{t-1}, stems from the long-run equation (12.35), which is the error-correction term in this model. A correct way to publish the estimation results in a correct notation is:

Long run: $Y_t = \widehat{\beta}_1 + \widehat{\beta}_2 X_t + e_t$

Short run: $\widehat{\nabla Y_t} = \widehat{\beta}_0 + \widehat{\gamma}_0 \nabla X_t + \sum \widehat{\gamma}_i \nabla X_{t-i} + \sum \widehat{\alpha}_j \nabla Y_{t-j} + \widehat{\gamma} e_{t-1}.$

The long-run equation is written with a residual term and the short-run model with a 'hat' above the dependent variable. When the conditions for cointegration are not satisfied, equation (12.34) is a spurious regression, Y_t and X_t are not related. Then the residuals are not stationary, $e_t \sim I(1)$, they have a unit root and so the DW-statistic is not significantly different from zero, the variables are TSP. If the model were to be estimated in first differences (variables are stationary in that case) nothing is left of the 'good statistics'. DW goes up, R^2 reduces to zero, and t- and F-values are no longer 'significant'.

Remark 12.2 Procedure
It is possible that one of the null hypotheses in the scheme above is not rejected whereas it is actually true (or the other way around) because of the ADF-test's low power. However, still go on and estimate the ECM and test whether e_{t-1} has a clearly significant influence (t-statistic with a low p-value), which can also be considered as a test for cointegration. Draw conclusions only when the 'complete picture' of all the results can be considered.

Remark 12.3 Specification
The short-run model and the long-run model can be different with respect to the number of specified variables. Variables that are not included in the long-run equation can be included in the short-run model, or the other way around.

Example 12.3   A cointegration analysis

This chapter is concluded with an example concerning the relationship with the two commodity prices P_t^{coc} and P_t^{cof} in logs. We will investigate whether a long-run relationship exists between the two world-market prices along the lines as discussed above. A graph of the logs of the prices is shown in Figure 12.12. The prices clearly move in a similar way in time. Therefore, it is interesting to investigate the hypothesis that P_t^{coc} and P_t^{cof} are cointegrated. If not rejected, the static regression will be compared with the solution of the estimated short-run model shown in Figure 4.4. At the end of the example, these results will be evaluated. For notational convenience we write P_t^{coc} and P_t^{cof} instead of ln (P_t^{coc}) and ln (P_t^{cof}) in this example.

In this chapter, we have already established that P_t^{coc} is a unit-root process. The same can be found for P_t^{cof} (show that yourself by using the available coffee data). Next the analysis proceeds with investigating the properties of the static relationship between the two prices. The result of the OLS estimation of the static equation

$$P_t^{coc} = \beta_0 + \beta_1 P_t^{cof} + u_t,$$

is given in Figure 12.13.

Observe the low value of the DW-statistic. With respect to the interpretation of the value of the determination coefficient, remember that for a bivariate model we have established in Section 5.3 that $R^2 = r^2_{P_t^{coc}, P_t^{cof}}$. Next, store the residuals ('Procs', 'Make Residual Series ...'), which has been done under the name $RESID\_COIN$, and apply the unit-root test for the null hypothesis that the prices are not cointegrated:

$$H_0 : RESID\_COIN \sim I\,(1)\,.$$

The output of the ADF t-test is shown in Figure 12.14.

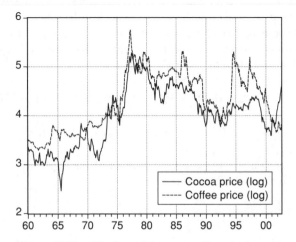

Figure 12.12:   The logs of the commodity prices

Equation: UNTITLED Workfile: COFCOCTEA

View | Procs | Objects | Print | Name | Freeze | Estimate | Forecast | Stats | Resids

Dependent Variable: LPCOCOA
Method: Least Squares
Date: 04/08/03 Time: 13:34
Sample: 1960:01 2002:09
Included observations: 513

Variable	Coefficient	Std. Error	t-Statistic	Prob.
LPCOFFEE	0.897914	0.020590	43.60908	0.0000
C	0.136019	0.089273	1.523628	0.1282

R-squared	0.788209	Mean dependent var	3.992180
Adjusted R-squared	0.787794	S.D. dependent var	0.603299
S.E. of regression	0.277915	Akaike info criterion	0.280886
Sum squared resid	39.46789	Schwarz criterion	0.297417
Log likelihood	-70.04726	F-statistic	1901.752
Durbin-Watson stat	0.090501	Prob(F-statistic)	0.000000

Figure 12.13: The static regression

Do *not* use the critical values and the p-value that are shown in the output in Figure 12.14. If we want to test the null hypothesis at a significance level of 5%, we compare the value -3.30 of the DF-statistic with the value -2.76 from Table 12.7. The result is that the null hypothesis of no cointegration is rejected, even at the 2.5% level. So we conclude that P_t^{coc} and P_t^{cof} are cointegrated and that the equation

$$P_t^{coc} = 0.1360 + 0.8979 P_t^{cof} + e_t \tag{12.40}$$

is a long-run equilibrium relationship between the logs of the both prices.

Next (as step 2 in the EG procedure) a short-run error-correction model is estimated by modelling from general to specific. The final result of that procedure is shown in Figure 12.15. The option 'White Heteroskedasticity-Consistent Standard Errors' has been used because of the heteroskedastic disturbances.

We observe that all the estimated parameters, except the constant term but including the error-correction coefficient, are significantly different from zero. So the corresponding short-run ECM to (12.40) is written as:

$$\widehat{\nabla P_t^{coc}} = \underset{(0.00)}{0.002} + \underset{(0.047)}{0.122}\ \nabla P_t^{cof} + \underset{(0.050)}{0.352}\ \nabla P_{t-1}^{coc} - \underset{(0.043)}{0.110}\ \nabla P_{t-2}^{coc} - \underset{(0.011)}{0.023}\ e_{t-1},$$

$$R^2\ :\ 0.13,\ JB : 48.95\ (0.00)\,,\ BG\,(3) : 2.93\ (0.40)\,,\ White : 30.85\ (0.00)\,.$$

It is interesting to compare these results with the originally obtained unrestricted results from Section 4.9. That result was:

$$\widehat{P_t^{coc}} = \underset{(0.020)}{0.016} + \underset{(0.041)}{0.121}\ P_t^{cof} - \underset{(0.041)}{0.103}\ P_{t-1}^{cof} + \underset{(0.044)}{1.328}\ P_{t-1}^{coc} - \underset{(0.071)}{0.462}\ P_{t-2}^{coc} + \underset{(0.044)}{0.110}\ P_{t-3}^{coc},$$

$$R^2\ :\ 0.99,\ JB : 49.07\ (0.00),\ BG(3) : 3.14\ (0.370),\ White : 12.04\ (0.28).$$

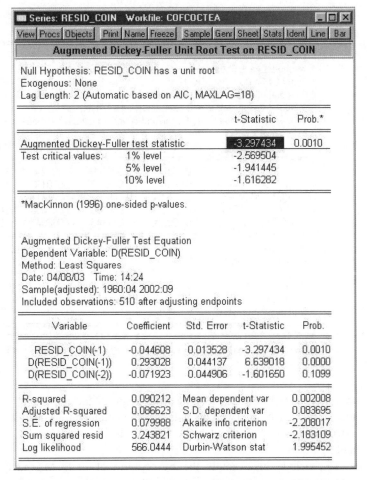

Figure 12.14: Dickey–Fuller t-test applied on the cocoa residuals

Rewrite this model by making use of the lag operator:

$$\widehat{P_t^{coc}} = \frac{0.016}{1 - 1.328 + 0.462 - 0.110} + \frac{0.121 - 0.103L}{1 - 1.328L + 0.462L^2 - 0.110L^3}P_t^{cof}.$$

Next, the long-run implication of this model is found by the substitution of $L = 1$:

$$\widehat{P_t^{coc}} = 0.667 + 0.75P_t^{cof}.$$

This result looks like an acceptable relationship too. The estimated long-run parameter is 0.90, whereas the solution of the unrestrictedly estimated short-run model gives a long-run response of 0.75. As the quotient of the sample means of $\ln\left(P_t^{coc}\right)$ and $\ln\left(P_t^{cof}\right)$ is $3.99/4.29 = 0.93$, the estimated long-run equation (12.40) seems reasonably close

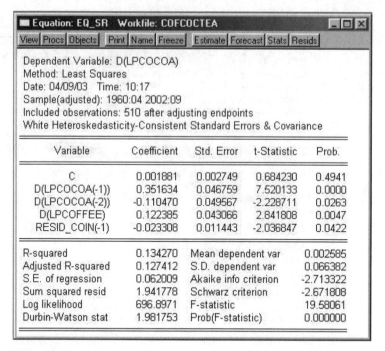

Figure 12.15: The estimated error-correction model for ln (P_t^{coc})

to what can be expected. (See also the graph of the logs of P_t^{coc} and P_t^{cof} in Figure 12.12.) Therefore, we conclude that the cointegration analysis of the commodity prices has resulted in acceptable models for the investigated relationship between P_t^{coc} and P_t^{cof}.

To conclude this example, the irreversibility of the ECM is investigated: has an increase of the coffee price an identical influence on the cocoa price as a price decrease? The variables $\nabla^+ P_t^{cof}$ and $\nabla^- P_t^{cof}$ have already been computed in Section 12.4. In Figure 12.16 the estimation result of the irreversible ECM is shown.

The point estimates show that an increase of P_t^{cof} has more influence than a decrease, but is that difference statistically significant? That question is quickly answered by computing a Wald F-test or an LR-test. The result of the F-test is given in Figure 12.17.

The null hypothesis that $\nabla^+ P_t^{cof}$ and $\nabla^- P_t^{cof}$ have the same influence on P_t^{coc} is clearly not rejected with a probability of 57.13%. The same result is obtained with the LR-test:

$$-2\ln(\lambda) = -2\,(696.8971 - 697.0516)$$

$$= 0.309.$$

The LR-statistic has a $\chi^2(1)$ distribution; the value 0.309 has a probability of 57.83%. The null hypothesis is not rejected, implying that the model can be estimated in reversible (symmetrical) form for the entire sample period.

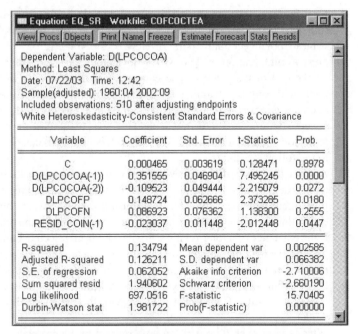

Figure 12.16:   The estimated irreversible error-correction model

Figure 12.17:   Testing the irreversibility property

12.7   Case 10: cointegration analysis

In this case, we take up again the papers written relating to Cases 2 and 6. In Case 6, the parameters of the original dynamic model from Case 2 were re-estimated in a consistent way with 2SLS. Your model is a dynamic model for the short run that will be analysed further.

- First, compute the long-run multipliers and/or elasticities from that unrestrictedly estimated dynamic model. Conclude whether these long-run parameters have realistic values from an economic point of view.

  Next, a cointegration analysis will be done along the lines as discussed in this chapter. At the end of the exercise you can compare these results with the unrestrictedly computed long-run parameters. Depending on the conclusions from the interim results it is possible that a decision can be taken to stop the analysis, for example, because common trends do not occur. However, in this case the complete exercise has to be done (see Remark 12.2). Then overall conclusions can be drawn. Pay attention to the following points.

- Analyse the data to determine which variables are integrated of first order and follow a unit-root process. It is possible that not all the variables are $I(1)$.

- Investigate whether a long-run relationship exists between the $I(1)$ variables, by estimating the static equation and testing the residuals for the presence of a unit root.

- If the existence of a long-relationship has not been rejected, compare these long-run parameters with the computed long-run parameters of the unrestrictedly estimated model. Draw conclusions about the sense of reality of the different long-run results.

- Next, estimate a short-run ECM. Decide which estimator can be used to obtain consistent results. Compare this ECM with the unrestrictedly estimated short-run model.

- What is your overall conclusion with respect to the presence or absence of cointegration?

- Write a clear paper about your analysis of the short-run and long-run behaviour of the model. Summarise the results from the unit-root tests in a compact table.

Practical remarks

- Read once more Remarks 12.2 and 12.3, and remember that an $I(0)$ variable does not form part of a long-run model but can be included in the short-run model.

- Attention! In the 'Equation Specification' window in EViews it is not possible to specify lags for differenced variables in the same convenient way as can be done for variables in levels: $X_t, X_{t-1}, X_{t-2}, X_{t-3}$ can be written as $X(0 \text{ to } -3)$. The variables $\nabla X_t, \nabla X_{t-1}, \nabla X_{t-2}, \nabla X_{t-3}$ cannot be specified as $D(X)(0 \text{ to } -3)$ or similar. All the variables have to be specified: $D(X)$ $D(X(-1)) \, D(X(-2)) \, D(X(-3))$. When, for example, the variable DX has been generated as the first difference of X_t, then $DX(0 \text{ to } -3)$ can of course be used.

Chapter 13

Distributed Lag Models

13.1 Introduction

A distributed lag model is another dynamic causal model. Two types of distributed lag models and some related models will be discussed . As an introduction to the concept of distributed lags, the two kinds of distributed lag models for two variables are distinguished. One concerns a model with many but a finite number of lags of an explanatory variable, like model (13.1), and the other with an infinite number of lags of an explanatory variable, like model (13.2).

$$Y_t = \beta_0 + \gamma_0 X_t + \gamma_1 X_{t-1} + \ldots + \gamma_q X_{t-q} + u_t, \tag{13.1}$$

or

$$Y_t = \beta_0 + \gamma_0 X_t + \gamma_1 X_{t-1} + \gamma_2 X_{t-2} + \ldots + u_t. \tag{13.2}$$

In both models, the variable X_t is assumed to be exogenous, and the disturbance term has the usual assumptions:

$$u_t \sim NID\left(0, \sigma_u^2\right).$$

The name *distributed lag model* will become clear in Section 13.3. The estimation problems, caused by the specification of a distributed lag, are multicollinearity, and too few or no degrees of freedom. The parameters cannot, or cannot accurately, be estimated. These problems and some possible solutions will be discussed in the following sections. At the end of this chapter, we will look at some specific dynamic models that are encountered in the econometrics literature. These models are related to each other owing to the specification of a lagged dependent variable because of economic model building.

13.2   A finite distributed lag model

In this section, an adequate estimation method will be discussed for the parameters of model (13.1). If sufficient degrees of freedom are available, then the OLS estimator can be used to estimate the parameters of model (13.1), with an unbiased, consistent and efficient result, but inaccurate estimates can be caused by the multicollinearity problem. A well-known solution to these problems is the method of Almon (1962). The procedure will reduce the number of parameters by a transformation of the model and also the multicollinearity problem. The idea behind the method is that you have knowledge about the development of the influence of the explanatory variable in time, based on the economic theory. In other words, you have an idea about the form of the graph of the parameters γ_i for $i = 0, 1, 2, \cdots, q$. The Almon method suggests you approximate the 'graph' of the parameters γ_i against the lag length i by a continuous function. An example of an arbitrarily chosen graph that suggests an increasing influence of X_t for two periods after which the influence fades away till it is zero after nine lags, is shown in Figure 13.1.

The method assumes that the form of the graph can be approximated by a polynomial in i of a suitable degree. Consider the following polynomial of degree r, with $r < q$, for the unknown parameters γ_i:

$$\gamma_i = \alpha_0 + \alpha_1 i + \alpha_2 i^2 + \ldots \alpha_r i^r. \tag{13.3}$$

The approximation of the lag structure with this polynomial of degree r implies restrictions on the parameters γ_i. Substitution of the polynomial in the model will replace the q parameters γ_i by the r parameters α_i. Probably the degree r will be larger than 2, as a

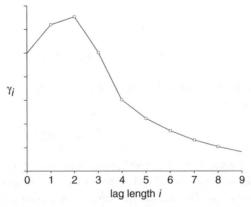

Figure 13.1:   A hypothetical path of lag coefficients

second-degree polynomial is a parabola, which is rather restrictive as it has no inflexion point and so no 'tail' that makes it possible to let the influence of X_t fade away over time. The procedure will be explained by using an example where the degree of the polynomial $r = 3$. Then the original q parameters γ_i are expressed in the parameters α_i in the following way:

$$\gamma_0 = \alpha_0$$
$$\gamma_1 = \alpha_0 + \alpha_1 + \alpha_2 + \alpha_3$$
$$\gamma_2 = \alpha_0 + 2\alpha_1 + 4\alpha_2 + 8\alpha_3$$
$$\gamma_3 = \alpha_0 + 3\alpha_1 + 9\alpha_2 + 27\alpha_3$$
$$\vdots$$
$$\gamma_q = \alpha_0 + q\alpha_1 + q^2\alpha_2 + q^3\alpha_3.$$

Substitute these expressions in model (13.1):

$$Y_t = \beta_0 + \alpha_0 X_t + (\alpha_0 + \alpha_1 + \alpha_2 + \alpha_3)\, X_{t-1} + (\alpha_0 + 2\alpha_1 + 4\alpha_2 + 8\alpha_3)\, X_{t-2}$$
$$+ (\alpha_0 + 3\alpha_1 + 9\alpha_2 + 27\alpha_3)\, X_{t-3} + \ldots + \left(\alpha_0 + q\alpha_1 + q^2\alpha_2 + q^3\alpha_3\right) X_{t-q} + u_t.$$

Then rewrite this equation by collecting the variables for identical α_i:

$$Y_t = \beta_0 + \alpha_0 \left(X_t + X_{t-1} + X_{t-2} + \ldots + X_{t-q}\right)$$
$$+ \alpha_1 \left(X_{t-1} + 2X_{t-2} + 3X_{t-3} + \ldots + qX_{t-q}\right)$$
$$+ \alpha_2 \left(X_{t-1} + 4X_{t-2} + 9X_{t-3} + \ldots + q^2 X_{t-q}\right)$$
$$+ \alpha_3 \left(X_{t-1} + 8X_{t-2} + 27X_{t-3} + \ldots + q^3 X_{t-q}\right) + u_t.$$

Next redefine the explanatory variables:

$$Z_{t1} = X_t + X_{t-1} + X_{t-2} + \ldots + X_{t-q}$$
$$Z_{t2} = X_{t-1} + 2X_{t-2} + 3X_{t-3} + \ldots + qX_{t-q}$$
$$Z_{t3} = X_{t-1} + 4X_{t-2} + 9X_{t-3} + \ldots + q^2 X_{t-q}$$
$$Z_{t4} = X_{t-1} + 8X_{t-2} + 27X_{t-3} + \ldots + q^3 X_{t-q},$$

which gives the equation:

$$Y_t = \beta_0 + \alpha_0 Z_{t1} + \alpha_1 Z_{t2} + \alpha_2 Z_{t3} + \alpha_3 Z_{t4} + u_t. \tag{13.4}$$

This model has five unknown parameters to estimate, instead of the original $q + 2$ parameters! Model (13.4) has the same disturbance term u_t as the original model (13.1), so the disturbance-term assumptions have not changed by the respecification of the model. The new variables $Z_{t1}, \ldots, Z_{t4}$ will be less correlated than the original lagged variables X_{t-i}, implying fewer or no multicollinearity problems. Just estimate the parameters $\alpha_0, \ldots, \alpha_3$ from model (13.4) with OLS and compute the corresponding values for the $\widehat{\gamma}_i$ and their standard errors.

In practice, we do not know the degree of the polynomial, but the Student's t-test can be used to test the significance of the last parameter $\hat{\alpha}_3$ in equation (13.4). In case of residual autocorrelation being absent, this t-statistic gives information about the suitability of the degree of the used polynomial. Also, the validity of the Almon procedure can be tested with a standard F-test as model (13.4) is a restricted model with regard to model (13.1). Estimate both models, which gives the restricted (S_R) and unrestricted (S) sum of residual squares, and compute the F-statistic:

$$F = \frac{(S_R - S)/(q-r)}{S/(n-K)} \overset{H_0}{\sim} F(q-r, n-K).$$

The Almon procedure does not always directly give a satisfactory result. It is possible that the estimation result is unsatisfactory if, for example, the γ_i start at a level that is too high from an economic point of view or the graph of the γ_i decreases too slowly to zero. Then this behaviour can be 'repaired' by restricting the graph (and so the parameters) by the imposition of a 'near-end' and/or 'far-end' restriction on one or two parameters that do not occur in the model. This is done by setting: $\gamma_{-1} = 0$ and/or $\gamma_{q+1} = 0$. Substituting the restrictions in (13.3) gives:

$$\alpha_0 - \alpha_1 + \alpha_2 - \alpha_3 = 0,$$

and/or

$$\alpha_0 + \alpha_1 (q+1) + \alpha_2 (q+1)^2 + \alpha_3 (q+1)^3 = 0.$$

These restrictions are substituted in model (13.4) and have to be elaborated. This exercise results in fewer regressors in equation (13.4). For example, if only a near-end restriction is imposed, then substitute α_0 in equation (13.4):

$$\alpha_0 = \alpha_1 - \alpha_2 + \alpha_3, \tag{13.5}$$

$$Y_t = \beta_0 + (\alpha_1 - \alpha_2 + \alpha_3) Z_{t1} + \alpha_1 Z_{t2} + \alpha_2 Z_{t3} + \alpha_3 Z_{t4} + u_t$$
$$= \beta_0 + \alpha_1 (Z_{t2} + Z_{t1}) + \alpha_2 (Z_{t3} - Z_{t1}) + \alpha_3 (Z_{t4} + Z_{t1}) + u_t.$$

This yields the restricted regression equation:

$$Y_t = \beta_0 + \alpha_1 W_{t1} + \alpha_2 W_{t2} + \alpha_3 W_{t3} + u_t,$$

with the new variables W_{ti} defined as:

$$W_{t1} = Z_{t2} + Z_{t1}$$
$$W_{t2} = Z_{t3} - Z_{t1}$$
$$W_{t3} = Z_{t4} + Z_{t1}.$$

The parameters β_0, α_1, α_2 and α_3 are estimated, for example, with OLS, after which $\hat{\alpha}_0$ is computed by substitution of the $\hat{\alpha}_1$, $\hat{\alpha}_2$, $\hat{\alpha}_3$ in the restriction (13.5). If both end-point restrictions are imposed one more regressor disappears, but the derivation is done in a similar way.

In empirical work, the application of the Almon procedure is very simple in EViews. The procedure is used by specifying a *polynomial distributed lag (PDL)* in the 'Equation' window. For example, if model (13.1) is estimated unrestrictedly with Almon's method, the specification in the window is done as follows (but with concrete numbers for q and r in parenthesis):

$$Y \; C \; PDL\,(X, q, r)\,.$$

The specification $PDL\,(X, q, r)$ means that a polynomial distributed lag is applied to X that has been specified with q lags in the original model and that will be estimated by using a polynomial of degree r for the parameters. 'Near-end' and 'far-end' restrictions can be imposed by specifying one more parameter m:

$$Y \; C \; PDL\,(X, q, r, m)\,,$$

with the following explanation:

$$m = 0, \text{ or no } m \text{ specified: no restrictions,}$$
$$m = 1\text{: near-end restriction, } (\gamma_{-1} = 0),$$
$$m = 2\text{: far-end restriction, } (\gamma_{q+1} = 0),$$
$$m = 3\text{: both ends are restricted.}$$

To end this section, an example is given of the use and the output of the Almon procedure in EViews. This example will show a failed attempt to find a good fit to the data by using the Almon procedure. In empirical econometric research we are often confronted with failures so it is good to give some unsuccessful examples in a textbook; especially as it makes no difference whether the example is successful or not in showing the output of the Almon procedure that is given by EViews.

The Almon procedure is applied to the relationship between the commodity prices. We will investigate whether more lags of P_t^{cof} and P_{t-1}^{coc} (in logs) have an influence on the price formation of cocoa by specifying polynomial distributed lags for both the variables. Both the polynomials are of degree 4 and have been specified for 12 lags. Only 'far end' restrictions have been specified. The specification in the 'Equation Specification' window is shown in Figure 13.2 and the output has been split up in Figures 13a to 13c. In Figure 13a, the regression output is shown. The parameters of the distributed lags are calculated together with their standard errors and t-values. The results, which are asymptotic because of the lagged dependent variables, are given in Figures 13b and 13c, where also the estimated original parameters have been plotted, showing the lag patterns.

The 'variables' PDL01–PDL08 are the transformed variables Z_{ti} from equation (13.4); PDL01–PDL04 for P_t^{cof} and PDL05–PDL08 for P_{t-1}^{coc}. Lags of P_{t-1}^{coc} clearly have more influence.

However, the residuals are highly autocorrelated; all the Q-statistics have probabilities equal to zero. This implies that the parameters of this specification have been inconsistently estimated. From the estimation results we see that only two coffee prices have a significant

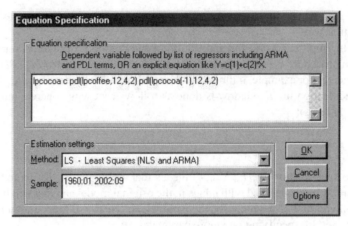

Figure 13.2: Specification of a polynomial distributed lag for P_t^{cof} and P_{t-1}^{cof} (in logs)

influence, just as before. But we cannot draw any conclusion from this result. The only conclusion is that the estimation results, because of the residual serial correlation, indicate that the PDL specification is not a good method for determining the relationship between P_t^{cof} and P_t^{coc}. However, the use of EViews' PDL procedure has been clarified by this example.

■ Equation: EQ_PDL Workfile: COFCOCTEA   _ □ ✕

View Procs Objects Print Name Freeze Estimate Forecast Stats Resids

Dependent Variable: LPCOCOA
Method: Least Squares
Date: 04/14/03   Time: 13:20
Sample(adjusted): 1961:02 2002:09
Included observations: 500 after adjusting endpoints

Variable	Coefficient	Std. Error	t-Statistic	Prob.
C	0.039687	0.024815	1.599282	0.1104
PDL01	-0.005297	0.008027	-0.659822	0.5097
PDL02	0.002952	0.004225	0.698761	0.4850
PDL03	-6.08E-06	0.001418	-0.004288	0.9966
PDL04	-0.000185	0.000174	-1.060838	0.2893
PDL05	0.017796	0.008829	2.015758	0.0444
PDL06	0.053430	0.004600	11.61603	0.0000
PDL07	-0.008903	0.001534	-5.802482	0.0000
PDL08	-0.003496	0.000189	-18.45517	0.0000

R-squared	0.985521	Mean dependent var	4.010957
Adjusted R-squared	0.985285	S.D. dependent var	0.599500
S.E. of regression	0.072722	Akaike info criterion	-2.386505
Sum squared resid	2.596661	Schwarz criterion	-2.310642
Log likelihood	605.6262	F-statistic	4177.544
Durbin-Watson stat	1.199175	Prob(F-statistic)	0.000000

Figure 13.3a: The regression output

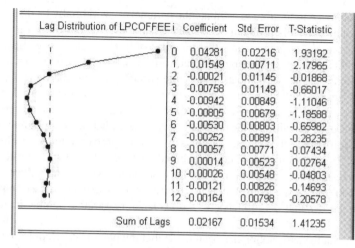

Lag Distribution of LPCOFFEE i	Coefficient	Std. Error	T-Statistic
0	0.04281	0.02216	1.93192
1	0.01549	0.00711	2.17965
2	-0.00021	0.01145	-0.01868
3	-0.00758	0.01149	-0.66017
4	-0.00942	0.00849	-1.11046
5	-0.00805	0.00679	-1.18588
6	-0.00530	0.00803	-0.65982
7	-0.00252	0.00891	-0.28235
8	-0.00057	0.00771	-0.07434
9	0.00014	0.00523	0.02764
10	-0.00026	0.00548	-0.04803
11	-0.00121	0.00826	-0.14693
12	-0.00164	0.00798	-0.20578
Sum of Lags	0.02167	0.01534	1.41235

Figure 13.3b: The estimated polynomial distributed lag of ln (P_t^{cof})

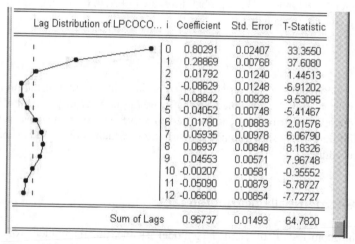

Lag Distribution of LPCOCO... i	Coefficient	Std. Error	T-Statistic
0	0.80291	0.02407	33.3550
1	0.28869	0.00768	37.6080
2	0.01792	0.01240	1.44513
3	-0.08629	0.01248	-6.91202
4	-0.08842	0.00928	-9.53095
5	-0.04052	0.00748	-5.41467
6	0.01780	0.00883	2.01576
7	0.05935	0.00978	6.06790
8	0.06937	0.00848	8.18326
9	0.04553	0.00571	7.96748
10	-0.00207	0.00581	-0.35552
11	-0.05090	0.00879	-5.78727
12	-0.06600	0.00854	-7.72727
Sum of Lags	0.96737	0.01493	64.7820

Figure 13.3c: The estimated polynomial distributed lag of ln (P_t^{coc})

13.3 Infinite distributed lags

Model (13.6) is a model that is specified with an infinite distributed lag pattern for the explanatory variable X_t:

$$Y_t = \beta_0 + \gamma_0 X_t + \gamma_1 X_{t-1} + \gamma_2 X_{t-2} + \ldots + u_t, \qquad (13.6)$$
$$u_t \sim NID\left(0, \sigma_u^2\right).$$

It is clear that the infinite number of parameters γ_i cannot be estimated without making further assumptions about the lag pattern. Such assumptions and accompanying procedures, which make it possible to estimate the parameters, will briefly be discussed in this section. A solution to this problem is to make assumptions about the form of the lag structure. For example, we can assume that the form of the lag pattern is comparable with the form of some probability distribution. The form of the lag structure is in accordance with the economic theory idea about the way the variable X_t influences the dependent variable Y_t over time. A suitable probability distribution is a distribution with a form that corresponds to the expected shape for the course of the parameters. The number of parameters γ_i can be reduced, by substituting the parameter(s) of that probability distribution in the model (13.6). The form of the chosen distribution is used as an approximation for the theoretical lag structure. This explains the name 'distributed lag'. A well-known and often-used distribution is the *geometric distribution*. With this distribution a declining influence of the exogenous variable can be specified, which can be an acceptable and realistic assumption. This assumption implies that the influence of the explanatory variable geometrically fades away over time.

When the assumption has been made that the parameters stem from a probability distribution, the parameters must be positive and sum to one. In general, the parameters will not sum to one, so they have to be rescaled. Denote the probabilities with p_i, then $\sum p_i = 1$, with $p_i \geq 0$ for all i. These probabilities are linked to the parameters in a simple way: there is a constant γ such that:

$$\gamma_i = p_i \gamma.$$

The parameters γ_i are replaced by $p_i \gamma$. Next the formula of the probability distribution for the p_i can be substituted. In that way, the number of parameters is reduced. Various probability distributions can be used to solve this distributed lag problem, but we will limit ourselves to the geometric distribution, which is discussed as an example of such a procedure.

Geometrically distributed lags

The geometrically distributed lag model assumes that the influence of a change in X_t on Y_t declines geometrically in the course of time. Write the specification of the distributed lag model (13.6) once more in general notation:

$$Y_t = \beta_0 + \gamma_0 X_t + \gamma_1 X_{t-1} + \gamma_2 X_{t-2} + \ldots + u_t,$$

$$= \beta_0 + \sum_{i=0}^{\infty} \gamma_i X_{t-i} + u_t, \tag{13.7}$$

$$u_t \sim NID\left(0, \sigma_u^2\right).$$

Historically, Koyck (1954) assumed that the influence of the exogenous variable X_t geometrically declines over time. That implies for the parameters γ_i that a parameter λ exists such that:

$$\gamma_i = \lambda \gamma_{i-1}, \text{ with } |\lambda| < 1, \text{ and } i = 1, 2, 3, \ldots.$$

Recursive substitution of this relationship gives:

$$\gamma_i = \lambda^i \gamma_0. \tag{13.8}$$

This suggests that the infinite number of parameters γ_i can be replaced by two parameters γ_0 and λ. Substitution of (13.8) in the model results in the respecified model (13.9):

$$Y_t = \beta_0 + \sum_{i=0}^{\infty} \lambda^i \gamma_0 X_{t-i} + u_t$$

$$Y_t = \beta_0 + \gamma_0 \sum_{i=0}^{\infty} \lambda^i X_{t-i} + u_t$$

$$Y_t = \beta_0 + \gamma_0 X_t + \lambda \gamma_0 L X_t + \lambda^2 \gamma_0 L^2 X_t + \ldots + u_t$$

$$Y_t = \beta_0 + \gamma_0 \left(1 + \lambda L + \lambda^2 L^2 + \ldots \right) X_t + u_t$$

$$Y_t = \beta_0 + \frac{\gamma_0}{1 - \lambda L} X_t + u_t. \tag{13.9}$$

This is the geometrically distributed lag model in its standard notation with the lag operator. The notation of equation (13.9) defines the sum of a geometrically declining time-series, as introduced in Chapter 12:

$$\frac{1}{1 - \lambda L} X_t = \sum_{i=0}^{\infty} \lambda^i X_{t-i}, \text{ with } |\lambda| < 1.$$

The infinite number of parameters of the original model has been reduced to three. However, model (13.9) is a non-linear model in the parameters that cannot be estimated with OLS.

Because of the solution mentioned in the introduction, using a probability distribution, it is more correct to use explicitly the formula of the *geometric distribution*,

$$p_i = (1 - \lambda) \lambda^i, \ |\lambda| < 1.$$

Then everything follows in similar way. First, rescale the probabilities to link them to the parameters:

$$\gamma_i = p_i \gamma, \text{ for } i = 0, 1, 2, \ldots$$

$$\gamma_i = \gamma (1 - \lambda) \lambda^i \tag{13.10}$$

Next substitute (13.10) in the model:

$$Y_t = \beta_0 + \sum_{i=0}^{\infty} \gamma (1 - \lambda) \lambda^i X_{t-i} + u_t$$

$$= \beta_0 + \gamma (1 - \lambda) \sum_{i=0}^{\infty} \lambda^i X_{t-i} + u_t,$$

with the parameter γ_0 written as:

$$\gamma_0 = \gamma(1 - \lambda)$$

the result is identical to model (13.9).

How can the parameters of model (13.9) be estimated? Historically, the parameters were estimated by transforming model (13.6), this can be demonstrated by 'multiplying' both sides of equation (13.9) with $(1 - \lambda L)$:

$$Y_t = \beta_0 + \frac{\gamma_0}{1 - \lambda L} X_t + u_t$$
$$(1 - \lambda L) Y_t = \beta_0 (1 - \lambda L) + \gamma_0 X_t + (1 - \lambda L) u_t$$
$$Y_t = \beta_0 (1 - \lambda) + \gamma_0 X_t + \lambda Y_{t-1} + (u_t - \lambda u_{t-1}) \qquad (13.11)$$

However, this is not a simple equation. When this model is estimated with OLS in the form:

$$Y_t = \alpha_1 + \alpha_2 X_t + \alpha_3 Y_{t-1} + v_t \qquad (13.12)$$
$$v_t = u_t - \lambda u_{t-1},$$

then the OLS estimates are *biased, inconsistent* and *inefficient*. The disturbance term v_t is an MA(1) process, so this model has an autocorrelated disturbance term that belongs to the model. This model was introduced in Section 8.5, where the GLS estimator was also introduced. In Section 8.5, the statement was made that no a priori reasons exist to assume an AR(1) disturbance term, but that an MA(1) disturbance is possible after a transformation of the model. However equation (13.11) has more problems than just autocorrelation. The lagged dependent variable (Y_{t-1}) and the disturbance term (v_t) are dependently distributed, and a restriction exists that the MA(1) parameter of u_t and the AR(1) parameter of Y_t are identical. So the OLS or GLS estimator cannot be used in a correct way. With the use of instrumental variables (IV) only consistent estimates can be obtained. Solutions for all the estimation problems can be found in, for example, Dhrymes (1971). They concern methods, like search and iterative methods, to find the maximum of the likelihood function of the non–transformed model (13.9). These procedures are not standard in EViews, but can be applied by writing a program of EViews procedures. However, these methods are beyond the scope of this book and are not discussed further. Finally, two more aspects of this model will be introduced, which can be used for the evaluation of the obtained estimated model.

The long-run response and the mean lag

The *long-run response* of Y_t to a unit change of X_t is found by substituting $L = 1$ in model (13.9) and is equal to the following expression:

$$\frac{\gamma_0}{1 - \lambda}.$$

One more convenient, and simply to compute, statistic that can be used as an evaluation tool with dynamic models is the *mean lag*. The mean lag can also be used to check the economic reliability concerning the assumption about the distribution of the lags. We have an idea about the mean number of periods that the adjustment to a shock from an exogenous variable on the dependent variable will last. In general notation, the formula for the mean lag is:

$$mean\_lag = \frac{\sum i\gamma_i}{\sum \gamma_i}. \tag{13.13}$$

In practice, the mean lag can be computed and evaluated when formula (13.13) has been made concrete and after the parameters have been estimated. Here the mean lag will be computed for the geometrically distributed lags. Substitute the formula of the geometric distribution in (13.13), and calculate separately the numerator (S_{num}) and the denominator (S_{denom}) – see, for example, Stewart and Wallis (1981: p.36):

$$mean\_lag = \frac{\sum i\gamma_i}{\sum \gamma_i} = \frac{\gamma(1-\lambda)\sum i\lambda^i}{\gamma(1-\lambda)\sum \lambda^i} = \frac{S_{num}}{S_{denom}}.$$

The denominator S_{denom} is computed straightforwardly:

$$S_{denom} = \sum \lambda^i = \frac{1}{1-\lambda}.$$

The numerator S_{num} is computed in the following way:

$$S_{num} = \sum i\lambda^i = \lambda + 2\lambda^2 + 3\lambda^3 + 4\lambda^4 + \ldots \tag{13.14}$$

$$\lambda S_{num} = \lambda^2 + 2\lambda^3 + 3\lambda^4 + \ldots. \tag{13.15}$$

Next compute the difference (13.14)–(13.15):

$$S_{num} - \lambda S_{num} = \lambda + \lambda^2 + \lambda^3 + \lambda^4 \ldots$$
$$= \frac{\lambda}{1-\lambda}.$$

Also it is true that:

$$S_{num} - \lambda S_{num} = S_{num}(1-\lambda).$$

Combine the two equations to determine S_{num}:

$$S_{num}(1-\lambda) = \frac{\lambda}{(1-\lambda)}$$
$$S_{num} = \frac{\lambda}{(1-\lambda)^2}.$$

Next compute the mean lag:

$$mean\_lag = \frac{\lambda/(1-\lambda)^2}{1/(1-\lambda)} = \frac{\lambda}{1-\lambda}.$$

In practice, the mean lag can easily be computed when the three parameters of model (13.12) have been estimated. The mean lag is equal to the coefficient of Y_{t-1} divided by 1 minus the value of that coefficient.

Remark 13.1
It is possible to estimate model (13.9) in a less restrictive way by assuming that the geometric decline does not start immediately but starts after several periods. For example:

$$Y_t = \beta_0 + \gamma_0 X_t + \gamma_1 X_{t-1} + \gamma_2 X_{t-2} + \ldots + u_t,$$

with

$$\gamma_i = \lambda \gamma_{i-1} \text{ for } i = 3, 4, 5, \ldots,$$

which results in the following model:

$$Y_t = \beta_0 + \gamma_0 X_t + \gamma_1 X_{t-1} + \frac{\gamma_2}{1 - \lambda L} X_t + u_t.$$

The parameters γ_0, γ_1, and γ_2 are estimated unrestrictedly.

13.4 Models with a lagged dependent variable

In the previous section, we saw that a lagged dependent variable appeared in model (13.12) by transforming the original model (13.6), because of a geometrically distributed lag. In this section, we look at some more economic models that result in a specification with a lagged dependent variable. Theoretical reasons exist for the 'popular' specification of a *lagged dependent variable*. Popular because a lagged dependent variable often eliminates first-order autocorrelation when we have started with the specification of a static model (which is not always the best idea to start with). The question that is raised in this section is: what is the *economic interpretation* of Y_{t-1} in the equation:

$$Y_t = \beta_0 + \gamma_0 X_t + \beta_1 Y_{t-1} + v_t? \tag{13.16}$$

Five hypotheses are discussed in this section, which are all examples of models that result in a specification such as (13.16). Special attention will be paid to their economic interpretation and to the disturbance term. The disturbance term v_t is either just randomly specified or it is a transformed disturbance term. If model (13.16) is correct with respect to one of these hypotheses and the estimated parameters have economically relevant values, then the mean lag is:

$$\frac{\beta_1}{1 - \beta_1},$$

and the long-run response is:

$$\frac{\gamma_0}{1 - \beta_1}.$$

Habit formation

First, model (13.16) can directly be specified by the researcher to show habit formation in the behaviour of economic subjects, for example. It shows the stochastic trend in the dependent variable. Just a dynamic model has been specified, probably with more dynamics for the other involved variables also. The disturbance term v_t is not a transformed disturbance term. Then we make the usual assumptions for the disturbance term v_t, $v_t \sim NID\left(0, \sigma_v^2\right)$, and OLS can be used to obtain consistent estimates of the parameters.

A geometrical distributed lag

A second model with the specification (13.16) is a transformed model that has arisen by transforming a causal model with a geometric distributed lag (with parameter λ) for an explanatory variable. The model has been transformed according to Koyck's method as was shown in the previous section. There we saw that the disturbance term v_t is an MA(1) process, $v_t = u_t - \lambda u_{t-1}$, with u_t as the disturbance term of the original model:

$$\mathbf{u} \sim N\left(\mathbf{0}, \sigma_u^2 \mathbf{I}_n\right),$$
$$\mathbf{v} \sim N\left(\mathbf{0}, \mathbf{\Omega}\right).$$

OLS results in inconsistent estimates of the parameters.

Partial adjustment

The model that will be discussed as the third model with specification (13.16) is also the result of a transformation. It is a model with a clear economic interpretation. The original model is one with a partial adjustment mechanism; it makes the economic assumption that a change in X_t in period t is fully reflected in Y_t in the same period t. If the dependent variable Y_t does not completely adjust to a change in X_t in the same period t, then we specify Y_t^* as the desired level of Y_t after a change in X_t, and specify a partial adjustment mechanism for the real change ∇Y_t. The desired level Y_t^* is determined by the static equation without a disturbance term:

$$Y_t^* = \beta_1 + \beta_2 X_t, \tag{13.17}$$

and the actual adjustment $(Y_t - Y_{t-1})$ is specified as part of the desired adjustment $(Y_t^* - Y_{t-1})$, and a random disturbance term u_t:

$$(Y_t - Y_{t-1}) = \lambda (Y_t^* - Y_{t-1}) + u_t; \ 0 < \lambda \le 1, \tag{13.18}$$

$$u_t \sim NID\left(0, \sigma_u^2\right).$$

The real change from Y_{t-1} to Y_t is a fraction of the desired change. When λ is close to one, the adjustment is fast, and there is slow adjustment with a value of λ close to zero. Substitution of the desired level (13.17) in the adjustment equation (13.18) yields a specification similar to (13.16), but still with the original disturbance term:

$$Y_t = \lambda\beta_1 + \lambda\beta_2 X_t + (1 - \lambda) Y_{t-1} + u_t.$$

In this equation, the lagged endogenous variable Y_{t-1} and the disturbance term u_t are independently distributed, because the transformation does not affect the disturbance term u_t. Its parameters can consistently be estimated with OLS. Notice that the parameter $(1 - \lambda)$ of Y_{t-1} is not the adjustment parameter. A value close to zero of the estimated parameter of Y_{t-1} implies a value close to one for the estimated adjustment parameter $\widehat{\lambda}$, and so a fast adjustment process!

Expectation variables

With this fourth model, an historical model that has not disappeared from econometrics literature will be mentioned. The original model is one which has an explanatory variable that represents an expected future value of an exogenous variable X_t:

$$Y_t = \beta_1 + \beta_2 X_{t+1|t}^* + u_t, \tag{13.19}$$

where $X_{t+1|t}^*$ is the expectation of X_t for period $t + 1$ that is formed in period t. No observations are available for this variable $X_{t+1|t}^*$. So an assumption about the way the expectation is formed has to be made. By substituting this assumption in (13.19) the variable $X_{t+1|t}^*$ can be eliminated. In the past, it was not unusual to assume an adaptive expectations mechanism. The adaptive expectations mechanism is formulated as:

$$\left(X_{t+1|t}^* - X_{t|t-1}^*\right) = \lambda \left(X_t - X_{t|t-1}^*\right), \ 0 < \lambda \le 1. \tag{13.20}$$

Equation (13.20) means that the change in the expectation from period t to $t + 1$ is a fraction of the expectations error $\left(X_t - X_{t|t-1}^*\right)$ that was made in the previous period.

Rewrite equation (13.20) to get an expression for $X^*_{t+1|t}$ in a variable that is observed:

$$\left(X^*_{t+1|t} - X^*_{t|t-1}\right) = \lambda \left(X_t - X^*_{t|t-1}\right)$$
$$X^*_{t+1|t} - X^*_{t|t-1} + \lambda X^*_{t|t-1} = \lambda X_t$$
$$X^*_{t+1|t} - (1-\lambda) X^*_{t|t-1} = \lambda X_t$$
$$X^*_{t+1|t} - (1-\lambda) L X^*_{t+1|t} = \lambda X_t$$
$$(1 - (1-\lambda) L) X^*_{t+1|t} = \lambda X_t$$

$$X^*_{t+1|t} = \frac{\lambda X_t}{(1 - (1-\lambda) L)}.$$

Substitute this expression in the original equation:

$$Y_t = \beta_1 + \beta_2 \frac{\lambda X_t}{(1 - (1-\lambda) L)} + u_t.$$

Multiply both sides of the equation with $(1 - (1-\lambda) L)$:

$$(1 - (1-\lambda) L) Y_t = \beta_1 (1 - (1-\lambda)) + \beta_2 \lambda X_t + (1 - (1-\lambda) L) u_t,$$

and rearrange the variables:

$$Y_t = \beta_1 (1 - (1-\lambda)) + \beta_2 \lambda X_t + (1-\lambda) Y_{t-1} + (u_t - (1-\lambda) u_{t-1}). \tag{13.21}$$

Again the specification of model (13.16) has been obtained as the result of a transformation. Equation (13.21) has a transformed disturbance term that has an MA(1) process,

$$v_t = u_t - (1-\lambda) u_{t-1}.$$

So, identical estimation problems arise to those with the geometric distributed lag model after using Koyck's transformation.

The procedure of using adaptive expectations is rather old-fashioned and restrictive. It can be shown that the result of the adaptive hypothesis is comparable with the specification of a specific time-series model for X_t, an IMA(1,1) process: $\nabla X_t = v_t - (1-\lambda) v_{t-1}$ (see, for example Stewart and Wallis (1981: p.48)). A more general approach is to identify and estimate a suitable ARIMA model for the variable X_t and to compute forecasts with that model that will serve as 'observations' for the expectations. The ARIMA models are discussed in Chapter 14.

Error-correction models

The last example of a model with a lagged endogenous variable in the specification is an error-correction model (ECM). An error-correction model can have a specification with a lagged dependent variable when the degree of the lag polynomial of the dependent variable is larger than or equal to one, as has been shown in Section 12.4. We have seen that the disturbance term u_t of the ECM has not been transformed, and so it has the usual assumptions: $u_t \sim NID\left(0, \sigma_u^2\right)$.

Knowledge about the interpretation of the value of the parameter β_1 that has been obtained when discussing the partial adjustment model can be used here to derive a property of the parameter of the error-correction term. That result will yield relevant information about the interpretation of the parameter of the error-correction term. Its value indicates the speed of convergence to the equilibrium relationship. This will be demonstrated with a simple example. Remember the unrestricted bivariate model with first-order lag polynomials, as discussed in Section 12.4:

$$Y_t = \beta_0 + \gamma_0 X_t + \gamma_1 X_{t-1} + \beta_1 Y_{t-1} + u_t,$$
$$u_t \sim NID\left(0, \sigma_u^2\right).$$

Now we know the interpretation of β_1. A low value of β_1 implies a fast adjustment to the long-run equilibrium. The long-run equilibrium in the example was $Y_t = X_t$ and the restricted error-correction model for this relationship was:

$$\nabla Y_t = \beta_0 + \gamma_0 \nabla X_t + (\beta_1 - 1)\left(Y_{t-1} - X_{t-1}\right) + u_t$$
$$u_t \sim NID\left(0, \sigma_u^2\right).$$

Once again: a low value of β_1 is identical to a coefficient close to one for the error-correction term $(\beta_1 - 1)$. So fast adjustment to the long-run equilibrium occurs when the parameter of the error-correction term is close to one. That is useful knowledge for empirical econometricians.

Chapter 14

Univariate Time-Series Models

14.1 Introduction

In this chapter, a type of model that is clearly different from the causal models that have been discussed so far is considered. It concerns the *autoregressive integrated moving average models* (ARIMA models), which are statistical models. In previous chapters, we became familiar with the concepts of AR(1), AR(p) and MA(1) processes for the disturbance term of a causal model. These models can be considered for one variable, but also for a vector of variables in a multivariate context. We will not consider multivariate time-series models in this book, instead limiting ourselves to the discussion of univariate ARIMA models. A univariate time-series (TS) model explains one variable (e.g. Y_t in general notation) with regard to its own past and the history of the random disturbance term u_t. The variable Y_t is considered as a stochastic process and the time-series with observations on Y_t are realisations of that process. Why have these models been developed? The idea behind them is that it is sometimes possible to get more accurate predictions for a variable with a TS model than with a causal model. However, do not think that two completely different models exist that explain and forecast the variable Y_t. There is a link between a causal model and TS model for an economic variable (see, for example, Zellner and Palm (1974, 1975)). In case the objective of the research is to produce predictions for an economic variable you can consider estimating a TS model for that variable. One more advantage is that only data for that variable have to be collected.

Besides an ARIMA model, a deterministic TS model can be distinguished. That is, for example, a model with a deterministic or exponential trend as explanatory variables only. In this chapter, the stochastic TS models are discussed. An accessible comprehensive introduction to many aspects of time-series analysis is, for example, Chatfield (1996). The

TS models have originally been developed by Box and Jenkins in the 1960s (see Box and Jenkins (1976)). Their methods will be explained in this chapter and the use of these procedures in EViews will be clarified. As an introduction to the models, the idea of the *linear filter model* (or linear statistical model) is briefly discussed. That model can be represented schematically in the following way.

$$u_t \rightarrow \boxed{\psi(L)}_{\text{model}} \rightarrow Y_t \tag{14.1}$$

There is a random input (u_t) into a model $(\psi(L))$ that results in an output series Y_t. This process can be written in an equation, possibly with a constant term, such as:

$$Y_t = \psi(L) u_t,$$

with $\psi(L)$ written as an infinite lag polynomial:

$$
\begin{aligned}
\psi(L) &= 1 + \psi_1 L + \psi_2 L^2 + \psi_3 L^3 + \dots \\
Y_t &= u_t + \psi_1 u_{t-1} + \psi_2 u_{t-2} + \dots \\
u_t &\sim NID\left(0, \sigma_u^2\right) \text{ for all } t.
\end{aligned} \tag{14.2}
$$

The input u_t is not observed. The output series Y_t is observed as a realisation of a stationary stochastic process that is assumed to be a Gaussian process:

$$\mathbf{y} \sim N\left(\mathbf{0}, \boldsymbol{\Omega}\right),$$

or with a constant in the model:

$$\mathbf{y} \sim N\left(\boldsymbol{\mu}, \boldsymbol{\Omega}\right)$$

Without loss of generality, it is assumed that the mean is zero in the following discussions. To determine the model $\psi(L)$ consider the opposite direction of the process (14.1): Y_t is 'filtered' to become a white-noise process:

$$Y_t \rightarrow \boxed{\psi^{-1}(L)}_{\text{filter}} \rightarrow u_t,$$

with the condition that the inverse $\psi^{-1}(L)$ has to exist. The necessary conditions of being invertible and stationary of the process imply restrictions on the parameters of the model. The linguistic terminology in the literature of time-series analysis is somewhat different from what has been used so far around causal models. For example, the process u_t is called a 'white noise process' because of the assumption that it is $NID\left(0, \sigma_u^2\right)$ for all observations. So when the observed Y_t has been filtered to a white noise process, the model has been found, as the inverse of the filter.

To check the stationarity of a Gaussian process, it is sufficient to check that the process is stationary of the second order, as the normal distribution is completely determined when the first two moments of the distribution are known, as was mentioned in Chapter 12. For example, consider the mean and variance of model (14.2):

$$E\left(Y_t\right) = E\left(u_t + \psi_1 u_{t-1} + \psi_2 u_{t-2} + \ldots\right)$$
$$= 0 \cdot \left(1 + \psi_1 + \psi_2 + \psi_3 + \ldots\right)$$
$$= 0,$$

if the series $1 + \psi_1 + \psi_2 + \psi_3 + \ldots$ converges to a finite constant:

$$E\left(Y_t^2\right) = E\left(u_t^2\right) + \psi_1^2 E\left(u_{t-1}^2\right) + \psi_2^2 E\left(u_{t-2}^2\right) + \ldots$$
$$= \sigma_u^2 \left(1 + \psi_1^2 + \psi_2^2 + \psi_3^2 + \ldots\right)$$

The variance exists as the series $1 + \psi_1^2 + \psi_2^2 + \psi_3^2 + \ldots$ will also converge to a finite constant. The process is stationary by imposing restrictions on the parameters ψ_i in such a way that the variance of Y_t is constant. If the variable Y_t is not stationary (and most economic time-series are not), the variable has to be transformed to a stationary variable. Mostly this is done by using transformations that we considered in Chapter 12, like differencing $\left(\nabla^d \text{ with } d \leq 2\right)$, by taking the logs (ln), or by doing both $\left(\nabla^d ln\right)$; with the condition $d \leq 2$ for economic reasons. When $d = 1$ the variable Y_t has a linear trend (constant growth) and when $d = 2$ there is a trend in the first differences, so a linear trend in the growth rate.

An ARMA(p,q) model without a constant term, for a stationary variable Y_t, is usually defined as:

$$\varphi\left(L\right) Y_t = \theta\left(L\right) u_t. \tag{14.3}$$

The model has an autoregressive polynomial $\varphi\left(L\right)$ of degree p and a moving-average polynomial $\theta\left(L\right)$ of degree q that are written as usual:

$$\varphi\left(L\right) = 1 - \varphi_1 L - \varphi_2 L^2 - \ldots - \varphi_p L^p$$
$$\theta\left(L\right) = 1 + \theta_1 L + \theta_2 L^2 + \ldots + \theta_q L^q.$$

Non-stationarity of Y_t might be caused by a unit root in $\varphi\left(L\right)$, as seen in Section 12.5. In case of one unit root, the polynomial $\varphi\left(L\right)$ can be written as:

$$\varphi\left(L\right) = \left(1 - L\right) \left(1 - \varphi_1^* L - \varphi_2^* L^2 - \ldots \varphi_{p-1}^* L^{p-1}\right)$$
$$= \left(1 - L\right) \varphi^*\left(L\right)$$
$$= \nabla \varphi^*\left(L\right).$$

Substitute this in model (14.3) and we have an ARMA(p-1,q) model for ∇Y_t, which is defined as an ARIMA(p,1,q) process for Y_t:

$$\varphi^*\left(L\right) \nabla Y_t = \theta\left(L\right) u_t.$$

The process is integrated of order one, because $\varphi(L)$ has one unit root. In general terms, a process with d $(d \leq 2)$ unit roots in the autoregressive polynomial is called an ARIMA(p,d,q) process; an autoregressive integrated moving average process:

$$\varphi(L) Y_t = \theta(L) u_t \Longrightarrow$$
$$\varphi^*(L) \nabla^d Y_t = \theta(L) u_t,$$

with $\varphi^*(L)$ a polynomial of order $p - d$.

In the next section, some examples of AR, MA and ARMA models will be considered first.

14.2 Time-series models and some properties

In this section, we look at the properties of some TS models – a pure AR and MA model, and the mixed ARMA model. The conditions for stationarity and invertibility of the polynomials are discussed in a more concrete manner.

Autoregressive models

The AR(p) model, without a constant term, is written as:

$$Y_t = \varphi_1 Y_{t-1} + \varphi_2 Y_{t-2} + \ldots + \varphi_p Y_{t-p} + u_t$$

or

$$\varphi(L) Y_t = u_t, \tag{14.4}$$

with

$$\varphi(L) = 1 - \varphi_1 L - \ldots - \varphi_p L^p.$$

We know already that the process is stationary if all the p solutions of $\varphi(L) = 0$ are outside the unit circle. Because this polynomial is a finite polynomial, the process is always invertible, and the model can be written as an MA(∞) process:

$$Y_t = \varphi^{-1}(L) u_t.$$

The AR-process is stationary if the parameters φ_i of (14.4) are such that the coefficients of the infinite polynomial $\varphi^{-1}(L)$ converge, which is identical with the previous mentioned condition for the roots of $\varphi(L) = 0$ lying outside the unit circle.

The range for the parameters where the AR(p) model is stationary can be determined a priori. This has been done earlier in Section 12.2 for the AR(1) model and is shown here once more to complete the overview of this section.

$$Y_t = \varphi_1 Y_{t-1} + u_t$$

or written with the polynomial $\varphi(L)$:

$$(1 - \varphi_1 L) Y_t = u_t$$

so solve L from:

$$\varphi(L) = 1 - \varphi_1 L$$
$$1 - \varphi_1 L = 0,$$
$$L = \frac{1}{\varphi_1}$$

giving the restriction for φ_1:

$$|L| > 1 \implies |\varphi_1| < 1.$$

The same can be done for the AR(2) model:

$$Y_t = \varphi_1 Y_{t-1} + \varphi_2 Y_{t-2} + u_t,$$

or again written with the lag polynomial $\varphi(L)$:

$$\left(1 - \varphi_1 L - \varphi_2 L^2\right) Y_t = u_t.$$

It is possible to derive the following region for the parameters where the AR(2) model is stationary:

$$-1 < \varphi_2$$
$$\varphi_1 + \varphi_2 < 1$$
$$-\varphi_1 + \varphi_2 < 1. \tag{14.5}$$

The interested reader can find detailed descriptions concerning the computation of these inequalities in econometric books such as Anderson (1976), Box and Jenkins (1976), Chatfield (1996), Greene (2000) and Hamilton (1994).

Moving average models

Similar examples can be given for moving average models. The MA(q) model, without an intercept, is written as:

$$Y_t = u_t + \theta_1 u_{t-1} + \theta_2 u_{t-2} + \ldots + \theta_q u_{t-q},$$

or with the MA polynomial $\theta(L)$:

$$Y_t = \theta(L) u_t,$$

with

$$\theta(L) = 1 + \theta_1 L + \theta_2 L^2 + \ldots + \theta_q L^q.$$

The process is always stationary because the polynomial $\theta\left(L\right)$ is a finite polynomial. This means that the moments of the distribution of Y_t are finite constants, as can be checked quickly by looking at, for example, the mean and variance:

$$E(Y_t) = 0$$

$$E(Y_t^2) = \sigma_u^2 + \theta_1^2\sigma_u^2 + \theta_2^2\sigma_u^2 + \ldots + \theta_q^2\sigma_u^2$$

$$= \sigma_u^2 \left(1 + \theta_1^2 + \theta_2^2 + \ldots + \theta_q^2\right).$$

The MA(q) process is invertible if the coefficients of the infinite polynomial $\theta^{-1}\left(L\right)$ converge, and this is identical to the condition that the q solutions of $\theta\left(L\right) = 0$ are all outside the unit circle.

As a first example, look at the MA(1) process:

$$Y_t = u_t + \theta_1 u_{t-1}$$

or with a lag polynomial:

$$Y_t = \left(1 + \theta_1 L\right) u_t$$

$$\frac{1}{1 + \theta_1 L}Y_t = u_t.$$

The infinite sum $\left(1 + \theta_1 L\right)^{-1}$ converges if $|\theta_1| < 1$ or, the other way around, the root of the polynomial $\theta\left(L\right)$ has to lie outside the unit circle:

$$\theta\left(L\right) = 1 + \theta_1 L$$

$$1 + \theta_1 L = 0$$

$$L = -\frac{1}{\theta_1}.$$

This gives the restriction for θ_1:

$$|L| > 1 \Longrightarrow |\theta_1| < 1.$$

For the MA(2) model, restrictions for the parameters can be derived in a similar way:

$$Y_t = u_t + \theta_1 u_{t-1} + \theta_2 u_{t-2},$$

or with the lag polynomial:

$$Y_t = \left(1 + \theta_1 L + \theta_2 L^2\right) u_t.$$

The conditions for invertibility of the MA polynomial resemble the stationarity conditions of the AR(2) process (14.5) except for the signs of the parameters:

$$-1 < -\theta_2$$
$$-\theta_1 - \theta_2 < 1$$
$$\theta_1 - \theta_2 < 1.$$

Autoregressive moving average models

Finally, we look at the ARMA(p,q) model, which is a mix of the previously introduced AR and MA model. The ARMA(p,q) model is written as (14.3).

$$\varphi\left(L\right)Y_t = \theta\left(L\right)u_t.$$

It will be clear that the conditions for stationarity and invertibility are a combination of the conditions for the AR and MA models. The roots of both the polynomials $\varphi\left(L\right)$ and $\theta\left(L\right)$ have to be outside the unit circle, resulting in restrictions on the parameters.

A useful property of the estimation procedure in EViews is that the (inverse) roots of the polynomials are printed in the output, making it possible to check the conditions. With regard to the roots of the AR polynomial, we are sure that they comply with the conditions, because the variable has been transformed to become stationary.

14.3 Box–Jenkins procedures

In practice, we do not know the orders p and q of the lag polynomials $\varphi\left(L\right)$ and $\theta\left(L\right)$. The Box–Jenkins procedures provide us with tools that are useful in identifying the order of the polynomials. Then we will estimate the parameters φ_i and θ_i, and check the residuals of the TS model as to whether or not they are white noise. Then we will compute predictions for the concerned variable, which is the final goal of this exercise. In this section, the Box–Jenkins procedures are discussed in the following four stages.

Identification of the TS model.

First the stationarity of the variable has to be checked, for example, by applying an ADF unit-root test. If the variable is not stationary it has to be transformed into first differences or first differences of the logs of the observations. Next, the orders of the polynomials p and q have to be determined. The tools to determine p and q are the autocorrelation function (ACF) and the partial autocorrelation function (PACF). Each TS model has a unique theoretical ACF and PACF. In practice, the sample ACF and the sample PACF of the time-series are computed. The pictures of the sample functions are visually compared with figures showing forms of known theoretical ACFs and PACFs. Matching functions makes it possible to identify some ARIMA model. The ACF is introduced in Section 14.4 and the PACF will be discussed in Section 14.5. Both functions are necessary for the identification of the TS model. Examples are given in Section 14.6. The relationship between ACF, PACF and the theoretical TS model is unique. Theoretical forms of the ACF and PACF of many TS models have been determined and are known in the econometrics literature.

Estimation of the parameters of the polynomials $\varphi(L)$ and $\theta(L)$

After an initial identification, the parameters of the selected TS model will be estimated. As invertibility of the polynomial $\theta\left(L\right)$ has been required, model (14.3) can be rewritten as:

$$u_t = \theta^{-1}\left(L\right)\varphi\left(L\right)Y_t.$$

The disturbance term u_t is a non-linear function of the unknown parameters φ_i and θ_i. The maximum of the likelihood function is found by minimising $\sum u_t^2$ with respect to these parameters. EViews estimates the parameters with a non-linear optimisation procedure and computes the roots of the polynomials which are printed as 'inverted roots'. Then you can check whether these inverted roots are *within* the unit circle.

Diagnostic checking

After the TS model has been estimated the absence of residual autocorrelation has to be checked. The presence of autocorrelation will have been caused by model mis-specification. In the TS-analysis literature this step is called 'diagnostic checking'. If residual autocorrelation is absent, the significance of the parameter estimates can be considered. The earlier introduced Q-test of Ljung–Box will be used to test the hypothesis of random residuals.

Forecasting

The polynomial $\varphi(L)$ is invertible, so model (14.3) can be written as:

$$Y_t = \varphi^{-1}(L)\,\theta(L)\,u_t,$$

or with the estimated parameters as:

$$\widehat{Y}_t = \widehat{\varphi^{-1}(L)}\widehat{\theta(L)}u_t.$$

This expression is used for forecasting Y_t. Forecasting the last observations of the known sample belongs more or less to the diagnostic checking stage also. But remember that data from outside the estimation period cannot be used to test the quality of the estimated model for the sample. When the results are satisfactory, short-run post-sample forecasts can be computed with their prediction errors.

All these procedures are implemented in EViews. In the following section, the identification tools, the ACF and the PACF, are introduced and illustrated with examples, after which the econometric practice of the Box–Jenkins procedures is discussed and clarified with examples.

14.4   The autocorrelation function (ACF)

The autocorrelation function had been introduced in Section 6.3 as a tool for the Ljung–Box Q-test, to test the null hypothesis of an independently distributed disturbance term. The concept of stationarity was introduced in Chapter 12 and is considered here in more detail. A stochastic process is said to be *covariance stationary* if the means, the variances and the covariances of the process are constant through time. Therefore, the following conditions for the moments of the distribution of Y_t are required:

$$E\left(Y_t\right) = E\left(Y_{t-s}\right), \text{ for all } s \text{ and } t,$$

$$var\left(Y_t\right) = var\left(Y_{t-s}\right), \text{ for all } s \text{ and } t,$$

$$cov\left(Y_t, Y_{t-k}\right) = cov\left(Y_t, Y_{t+k}\right)$$

$$= cov\left(Y_{t-s}, Y_{t-k-s}\right)$$

$$= cov\left(Y_{t+s}, Y_{t+k+s}\right), \text{ for all } s, t \text{ and } k.$$

For notational convenience, it is common practice in the econometrics literature to define the autocovariance between Y_t and Y_{t-k} as γ_{kt}:

$$\gamma_{kt} = cov\left(Y_t, Y_{t-k}\right) = cov\left(Y_t, Y_{t+k}\right).$$

If the moments are not time dependent because of the stationarity requirement, then the only relevant parameter is the lag or the lead k:

$$\gamma_k = \gamma_{kt}.$$

The autocovariance with k lags is identical to the autocovariance with k leads:

$$\gamma_k = \gamma_{-k}.$$

Notice that γ_0 denotes the variance of Y_t for all t:

$$\gamma_0 = var\left(Y_t\right).$$

The autocovariances γ_k for $k = 0, 1, 2, \ldots$ form the discrete *autocovariance function* of Y_t. The 'autocorrelation coefficients' of the process Y_t are defined as:

$$\rho_{kt} = \frac{cov\left(Y_t, Y_{t+k}\right)}{\sqrt{var\left(Y_t\right)} \cdot \sqrt{var\left(Y_{t+k}\right)}}.$$

Because of the stationarity property of the process it follows that:

$$\rho_{kt} = \rho_k = \rho_{-k}.$$

Then the theoretical discreet *autocorrelation function* ρ_k of Y_t, is written as:

$$\rho_k = \frac{\gamma_k}{\gamma_0}; \text{ with } k = 0, 1, 2, \ldots \tag{14.6}$$

The theoretical ACF can be computed for all TS models of economic variables. This ACF will be estimated by computing the 'sample autocorrelation coefficients' from the data on Y_t. Comparing the sample ACF with theoretical ACF can yield indications about the kind of process that may have generated the data. But the use of only the ACF is not sufficient to identify all characteristics of the process, we also need the PACF of the variable. The PACF is introduced in the next section. Both functions give information about the type and order of the process.

14.5 The partial autocorrelation function (PACF)

The PACF is necessary as a second tool in the process to identify a TS model together with the ACF. The concept of a 'partial correlation coefficient' may be well-known from statistics, but it is useful to discuss it briefly here as an introduction to the partial autocorrelation coefficient. To understand the concept of a partial autocorrelation coefficient, an example of a partial correlation coefficient of two variables is given. For example, we consider a linear relationship among three variables: Y_t, X_t and Z_t. What is, for example, the partial correlation coefficient between Y_t and X_t within this group of variables? A partial correlation coefficient measures the correlation between two variables after the influence of other involved variables (in this example only Z_t) has been eliminated from these two variables. How can the partial correlation coefficient between Y_t and X_t (notation: $\widehat{\rho}^*_{Y,X}$) be computed? This can be done by first regressing both variables on Z_t. The residuals of these regressions (in notation: e^Y_t and e^X_t) are equal to the variables Y_t and X_t, but 'corrected' for the influence of Z_t. Next, compute the partial correlation coefficient $\widehat{\rho}^*_{Y,X}$ of Y_t and X_t as the correlation coefficient between the two residuals e^Y_t and e^X_t, which is shown with the following formulae:

$$e^Y_t = Y_t - \widehat{\alpha}_1 - \widehat{\beta}_1 Z_t,$$

$$e^X_t = X_t - \widehat{\alpha}_2 - \widehat{\beta}_2 Z_t,$$

$$\widehat{\rho}^*_{Y,X} = \widehat{\rho}_{e^Y,e^X} = \frac{\sum e^Y_t e^X_t}{\sqrt{\sum \left(e^Y_t\right)^2}\sqrt{\sum \left(e^X_t\right)^2}}.$$

The partial autocorrelation coefficient $\widehat{\rho}^*_{kt}$ between Y_t and Y_{t-k}, written as $\widehat{\rho}^*_k$ between Y and Y_{-k}, is computed in a similar way. It is the simple correlation between Y_t and Y_{t-k}, corrected for the influence of the intervening $k-1$ periods $Y_{t-1}, \ldots, Y_{t-k+1}$. That means that we can only correct Y_t for the influence of its past: $Y_{t-1}, \ldots, Y_{t-k+1}$. The residuals e^Y_t are now defined as:

$$e^Y_t = Y_t - \widehat{\alpha}_0 - \widehat{\alpha}_1 Y_{t-1} - \ldots - \widehat{\alpha}_{k-1} Y_{t-k+1}.$$

The partial autocorrelation coefficient $\widehat{\rho}^*_{kt}$ can be computed as the correlation coefficient of e^Y_t and Y_t:

$$\widehat{\rho}^*_{kt} = \widehat{\rho}_{Y,e^Y}.$$

The theoretical PACF ρ^*_k for a stationary process is defined as:

$$\rho^*_k = \rho^*_{kt}, \text{ with } k = 1, \ldots, p.$$

As an example, we look at an AR(p) process. As the maximum number of lags is equal to p, it is clear that:

$$\rho_k^* = 0 \text{ if } k > p.$$

This is an important property for determining the order of the process.

In the econometrics literature, the sample PACF is computed by solving a number of equations that are called the *Yule–Walker equations*. The derivation of these equations is briefly summarised. Proceed as follows with the AR(p) model:

$$Y_t = \varphi_1 Y_{t-1} + \varphi_2 Y_{t-2} + \ldots + \varphi_p Y_{t-p} + u_t.$$

Multiply both sides of the equation by Y_{t-i}:

$$Y_t Y_{t-i} = \varphi_1 Y_{t-1} Y_{t-i} + \varphi_2 Y_{t-2} Y_{t-i} + \ldots + \varphi_p Y_{t-p} Y_{t-i} + u_t Y_{t-i}.$$

Take the expectation at both sides of the equation giving a similar equation, but now for the autocovariances:

$$\gamma_i = \varphi_1 \gamma_{i-1} + \varphi_2 \gamma_{i-2} + \ldots + \varphi_p \gamma_{i-p}. \tag{14.7}$$

Obtain the same relationship for the autocorrelations by dividing both sides of the equation by the variance γ_0:

$$\rho_i = \varphi_1 \rho_{i-1} + \varphi_2 \rho_{i-2} + \ldots + \varphi_p \rho_{i-p}. \tag{14.8}$$

Define the partial autocorrelation coefficient of order k for any AR(p) process as φ_{kk}. Solve φ_{kk} (with $k = 1, \ldots, p$) from the set of k linear equations in φ_{kj} $(j = 1, \ldots, k)$ that are given as:

$$\rho_i = \varphi_{k1} \rho_{i-1} + \varphi_{k2} \rho_{i-2} + \ldots + \varphi_{kk} \rho_{i-k}, \text{ with } i = 1, \ldots, k. \tag{14.9}$$

Then the PACF is defined by the series $\{\varphi_{kk} : k = 1, \ldots, p\}$, and $\varphi_{kk} = 0$ for $k > p$. We will look at some examples.

When we have an AR(1) process, then $k = 1$, which implies that one equation is solved for one parameter φ_{11} (with $\rho_0 = 1$):

$$\rho_1 = \varphi_{11} \rho_0 \Longrightarrow \varphi_{11} = \rho_1,$$
$$\varphi_{kk} = 0 \text{ for } k \geq 2.$$

For an AR(2) process, two parameters (φ_{11} and φ_{22})are unequal to zero and are solved for $k = 1$ and $k = 2$. For $k = 1$ the result for φ_{11} is identical to that above. For $k = 2$ there are two linear equations that can be solved for two parameters, φ_{21} and φ_{22} as $i = 1, \ldots, k$, but only the solution for φ_{22} is relevant:

$$\rho_1 = \varphi_{21} \rho_0 + \varphi_{22} \rho_1$$
$$\rho_2 = \varphi_{21} \rho_1 + \varphi_{22} \rho_0,$$
$$\varphi_{kk} = 0 \text{ for } k \geq 3.$$

So, in general, the PACF for an AR(p) process consists of p coefficients unequal to zero:

$$\{\varphi_{kk} : k = 1, \ldots, p\},$$
$$\varphi_{kk} = 0 \text{ for } k > p.$$

The p coefficients are computed by solving φ_{11} from one equation, φ_{22} from a system of two equations, φ_{33} from a system of three equations, and finally solving φ_{pp} from a system of p equations.

This can compactly be written in matrix notation. The series φ_{kk} is derived from the solutions from the system (14.9) of k linear equations in the k unknown parameters φ_{kj}, written as:

$$
\begin{pmatrix} \rho_1 \\ \rho_2 \\ \cdot \\ \cdot \\ \cdot \\ \rho_k \end{pmatrix}
=
\begin{pmatrix}
1 & \rho_1 & \cdot & \cdot & \cdot & \rho_{k-1} \\
\rho_1 & 1 & \cdot & \cdot & \cdot & \rho_{k-2} \\
\cdot & & \cdot & & & \cdot \\
\cdot & & & \cdot & & \cdot \\
\cdot & & & & \rho_1 & \\
\rho_{k-1} & \cdot & \cdot & \cdot & \rho_1 & 1
\end{pmatrix}
\begin{pmatrix} \varphi_{k1} \\ \varphi_{k2} \\ \cdot \\ \cdot \\ \cdot \\ \varphi_{kk} \end{pmatrix}
, \quad \text{for } k = 1, \ldots p.
$$

These equations are the earlier mentioned Yule–Walker equations in the k unknown parameters φ_{kj}. But we will only calculate φ_{kk}. This is simply done by using the Cramer's rule:

$$
\varphi_{kk} = \frac{
\begin{vmatrix}
1 & \rho_1 & \cdot & \rho_{k-2} & \rho_1 \\
\rho_1 & 1 & \cdot & \rho_{k-3} & \rho_2 \\
\cdot & & \cdot & & \cdot \\
\cdot & & & \cdot & \rho_{k-1} \\
\rho_{k-1} & \cdot & \cdot & \rho_1 & \rho_k
\end{vmatrix}
}{
\begin{vmatrix}
1 & \rho_1 & \cdot & \rho_{k-2} & \rho_{k-1} \\
\rho_1 & 1 & \cdot & \rho_{k-3} & \rho_{k-2} \\
\cdot & & \cdot & & \cdot \\
\cdot & & & \cdot & \rho_1 \\
\rho_{k-1} & \cdot & \cdot & \rho_1 & 1
\end{vmatrix}
}
= \frac{|P_k^*|}{|P_k|}.
$$

Then the PACF, earlier defined by the sequence φ_{kk}, is written as:

$$\varphi_{kk} = \frac{|P_k^*|}{|P_k|}, \text{ for } k = 1, \ldots, p, \text{ whereas } \varphi_{kk} = 0, \text{ for } k > p. \tag{14.10}$$

The *theoretical* ACF ρ_k and *theoretical* PACF φ_{kk} can analytically be determined for every ARMA model. Both functions are expressed in the autocorrelation coefficients ρ_k. In practice, when modelling a variable, these coefficients will be estimated by the sample autocorrelation coefficients $\hat{\rho}_k$. The order of the process is unknown and will be estimated by determining the lag where the PACF becomes not significantly different from zero. Both functions are available in EViews and computed by double-clicking on the variable and selecting 'View' and 'Correlogram', as will be shown in the next section.

14.6 Examples of theoretical ACFs and PACFs for some TS models

In this section, a few examples are given of the computation of theoretical ACFs and PACFs of some simple TS models, together with their plots. Various examples of theoretical ACFs and PACFs can be found in the econometrics literature (see, for example, Anderson (1976) for many examples and a compact description of theoretical correlograms and sample correlograms of matching simulated processes). In all the examples we assume that:

$$u_t \sim NID\left(0, \sigma_u^2\right).$$

Example 14.1 The AR(1) model

The AR(1) model is:

$$Y_t = \varphi_1 Y_{t-1} + u_t, \quad |\varphi_1| < 1.$$

Use equation (14.7) as a basis for the computation of the ACF. For the AR(1) model the relationship for the γ_i is:

$$\gamma_i = \varphi_1 \gamma_{i-1}.$$

Recursive substitution of this relation gives:

$$\gamma_i = \varphi_1^i \gamma_0.$$

The ACF is computed as:

$$\rho_i = \frac{\gamma_i}{\gamma_0}$$
$$= \frac{\varphi_1^i \gamma_0}{\gamma_0}$$
$$= \varphi_1^i,$$

which is a geometrically declining function.
Also (14.8) can be used to get a similar relationship for ρ_i:

$$\rho_i = \varphi_1 \rho_{i-1}.$$

Compute the autocorrelation coefficients:

$$\rho_0 = 1$$
$$\rho_1 = \varphi_1 \rho_0 = \varphi_1$$
$$\rho_2 = \varphi_1 \rho_1 = \varphi_1^2$$
$$\rho_i = \varphi_1 \rho_{i-1}.$$

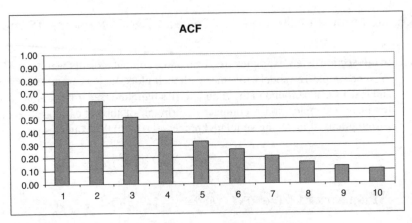

Figure 14.1a: The ACF of the AR(1) process $Y_t = 0.8Y_{t-1} + u_t$

The PACF is computed by using equation (14.10). For the AR(1) model:

$$p = 1 \Longrightarrow k = i = 1.$$

This implies that no intervening lags are present, which already means that $\varphi_{11} = \rho_1$. This result is also obtained by solving equation (14.10):

$$\varphi_{11} = \frac{|\rho_1|}{|1|} = \rho_1.$$

Although it is clear that $\varphi_{kk} = 0$ for $k \geq 2$, this can also be shown arithmetically by computing φ_{22} from (14.10):

$$\varphi_{22} = \frac{\begin{vmatrix} 1 & \rho_1 \\ \rho_1 & \rho_2 \end{vmatrix}}{\begin{vmatrix} 1 & \rho_1 \\ \rho_1 & 1 \end{vmatrix}}$$

$$= \frac{\rho_2 - \rho_1^2}{1 - \rho_1^2}$$

$$= \frac{\varphi_1^2 - \varphi_1^2}{1 - \varphi_1^2}$$

$$= 0, \ (\varphi_1 \neq 1).$$

An example[*] of the ACF and PACF of the AR(1) model,

$$Y_t = 0.8Y_{t-1} + u_t,$$

is given in Figures 14.1a and 14.1b.

---

[*] The plots of the theoretical ACFs and PACFs in this section have been made by using Microsoft Excel.

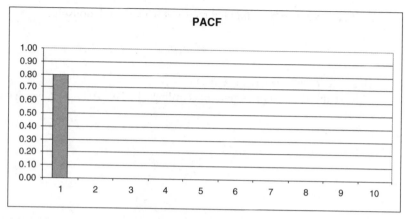

Figure 14.1b: The PACF of the AR(1) process $Y_t = 0.8Y_{t-1} + u_t$

Although the form of the two functions and the number of coefficients are identical for every AR(1) model, the figures are different for every value of φ_1.

Example 14.2 The AR(2) model

The AR(2) model is:

$$Y_t = \varphi_1 Y_{t-1} + \varphi_2 Y_{t-2} + u_t,$$

with the stationarity restrictions on the parameters as given in the inequalities (14.5). The ACF is computed by using equation (14.8):

$$\rho_i = \varphi_1 \rho_{i-1} + \varphi_2 \rho_{i-2}.$$

$i = 0$:

$$\rho_0 = 1$$

$i = 1$:

$$\rho_1 = \varphi_1 \rho_0 + \varphi_2 \rho_{-1}$$
$$= \varphi_1 + \varphi_2 \rho_1$$
$$= \frac{\varphi_1}{1 - \varphi_2},$$

$i = 2$:

$$\rho_2 = \varphi_1 \rho_1 + \varphi_2 \rho_0$$
$$= \frac{\varphi_1^2}{1 - \varphi_2} + \varphi_2.$$

Further, the ρ_i can be computed recursively by the relationship:

$$\rho_i = \varphi_1 \rho_{i-1} + \varphi_2 \rho_{i-2}.$$

This function will decay to zero as $i \to \infty$.

Next the PACF is computed according (14.10). As $p = 2$, we have $k = 1, 2$ and $i = 1, 2$.

First, $k = 1$:

$$\varphi_{11} = \frac{|\rho_1|}{|1|}$$

$$= \frac{\varphi_1}{1 - \varphi_2}.$$

Secondly, $k = 2$:

$$\varphi_{22} = \frac{\begin{vmatrix} 1 & \rho_1 \\ \rho_1 & \rho_2 \end{vmatrix}}{\begin{vmatrix} 1 & \rho_1 \\ \rho_1 & 1 \end{vmatrix}}$$

$$= \frac{\rho_2 - \rho_1^2}{1 - \rho_1^2}$$

$$= \frac{\varphi_1 \rho_1 + \varphi_2 - \rho_1^2}{1 - \rho_1^2}$$

$$= \frac{\rho_1^2 (1 - \varphi_2) + \varphi_2 - \rho_1^2}{1 - \rho_1^2}$$

$$= \frac{\rho_1^2 - \varphi_2 \rho_1^2 + \varphi_2 - \rho_1^2}{1 - \rho_1^2}$$

$$= \frac{\varphi_2 (1 - \rho_1^2)}{1 - \rho_1^2}$$

$$= \varphi_2.$$

The higher-order partial autocorrelation coefficients are zero:

$$\varphi_{kk} = 0, \text{ for } k \geq 3.$$

The ACF of the AR(2) model is an infinite decreasing function and the PACF has only two non-zero values. An example of the ACF and PACF of the AR(2) model:

$$Y_t = -0.40 Y_{t-1} + 0.25 Y_{t-2} + u_t$$

has been plotted in the Figures 14.2a and 14.2b.

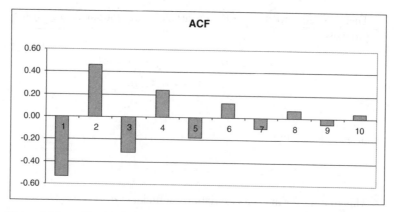

Figure 14.2a: The ACF of the AR(2) process $Y_t = -0.40Y_{t-1} + 0.25Y_{t-2} + u_t$

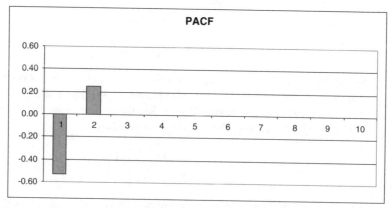

Figure 14.2b: The PACF of the AR(2) process $Y_t = -0.40Y_{t-1} + 0.25Y_{t-2} + u_t$

Conclusion

On the basis of the preceding examples we conclude the following about the ACF and PACF of the AR(p) model. Generalising the result of the AR(1) and AR(2) processes, it can be shown that the AR(p) model has an ACF that decays to zero, and an PACF that cuts off after p lags.

Example 14.3   The MA(1) model

The MA(1) model is:

$$Y_t = u_t + \theta_1 u_{t-1}, \quad |\theta_1| < 1.$$

The computation of the ACF is done as follows. Start with the autocovariance function:

$$\gamma_i = cov(Y_t, Y_{t-i})$$
$$= E[(u_t + \theta_1 u_{t-1})(u_{t-i} + \theta_1 u_{t-i-1})].$$

Then it is easy to see that the covariances are not equal to zero for contemporaneous products:

$$i = 0 \Longrightarrow \gamma_0 = (1 + \theta_1^2)\sigma_u^2$$
$$i = 1 \Longrightarrow \gamma_1 = \theta_1\sigma_u^2$$
$$i = 2 \Longrightarrow \gamma_2 = 0,$$

or more generally:

$$i \geq 2 \Longrightarrow \gamma_i = 0.$$

This implies for the autocorrelation coefficients $\rho_i = \gamma_i/\gamma_0$:

$$\rho_0 = 1$$
$$\rho_1 = \frac{\theta_1}{1 + \theta_1^2}$$
$$\rho_i = 0 \text{ for } i \geq 2.$$

So the ACF of an MA(1) process cuts off after one lag. Further, it is important to notice that $|\rho_1| < \frac{1}{2}$ because $|\theta_1| < 1$ (see also Figure 14.3a). This is always valid for an MA(1) model. The PACF is less easy to derive. See the econometrics literature (e.g. Anderson (1976)) for its derivation. The PACF is computed by:

$$\varphi_{kk} = \frac{(-1)^{k-1}\theta_1^k(1 - \theta_1^2)}{1 - \theta_1^{2(k+1)}}.$$

This is an infinite function that decays to zero. An example of the ACF and PACF of the MA(1) model,

$$Y_t = u_t + 0.70u_{t-1},$$

is given in Figures 14.3a and 14.3b.

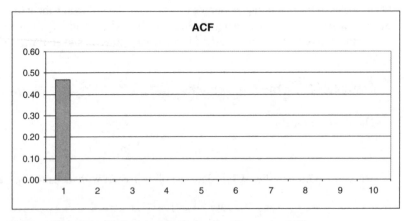

Figure 14.3a: The ACF of the MA(1) process $Y_t = u_t + 0.70u_{t-1}$

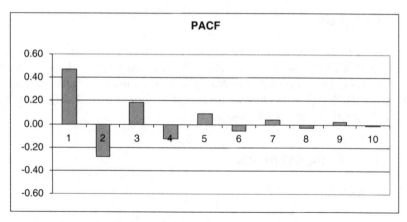

Figure 14.3b: The PACF of an MA(1) process $Y_t = u_t + 0.70u_{t-1}$

Example 14.4   The MA(2) model

The MA(2) model is:

$$Y_t = u_t + \theta_1 u_{t-1} + \theta_2 u_{t-2}.$$

For the determination of the ACF the autocovariances are computed again:

$$\gamma_i = cov(Y_t, Y_{t-i})$$
$$= E[(u_t + \theta_1 u_{t-1} + \theta_2 u_{t-2})(u_{t-i} + \theta_1 u_{t-i-1} + \theta_2 u_{t-i-2})].$$

In the same way as for the MA(1) model, the expectations of contemporaneous products are not equal to zero. The autocovariance function γ_i is:

$$i = 0 \Longrightarrow \gamma_0 = (1 + \theta_1^2 + \theta_2^2)\sigma_u^2$$
$$i = 1 \Longrightarrow \gamma_1 = (\theta_1 + \theta_2\theta_1)\sigma_u^2$$
$$i = 2 \Longrightarrow \gamma_2 = \theta_2\sigma_u^2$$
$$i \geq 3 \Longrightarrow \gamma_i = 0.$$

Next compute the ACF again from $\rho_i = \gamma_i/\gamma_0$:

$$\rho_0 = 1$$
$$\rho_1 = \frac{\theta_1(1 + \theta_2)}{1 + \theta_1^2 + \theta_2^2}$$
$$\rho_2 = \frac{\theta_2}{1 + \theta_1^2 + \theta_2^2}$$
$$\rho_i = 0 \text{ for } i \geq 3.$$

The ACF of an MA(2) process cuts off after two lags. Notice that it is possible that $\rho_1 > \frac{1}{2}$ for an MA(2) model. The PACF can be shown to have no cut-off; the function decays to zero.

Conclusion

On the basis of the preceding examples the following conclusions concerning the ACF and PACF of an MA(q) model are drawn. Generalising the result of the MA(1) and MA(2) process it can be shown that the MA(q) model has an ACF that has a cut off after q lags, and has a PACF that decays to zero. So the behaviour of the ACF and the PACF of MA models is 'contrary' to that of AR models.

The ARMA(p,q) model

The ARMA(p,q) model:

$$\varphi(L) Y_t = \theta(L) u_t,$$

has a combination of AR and MA properties resulting in the following property. The ACF and PACF are a mixture of damped exponentials or sine waves. They do not have clear cut-off points.

In practice, adequate representations for many stationary variables can be achieved by models that do not have too high values for p and q. An empirical example is given in the next section.

Remark 14.1 A property of the sample autocorrelations
In practice, we will compute a series of sample autocorrelations $\{\widehat{\rho}_k\}$ and try to recognise a matching known theoretical pattern to identify a TS model. Good advice is to use only a small number of the autocorrelations for the following reason. If you have a sample of n observations, then it can be proved that:

$$\sum_{k=1}^{n-1} \widehat{\rho}_k = -0.5.$$

This property works as a 'restriction' when many $\widehat{\rho}_k$ are computed and disturbs the theoretical pattern, making it difficult to determine the order p and q of the ARIMA model. You will observe waves in the pattern of $\widehat{\rho}_k$ because of this.

14.7 The Box–Jenkins approach in practice

In this section the Box–Jenkins procedures are discussed on the basis of an example of a TS model for the cocoa price. In Section 7.3, the relationship between P_t^{coc} and P_t^{cof} was used to illustrate the computation of predictions for the cocoa price with a causal model. Therefore the identification and estimation of an ARIMA model for the log of the cocoa price will be discussed. Predictions for $\ln(P_t^{coc})$ will be computed with a TS model and compared with the previous results.

The identification procedure has been discussed rather extensively in the previous section but here the computational aspects of estimation and forecasting procedures will only briefly be discussed. (See the more advanced textbooks for more detailed information about these aspects.) Of course, more examples of identifying TS models can also be found in the literature (see, for example, Granger and Newbold (1977) for some clear empirical examples).

Identification of a TS model for ln (P_t^{coc})

To identify a univariate time-series model for ln (P_t^{coc}), the ACF and PACF are estimated for the sample data of the stationary transformed variable. In Section 12.5, we concluded that ln (P_t^{coc}) $\sim I(1)$, therefore we will try to identify a TS model for ∇ ln (P_t^{coc}). Look for values of $\widehat{\rho}_k$ in the ACF and PACF that are significantly different from zero by using the interval

$$0 \pm 2 \times se\left(\widehat{\rho}_k\right).$$

Next, the sample ACF and PACF are compared with pictures of theoretical ACFs and PACFs as derived in the previous section. The standard errors $se\left(\widehat{\rho}_k\right)$ of the estimated autocorrelation coefficients are approximately computed as:

$$se\left(\widehat{\rho}_k\right) = \sqrt{\frac{1}{n}\left(1 + 2\sum_{i=1}^{k-1}\widehat{\rho}_i^2\right)},$$

under the null hypothesis that

$$\rho_i = 0 \text{, for } i \geq k.$$

For example, if you want to test that the process is a white noise process (such as the residuals of an estimated model), then the standard errors are computed under $H_0 : \rho_i = 0$ for $i \geq 1$:

$$se(\widehat{\rho}_k) = \sqrt{\frac{1}{n}}, \text{ for all } k.$$

These are the standard errors that are plotted in the EViews window. To identify an ARIMA model by using EViews, double-click on the variable name, click on 'View' and select 'Correlogram'. A window opens where the order of integration of the variable has to be indicated. In Figure 14.4 the window is shown that appears after the option correlogram has been selected for ln (P_t^{coc}). Next the sample ACF and PACF of the variable are computed.

From section 12.5, we know already that ln (P_t^{coc}) is not stationary, so we can directly select '1st difference'. But in case we do not have that knowledge a priori, then the non-stationarity is immediately observed in the correlogram that is given in Figure 14.5. The figure shows the typical form of a correlogram of a non-stationary variable. In fact it shows the unit root in the process: $\widehat{\rho}_1 = 0.992$, as had been tested previously with an ADF test. It is clear that the ACF cannot decline in a fast way.

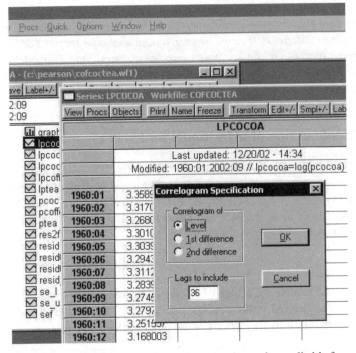

Figure 14.4: Defining which transformation has to be applied before the correlogram is computed

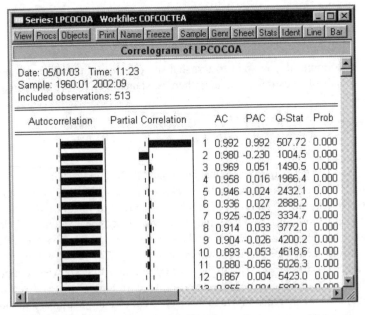

Figure 14.5: The correlogram of $\ln\left(P_t^{coc}\right)$

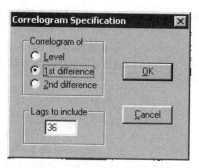

Figure 14.6: Selection of the transformation before the correlogram is computed

The dotted lines around the correlation coefficients are twice the standard errors ($\pm 2 \times \sqrt{1/n}$). Notice in Figure 14.5 that a button 'Ident' has appeared. This button can now be used to get the 'Correlogram Specification' window at once. Next in Figure 14.6, the first difference of $\ln\left(P_t^{coc}\right)$ has been selected and the correlogram of $\nabla \ln\left(P_t^{coc}\right)$ is given in Figure 14.7.

In the first place, we notice that all the probabilities of the Q-test are zero, indicating that the process clearly differs from a white noise process. The correlogram in Figure 14.7 is used for the identification of a TS model for $\nabla \ln\left(P_t^{coc}\right)$. The ACF and PACF suggest, for example, estimating an MA(1) or maybe an ARMA(1,2) model.

Series: LPCOCOA Workfile: COFCOCTEA

View | Procs | Objects | Print | Name | Freeze | Sample | Genr | Sheet | Stats | Ident | Line | Bar

Correlogram of D(LPCOCOA)

Date: 05/01/03 Time: 11:44
Sample: 1960:01 2002:09
Included observations: 512

Autocorrelation	Partial Correlation		AC	PAC	Q-Stat	Prob
		1	0.314	0.314	50.935	0.000
		2	-0.007	-0.117	50.958	0.000
		3	-0.006	0.038	50.976	0.000
		4	0.014	0.004	51.082	0.000
		5	-0.030	-0.042	51.547	0.000
		6	0.008	0.038	51.580	0.000
		7	-0.032	-0.058	52.105	0.000
		8	0.023	0.062	52.382	0.000
		9	0.076	0.052	55.439	0.000
		10	0.108	0.074	61.553	0.000
		11	0.029	-0.021	62.003	0.000
		12	-0.012	-0.010	62.075	0.000
		13	-0.016	-0.006	62.216	0.000

Figure 14.7: The correlogram of $\nabla \ln\left(P_t^{coc}\right)$

Estimation of the parameters of the TS model

The parameters are estimated by minimising the sum of squared disturbances, which is identical to maximising the likelihood function. The (squared) disturbances are a non-linear function of the parameters:

$$u_t = \theta^{-1}(L)\,\varphi(L)\,Y_t.$$

The minimum is found by using an iterative procedure (see the EViews User's Guide for the details as to how this is done in EViews). In EViews, AR and MA terms can be specified in the 'Equation Specification' window by specifying AR(1), AR(2), MA(1) or MA(2), etc. When an ARMA(2,2) model for ∇Y_t has to be estimated, for example, the following must be done. Click on 'Quick' and 'Estimate' as usual, and specify in the 'Equation Specification' window:

$$d(Y)\ c\ ar(1)\ ar(2)\ ma(1)\ ma(2).$$

ARIMA models are statistical models; they are related to economic models but they are not economic models themselves. That makes it sometimes difficult to make a choice between different model specifications, especially when specifications are very close to each other and estimation results hardly differ. A helpful tool in making a choice is the use of an information criterion that is often part of the computer regression output. In EViews, you always find the 'Akaike information criterion' (AIC) and the 'Schwarz information criterion' (SIC). Both criteria are based on the residual variance. You want to have a model that has the smallest residual variance. However, we have seen that the residual variance is reduced by increasing the number of regressors, therefore a 'penalty' is added for the number of parameters in the model. For two models based on *the same series* you would choose the specification with the lowest value of the AIC or the SIC. The values of the criteria can only be interpreted relatively. Because series of different length can be used, the criteria are normalised by dividing them by the number of observations that have been used to estimate the model. The AIC and the SIC are defined as:

$$AIC = ln(\widehat{\sigma}_u^2) + \frac{2K}{n},$$

$$SIC = ln(\widehat{\sigma}_u^2) + \frac{K \cdot ln(n)}{n}.$$

The SIC is an alternative to the AIC. It has a similar interpretation but it gives a larger 'penalty' for the number of parameters. For that reason, the SIC will indicate a simpler model than the AIC, which can be an advantage. These criteria cannot be used to compare models that have different levels of differencing.

The example of estimating a TS model for the cocoa price is continued. An ARIMA(0,1,1) and an ARIMA(1,1,2) are estimated. In Figure 14.8 the 'Equation Specification' window is shown.

Initially, the ACF and PACF gave some indication of the order of an ARIMA specification. Next the number of p and q have to be chosen in such a way that absence of residual

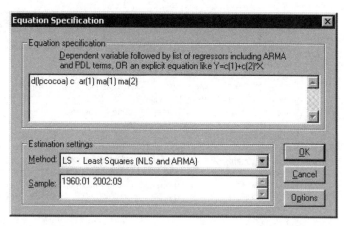

Figure 14.8: Specification of an ARIMA(1,1,2) model for ln (P_t^{coc})

autocorrelation is also found, and the estimated parameters are significantly different from zero. In Figures 14.9 and 14.10 the two output windows are shown.

The estimated ARIMA(0,1,1) model has a lower value both for the AIC and the SIC. Autocorrelation in the residuals will be checked later. Notice that the roots of the lag polynomials have been computed and have been printed as the *inverted roots.* The inverted roots should be within the unit circle.

```
■ Equation: EQ_ARMA   Workfile: COFCOCTEA                              _ □ X
View Procs Objects   Print Name Freeze   Estimate Forecast Stats Resids

Dependent Variable: D(LPCOCOA)
Method: Least Squares
Date: 05/01/03   Time: 14:33
Sample(adjusted): 1960:03 2002:09
Included observations: 511 after adjusting endpoints
Convergence achieved after 21 iterations
Backcast: 1960:01 1960:02
```

Variable	Coefficient	Std. Error	t-Statistic	Prob.
C	0.003280	0.003372	0.972740	0.3311
AR(1)	0.966348	0.057950	16.67548	0.0000
MA(1)	-0.617571	0.069076	-8.940414	0.0000
MA(2)	-0.346508	0.043644	-7.939449	0.0000

R-squared	0.113498	Mean dependent var		0.002484
Adjusted R-squared	0.108252	S.D. dependent var		0.066356
S.E. of regression	0.062662	Akaike info criterion		-2.694338
Sum squared resid	1.990726	Schwarz criterion		-2.661176
Log likelihood	692.4033	F-statistic		21.63688
Durbin-Watson stat	1.984577	Prob(F-statistic)		0.000000

Inverted AR Roots	.97	
Inverted MA Roots	.97	-.36

Figure 14.9: An estimated ARIMA(1,1,2) for ln (P_t^{coc})

```
■ Equation: EQ_ARMA  Workfile: COFCOCTEA                    _ □ ×
View Procs Objects  Print Name Freeze  Estimate Forecast Stats Resids

Dependent Variable: D(LPCOCOA)
Method: Least Squares
Date: 05/01/03   Time: 14:36
Sample(adjusted): 1960:02 2002:09
Included observations: 512 after adjusting endpoints
Convergence achieved after 6 iterations
Backcast: 1960:01
```

Variable	Coefficient	Std. Error	t-Statistic	Prob.
C	0.002454	0.003738	0.656614	0.5117
MA(1)	0.352651	0.041550	8.487292	0.0000

R-squared	0.112273	Mean dependent var	0.002398
Adjusted R-squared	0.110532	S.D. dependent var	0.066320
S.E. of regression	0.062548	Akaike info criterion	-2.701880
Sum squared resid	1.995221	Schwarz criterion	-2.685324
Log likelihood	693.6813	F-statistic	64.50096
Durbin-Watson stat	1.987519	Prob(F-statistic)	0.000000

Inverted MA Roots	-.35

Figure 14.10: An estimated ARIMA(0,1,1) for $\ln{(P_t^{coc})}$

The interpretation of the printed signs is often not clear in software output, because the convention of writing the lag polynomial of the MA-part is not standard in econometrics literature. Some authors write the MA parameters with positive signs (as in this book), whereas others write them with negative signs. Similar problems exist with respect to the AR polynomial: are the parameters initially written at the left- or right-hand side of the equation?

The estimation results of the two models, obtained with EViews, have the following interpretation.

The ARIMA(1,1,2) model:

$$\nabla \widehat{\ln{(P_t^{coc})}} = \underset{(0.003)}{0.00328} + \widehat{v}_t$$

$$\left(1 - \underset{(0.058)}{0.966}\, L\right) \widehat{v}_t = \left(1 - \underset{(0.069)}{0.618}\, L - \underset{(0.044)}{0.347}\, L^2\right) u_t.$$

That is equivalent to:

$$\left(1 - \underset{(0.058)}{0.966}\, L\right)\left(\nabla \widehat{\ln{(P_t^{coc})}} - \underset{(0.003)}{0.00328}\right) = \left(1 - \underset{(0.069)}{0.618}\, L - \underset{(0.044)}{0.347}\, L^2\right) u_t,$$

$$\left(1 - \underset{(0.058)}{0.966}\, L\right) \nabla \widehat{\ln{(P_t^{coc})}} = 0.00011 + \left(1 - \underset{(0.069)}{0.618}\, L - \underset{(0.044)}{0.347}\, L^2\right) u_t.$$

This can also be rewritten as:

$$\nabla \widehat{\ln \left(P_t^{coc} \right)} = 0.000111 + \underset{(0.058)}{0.966} \nabla \ln \left(P_{t-1}^{coc} \right) + u_t - \underset{(0.069)}{0.618} \, u_{t-1} - \underset{(0.044)}{0.347} \, u_{t-2}.$$

The ARIMA(0,1,1) model:

$$\nabla \widehat{\left(\ln P_t^{coc} \right)} = \underset{(0.004)}{0.002} + \widehat{v}_t$$

$$\widehat{v}_t = \left(1 + \underset{(0.042)}{0.353} \, L \right) u_t,$$

or

$$\nabla \widehat{\left(P_t^{coc} \right)} = \underset{(0.004)}{0.002} + \left(1 + \underset{(0.042)}{0.353} \, L \right) u_t.$$

So this is equivalent to the model:

$$\nabla \widehat{\ln \left(P_t^{coc} \right)} = \underset{(0.004)}{0.002} + u_t + \underset{(0.042)}{0.353} \, u_{t-1}.$$

Remark 14.2 Common factors

You must be aware of 'common factors' in the model specification. For example, the following two models have the same correlogram because of a common factor in the AR and MA part of the model:

$$
\begin{aligned}
\text{AR(1):} \quad & (1 - \varphi_1 L) Y_t = u_t \\
\text{ARMA(2,1):} \quad & (1 + \theta_1 L)(1 - \varphi_1 L) Y_t = (1 + \theta_1 L) u_t
\end{aligned}
\quad \text{for any } |\theta_1| < 1.
$$

The model specification is unique for a particular ACF and PACF, except in the case of common factors. So be cautious or economical with the specification of a TS model. Try to find the most parsimonious model, with respect to the number of parameters, that is free of residual autocorrelation and has significant parameter estimates. See the common factor in Figure 14.9!

Diagnostic checking (testing the residuals to be white noise)

Obviously, the residuals have to be tested for the absence of autocorrelation. In time-series terminology this is called 'diagnostic checking'. Diagnostic checking concerns the evaluation of the estimation result. In time-series analysis, it is usual to compute the Ljung–Box (Q) test, earlier introduced in Section 6.3 as the Q-statistic, in expression (6.6). With the Ljung–Box test, we test whether the residuals behave like a white noise process. The formula is given once more in expression (14.11).

$$Q = n(n+2) \sum_{k=1}^{K} \frac{\widehat{\rho}_k^2}{n - k}, \tag{14.11}$$

where $\widehat{\rho}_k^2$ is now the squared *residual* autocorrelation coefficient of lag length k. Under the null hypothesis of white noise residuals of an estimated ARMA(p,q) model, the Q-test has a $\chi^2(K - p - q)$ distribution:

$$Q \stackrel{H_0}{\sim} \chi^2(K - p - q).$$

You should choose an appropriate value for K, which is not too high or too low. In EViews the 'Residual Tests' have to be used again, where 'Correlogram - Q-statistics' is selected with all the values of the Q-statistic and the corresponding probabilities. As usual, it is informative to look at the whole range of probabilities of the Q-test. As an example, the correlograms of the residuals of both the ARIMA models for the cocoa price are given in Figure 14.11. The null hypothesis of white noise residuals is not rejected for both models, although the p-values of the MA(1) model are higher. In the ARIMA(1,1,2) model, $p + q = 3$, because the probabilities are given starting at lag 4, and for the ARIMA(0,1,1) model they are given with lag 2; it is a mistake to double-click on RESID and to use that correlogram, because it always starts at lag 1!

The determination coefficient R^2 is not very useful in TS models. It can be shown that very high R^2s can belong to very poor TS models. (See Section 13.7 in Maddala (2001) for a discussion of this topic.) For example, for a stationary AR(1) process with zero mean it can be shown that $R^2 \approx \widehat{\varphi}_1^2$. The best thing to do is to judge a model by looking at the residual correlogram, by using the information criteria and evaluating its forecasting power.

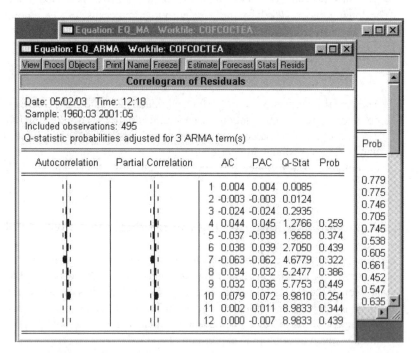

Figure 14.11: Correlograms of the residuals of the estimated ARIMA models for ln (P_t^{coc}), the (1,1,2) comes first, the p-values of the (0,1,1) are visible in the background

Forecasting with a TS model

Forecasting future values of an economic variable with an ARIMA model follows a similar route to that of the causal model discussed in Chapter 7 (see also Clemens and Hendry (1998)). Remember the remark that was made in Section 7.3 concerning the specification of a differenced variable. For example, an ARIMA(1,1,1) model can be estimated as:

$$d(y) \; c \; ar(1) \; ma(1) \tag{14.12}$$

and can also be estimated as:

$$dy \; c \; ar(1) \; ma(1), \tag{14.13}$$

with the variable dy generated in advance as:

$$\text{genr } dy = y - y(-1).$$

With the specification (14.12) the choice has to be made whether forecasts will be computed for the level of y_t or its first difference ∇y_t. With specification (14.13) only predictions for ∇y_t can be computed. In most cases, you want to predict the level of the variable.

In EViews, a forecast window appears after clicking on the button 'Forecast' in the 'Equation' window (see Figure 14.12). The forecast sample and the choice between dynamic or static simulation have to be indicated, just as earlier discussed. See the chosen options in Figure 14.12 with the option to predict the level of $\ln P_t^{coc}$ and to save the standard errors of the forecasts. The same prediction period has been chosen as in Section 7.3.

The models have been estimated for the reduced sample period and the predictions are computed for the chosen prediction period. In Table 14.1, the forecast evaluations have been summarised; in the last column the result from Section 7.3 has been repeated.

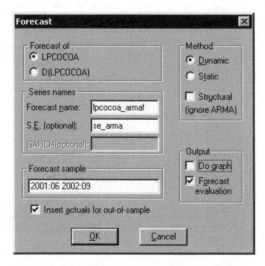

Figure 14.12: The 'Forecast' window

Forecast evaluations of various models for $\ln P_t^{coc}$ Forecast sample: 2001:06 2002:09			
Inequality coefficient	**ARIMA(1,1,2)**	**ARIMA(0,1,1)**	**Causal model**
Root Mean Squared Error	0.330472	0.346024	0.504822
Mean Absolute Error	0.272837	0.284123	0.416260
Mean Abs. Perc. Error	6.347836	6.604259	9.665497
Theil Inequality Coefficient	0.040965	0.042970	0.063902

Table 14.1: Forecast evaluations of the two ARIMA models and the causal model

The inequality coefficients of the ARIMA(1,1,2) model are marginally smaller than those of the ARIMA(0,1,1) model, but they are clearly smaller than the coefficients belonging to the predictions obtained from the causal relationship between the commodity prices. Although we ought to realise that the causal model is not really a model for the price formation of cocoa on the cocoa market, in Figure 14.13 the results for the ARIMA(1,1,2) model are plotted in the same way as was done in Section 7.3.

In Figure 7.3, we observed a decreasing trend in the forecasts, whereas the ARIMA model yields increasing trends. This is the reason for the smaller values of the inequality coefficients as P_t^{coc} is also increasing.

Although you cannot see it in Figure 14.13, a property of predictions from an ARIMA model is that they vary in the short run after which they become constant. That can be demonstrated as follows. The ARIMA(1,1,2) model that has been estimated for the sample period is:

$$\nabla \widehat{\ln\left(P_t^{coc}\right)} = 0.00011 + \underset{(0.058)}{0.966}\ \nabla \ln\left(P_{t-1}^{coc}\right) + u_t - \underset{(0.069)}{0.618}\ u_{t-1} - \underset{(0.044)}{0.347}\ u_{t-2}.$$

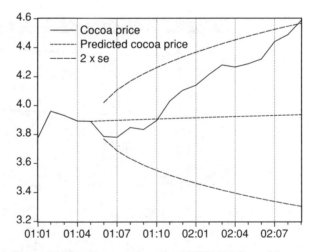

Figure 14.13: Forecasts from the ARIMA(1,1,2) model

Then, for period $n + 1$, the model is:

$$\nabla \ln \left(P_{n+1}^{coc} \right) = \varphi_0^* + \varphi_1 \nabla \ln \left(P_n^{coc} \right) + u_{n+1} + \theta_1 u_n + \theta_2 u_{n-1}.$$

The conditional expectation of $\nabla \ln \left(P_n^{coc} \right)$, given its past, is $\nabla \ln \left(P_n^{coc} \right)$, and the conditional expectation of u_n and u_{n-1}, given the past, is u_n and u_{n-1}. However, the conditional expectation of u_{n+1} is zero. Hence $\nabla \ln \left(P_{n+1}^{coc} \right)$ is forecasted as follows:

$$\widehat{\nabla \ln \left(P_{n+1}^{coc} \right)} = 0.00011 + 0.966 \nabla \ln \left(P_n^{coc} \right) + 0 - 0.618 u_n - 0.347 u_{n-1}.$$

In practice, the forecast is computed according to the estimated model and using the last residuals e_n and e_{n-1}:

$$\widehat{\nabla \ln \left(P_{n+1}^{coc} \right)} = 0.00011 + 0.966 \nabla \ln \left(P_n^{coc} \right) - 0.618 e_n - 0.347 e_{n-1}.$$

To forecast $\nabla \ln \left(P_{n+2}^{coc} \right)$ the model is:

$$\nabla \ln \left(P_{n+2}^{coc} \right) = \varphi_0^* + \varphi_1 \nabla \ln \left(P_{n+1}^{coc} \right) + u_{n+2} + \theta_1 u_{n+1} + \theta_2 u_n.$$

That implies for the computation of the forecast $\nabla \ln \left(P_{n+2}^{coc} \right)$:

$$\widehat{\nabla \ln \left(P_{n+2}^{coc} \right)} = 0.00011 + 0.966 \nabla \ln \left(P_{n+1}^{coc} \right) + 0 - 0.618 \cdot 0 - 0.347 \cdot u_n$$
$$= 0.00011 + 0.966 \nabla \ln \left(P_{n+1}^{coc} \right) - 0.347 \cdot u_n.$$

The forecast is computed by using the last residual e_n:

$$\widehat{\nabla \ln \left(P_{n+2}^{coc} \right)} = 0.00011 + 0.966 \nabla \ln \left(P_{n+1}^{coc} \right) - 0.347 \cdot e_n.$$

It will be clear that $\nabla \ln \left(P_{n+3}^{coc} \right)$ is forecasted by:

$$\widehat{\nabla \ln \left(P_{n+3}^{coc} \right)} = 0.00011 + 0.966 \nabla \ln \left(P_{n+2}^{coc} \right).$$

The last expression shows that the computation of forecasts has become recursive. Then the ARIMA forecasts from this model will converge to a constant value. In this example, the forecasts of $\nabla \ln \left(P_{n+i}^{coc} \right)$, with $i \geq 3$, converge to the constant term of the model, 0.00328 as shown below in 'general' terms:

$$\left(\widehat{\nabla \ln \left(P_{n+i}^{coc} \right)} - 0.00328 \right) = \varphi^{-1} \left(L \right) \theta \left(L \right) e_t$$

$$e_t = 0, \text{ for } t \geq n + 1,$$

so

$$\left(\nabla \widehat{\ln\left(P_{n+i}^{coc}\right)} - 0.00328\right) \rightarrow 0, \text{ for } i \rightarrow \infty$$

$$\nabla \widehat{\ln\left(P_{n+i}^{coc}\right)} \rightarrow 0.00328.$$

After a number of periods, the forecasts have become nearly constant. However, the variable is in first differences, which means that the forecast of the change of $\ln\left(P_t^{coc}\right)$ has become constant. This result is illustrated in Figure 14.13 above, where the forecasts show the growth of 0.328% per month in the log of P_t^{coc}. This implies that the trend in $\ln\left(P_t^{coc}\right)$ has become constant.

These (long-run) forecasts are not very interesting, which underpins the statement that an ARMA model can be useful for the computation of short-term predictions. Long-run model simulations are better carried out using a causal econometric model.

14.8   Case 11: Box–Jenkins procedures

In this case the Box–Jenkins procedures will be applied to a series from one of the time-series data sets. In Case 3, predictions for an endogenous variable have been computed by using a causal econometric model. It is interesting to estimate an ARIMA model for the same endogenous variable, which makes it possible to compare the quality of both the predictions. But each time-series from a data set can be selected for this exercise.

■   Identify and estimate a TS model for one of the variables from a data set; pay attention to stationarity (also seasonality). Check the residual behaviour for the absence of autocorrelation (diagnostic checking). Do this for a sample without the last couple of periods.

■   Compute forecasts for the omitted periods at the end of the sample period. Compare these forecasts with the real values of the observations and, if relevant, compare the forecasts with the earlier obtained predictions made with the causal model.

■   Write an illustrated paper about your analysis, showing the graphs of the ACF and PACF. Include a figure with the newly calculated predictions, the predictions from Case 3 and the actual values.

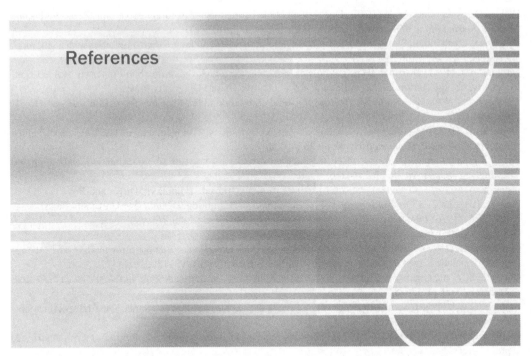

References

Almon, S. (1962) 'The distributed lag between capital appropriations and expenditures', *Econometrica* 30, pp.407–423.

Amemiya, T. (1981) 'Qualitative Response Model: A survey', *Journal of Economic Literature*, p.1488.

Anderson, O.D. (1976) *Time Series Analysis and Forecasting, The Box-Jenkins approach*, London: Butterworths.

Baltagi, B.H. (2001) *Econometric Analysis of Panel Data*, 2nd ed., Chichester: John Wiley & Sons.

Bollerslev, T. (1986) 'Gereralized Autoregressive Conditional Heteroskedasticity', *Journal of Econometrics* 31, pp.307–327.

Box, G.E.P. and Jenkins, G.M. (1976) *Time Series Analysis, Forecasting and Control*, revised ed., San Francisco: Holden Day.

Box, G.E.P. and Pierce, D.A. (1970) 'Distribution of residual autocorrelations in autoregressive-integrated moving average time series models', *Journal of the American Statistical Association* 65, pp.1509–1526.

Breusch, T.S. (1978) 'Testing for autocorrelation in dynamic linear models', *Australian Economic Papers* 17, pp.334–355.

Breusch, T.S. and Pagan, A.R. (1979) 'A simple test for heteroscedasticity and random coefficient variation', *Econometrica* 47, pp.1287–1294.

Charemza, W. and Deadman, D.F. (1992) *New directions in econometric practice*, Hants: Edward Elgar.

Chatfield, C. (1996) *The Analysis of Time Series: An introduction*, 5th ed., London: Chapman and Hall.

Clemens, M.P. and Hendry, D.F. (1998) *Forecasting economic time series*, Cambridge: Cambridge University Press.

Cramer, J.S. (1989) *Econometric Applications of Maximum Likelihood Methods*, Cambridge: Cambridge University Press.

Cuthbertson, K., Hall, S.G. and Taylor, M.P. (1992) *Applied Econometric Techniques*, Hemel Hempstead: Philip Allan.

Davidson, J.E.H., Hendry, D.F., Srba, F. and Yeo, S. (1978) 'Econometric modelling of the aggregate time-series relationship between consumers' expenditure and income in the United Kingdom', *The Economic Journal* 88, pp.661–692.

Dickey, D.A. and Fuller, W.A. (1979) 'Distribution of the Estimators for Autoregressive Time Series with a unit root', *Journal of the American Statistical Association* 74, pp.427–431.

Dickey, D.A. and Fuller, W.A. (1981) 'Likelihood ratio statistics for autoregressive time series with a unit root', *Econometrica* 49, p.1063.

Dhrymes, P.J. (1971) *Distributed lags: Problems of Estimation and Formulation*, San Francisco: Holden-Day.

Dougherty, C. (2002) *Introduction to Econometrics*, Oxford: Oxford University Press.

Durbin, J. and Watson, G.S. (1950) 'Testing for serial correlation in least squares regression', *Biometrika* 37, pp.409–428.

Engle, R. F. (1982) 'Autoregressive conditional heteroskedasticity with estimates of the variance of United Kingdom inflation', *Econometrica* 50, pp.987–1008.

Engle, R.F. and Granger, C.W.J. (1987) 'Co-integration and error correction: representation, estimation and testing', *Econometrica* 55, pp.251–276.

Fisher, R.A. (1948) *Statistical methods for research workers*, 10th ed., Edinburgh: Oliver and Boyd.

Franses, P.H. (2002) *A Concise Introduction to Econometrics,* Cambridge: Cambridge University Press.

Fuller, W.A. (1976) *Introduction to Statistical Time Series*, New York: John Wiley & Sons.

Ghisler, C. (2003) *Total Commander*, Switzerland: Ghisler & Co.

Godfrey, L.G. (1978) 'Testing against general autoregressive and moving average error models when the regressors include lagged dependent variables', *Econometrica* 46, pp.1293–1302.

Goldfeld, S.M. and Quandt, R.E. (1965) 'Some tests for homoscedasticity', *Journal of the American Statistical Association* 60, pp.539–547.

Granger, C.W.J. (1981) 'Some properties of time series data and their use in econometric model specification', *Journal of Econometrics* 16, pp.121–130.

Granger, C.W.J. and Newbold, P. (1974) 'Spurious regressions in econometrics', *Journal of Econometrics* 2, pp.111–120.

Granger, C.W.J. and Newbold, P. (1977) *Forecasting Economic Time Series,* London: Academic Press.

Greene, W.H. (2000) *Econometric Analysis*, 4th ed., Upper Saddle River: Prentice Hall.

Gujarati, D.N. (2003) *Basic Econometrics*, New York: McGraw-Hill.

Haldrup, N. (1999) 'An Econometric Analysis of I(2) Variables' in *Practical Issues in Cointegration Analysis*, Oxley, L. and McAleer, M. (Eds.), Oxford: Blackwell Publishers, pp.179–234.

Hamilton, J.D. (1994) *Time Series Analysis*, Princeton: Princeton University Press.

Harvey, A.C. (1990) *The Econometric Analysis of Time Series*, 2nd ed., Hemel Hempstead: Philip Allan.

Hendry, D.F. (1995) *Dynamic econometrics*, Oxford: Oxford University Press.

Intrilligator, M.D., Bodkin, R.G. and Hsiao, C. (1996) *Econometric Models, Techniques, and Applications*, 2nd ed., Upper Saddle River: Prentice Hall.

Jarque, C.M. and Bera, A.K. (1980) 'Efficient tests for normality, homoskedasticity and serial independence of regression residuals', *Economics Letters* 6, pp.255–259.

Johansen, S. (1988) 'Statistical Analysis of Cointegration Vectors', *Journal of Economic Dynamics and Control* 12, pp.231–254.

Johansen, S. and Juselius, K. (1990) 'Maximum Likelihood Estimation and Inference on Cointegration, with Applications for the Demand for Money', *Oxford Bulletin of Economics and Statistics* 52, pp.169–210.

Johnston, J. (1972 2nd ed., 1984 3rd ed.) *Econometric Methods*, New York: McGraw-Hill.

Johnston, J. and DiNardo, J. (1997) *Econometric Methods* 4th ed., New York: McGraw-Hill.

Koyck, L.M. (1954) *Distributed Lags and Investment Analysis*, Amsterdam: North-Holland.

Ljung, G.M., and Box, G.E.P. (1978) 'On a measure of lack of fit in time series models', *Biometrika* 65, pp.297–303.

Maddala, G.S. (1983) *Limited-Dependent and Qualitative Variables in Econometrics*, Cambridge: Cambridge University Press.

Maddala, G.S. (2001) *Introduction to Econometrics*, 3rd ed., Chichester: John Wiley & Sons.

Maddala, G.S. and Kim, In Moo (1998), *Unit roots, cointegration and structural change*, Cambridge: Cambridge University Press.

Phillips, P.C.B. (1987) 'Time-series regression with a unit root', *Econometrica* 55, pp.277–301.

Phillips, P.C.B. and Perron, P. (1988) 'Testing for a unit root in time-series regression', *Biometrica* 75, pp.335–346.

Quantitative Micro Software (2000) *EViews 4.1 User's Guide*, Irvine: Quantitative Micro Software.

Stewart, J. (1991) *Econometrics*, Hemel Hempstead: Philip Allan.

Stewart, J. and Gill, L. (1998) *Econometrics*, 2nd ed., Hemel Hempstead: Prentice Hall Europe.

Stewart, M.B. and Wallis, K.F. (1981) *Introductory Econometrics*, 2nd ed., Oxford: Blackwell Publishers.

Stock, J.H. and Watson, M.W. (2003) *Introduction to Econometrics*, Boston: Pearson Education.

Studenmund, A.H. (2001) *Using Econometrics: a Practical Guide*, 4th ed., Boston: Addison Wesley Longman.

Thomas, R.L. (1997) *Modern Econometrics, an introduction*, Harlow: Addison Wesley Longman.

Van Montfort, K., Ridder, G. and Kleinknecht, A. (2002), 'The innovation decision and fixed costs' in *The emergence of the knowledge economy,* Acs, Z.J., Groot, H.L.F. and Nijkamp, P. (Eds.), New York: Springer Verlag, pp.81–106.

Verbeek, M. (2000) *A Guide to Modern Econometrics*, Chichester: John Wiley & Sons.

Vogelvang, E. (1988) *A quarterly econometric model of the world coffee economy*, Amsterdam: Free University Press.

Vogelvang, E. (1992) 'Hypotheses Testing Concerning Relationships between Spot Prices of Various Types of Coffee', *Journal of Applied Econometrics* 7, 191–201.

Vogelvang, E. (1994) 'Analysis of Long-run and Short-run Price Behaviour of Related Agricultural Commodities for Modelling and Forecasting', Tinbergen Institute Discussion Papers, TI 94–113.

White, H. (1980) 'A heteroskedasticity-consistent covariance matrix estimator and a direct test for heteroskedasticity', *Econometrica* 48, pp.817–838.

Wooldridge, J.M. (1999) *Introductory Econometrics: A Modern Approach*, USA: South-Western College Publishing.

Zellner, A. and Palm, F.C. (1974) 'Time Series analysis and simultaneous equation models', *Journal of Econometrics* 2, pp.17–54.

Zellner, A. and Palm, F.C. (1975) 'Time Series and structural analysis of monetary models of the U.S. economy', *Sankhyā: The Indian Journal of Statistics* 37, Series C, Pt.2, pp.12–56.

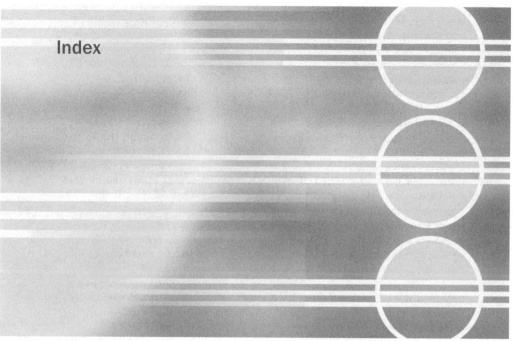

Index